Rock-n-Roll is everybody's fucking music... I would certainly hope that it's the Devil's music, but it's not just the Devil's music. I think that's where God and the Devil shake hands – right there.

Neil Young

MAGIC, MURDER, MAYHEM AND THE DIABOLICAL NOTES OF THE DEVIL'S MUSIC

A SONG OF DANCE & DEATH

TROY TAYLOR

Original Cover Artwork Designed by

© Copyright 2019 by April Slaughter & Troy Taylor

This Book is Published By:

American Hauntings Ink
Jacksonville, Illinois | 217.791.7859
Visit us on the Internet at http://www.americanhauntingsink.com

First Edition – April 2019
ISBN: 978-1-7324079-5-4

Printed in the United States of America

INTRODUCTION

You can find the song almost anywhere. Times have changed. It's not as though you have to blow the dust off an old vinyl recording that you found in a rundown record store somewhere – unless you just want to, that is. When you call up the playlist for Billie Holiday – and you really should have one – find what was once one of her most popular songs, a tune with the uplifting name of "Gloomy Sunday."

Go ahead and give it a listen, I'll wait.

Before you turn it on, though, make sure the windows are closed, the medicine cabinet is locked, the knives have all been put away, and the gas has been turned off on the stove.

Why? Well, because "Gloomy Sunday" is also known by the moniker of the "Hungarian Suicide Song." Legend has it that it's sent a lot of people to their deaths and ruined the lives of others, including the beautiful and talented Billie Holiday.

The song was written in 1933 by a Hungarian pianist and composer named Rezso Seress. It had a different title then, which translated roughly to "The World is Ending." It was a not-so-cheerful tune about the despair that had been caused by the Great War and ended with a prayer for the sins of people everywhere. Needless to say, it never really took off. A short time later, however, a poet named Laszlo Javor got hold of it and added his own lyrics to the melody. He turned it into a song about a young man who wanted to kill himself after his lover's death. It was just as morbidly sad, but at least it was a little more relatable.

Maybe too relatable, as it turned out.

"Gloomy Sunday" was first recorded in English in 1936 and, almost immediately, gained a grim reputation. The song was so depressing that even the record label described it as a "suicide song." In the 1930s, radio networks started banning the song after stories began to circulate that people were killing themselves after hearing it. The stories claimed that a "suicidal mania" swept through Europe as confirmed cases of "Gloomy Sunday" madness reached epidemic proportions.

One press report attributed 19 suicides to "Gloomy Sunday," although those deaths are hard to verify – except for two.

In January 1968, the song's original composer, Rezso Seress, took his own life. He survived his initial attempt – jumping from a third-floor window in Budapest – but managed to choke himself to death with a wire while in the hospital.

Laszlo Javor, who penned the most heartbreaking lyrics for the song, had been inspired by his own broken heart. As the controversy over the song increased, so did his fortunes from the sales of sheet music. Encouraged by his dubious good fortune, he attempted to reconcile with his ex-sweetheart. He sent her a letter filled with tender words, but she never responded. A day later, her body was discovered. She had taken poison. The letter that Laszlo had sent her was found next to her body. She had scrawled two words on it: "Gloomy Sunday."

But verified or not, the stories of suicides continued. But why? Yes, the words and music were eerie, but there had been stranger songs that were written that didn't compel men and women to commit suicide. Fifteen different countries became convinced that the song was "cursed" in some way and banned its playing on the radio. Regardless, sales continued to climb. In places where records were banned in stores, black-market copies were sold. Rumors of "Gloomy Sunday" suicides continued, like the young boy who was cycling through the streets of Rome and heard the strains of "Gloomy Sunday" being sung by a street beggar. The boy emptied his pockets, giving his money to the singer, and then climbed the railing of a nearby bridge and plunged to his death in the water below. An elderly man threw himself from the window of a seven-story building after listening to the so-called "suicide song" in his apartment.

And the stories went on, remaining a European phenomenon until it was introduced to American audiences in 1941. When the instrumental version was first recorded in the United States by Hal Kemp (who himself died an early and tragic death), many of the musicians failed to show up for the recording session – over half were absent. So many weird, unexplainable things happened during the session that 21 different master copies were attempted before a final one was successfully made.

One would think that the omission of the gloomy, depressing words alone would have ended the parade of suicides, but it was Kemp's instrumental record that was heard from an apartment window by a passing London police officer when he discovered the body of a young woman inside. She had taken an overdose of prescription drugs.

And then came Billie Holiday's recording of the song later that same year, creating a sensation like nothing American audiences had experienced before.

Billie had been born Eleanora Fagan on April 7, 1915. Her parents, Sadie Fagan, 12, and Clarence Holiday, 15, were children themselves. Billie attended their wedding three years later. She was raised as a Catholic girl in the slums of Baltimore, Maryland. Alice Dean, a neighbor who ran a brothel in Baltimore's red-light district, allowed Billie to clean for her in return for listening to Alice's collection of jazz records. She spent hours imitating the great blues singer Bessie Smith and singing along to Louis Armstrong's famous horn.

Billie Holiday

Billie lived a hard life in the slums and back alleys of the city and spent time at a Catholic institution for wayward girls. She had been placed there when she was 10 for being the underage victim of an attempted forcible rape. After her mother got her out, they moved to New York, but things were no better for her there – until music literally saved her life.

The girl who was later nicknamed "Lady Day" by her friend and musical partner Lester Young, became a tremendous influence on jazz, blues, and popular music. Her career spanned more than 30 years and her vocal style, strongly inspired by jazz instrumentalists, pioneered a new form of vocal delivery and improvisation. Her childhood was difficult, and her young adult life was no better. She became involved in violence, prostitution, drugs and alcohol -- but no one could sing like Billie. She worked with the best in the business, recorded amazing music but then descended into a haze from which she never returned – starting, some say, with her recording of the cursed suicide song, "Gloomy Sunday."

Billie's early career began with her singing in Harlem nightclubs, where she was heard by producer John Hammond, who was determined to make her a star. She signed a recording contract with Brunswick Records in 1935. Collaborations with Teddy Wilson produced the hit "What a Little Moonlight Can Do," which became a jazz standard. Throughout the 1930s, Billie had mainstream success on labels such as Columbia Records and Decca Records. It seemed nothing could go wrong – and then she recorded "Gloomy Sunday." It became a huge hit, but her life soon went into a tailspin.

Billy married Jimmy Monroe in 1941, the same year that she recorded "Gloomy Sunday." She quickly discovered that he had a vicious heroin habit, and soon, Billie was using, too. She was soon beset with legal troubles, thanks to drug use, drinking, and Jimmy's abuse. After a short stint in prison, she performed at a sold-out concert at Carnegie Hall, but that was nearly at the end of the road for Billie. Her drug and alcohol problems continued, and her health began to deteriorate. In early 1959, she was diagnosed with cirrhosis of the liver. She stopped drinking for a time and then relapsed.

On May 31, she was taken to Metropolitan Hospital in New York with liver and heart disease, only to be arrested in the hospital for drug possession. She was under police guard when she died on July 17. In her final years, she had been swindled out of her royalties and earnings and died with just 70-cents in the bank. She was only 44-years-old.

It was "Gloomy Sunday," her friends said. It ruined her life.

Perhaps the BBC had been right. The song was so depressing that they had banned it from British airwaves in 1941. They felt it was detrimental to wartime morale.

The ban wasn't lifted until 2002.

The story of Billie Holiday and "Gloomy Sunday" serves as a fitting introduction to this book – a history of legends, lies, myths, murders, curses, and the influence of the occult on music. The diabolical and the darkness has always been a part of music, even long before religious authorities began calling jazz, the blues, and rock-n-roll "the work of the devil."

There was always something strange about music, dating back to medieval times. It captured the imaginations of people in ways that nothing else had ever been able to do. This was true during the days of traveling minstrels, when folk music emerged from the Appalachian Mountains, when the first jazz music was played in the brothels of New Orleans, and when the first bluegrass songs rattled across the American South. But when the first notes of the blues – which eventually gave birth to rock-n-roll – began to be heard from roadhouses and juke joints, the fundamentalists were convinced that Satan himself had invented his own brand of music.

And perhaps they were right. The origins of rock-n-roll are murky, at best. It is, by its nature, difficult to define, and even harder to explain. There may never be a single, clear-cut, universally-accepted explanation for the origins of rock music. It has always had a turbulent history, as we'll see in the pages that follow. From its inception, rock-n-roll has been twisted by myth, folklore, legend, rumor, and fact. There is no other kind of music – or even type of popular culture – that has such a rich history. It's a history that includes untimely deaths, lives filled with excess, strange curses, and bizarre coincidences. The Grateful Dead best described the history of rock music when they sang "What a long strange trip it's been." How it began, where it started, and why it seems so closely linked to the unexplained is an enigma.

One thing we do know is that it started in the American South, springing forth, so to speak, from the loins of the blues. What inspired it? Good question. We'll explore the nature of the blues and rock-n-roll within these pages, but I'll be honest with you right up front – I really don't think I have a solution to the mystery for you. Music is strange, and rock-n-roll is stranger, as are the people who find themselves drawn to it.

Let's get weird for a minute – or weirder – and maybe get a little off track.

Many believe there is a reason why rock-n-roll and the occult go hand-in-hand. They feel that rock musicians and their audiences make an almost unconscious pact to expand their consciousness together and push beyond the restraints of all other forms of music. Rock, they say, is the sound of both spiritual and musical rebellion and is the perfect vehicle for revitalization of ancient rituals and for penetrating the veil between this world and the realm of the spirits.

Huh?

Yeah, I promised this would get weird, but hang in there.

It's at rock concerts where musicians have staged their events to appear as moments of shamanic and religious rites, creating personas simulating magicians, demons, the gods Pan and Dionysus, even appearing as people possessed by gods and devils. They design their album covers with images of the occult, conjure lyrics from legend and myth, and fill their personal lives with quests for mystical and magical experiences.

Trust me, that's not the way they do things at the Grand Ole Opry.

But let's dig a little deeper.

Rock's affinity for the occult is due in large part to the nature of the occult itself. The occult – a popular term for anything to do with beliefs and activities linked to the supernatural, magical, and mystical ideas – operates on an unorthodox and nonconformist stage, at odds with the traditional and established religious order. Occult ideas are an attempt by an individual or group to take a more active role in their own spiritual destiny and to commune with the divine. Spirits, divination, amulets, charms, and the worship of alternate deities are a large part of the experience.

This kind of purposeful drive toward a divine encounter has surfaced in various ways throughout history and all over the world. Christianity often saw it as the work of the Devil, even within its own ranks. Renaissance magicians and alchemists were called heretics and other American sects looked on those who spoke in tongues or handled snakes as confused, at best, and as devil worshippers, at worst. In many cases, it was Christianity that perpetrated a belief in pagan activities through laws against magic and through often false accusations of witchcraft during the infamous witch trials. By creating a fear of the occult for political gain, religious authorities breathed life into the superstitions and alternate beliefs they claimed to want to eradicate.

Christianity did its best to get rid of all pagan beliefs and it mostly succeeded. It appropriated the pagan holidays that celebrated the solstice and the resurrecting god and turned them into something blander and less powerful. The original pagan rites, both theatrical and hypnotic, were lost – until rock-n-roll brought them back. In spirit, at least.

The heart of rock-n-roll was forged in the fires of ancient mystery cults, when myth and initiation were celebrated by dance, intoxication, and ecstatic revelry. In addition to this kind of worship, there was still the need for community, for myth and ritual, and for direct communion with the spirits, all played out in a theatrical setting.

It's best to imagine the history of rock-n-roll as a sort of gumbo. Early rock can be traced directly to the blues, gospel, folk, jazz, and even early experimental and classical music. In each of these, the influence of the occult was also present, often doing the same thing that rock-n-roll would be – looking for ways to revolt against convention. While rock-n-roll is a somewhat recent invention, it's like many other things that make up the human experience. Rock is part of the ancient impulse to hammer out sounds on whatever tools are available, expressing what it means to be human. For thousands of years, making music has been inseparable from religious activity. Rock-n-roll's origins are in blues and folk – forms of music deeply ingrained with Christian tradition, but whose own roots grew in soil where pagan gods were worshipped. As popular music developed, it struggled with the tension that developed between fundamental religion and the shadow of older forms of worship that were just as much a part of American music.

Just as mainstream religions have always tried to make sense of their own pagan origins – usually by replacing and demonizing the old gods – ministers, parents, and record-burning do-gooders have recognized the threat of sex and chaos that exists in all kinds of popular music, especially rock-n-roll. The response of the musicians was what saved music itself – they pushed back, conjuring up spirits with their strings and using sex as an agitation that everyone could relate to. They literally shook their hips in the face of the religious authority. Rock turned the values of traditional religion on its head. Because the mainstream church often saw sex – especially in the 1950s, when rock was truly born – as a symptom of ungodliness and the influence of evil spirits, rock musicians started a rebellion when they plugged in their amps and got teenagers dancing.

Rock-n-roll became the next "Devil's Music." It wasn't the first musical form to wear that moniker – as we'll soon see – but the label has certainly stuck. Rock's first words were sexual, drawn from deeply explicit blues lyrics and the very physicality of its rhythms. Those rhythms dated back to the arrival of the first slaves on American shores. As the slaves developed their own form of Christianity, they used song as an essential form of worship, carefully incorporating African tribal music and movement. They would shuffle in a circle, calling out and shaking in the throes of religious ecstasy. But their feet had to remain firmly on the ground. If they didn't, they risked being accused of turning their precise religious devotion into something profane – dancing. Unless it was glorifying God, music was considered profane and led to dancing, one of the most sexually charged pastimes imaginable.

And, of course, where sex is, the Devil is always lurking nearby.

Rock-n-roll, like sex, was something that religious authorities and parents wanted young people to be afraid of. But fear can be a funny thing. Fear often leads to attraction. We want to feel afraid, which strengthens our desire for things like music, sex, the supernatural, and the occult. They are temptations, especially when they lead us to people who dare to defy convention and who place themselves outside of the mainstream.

Society has long believed that music contains some enchanting attributes, going back to the story of the Pied Piper of Hamlin, who lured the children of the village away with his flute. Music can electrify both the listener and the player. Rumors of the occult, particularly stories of deals with the Devil, both attract and repel. We'll later delve into the story of blues player Robert Johnson and the legend of the deal he made at the crossroads, but Robert was far from the first musician linked to pacts with Satan.

Niccolo Paganini, a nineteenth-century composer and violin virtuoso, was accused of consorting with the Devil, who enabled Niccolo to astonish listeners with his skilled playing. The young man's physical appearance only encouraged the rumor. He was pale and extremely thin, with long black hair that fell across his face as he performed. Women were said to have screamed and fainted as he produced music that was described as otherworldly. Rumors swirled – he was a gambler, a killer, a cruel seducer of women, but it was his musical ability that caused the most speculation. Surely, he had sold his soul to the Devil – no one was naturally as good as Niccolo was. Some claimed they even saw the Devil himself pulling the violin bow as Niccolo's fingers flew across the instrument's neck. Once before a performance in France, Niccolo was forced to bring a note from his mother stating that the Devil was not his father.

But rumors of Niccolo selling his soul to the devil Did not keep devout Italian Catholics away from his music. While it took a mental toll on the musician – who wanted to be recognized for his own talent – it added to his reputation and increased the size of the audiences at his concerts.

Paganini began a long tradition of musicians that flirted with – or openly embraced – the occult. All the essential genres, from blues to heavy metal, from goth to glam, toyed with the supernatural. Magic and mysticism became an integral part of rock-n-roll, beginning in the 1960s. It could have gone another way and became merely a fusion of American blues and folk without its own identity. Instead, some of the biggest names in popular music willingly participated in a sort-of spiritual rebellion. The Beatles, Led Zeppelin, David Bowie, the Rolling Stones, Black Sabbath, and many others not only transformed rock by embracing the occult but kept it from remaining a series of redundant chord records that were spinning away the hours on AM radio.

It would be futile with this book to try and list every album that featured a pentagram, a Devil's face, a sigil, or some other mystical or occult symbol. It would be impossible to name every song that references wizards and warlocks, devils and demons, tarot cards, ghosts, or Aleister Crowley. It would be overwhelming – and pretty boring – to try and examine every musician that has dabbled in the occult.

What I have tried to do instead is to chronicle the "dark side" of music, from the earliest influences of the occult to the way that music has even inspired some pretty famous crimes. We'll look at rock-n-roll curses, assorted mayhem, strange, possibly supernatural coincidences, and the way that many artists saw their lives turned upside down by fame, excess, and weird influences.

This is a book that I have probably wanted to write for most of my life. I was exposed to music – specifically to rock-n-roll – when I was very young. The Doors, Janis Joplin, Eagles, Bob Seger – they're all part of my early memories. There was never a time in my life that I was not a fan of rock-n-roll, and I've never been able to shake it. Although, really, I've never tried. Because of my fascination with the supernatural, I've always looked at the way that music and the occult have gone hand in hand. So, this book was really a natural one for me and I always knew I'd get to it eventually.

I guess what I'm saying is that I didn't write this book for you. This one was just for me. Don't get me wrong – I appreciate you buying it and I hope you enjoy it. But even if you don't, I'm okay with that. I did this one for me – like Elvis once said about the way the music made his hips shake, "I can't help it."

Troy Taylor
Winter 2018-2019

PART ONE:
THE DEVIL'S MUSIC

THe DeVIL'S mUSIC...
LITeRaLLY

It's the "Devil's Music." You're going to hear that a lot in this book – in fact, you already have – and it's been used to describe everything from jazz, to the blues, to, of course, rock-n-roll. But at one time, religious leaders weren't just referring to a certain type of music as being detrimental to the souls of those who listened to it. They were serious. They actually believed that some types of music were literally the work of the Devil himself.

Of course, we have to keep in mind that during the Middle Ages, the Catholic Church taught that music was a gift from God and that it was only supposed to be played in celebration of the Lord. This meant that any form of secular music was not only disapproved of by the Church, it was considered to be a glorification of the Devil. But even within some religious music, the Church tried to discourage composers from using certain intervals in music, such as the "augmented fourth interval" of the *Tritonus* – a spooky little ditty that was really only used by Gregorian monks when they sang about the apocalypse.

Playing music that was written in praise of God was supposed to sound pleasant. For composers of the day, this was easy to arrange. Take a C major scale – just the white keys on the piano – plunk out any two-note combination, and you'll find that they're all religious-grade harmonies.

Except one.

Played in sequence or together, the notes F, B, D sharp, and G sharp clash in a way that feels eerie, unnatural, and foreboding. If you're reading this and don't have a piano handy, think of the first notes of "Purple Haze" by Jimi Hendrix, or American police sirens. Spooky, right?

Before composers began using major and minor scales, this interval was considered so unnatural that it was dubbed "The Devil's Interval." It was actually believed that using it could summon the Devil – or so the legend goes.

To explain it further, if you change one of the notes slightly, the dissonance turns to harmony. What's really happening when we hear dissonance has to do with the relationship between frequencies—the two pitches of the Devil's Interval create a much more complicated ratio of frequencies than other intervals and are therefore much harder for the human ear to reconcile.

The demonic combination was considered largely off-limits in medieval times, though there's no historical evidence to say that it was banned outright. The Devil's Interval was occasionally used, although it as always in the gravest of musical circumstances – like when talking about the apocalypse or Christ's crucifixion.

Even during the seventeenth and eighteenth centuries, as the Church's influence over cultural traditions faded, composers continued to avoid the Devil's Interval. In the odd passages where tritones appeared, their use was technical: to create – and quickly resolve – tension. Then, suddenly, at the dawn of the Romantic era of classical music, it returned, in Act 2 of Beethoven's 1805 opera, *Fidelio*. As the scene opens in a dungeon – about the 1:20 point in the recording for those playing along at home – the kettle drums rumble menacingly, tuned in at the Devil's Interval.

After that, something like obsession followed, as composers used tritones to probe the darkest corners of humanity. Perhaps the best-known from this period is "Danse Macabre" by Camille Saint-Saëns, which we'll return to in a moment. Another Frenchmen, Hector Berlioz, boldly subjected listeners to the Devil's Interval in the opening of an aria – no surprise that it was about damnation. Another famous example appears in the combination of two tritone intervals during Siegfried's Funeral March in Götterdämmerung ("Twilight of the Gods"), the final opera of Wagner's Ring Cycle. Franz Listz, the Hungarian composer and piano virtuoso, also used tritones for ghastly effect—for example, to evoke Dante's descent into hell in the opening notes of his "Dante Sonata."

At the same time that Romantic composers were reveling in the Devil's Interval, they were also experimenting with another snippet of Catholic Church music that was used to evoke doom – the haunting theme from a thirteenth-century Gregorian chant called the *Dies Irae*, which translates from Latin to the uplifting phrase "Day of Wrath."

When it was sung acapella-style by monks it was plenty eerie but when composers began using it to conjure up music, it became downright sinister.

Hector Berlioz – the Frenchmen who gets credit for a lot of creepy music in his career – gets the credit for this bloodcurdling breakthrough when it invoked *Dies Irae* in his 1830 work, *Symphonie Fantastique*.

Go ahead, look it up – again, I'll wait.

As you may have heard, even without the apocalyptic refrain, it's a pretty freaky piece of music. It's essentially about a bad trip that turns ghastly. It tells the story of an artist who, believing himself rejected by the woman that he's stalking, tries to overdose on opium. In the hallucination that results, he ends up killing the woman, being beheaded, and then witnessing his funeral devolve into a witch's sabbath.

Good stuff, right?

Hector Berlioz – stalker, drug friend, and composer of scary music.

You may not be shocked to learn that Berlioz was a pretty accomplished stalker in real life, or that most historians believed that he composed *Symphonie Fantastique* while stoned on opium. He also once hatched a bumbling – and luckily, failed – plan to murder his former fiancée. The *Dies Irae* comes in during the final movement, in a fugue with the theme of the dancing witches, bubbling cauldron, and diabolical orgy. And so, you know, the orgy started at about 3:25 in the movement.

The use of the theme spread from Berlioz's dope trip and started showing up in the works of Johannes Brahms, Charles Gounod, Pyotyr Tchaikovsky, Frederic Chopin, and Sergei Rachmaninoff, who wins the prize for using *Dies Irae* the most. Although Franz Liszt – who happened to be in the audience at the 1830 premiere of *Symphonie Fantastique* – was the composer who became obsessed with *Dies Irae*.

A pioneer of infernally complicated piano pieces, Liszt had a real passion for the Devil, death, and other dark subjects and – unsurprisingly – featured either the *Dies Irae* or the Devil's Interval or both in several pieces, including "Dante Sonata" and "Mephisto Waltz." His "Totentanz" – "Dance of Death," or "Danse Macabre" in French – was a devilishly frenzied work for piano and orchestra. It opens with the *Dies Irae* and uses the Devil's Interval throughout.

The "Dance of Death" refers to a medieval allegory in which the dead rise to dance with the living to remind them of their mortality. This idea became a popular subject of frescoes and cemetery murals across Europe.

The French weren't content to just leave the idea to the Church. They pushed the "Dance of Death" into the realm of celebration. And it wasn't just in their artwork. They dressed up corpses at village fairs and court parties to act out the *Danse Macabre*. A superstition was even born that claimed that at the stroke of midnight on All Hallow's Eve, Death walked forth and summoned the dead to dance with him.

Romantic-era heavyweights like Gustav Mahler and Modest Mussorgsky used the "Dance of Death" in their music. But given France's rich traditions with the idea, it should come as no surprise that the most enduring rendition – and the biggest Halloween hit of the nineteenth century – came from a Frenchmen: Camille Saint-Saëns. And as with Liszt's "Totentanz," Saint-Saëns's 1872 work *Danse Macabre* uses the doom-laden combination of the Devil's Interval" and the *Dies Irae*.

The piece begins with 12 plucks of a harp string depicting a bell tolling at midnight. Then, in comes the "Devil's Interval" – raw, savage, almost painful screeches of a solo violin that is played by Death.

Camille Saint-Saëns – creator of Danse Macabre, one of the classic occult music pieces of all time

Seriously, go listen to this one. You're going to recognize it from a dozen different films and commercials – and it shows up in horror films for a very good reason. I have to confess that I'm not an aficionado of classical music, but this is one of my favorites.

Now that you're back, I think we can agree on how eerie this music is. The Dies Irae appears about halfway through the piece, but by then, it was an old trope. More innovative were Saint-Saëns's other eerie methods of celebrating the horror – like the xylophone being used to emulate the cracking of bones. When the oboe sounds the crowing of the rooster, the dead retreat back to their graves, and the whole ghoulish thing comes to an end.

The "Devil's Interval," of course, has never gone away. Stanley Kubrick used it in the opening music for *The Shining* and it also made it into horror classics like *The Exorcist* and *Poltergeist*. As mentioned already, Jimi Hendrix used it, and among heavy metal bands, it approaches cult status. Lots of groups have included it in their music, but perhaps the most famous use of its unholy eeriness is the opening of Black Sabbath's song, "Black Sabbath" in 1970.

While metal bands have carried on the innovation of the "Devil's Interval" from the Romantic era, other genres have broadened its appeal. In the first notes of the song "Maria," from *West Side Story*, composer Leonard

Bernstein used it to create a weird tension that resolves. Danny Elfman did the same thing in the opening notes of the theme song to *The Simpsons*. Thanks to its unique ambiguity, it's found everywhere in jazz chords. Its wider popularity these days probably has something to so with the fact that Death and the Devil aren't quite as frightening as they were 200 years ago.

Or that the Church soon found other kinds of "Devil's Music" to worry about.

"THE DEVIL'S TRILL"

The Devil might not be as terrifying to most people as he was two centuries ago, but I think that we can all agree that music written to explore the fear of death and evil still has a power that endures. Throughout history, however, people have tried to find words to explain the power that music possesses. As author Aldous Huxley put it, "After silence, that which comes nearest to expressing the inexpressible is music."

But that really doesn't make it much clearer.

The profound effect that music has on us has been the subject of many scientific studies. It seems that our brains are wired to be influenced by different harmonies and tones, which invoke different responses in our brains.

We have already discussed the so-called "Devil's Interval," which first achieved notoriety in the Middle Ages. The human ear by nature was more accustomed to simpler-sounding tones than complex ones. The interval was complex and conflicting and was difficult to execute, earning it a reputation as something to be avoided. But, of course, it's never gone away, and used effectively, can cause a strong reaction in an audience, just the way that Camille Saint-Saëns did it with "Danse Macabre."

A century and a half before Saint-Saëns, though, there was a young, aristocratic youth from Venice who was a philosopher and dreamer by nature, but was forced to study to law at the University of Padua. He fled from school and traveled to a monastery in the province of Perugia. It was there, in 1716, that he met Francesco Maria Veracini, a master of the violin. The young man knew nothing of the instrument, but he was fascinated.

He eventually obtained his own violin – given to him by Antonio Stradivari – and locked himself in a room in Ancona. He was determined to learn to play. Months passed, and the boy emerged from his room transformed into a great musician. He developed a serious knowledge about the history of music, the principles of acoustics, and, most importantly, a vast

Tartini believed that the Devil came into his dreams and helped him to create the Violin Sonata in G Minor – the "Devil's Trill"

understanding of the "third sound" – the overtones produced when two notes are played simultaneously. He was able to play them in perfect harmony.

The name of the young man was Giuseppe Tartini, and he became known as *Il Maestro Delle Nazioni* in Italy and was considered one of the finest musicians in the world. He also composed one of the greatest pieces of music ever written: Violin Sonata in G Minor – the Devil's Trill. It was a sonata intended for one violin and with a series of swift changes in pace offers a melody that is haunting and deeply dramatic. There had been nothing written like it before – and not much since either. The dreamlike harmony goes from sadness to climax and from climax to sadness over and over again throughout its 15-minute recording time. The "Devil's Interval" is used in a commanding way throughout.

The composition – still considered one of the hardest scores to play – was unlike anything that anyone had heard before. Where had the talent come from to create something like it? Tartini had been a young boy with no experience with the violin before retreating from the world to become a master.

The legends say that he may have had some help.

Just before his death in 1770, Tartini told his friend, French astronomer Jerome Lalande, a strange story about the origin of the music. He explained:

"One night, in the year 1713, I dreamed I had made a pact with the Devil for my soul. Everything went as I wished: my new servant anticipated my every desire. Among other things, I gave him my violin to see if he could play. How great was my astonishment on hearing a sonata so wonderful and so beautiful, played with such great art and intelligence, as I had never even conceived in my boldest flights of fantasy.

"I felt enraptured, transported, enchanted: my breath failed me, and I awoke. I immediately grasped my violin in order to retain, in part at least, the impression of my dream. In vain! The music which I at this time composed is indeed the best that I ever wrote, and I still call it the 'Devil's Trill,' but the difference between it and that which so moved me is so great that I would have destroyed my instrument and have said farewell to music forever if it had been possible for me to live without the enjoyment it affords me."

Although not confirmed, Tartini's beautiful, intricate, seemingly impossible sonata was written during his time in seclusion when he was learning to use an instrument that he had never touched before. His eccentricity led people to believe that he was going mad during his isolated retreat and during the years of fanatical training that followed. Since then, many composers have tried to explain how Tartini managed to create his masterpiece. Some have suggested that perhaps he had six fingers on his hand.

Others, well, take the story of a deal with the Devil a little too seriously.

SOUNDS OF HORROR

We'll step away from the realm of classical music soon, but I can't do so without mentioning some of the other supernatural influences on music that occurred during the nineteenth century. Far too much of it continues to echo through popular culture today. Ghosts, evil creatures, and malevolent monsters were alive and well in the early 1800s, and their popularity became reflected in the music of the era.

For the most part, we can thank the "Goths." And no, I'm not talking about the fans of the Cure, Bauhaus, and Joy Division, although they're all indebted to the original followers of the Gothic who became enamored with crumbling castles, skeleton monks, and ancient family curses in the early nineteenth century.

It wasn't music that started the movement, though, it was a book – Horace Walpole's *The Castle of Otranto*. It's widely believed to be the first Gothic novel, setting the blueprint for a dark literary genre that was obsessed with terror, death, and the supernatural.

The Gothic sensibility – a fascination with the ghostly, the ghastly, and the terrifying – would not remain limited to the literary world. Much has been written about the genre's close relationship with art and architecture, but it had a great effect on the composers of music, too. The supernatural elements of it became a rich source of inspiration for composers in the nineteenth century and continues to inspire today. Attempts to represent the horrific, supernatural, and otherworldly led composers to explore new sounds and experiment beyond the conventional parameters of the era.

The rise in popularity of the Gothic came about with the height of the period known as the Enlightenment – an ironic twist, considering that the two movements were at the very opposite ends of the spectrum. The Gothic concerned itself with ghosts and the supernatural, while logic and reason were central to the philosophy of the age of Enlightenment.

The contrast was glaringly obvious in the early examples of the genre. Ann Radcliffe achieved a compromise of sorts with her brand of "rational Gothic" where – like in Scooby-Doo cartoons – the otherworldly occurrences were eventually given a logical explanation. As for Walpole, he tried to distance himself from his creation – which, by the way, included a giant ghost's head – by presenting his book as an alleged adaptation of an Italian medieval text that was supposedly discovered among the belongings of an ancient family in Northern England. When his anonymous first edition turned out to be a surprise hit, Walpole later revealed that the frame story was merely a literary device, which caused the novel to be panned by the same critics who had once praised it. *The Castle of Otranto* also managed to alternate its horrific scenes with comedic sections, further mitigating the more gruesome aspects of the novel.

That same kind of ambivalence was reflected in a major musical work of the same period – Mozart's opera *Il Dissoluto Punito ossia il Don Giovanni* (The Rake Punished or Don Giovanni). There are few more chilling moments in opera than the scene in which Don Giovanni is marched off to Hell by a statue that comes to life. And yet, these kinds of shocking moments are presented against the backdrop of a comic opera, making them more palatable to audiences of the period. Interestingly, changes in taste that soon came along meant that later productions chose to cut the work short, giving it a tragic finish, rather than the comedic one that concluded the original opera.

Mozart himself left little doubt about the tone he intended for the show. The very opening of the overture foreshadows the music that accompanies the ghostly entrance of the haunted statue. It's set in dark D Minor and accompanied by the scurrying sound of strings.

But explaining away the supernatural wouldn't last.

With the advent of the Romantic period, the excesses of the Gothic novel became more attuned to the spirit of the times. *The Monk* by Matthew Lewis adopted elements found in the works of Walpole, Radcliffe, and their many imitators and unapologetically took them to extremes. He threw in evil clerics, ghosts, shapeshifting demons, diabolical rituals, torture, violence, and lots and lots of sex. His book became known as one of the most shocking ever written and became a phenomenal bestseller. It also brought an end to the genre because no one at the time could ever possibly hope to imitate it. It was time for the genre to reinvent itself.

Industrialization and a changing social climate soon gave rise to new anxieties. New elements of the Gothic were born causing the novels of the Brontë sisters – such as *Jane Eyre* and *Wuthering Heights* – to abandon crumbling medieval castles and transpose their brand of terror into a domestic context. New "urban gothic" novels – like those of Charles Dickens and Wilkie Collins – discovered horror in the dirty streets and oppressive fog of the city, while Mary Shelley's *Frankenstein* explored what it meant to be human at a time when science was close to discovering the mysteries of life. In America, the works of Nathaniel Hawthorne and Edgar Allan Poe were unleashing their own brand of terror and the uncanny.

Literature had taken an even darker turn, so it should come as no surprise that similar themes began to haunt the music of the era. One of the best examples is *Der Freischütz* by Carl Maria von Weber. It became one of the landmarks of German Romantic opera and recounted the tale of a rifleman who struck a deal with an evil spirit in order to obtain magical bullets. The most original part of the score is the "Wolf Glen" scene where the very texture of the music, especially its use of the lowest notes of the orchestra, evokes a feeling of supernatural dread.

I know what you're thinking – it's opera. For most of us, just considering the idea of listening to it fills us with "supernatural dread," but one of the world's most influential opera critics called it "the most expressive rendering of the gruesome that is to be found in a musical score." That seems like a big deal to me.

The pact described in Weber's opera could be described as "Faustian," an adjective that is derived from a German legend about a scholar that sells his soul to the Devil in exchange for unlimited knowledge. It was a story with strong Gothic elements that was retold by various writers like Christopher Marlowe and Goethe. Several composers of the Romantic era were inspired by the supernatural legend to write both symphonies and operas and, let's be honest, it's a story that's never really died. It's still very much present in film, literature, and music today.

And some might say that a deal with the Devil led to the popularity of the blues, but we'll get to that soon.

Throughout the first half of the nineteenth century, scores of other operas appeared with plots that were inspired by supernatural events or elements of horror -- Giuseppe Verdi's *Macbeth* (1847) and *Rigoletto* (1851), Giacomo Meyerbeer's *Robert le Diable* (1831), Wagner's *The Flying Dutchman* (1843), to name just a few.

There were other Gothic operas which, like the novels of Ann Radcliffe, relied less on the otherworldly for effect and more on dark settings and borderline psychological states. In French and Italian operas of the middle nineteenth century, it became customary to include what was called a "mad scene," where one of the protagonists would descend into insanity. From a dramatic point of view, these scenes satisfied the audience's thirst for the extreme -- without descending into the supernatural – and musically, gave the performers a chance to display the limits of their vocal talents.

The best treatment of Gothic themes can be found in two compositions that I mentioned previously -- Hector Berlioz's *Symphonie Fantastique* and Camille Saint-Saëns's *Danse Macabre*. Seriously, this is good stuff and if you ignored my efforts to get you to listen to them in the last section, do it now. I'm not joking.

Both pieces are the musical equivalent of Matthew Lewis's *The Monk* in their intensity and were almost impossible to imitate. But if their excesses are not to your taste, there's also the suitable – but equally Gothic – *Winterreise* (Winter Journey) by Franz Schubert. It's a cycle of 24 songs, originally written for tenor and piano, that seems to be world's away from Berlioz and Saint-Saëns. However, its subject matter explores similar ground.

Later in the nineteenth century, there was an interesting development in the Gothic. Several composers – especially in Central and Eastern Europe – began combining supernatural themes with a nationalistic agenda, turning to horrific legends and myths of their countries as inspiration for patriotic works. The development reflected the late nineteenth century's growing interest in the study and publication of national sagas, myths, and legends. Composers of a nationalistic bent – and yes, that meant the same thing then as it does today, and it wasn't a good thing then either – tapped into these old, often macabre legends in order to find homegrown subjects that predated what they felt was the ruination of their country by political or cultural powers to which they were opposed.

Whatever the reason, these nationalistic composers seemed most inclined to portray dark and supernatural themes. This is evidenced by compositions like Lyadov's *Baba-Yaga* and Mussorgsky's *Night on Bald Mountain*, and, of course, pretty much anything by Wagner, who became known as "Hitler's favorite composer." His dredging up of old legends in his serious and intensely Teutonic music "struck a chord" with Hitler. Wagner was violently antisemitic and even wrote a booklet that insisted that the Jews had poisoned public taste in the arts.

You can understand why Hitler was such a fan.

Two different world wars effectively ended the Gothic movement in music and literature, but it remained very much alive in the film world, especially in productions from the British Hammer films of the 1950s and 1960s. Hammer revived nineteenth century favorites like Dracula and Frankenstein and set most of its films in the crumbling castles, secluded villages, and fog-shrouded graveyards.

It would not really be until the late 1960s and early 1970s that the Gothic would return to music – enjoying its heyday in the 1980s. The Gothic bands of the new era incorporated influences from nineteenth century literature, the Romantic and Victorian eras, from horror films, and from combinations of all of the above.

And they dressed in black. Lots of black.

According to music journalist Simon Reynolds, standard music fixtures of Gothic rock included "scything guitar patterns, high-pitched basslines that often usurped the melodic role [and] beats that were either hypnotically dirge-like or tom-tom heavy and 'tribal'."

And like the music inspired by the literature of the original Gothic era, it typically addressed dark themes through lyrics and the music's atmosphere. The poetic sensibilities of the genre led Gothic rock lyrics to delve into literary romanticism, existentialism, religious symbolism, or supernatural mysticism. The musicians who initially shaped the aesthetics and musical conventions of Gothic rock included the Velvet Underground, the Doors, David Bowie, Brian Eno, and even Alice Cooper, thanks to his theatrics and black humor.

Often described as the "first Goth album," Nico's 1969 album, *The Marble Index*, introduced a stark sound, somber lyrics, and Nico's deliberate change in her look to become a crucial music and visual prototype for the Gothic rock movement. But the Doors predated her – at least as far as music critics were concerned. Critic John Stickney had used the term "gothic rock" to describe Jim Morrison and the band in October 1967. Even so, it never really caught on.

It would again be a book that changed everything. In 1976, Anne Rice published *Interview with a Vampire*. The main character, although a dark and tortured soul, only wanted companionship and love, which he never believed he could truly have. The book spoke to legions of fans and slowly created an audience for Gothic rock by word of mouth.

By the late 1970s, the word "gothic" was used to describe the atmosphere of post-punk bands like Siouxsie and the Banshees and Joy Division. They were called the "masters of this gothic gloom." And when Joy Division's final album *Closer* came out a couple of months after the death of their singer, a review noted that there were "dark strokes of gothic rock."

In the early 1980s, more bands followed, like Bauhaus and the Cramps. The Cure's oppressively dispirited trio of albums, *Seventeen Seconds* (1980), *Faith* (1981) and *Pornography* (1982), cemented that group's stature in the genre. They were followed by others – Nick Cave, Killing Joke, Adam and the Ants, Flesh for Lulu, Play Dead, Gene Loves Jezebel, Blood and Roses, Cocteau Twins, Dead Can Dance, and others. The Icelandic group Kukl also appeared in this period, which included Björk and other musicians who later became part of the Sugarcubes.

Goth music went through many changes as the years went on, becoming heavier and – if possible – even darker. Bands like Sisters of Mercy, Fields of the Nephilim, Dream Disciples, Nosferatu, Rosetta Stone, and Suspiria began a crossover from the industrial, electronic, and metal scenes, and, by the late 1990s, Gothic metal fused the bleak atmospherics of the early Goth music with the loud guitars and aggression of heavy metal.

And it's still going strong, in one version or another. As one form of Gothic music embraces death through unintelligible lyrics and thrashing guitars, Robert Smith of the Cure just keeps putting out albums, so the movement endures.

And it all started because of ghost stories, old castles, and a handful of horror books that few people in the twenty-first century have ever read.

DEVIL'S MUSIC BORN IN A BROTHEL

Jazz music is, without a doubt, an American invention. That's about the only thing that we know for sure, other than it originated within the African-American communities of New Orleans in the late nineteenth and early twentieth centuries. Even though jazz has its roots in the blues, Ragtime, traditional African music, and spirituals, it's unlike any other kind of music that exists. It is one of America's original art forms, and, despite the title that I gave to this section, it was not actually born in the red-light districts of New Orleans – it just seemed that way. It was in the city's whorehouses that jazz became famous.

That also turned it into history's next version of the "Devil's Music."

The new sound was born sometime in the middle 1890s, in the working-class black clubs and honky-tonks near the poor Uptown neighborhood. You could hear it in the venues in and around South Rampart Street – like Dago Tony's and the Red Onion – and further away, in the dives on the other side of Canal Street. For a time, the music was only known to those who flocked to such places – the so-called "ratty people." But before long, the new sound was being heard in parks, on street corners, in dance halls, and well beyond the confines of the black neighborhoods.

And, of course, that's when the trouble started.

It's believed to have been a young cornet player from Uptown named Buddy Bolden who first played the music later known as jazz. Certainly, many others – black, mixed-race, and even white – would later lay claim to the distinction, but many of his contemporaries believe that it was Bolden who started it all. To hear them tell the story, he was extraordinary. "That boy could make women jump out windows," one of his listeners said. For many people in New Orleans, accustomed to straighter, more schooled forms of music, the new sound was a revelation.

Charles Joseph "Buddy" Bolden, like most of the jazzmen that followed him, grew up poor, with few prospects. The grandson of slaves, he was born on September 6, 1877, in a small house on Howard Street in the Uptown neighborhood. It was a tough place to live. On the edge of a fetid, foul-smelling canal, Buddy had lost his father, one sister, and his grandmother to various illnesses by the time he was six-years-old. Buddy and his sister, Cora, moved around with their mother, Alice, for a few years, staying with relatives and friends. They finally settled in a shotgun cottage on First Street, a tough but integrated neighborhood that was populated mostly by German and Irish immigrants who had little trouble getting along with their black neighbors. Alice made a modest living there taking in laundry, earning enough to keep her children in school.

Buddy grew up around music. In New Orleans – then, as now – it was everywhere. He heard it played on the streets, in parks, and in church, but he had no musical training of any kind until 1894, when his mother allowed him to take cornet lessons from a neighbor named Manuel Hall, a short-order cook. He was 16, which was a late start for a musician, but Buddy learned quickly. He soon found lots of opportunities to play. The city's established brass bands would sometimes have long work days, playing funerals or association affairs that went from early morning to late at night. When they needed a break or a beer, they'd have young men like Buddy fill in for them. By 1897, though, he was already playing with his own regular band at parades and picnics. And despite – or more likely, because of – his lack of formal training, he was soon attracting attention for taking street songs, hymns, and dance tunes and creating a musical sound that people were unfamiliar with.

Jazz icon "Buddy" Bolden

The Bolden sound, to hear witnesses describe it, was hot, wide-open, low-down and – like his most ardent fans – "ratty." It was bluesy and folksy and made you want to dance. You won't find any recordings of Buddy today, but you can get an idea of his sound by searching out the Buddy Bolden Legacy Band. Give them a listen and you'll understand how groundbreaking this sound was for the time.

Buddy couldn't read music very well, but that didn't matter much, since he could pick up anything he needed by ear. He "borrowed" sounds from other bands and got ideas from everywhere, including from the "Holy Roller" churches that he sometimes attended with his mother and sister. The music was electric. It was showy, improvisational, sometimes raunchy, and always very, very loud.

Soon, the Bolden Band was attracting a lot of attention – and a lot of imitators. Even some of the older musicians took notice. There were plenty of bandleaders in the city already making innovative music, but Buddy took things in a whole new direction. "Buddy was the first to play blues for dancing," one fellow musician summed it up. But it was younger musicians in particular that picked up the new sound. Not just other cornet players, either. It quickly became popular with clarinetists, trombone and bass players, drummers, and guitarists. Musicians like Freddie Keppard, Pops Foster, Bunk Johnson, "Big Eye" Louis Nelson, Willie Cornish, Frankie Dusen, and even a young Creole piano player named Jelly Roll Morton were soon doing their own innovations, taking old tunes -- and making up new ones – and putting their own personalities to them.

What exactly were they playing? That's still up for debate, but critics have tried to trace its lineage to African, Caribbean, French, or Spanish roots, to ragtime, to various religious forms, to traditions like the blues. But, in a way, it was completely new music created by untrained musicians who were doing whatever they wanted. As one old jazzman put it, "That's where jazz came from – from the routine men, you understand – the men that didn't know nothing about music. They just made up their own ideas."

Buddy was riding high with his new sound. Other musicians had noticed, but so had the ladies. He was soon a local celebrity in Uptown, traveling around with a harem of female admirers who would fight one another to hold his hat, his coat, and even his handkerchief. He loved the attention. One of the women – a slightly older neighbor named Hattie Oliver – even bore him a baby son before Buddy's twentieth birthday. Buddy took care of both mother and child, at least for a while.

Eventually, though, the new sound played by Buddy and his imitators became so popular – among working-class audiences both black and white – that it started drawing unwanted attention, too. The police would show up at so-called cutting contests – where two bands would meet and try and outplay each other – and starting cracking heads to "restore order." City reformers also started to take notice, and they didn't like what they heard. To their ears, the new sound was dangerous, an affront to their notions of respectability, restraint, temperance, and civil order. The new black music represented excess and sexuality, a direct violation of traditional moral values. Worst of all, it promoted contact – much of it the most scandalous type – across the color line. This was intolerable to most southern whites of the era.

Even before Buddy began to make his mark, reformers had already started protesting the detrimental effects of what they classily called "coon music." And now, with the rising popularity of Buddy and his peers, black music in New Orleans had taken an ominous new turn. Jazz represented the equivalent of "musical miscegenation" and for those self-styled white supremacists who wanted order, racial purity, and respectability, that meant it had to be suppressed. Many whites in the city believed that the music literally challenged the Jim Crow laws of the time, by bringing black and white audiences together. Jazz was, in a very real sense, an expression of defiance, rebelling against the increasing efforts to marginalize and suppress the African-American race. Because of this, it was viewed as a threat to the entire social order that was being reasserted in the post-Reconstruction era South.

Organized efforts to quash the growth of jazz were still a few years away. In the meantime, there were just sporadic acts of intimidation – a band

Storyville in New Orleans

at a party broken up here, a racially mixed street party raided by the police there. In 1896, during one of the city's occasional smallpox outbreaks, an effort was made to close the notorious "Negro dives" of Franklin Street. It was allegedly for health reasons, but it was really to shut down the jazz bands. Regardless, the effort failed.

And then came Storyville, where it was hoped that jazz music could be as easily segregated and contained as prostitution would be. It was the first phase of the city's efforts to reform. By putting everything disrespectable and disruptive in one place, it would make it easier to control.

Or so they thought.

Prostitution had been part of New Orleans since the very beginning. In fact, the first women who were shipped over from France when the colony began were prostitutes and criminals who were recruited from the prisons. Sporting houses did big business in the city but by the 1890s, city authorities finally came to the realization that unless some sort of suppressive or regulatory measures were carried out, the city would eventually be transformed into one large vice district. Several regulatory ordinances were proposed, but all failed, including one that provided for a segregated vice district and the issuing of licenses to prostitutes. The measure fell before the united opposition of clergymen and women's groups, who advanced the argument that such a law would recognize the existence of vice in New Orleans – which, at this point, was very hard to miss.

Nothing further was done about the matter until January 26, 1897, when the City Council adopted the now famous ordnance introduced by Alderman Sidney Story that would set aside an area where prostitution would not only be permitted but would actually be legal. The ordnance was changed and adapted several times before it was finally determined that this red-light district would comprise a five-block area on each of Customhouse, Bienville, Conti, and St. Louis Streets, and three each on North Basin, Treme, Villere, Marais, North Franklin, and North Robertson Streets – a total of 38 blocks occupied solely by brothels, saloons, cabarets, and other enterprises that depended on vice for their prosperity.

The removal of prostitutes to these streets, several of which were already well-filled with bordellos, began during the late summer of 1897 and was in full swing on October 1, when the Story ordnance went into effect. By the middle of 1898, the movement had been completed and the new district, popularly known as "Storyville" – much to the alderman's chagrin – began operating under the law. The brothels were now safe from interference by the police so long as they conducted themselves with restraint and no crimes were committed in them.

Within a few years, Storyville became the most celebrated red-light district in the United States and tourists came from all over to both see and experience it. The gateway to Storyville was the property of Thomas C. Anderson, saloon-keeper, political boss of the Fourth Ward, member of the legislature for two terms, owner of at least one of the most prosperous sporting houses in the district, and the unofficial "mayor" of Storyville. Anderson owned a restaurant and cabaret on Rampart Street, as well as several other places. His main establishment, the Annex, was the most important place in the district and served as the "town hall."

Storyville boomed during Anderson's years as the district's leader. The area along North Basin Street was the site of the new district's swankiest brothels. The imposing three- and four-story mansions were bordellos where business was conducted with considerable elegance and ceremony. Rudeness and lewd behavior on the part of the customers was frowned upon and drunken gentlemen were not accommodated. When a man entered the parlor, he was expected to buy a drink – incidentally, at great profit to the house – but the girls were not brought out for inspection unless he requested it. All the sporting houses were more or less expensively furnished and equipped, with as much gilt and velvet as the madams and their financial backers could afford. Many of them had one or more rooms with mirrored walls and ceilings, which were available at special rates; ballrooms with hardwood floors for dancing; and curtained stages for indecent performances and erotic displays that were given whenever sufficient money was offered.

Storyville became an important venue for jazz music. At first, the establishments of the district were reluctant to hire bands – if customers were busy dancing, after all, they wouldn't be buying drinks or women. But eventually, the new music became too popular to ignore. Buddy Bolden's band, as well as other hot ensembles, were soon playing regularly at Storyville clubs like Nancy Hank's Saloon and the Big 25. Tom Anderson's Annex began by hiring a string trio – piano, guitar, and violin – but eventually became a spot for larger bands, too. The brothels also wanted the new music. It was often in the form of a single piano "professor" playing in the parlor while clients chose their partners for the night, but it was something.

According to some reports, Countess Willie Piazza was the first madam to bring music into her sporting house, hiring a legendary pianist known as John the Baptist to play on her famous white grand. Other pianists like Tony Jackson, Clarence Williams, and Jerry Roll Morton eventually found their own regular gigs in the district, at Lulu White's, Gipsy Schaeffer's, Hilma Burt's, and other Basin Street brothels.

Storyville may not be the birthplace of jazz, as has sometimes been claimed, but the various venues in the district did provide many early jazzmen with employment and helped to bring their music to a wider – and usually non-black – audience. Of course, this was what earned jazz its early reputation as "whorehouse music," but the musicians that played it didn't much care so long as they had an audience and they were getting paid.

The groundbreaking musicians soon reached a new audience, including reporters who were writing stories about the brothels of Storyville, thus connecting jazz and vice for their readers. Whether the connection was deserved or not, Storyville began the careers of many musicians who went on to great fame like Joseph "King" Oliver, Manuel Manetta, Oscar "Papa" Celestin, Frank "Dude" Amacker, Steve Lewis, and many others. It also provided a home to perhaps 200 or more other musicians who worked the mansions of the district but of whom little record remains today. They are only recalled as whispered legends from a time when music rolled out of brothel windows and echoed down Basin Street.

Unlike jazz, though, Storyville didn't last. It was doomed by America's entrance into World War I in 1917. In August, Secretary of War Newton D. Baker issued an order forbidding open prostitution within five miles of an Army camp. A similar rule was made for naval bases and later that same month, Bascom Johnson, representing the War and Navy Departments, visited New Orleans, inspected Storyville, and informed Mayor Martin Behrman that it had to be shuttered. Mayor Behrman protested all the way to

Washington, but it was no use. If the city didn't close Storyville, the military would do it for them.

The deadline was November 12. After that, it would be illegal to operate a brothel anywhere in New Orleans. On Saturday night, November 10, two days before the new law went into effect, a large force of police officers was sent to Storyville to prevent the trouble that was expected to come from the closing. None developed and, in fact, the district was quieter than usual, as if in mourning. There were a few people in the streets but most of the saloons, cabarets, and brothels were empty. Many of them had already closed and the red lights had been removed from the windows of others.

On November 11, madam Gertrude Dix appealed to the civil courts for an injunction that would prevent the city from closing the district, but the request was refused. The exodus from Storyville had actually started two weeks earlier but most of the prostitutes had waited for the result of Gertrude Dix's application for a restraining order. When the news of her failure spread, wagons and vans began hauling away whatever furniture remained that had not been sold to the second-hand dealers. As late as midnight on November 12, there was still a parade of women, laden with property, leaving the district. The next afternoon, police officers visited every house and informed the women that if they remained in Storyville, they had to take down their red lights and that they would be watched and arrested if they continued to operate. Gertrude Dix was one of the few that remained. After a few months, she reopened her house and ran it secretly until she was arrested by agents from the Department of Justice on May 13, 1918. Four other places were also raided. Gertrude entered a guilty plea and spent five days in the House of Detention.

On November 14, the *New Orleans Item* announced that the police planned to round up any of the men who came looking for prostitutes in what was once Storyville and send them out into the countryside to help the farmers. Needless to say, nothing came of this idea.

The next day, many leading church women, and members of the Louisiana Federation of Women's Clubs, held a meeting and put together a committee to help the prostitutes that had been driven out. No one ever applied for the promised aid. Few of the women of Storyville needed it. They had simply moved on to new locations in various business and residential sections of New Orleans and continued plying their profession.

The jazzmen also kept working their trade in the clubs and dives throughout the city, although by the time that Storyville closed, Buddy Bolden was no longer playing the music that he essentially created. By 1917, Buddy had lost his mind.

Before that happened, though, Buddy was around to see jazz start attracting white audiences from every walk of life. Even so, given its association with sex, alcohol, a rise in cocaine use among blacks, and interracial mixing, the music had an image problem in the early twentieth century. The entire culture of jazz was often described as an affront to the decency of many people in New Orleans, including many middle-class blacks.

The bad image of jazz and jazzmen was not helped by the growing number of violent incidents occurring in places where the music was played. Jelly Roll Morton described one incident at a Bolden performance at Jackson Hall, probably in early 1905. A short, ill-tempered man was standing at the bar, listening to music, when a "great big, husky guy" stepped on his foot. An argument erupted between the two – with Morton standing right between them – during which the small man pulled out a very large gun and shot the other man at close range, just barely missing Jelly Roll. He later recalled, "This big guy laid there on the floor, dead. And, my goodness, Buddy Bolden – he was up on the balcony with his band – started blazing away with his trumpet, trying to keep the crowd together. Many of us realized it was a killing and we started breaking out windows and through doors and just run over by the police they had there."

Bolden himself was arrested in the incident, even though he was on stage blowing high notes to try and keep everyone quiet. "King" Bolden, as many now called him, seemed to be regarded by the white establishment as a threat. Buddy had a theme song – "I Thought I heard Buddy Bolden Say" – and rumor had it that the police would put a jazzman in jail if they heard him playing it.

Even the way the jazzmen dressed was considered a provocation. A lot of the players wouldn't wear anything but a coat, with no shirt, and trousers that had to be very tight. That was the look, and as Jelly Roll Morton commented, "I'm telling you, it was very seldom that you could button the top button of a person's trousers those days in New Orleans." For Buddy, one of his suspenders would always be hanging down, and his shirt would be open so that his undershirt could be seen beneath it. All of this was carried off with kind of a strut or "mosey walk," that allegedly made the women wild.

But Buddy's days as the leader of this defiant subculture would turn out to be tragically brief. The peak of his popularity was 1905. At that point, it was apparently enough to just see Buddy, fans didn't even have to hear him play. But whenever he practiced on his front steps, neighborhood children would gather around him on the sidewalk, shouting "King Bolden! King Bolden!" And his effect on women became the stuff of legend. In 1902, he had married one of his neighbors – not the one he already had a child with – named Nora Bass. They had a daughter the next year. But that didn't stop the attention he received from young female fans. According to one of his friends, "Sometimes, he would have to run away from the women."

But celebrity eventually took its toll. In March 1906, Buddy began to experience severe headaches. He seemed to be disoriented at times, failed to recognize his friends, and would walk the streets, speaking incoherently to strangers. Sometimes his mother and sister would send his friend, Louis Jones, to find him and bring him home. He even developed a fear of his own cornet.

No one really knows what caused Buddy to lose his grip on reality. Some said that he drank too much and slept too little. Others said that he simply succumbed to the pressure of having to stay one step ahead of the competition so that he didn't become yesterday's news. Louis Jones believed it was caused by an untreated ear infection.

Whatever the cause, he quickly fell apart. He was eventually even kicked out of his own band. After Buddy failed to pay his band members once too often, they started arranging their own gigs without him.

In the spring of 1906 – while bedridden and being cared for by his mother and mother-in-law, Ida Bass – Buddy became violent. Convinced that he was being poisoned, he jumped out of bed and attacked Mrs. Bass with a water pitcher. She suffered only a minor head wound and Buddy was soon calmed down again. But the two women, worried that more violence might follow, had him arrested on a charge of insanity. He was held in jail for a few days and then released.

But Buddy didn't get any better. His last gig was for the Labor Day parade later that same year. It was a huge parade and virtually every musician in the city was playing in it. Sometime before the march was over, though, Buddy had to drop out. He spent a troubled week at home and by Saturday, his mental state was bad enough that his mother had to have him arrested again on an insanity charge. He was released again after a few days, but now he was too far gone to help. He spent the winter self-medicating with liquor and little else. Then, on March 13, 1907, Alice Bolden had her son arrested for the third and final time.

Buddy was held in the House of Detention for several weeks before he was finally transferred to the State Insane Asylum in Jackson, Louisiana. He remained there for the rest of his life and died on November 4, 1931.

The first "King" of jazz was gone, but there were many musicians in New Orleans who carried on – and expanded upon – his legacy.

One of them was just a small boy when Buddy was put away. He would later tell conflicting stories about whether he really remembered hearing Buddy play, but it was likely that he did. He lived close to the Funky Butt Hall on Perdido and remembered listening – when he was a boy of 4 or 5, when Buddy was at his peak – to the band that played Saturday night dances at the hall.

The boy's name was Louis Armstrong and he would eventually do more than anyone in history to spread Buddy's new sound beyond the confines of New Orleans and out into the world.

But not every young musician in New Orleans at the time was pulled into the world of Buddy Bolden and the Uptown jazzmen. Jelly Roll Morton – whose actual name was Ferdinand Joseph La Menthe –was a Creole pianist who affected a casual disdain for the music of what he called "Uptown Negroes." He was a stunningly original musician himself and he was busy developing his own unique blend of piano-based ragtime, dance music, and blues. It was a style that would eventually have its own claim as the prototype for the kind of music still a decade away from being known as "jazz."

Like many Creoles of the era, Morton – who changed his name from La Menthe because he didn't want to be called "Frenchy" – grew up in an atmosphere saturated with music. His godmother, Eulalie Echo, paid for guitar lessons for him when he was very young and, by the time he was seven, he was an accomplished musician, playing in a three-piece string band that performed at night in the Seventh Ward. One day at a party, he heard a man playing ragtime on the piano and decided that was the instrument for him. He began studying with a series of teachers and was soon proficient enough to earn a reputation around town.

One Saturday night, he and some friends were on a wild jaunt through Storyville when he was approached by someone looking for a pianist to fill in at one of the district's sporting houses. Morton – who was only 15 at the time – agreed to go along but insisted that his friends come too for moral support. The madam – as well as some of her girls – were impressed by his talent and tipped him $20, a tidy sum at the time.

At the end of the night, he was offered a job as the brothel's regular "professor." He hesitated at first, worried what his proper Creole family might think, but he eventually took the position and told his family that he had switched to the night shift at his regular job at a barrel-making factory. He soon became a fixture of the district, one of its most evocative chroniclers, and perhaps the most famous musician to emerge from the confines of Storyville.

Jelly Roll became a favorite among the brothel women, who often wheedled big tips for him from their customers. Soon, he was making more money than he'd ever seen in his life. He eventually had a diamond implanted in one of his front teeth and bought a loud new suit with a Stetson hat and a pair of St. Louis Flats shoes with toes that turned up almost to his ankles.

Jelly Roll Morton

He was wearing those clothes when he ran into his great-grandmother on the street one Sunday morning. She was returning home from church, and it was obvious to her that her great-grandson was not. It turned out to be a life-changing encounter. When his grandmother – whom he'd been living with since his mother's death the year before – heard about it, she kicked him out of the house. At the age of 16, he was on his own.

And although Creole pride kept him somewhat aloof from the mainstream of the Uptown music scene, he soon became an important force in the development of New Orleans jazz.

But the closure of Storyville had an effect on the city's musicians. The jazzmen kept playing the clubs and dives around town, but the district's shutdown severely reduced the number of places where they could play. Bands reduced the number of players in their rosters, replacing their guitarist, bassist, and violinist with a single pianist. With fewer gigs available, many jazzmen were forced to return to their day jobs.

Some musicians, responding to the worsening employment picture, began to look for opportunities elsewhere. Many started new bands and began touring on the vaudeville circuit. Others followed their lead over the next few years.

Jelly Roll Morton was one of them. He had already been spending much of his time on the road and he was soon finding new opportunities – and more receptive audiences – in Chicago, New York, and Los Angeles. His reputation grew as time passed, and he became widely recognized for his originality and his influence on the world of jazz.

But, as with many great musicians, rumors swirled about his rise to fame. Legend had it that Jelly Roll's godmother, Eulalie Echo, who had first encouraged his love of music, was a practicing follower of "voodoo," an offshoot of the West African magic that slaves brought to New Orleans in the early nineteenth century. The stories claimed that Eulalie sold Jelly's soul to the Devil as part of a black-magic ritual to insure his success.

This turned out not to be Jelly Roll's only brush with the supernatural.

Throughout the 1930s, Jelly Roll was working in his own office, trying to break into the music publishing business, where all the big money was being made. One of his employees, a young man from the West Indies, stole many of Morton's music scores and sold them to another firm. Jelly Roll promptly fired him. The next day, a strange, colored powder was found sprinkled around his office door. Convinced that a voodoo curse had been placed on him, Jelly Roll's luck began to fail. His music scores, money, and collection of diamonds were stolen. Work that he had been promised was offered to Duke Ellington and Cab Calloway instead.

Jelly Roll became so discouraged that he decided to quit the music business and invest what money he had left in a cosmetics company that he had been assured was a "sure thing." It wasn't. After it failed, he had almost nothing left.

In desperation, he went to see an old voodoo woman, who told him that the only way to break the curse was to destroy all his clothing. Jelly Roll later recalled, "I always had a lot of clothes and the stack I made in my backyard was way over the top of my head. I poured on the kerosene and struck a match. It like to broke my heart to watch my suits burn."

Whether there was really a curse on him or not, the voodoo woman's advice worked. By the end of the 1930s, the jazz world developed a fascination with traditional New Orleans music, or what they called "authentic jazz," as opposed to the "swing style" that had taken American by storm.

Jelly Roll Morton, who had been playing for "coffee and cakes" in a Washington nightclub, his music all but forgotten, was suddenly considered a major attraction. White college students armed with notepads began to filter into the seedy night club where he'd been playing to gape at a living legend. Jelly Roll was perplexed. He felt his music was very much alive; he could easily out-swing the modern swingers such as Chick Webb and Count Basie. When Alan Lomax, the jazz historian, invited Morton to the Library of Congress to record his life-story in 1938, Jelly was down to his last dime.

But in 1939, Victor Records, in an effort to cash in on the New Orleans jazz revival, offered Jelly Roll a new recording contract. The publicity painted a picture of Jelly Roll emerging from seclusion to record a great new album, but, in truth, he had been saved from obscurity. At last, he was rightfully taking his place as one of the most important figures in an original American art form.

But Jelly Roll's days were numbered – and he knew it.

In 1941, his old voodoo godmother Eulalie Echo, died. As Jelly Roll's girlfriend, Anita Gonzales, told Alan Lomax, "Jelly always knew she'd sold him to Satan and that when she died, he'd die too - she would take him down with her."

Two months after Eulalie's death, Jelly Roll died on July 10, 1941. He was only 46-years-old.

I'd always like to think that even though Jelly Roll followed Eulalie to the grave, she undoubtedly failed in her dark mission. It's hard to believe that a musician as talented as Jelly Roll Morton would be stuck playing the piano for the Devil for eternity.

On the other hand, it's very likely that he's not alone down there.

I'm sure that the Devil has got a hell of a band.

DOWN AT THE CROSSROADS

Before the rise of rock-n-roll in the 1950s, there was nothing as maligned as the "Devil's Music" like the blues. In the Middle Ages, the Church was telling people that any kind of music that wasn't about God was the work of the Devil. That became a popular refrain for church leaders – then and now. By the early twentieth century, it was jazz music – forever linked to the whorehouses of Storyville – that was being blamed for lewd and lascivious behavior.

That was bad enough – and then came the blues.

It was said that the Devil himself presided over the birth of the blues in the Mississippi Delta in the 1920s, and he has kept a grip on the offspring of the blues ever since. It was not just the fact that blues players were black, and therefore, were considered a threat to the white population of the still-segregated region. No, it was the fact that African-Americans in those days were determined to enjoy what little life had to offer them and that meant dancing, drinking, and of course, music. But there was another, rarely acknowledged, reason why white society and the religious authorities were suspicious, even fearful, of black music – the blues sounded otherworldly to the whites, smacking of voodoo and African rhythms that could only be – you guessed it – the "Devil's Music."

For the Christians in the south – distrustful of anything that did not conform to mainstream religion and suspicious of secular music in general – the blues went beyond what anyone had seen before, challenging the idea that an American black identity had to be connected to the church. From the very beginning, the blues were the "Devil's Music," a questionable pastime that bumped right up against the sacred music of the church, which at that time was mostly gospel. The blues were not about faith, salvation, or redemption – they were about nothing but worldly things. While borrowing much of its musical form from slave spirituals, the blues were more in turn with songs sung about working in the fields or laying railroad track. Work was not what was sung about in church and, once the Civil War was over, no one could claim that hard labor done by slaves would be rewarded in heaven. Work songs for the freed blacks were honest in the way that work was honest – pure labor under a hot sun.

As the blues developed, becoming more and more liberated from the church, sex and relationships became the most common topic. Some of the more explicit songs were performed by women artists, which only highlighted how much the blues were about personal things and didn't need to conform to Christian ideals. Of course, not every song was sexually explicit, but all of them were emotionally explicit, dealing plainly with love and loss. The blues humanized the songs that had once been sung by slaves, making hope and suffering more earthbound and not a part of any kind of heaven and hell drama.

And while the blues often suggested that trouble was merely bad luck, there was also something you could do about it, if only that meant locating the source of the trouble. If you were heartsick over a lover who ran away, Jesus wouldn't help you, but a hoodoo woman might. If your lover was cheating, don't ask God to change their ways. The root of a certain orchid – the mojo hand – might help you in a way that the church was sure to frown upon. Freedom didn't necessarily mean that life would be easy, and work might still be hard to find. Manual labor for little money meant that gambling became more than a pastime. It was a hope that things could get better. And who knows, a little hoodoo might shake the odds loose in your favor.

The hand-in-hand nature of the blues and the supernatural gave birth to one of the most enduring legends in blues history – the story of Robert Johnson.

The stories said he'd been booed off the stage of every Mississippi roadhouse where he'd tried to perform just six months earlier, so when the awkward young man returned to the local juke joints, guitar in hand, whispers followed him as he took the stage again. The skinny, solitary bluesman took a chair and began conjuring up spooky riffs and moaning slide guitar lines that accompanied a voice that seemed to know the pain of the blues.

But some said it was a voice that hinted at worse pain to follow after death.

Robert Johnson – did he make a deal with the Devil at the Crossroads?

The whispers repeated the legend that was going around. Robert Johnson, they said, had sold his soul to the Devil at a crossroads on Mississippi's Highway 61 at midnight in exchange for some amazing guitar skills and a handful of tunes. He also got an escape from the poverty into which he'd been born and with that came the adoring company of women, whiskey, fortune, and fame.

His fame spread quickly, but at night, Robert was haunted by dreams in which the Devil pursued him down a long dirt road leading to a cemetery. These nightmares inspired his classic songs "Me and the Devil Blues," "Hellhound on my Trail," and, of course, "Crossroads Blues."

The legend goes that the Devil only allowed Johnson to live until his 27th birthday. He was apparently poisoned by a club owner who suspected the singer of seducing his wife. He was buried in an unmarked grave by the locals, who refused to put him in consecrated ground for fear that the Devil would come to claim his own.

As with any legend, it's hard to separate the fact from the fiction in Robert Johnson's life. He was apparently born on May 8, 1911, in Hazlehurst, Mississippi. He was the result of an extramarital affair between his mother, Julie Ann Majors, and a farmworker named Noah Johnson. Robert's "legal" father, Charles Dodds, Jr., had earlier abandoned his wife to live with his mistress in Memphis. By 1927, Robert was working in the cotton fields and was using several aliases, including Robert Sax and Robert Spenser, among others. He later told friends that he used the aliases in case a murder happened while he was in town. That way, the local lawmen wouldn't be able to pin it on him.

Robert was married twice. His first wife was Virginia Travis, who died in childbirth in 1930. Death claimed both mother and child. Around the time that he started to play music, he married Callie Craft. Robert's first musical instrument was a harmonica, but he later switched to guitar, which, of course, led to his reputation as a blues innovator and the father of what became rock-n-roll. Local blues legends like Willie Brown, Son House, and Charley Patton often let Robert sit in with them when they played the roadhouses. They weren't initially too impressed with his playing and tended to avoid him when they weren't on stage. Audiences were equally unimpressed, and his solo acts were often greeted with laughter and heckling from the crowd.

And then Robert disappeared for six months.

Some say that he went in search of his natural father, while others say that it was during this time that Robert, carrying a black cat's bone, went down to the crossroads and made his bargain with the Devil.

It was said that when he returned to the roadhouses, the older blues players were amazed by his new mastery of the guitar. According to legend, it was Son House who stated that, "He [Johnson] sold his soul to play like that."

Robert's guitar instructor was said to be a man named "Ike Zimmerman," a peculiar name for a bluesman, since all the great performers had legendary monikers like Blind Lemon Jefferson, Sonny Boy Williamson, Muddy Waters, and Howlin' Wolf. Even stranger than his name was the way that he taught Robert to play. He claimed to have learned guitar at night, sitting in old country churchyards, with the dead as his only companions. Some claimed "Zimmerman" was the Devil himself and most of the local bluesmen had no problem accepting that claim as fact. It's no surprise that whispers of a satanic pact followed Robert wherever he went.

The idea of selling one's soul to the Devil at a country crossroads actually precedes that of Robert Johnson. There were already stories about another early bluesman named Tommy Johnson – no relation to Robert – who had waited at a lonely crossroads to make his own deal with Satan. Tommy's brother, LaDell Johnson, explained how it worked to Francis Davis for the book *The History of the Blues*, "If you want to learn to play anything you want to play and learn how to make songs yourself, you take your guitar and you to where a crossroads is. A big black man will walk up there at the stroke of midnight and take your guitar, and he'll tune it."

The use of the crossroads as a spot where the Devil might appear comes from the concept of being the final resting place for suicides and those unworthy of being buried in hallowed ground. The crossroads were also supposed to be the site where witches held their gatherings. In Haitian folklore, the "guardian of the crossroads" was a deity known as Papa Legba. He had traveled across the oceans with the African slaves and became a part of the religion known as voodoo.

Was Papa Legba the "big black man" that LaDell Johnson claimed would appear at the crossroads looking for a deal? To white southerners, anything that smacked of voodoo had to be connected to the Devil, so it was all the same to them. It was a different story to the African-American bluesmen and their audiences, though. Many of them spoke in hushed tones about conjurers, spells, and gris-gris bags – those small bags that contained objects like bone and public hair that served as talismans – and many of them had likely paid someone for a good luck charm or for help to ward off evil.

The bluesmen knew of mojo hands and charms made from graveyard dust. The term "mojo" refers to magical powers that could be summoned to help someone achieve his desires. The great Muddy Waters sang of getting his "mojo workin'" and in "Hootchie-Cootchie Man" he listed several talismans to help him with his love life, including St. John the Conqueror root and a black cat bone – an accessory needed at the crossroads.

The black cat's bone possessed a supernatural power that would aid the owner in his quest for love, fame, and fortune. One legend stated that a dead black cat had to be boiled until only the bones remained. The bones then had to be placed in a running stream of water. When one of the bones floated away from the others, that would be the one needed for magic. With that bone, the owner was given the power to cast spells, and perhaps, in the case of Robert Johnson, the ability to summon the Devil.

If the story was true, well, it worked.

After Robert began to achieve fame as a stellar guitarist, he began traveling the South, rambling from town to town, jumping freight trains and landing in small towns with roadhouses that gladly offered him the stage. In 1936, at the insistence of a Jackson, Mississippi, music store owner, Robert began a short recording career with Ernie Oertle, a salesman from Columbia records. Within one year, he had recorded each of his now legendary songs with primitive equipment in dusty hotel rooms. In return for the recordings, he was only paid about $100 but the records were not how he achieved his fame during his lifetime – it was playing the blues on stage.

Robert's reputation packed the juke joints in which he performed. He had a cataract in one eye that many superstitious fans claimed was an "evil eye" that sent someone straight to hell. Some of the local musicians noticed that Robert turned his back to the audience when he performed. They believed that he was hiding the fact that the Devil helped him to pluck the chords. In truth, though, he was hiding his guitar licks from the other players. He wanted to keep his techniques a closely guarded secret. He also experimented with open tunings – which is when a base chord is played open and all similar chords in the chromatic scale are then played by barring all strings across a single fret – an unknown idea at the time but now a common technique in blues playing.

Robert spent his last years traveling around the Delta and to other parts of the country including Memphis, St. Louis, Chicago, Detroit, New York, and even Canada. He went from one roadhouse to another, never settling in one place, although he did have a home in Helena, Arkansas, for a time. Late in 1938, impresario John Hammond planned to present Johnson as part of the "From Spirituals to Swing" concert at Carnegie Hall, an appearance that would have undoubtedly made him a star.

Unfortunately, Robert died before that event could take place.

As with every good legend, the circumstances of Robert's death remain a mystery. Though it's evident that he was murdered, there are many variations to his early death at age 27. Some say that he was stabbed or shot to death by a jealous girlfriend or one of his many lovers' angry spouses or boyfriends. The most commonly reported method of murder involved Robert being poisoned – using either strychnine or wood alcohol -- by a jealous husband shortly before other musicians arrived to begin their performance. Johnny Shines and other musicians claimed that Robert died after three days of intense, excruciating pain on August 16, 1938.

The legend also states that Robert's family may have buried him in an unmarked grave and in unhallowed ground – but if that's true, it's hard to explain the multiple grave markers that exist in two different cemeteries and the unmarked grave that resides in another.

One of Robert's alleged gravesites can be found in the Zion Church graveyard just off Highway 7 in Morgan City, Mississippi. The marker was provided by Sony Music and all 29 of his songs are listed on it. There is also a cemetery near Greenwood, Mississippi, that is believed to hold the mortal remains of Robert Johnson. The headstone on this gravesite was donated by ZZ Top. To make things more confusing, another gravesite – with documentation – was found in 2000 that is believed to be Robert's actual resting place. This grave, which was not marked until 2002, is located at Little Zion Missionary Baptist Church, also in Greenwood. According to Mrs.

Rosie Eskridge, she saw her husband bury a body said to be that of Robert Johnson at the site in 1938. This location has since been deemed the "most reliable" burial spot and it's been added to the Mississippi Blues Trail – along with a certain crossroads in Clarksdale, Mississippi, where Highway 61 intersects with Highway 49.

The emergence of Robert Johnson's music is due to the many cover versions that have been done over the years by performers and bands like Eric Clapton and Cream, Elmore James, Led Zeppelin, and the Rolling Stones. Unfortunately, many performers have also duplicated the tragic elements of Robert's life as well as his music – leaving out the pacts with the Devil.

Well, maybe.

and GOD saiD, "LeT THeRe Be ROCK-n-ROLL…"

When blues artists left their rural backwaters for Chicago, searching for record contracts and regular gigs, they soon found that they needed to amplify their guitars to be heard above the rattle of the elevated trains and the noise of the traffic. Electric guitars, bass, drums, and amplified vocals made for a raunchier, rhythm-driven sound, and with it came ever earthier lyrics, which enhanced the music's reputation for promoting debauchery, drinking, and drugs.

And soon it turned into rock-n-roll.

The blues, rock-n-roll, and the Devil have been inseparable ever since. Rock music has evolved in many directions over the years, but the blues have remained the same. They still have that angry, wicked sound that conjures up visions of dive bars, pool halls, graveyards, and an abandoned crossroads in Mississippi where the Devil just might be waiting for the next hopeful guitar player to come along, looking for fame and fortune.

As rock-n-roll emerged on the American scene, it started a ripple of discontent among conservatives. But the religious groups did not come out in force against the new "race music" until it threatened to corrupt a white audience through the records of Elvis Presley, Chuck Berry, Little Richard, Carl Perkins, Jerry Lee Lewis, and many others. As rock and roll was unleashed upon a generation of teenagers who had never heard anything like it before, it was condemned from pulpits across America as – once again – the "Devil's Music."

Society blamed it for the subsequent rise in drunkenness, vandalism, violence, and juvenile delinquency. The Church was very clear about what would happen to you if you indulged in sinful activities like listening to records or dancing – you'd burn in hell.

But, as it turned out, fundamentalist churches had no one to blame for rock-n-roll but themselves.

In the 1980s, television preacher Jimmy Swaggart became a huge star. His services, broadcast from Baton Rouge, Louisiana, appeared on television sets across the country. At its peak, his ministry was raking in over $1 million every week. He had created an image for himself of a brash, bold, tell-it-like-it-is preacher that made him a respected figure in the Assemblies of God church – a group of affiliated churches that form the world's largest Pentecostal denomination -- and in the broader world of evangelical Christians. Critics hated his holier-than-thou posturing and his religious and cultural hostility. Some stations even took him off the air for it, which, of course, just emboldened his rabid fanbase.

Like many other television preachers – who were also moving in political circles – Swaggart stated that the Holy Ghost had emboldened him to pass along straight-arrow truths from the Bible. With his practiced Southern drawl, he raged against Hollywood celebrities, scientists, communists (it was the '80s), homosexuals, Catholics, feminists, liberals, and anyone he considered an "enemy of the faith." He warned his followers that Americans had lost interest in the Bible and the country deserved God's judgment. He tapped into the powerful resentments of the uneducated, the poor, and working class and built a massive audience for himself.

In the summer of 1985, Swaggart was on the road, conducting his mass revival crusades in rural parts of the country. In front of cameras and stage lights, he paced back and forth on the stage, waving his arms and swinging his Bible like a weapon. He shouted at audiences about the kinds of moral degeneracy that would drag them through the gates of hell. His favorite topic was rock-n-roll – the "Devil's Music."

How could Christians make peace with such a vile, hideous music, he asked with urgency in his voice. This was a personal issue with him, he confided night after night, pausing for emphasis and lowering his head in shame. And then he lunged at the crowd to exclaim, "My family started rock-n-roll!" he exclaimed, and his voice cracked with emotion. "I don't say that with any glee! I don't say it with any pomp or pride! I say it with shame and sadness, because I've seen the death and the destruction. I've seen the unmitigated misery and the pain. I've seen it! I speak of experience. My family – Jerry Lee Lewis, with Elvis Presley, with Chuck Berry ... started rock and roll!"

And he was right – well, about Jerry Lee Lewis anyway, who was Swaggart's cousin. He was also right in a much broader sense, though. His church "family" actually did help create rock-n-roll. The church had some help from the blues, Appalachian folk music, and a few other places, too, but it was the Pentecostals who provided the beat that America started dancing to in the 1950s.

Pentecostalism – that apocalyptic religion of spirit immersion, speaking in tongues, faith healing, and assorted mayhem – inspired many of the innovators of rock-n-roll. Jerry Lee Lewis, Swaggart's cousin, along with Elvis Presley, Johnny Cash, Little Richard, B.B. King, and others were all raised in or regularly attended Pentecostal services in their youth. Rock-n-roll, which became the soundtrack of rebellion and the music of juvenile delinquents and teenage sock-hoppers, owed a surprising debt to the religion of the Holy Ghost.

Growing up in the Assemblies of God church, Jerry Lee Lewis and Jimmy Lee Swaggart were as close as brothers. They bonded over their love of music and their shared Pentecostal experience. What they both lacked in formal education, they more than made up for in style, charisma, and stage presence.

Jerry Lee's aunt and Jimmy's grandmother, Ada, liked to tell family, friends, and anyone who would listen about her baptism by the Holy Ghost that she experienced as a camp meeting. "You've got to get it," she told them. "You've got to have it. You really don't know the Lord like you should until you receive it." When the power of the almighty struck her, she said, "the presence of God became so real. Suddenly, it seemed as if I had been struck by a bolt of lightning. Lying flat on my back, I raised my hands to praise the Lord. No English came out. Only unknown tongues."

James Brown, the "Godfather of Soul," used to reflect on his time in church as a boy. His family attended the United House of Prayer Church in Augusta, Georgia. Its flashy leader called himself Sweet Daddy Grace wore capes, shiny suits, and never failed to put on a show when he took the stage on Sunday morning. Sound familiar? Brown always said, "Those folks were sanctified. They had the beat. Sanctified people got more fire."

That beat certainly inspired Ray Charles. The brilliant pianist was a great admirer of religious music and especially black quartets. Ray admitted to lifting material from a song called "You Better Leave That Liar Alone" for his decidedly secular song "You Better Leave That Woman Alone." In 1954, he re-tooled a song called "It Must be Jesus" by the Southern Tones into "I've Got a Woman," which became a smash hit.

Such music – along with the unbridled religious services that went with them, which featured speaking in tongues, shouting, falling to the floor, jumping up and down, and running circles around the auditorium -- made a deep impression on Jerry Lee Lewis and other early rock-n-rollers. But when Jerry Lee ditched a Pentecostal ministry for a life of stardom, a major rift developed between him and cousin Jimmy. Jerry Lee recorded at Sun Records in Memphis in late 1956 and, soon after, became an international celebrity. The wild, piano-pounding performer was lured in by the girls, the sex, the drugs, and the alcohol.

Swaggart later made it clear what he thought of his cousin and his unsavory life. He asked: "Why do I need 40 suits? I'm clothed in a robe of righteousness! Why do I need Cadillacs and Lincolns when I can ride with the King of Kings? Jerry Lee can go to Sun Records in Memphis, but I'm on my way to heaven with a God who supplies all my needs according to His riches in glory by Christ Jesus."

Jerry Lee felt the sting of his cousin's rebukes. He wasn't the only one. Elvis Presley, who attended the Memphis First Assembly of God Church before fame made it impossible, was also hurt when Southern Baptists and Methodists lined up to denounce his shows and his "Devil's music." Billy Graham, America's most famous preacher, claimed that Elvis's fame was due to the "mystery of iniquity," which was "ever working in the world of evil."

Jerry Lee Lewis, caught between God and the Devil, was vocal about his burning sense of guilt. In 1979, critic and musician Robert Palmer asked him if he believed he was going to hell for playing rock-n-roll. '

"Yep," Lewis replied with certainty. "I know the right way. I was raised a good Christian. But I couldn't make it ... Too weak, I guess."

Then, in 1957, Jerry Lee married Myra Gale Brown. He'd been married twice before. His second marriage had caused quite a fuss when people realized it had taken place 23 days before his first divorce was final. But that was nothing to the fuss caused by his marriage to Myra. Though he had, again, gotten married before his divorce was final, it was also learned that his third wife was also his third cousin – his 13-year-old third cousin.

Myra was the daughter of J.W. Brown, Jerry Lee's cousin and the bass player in his band. At the time, Myra – who still believed in Santa Claus, by the way – didn't see anything wrong with the relationship. Elvis, the biggest rock star in the world, was dating 14-year-old Priscilla Beaulieu, who would later become his wife. Later, she would simply say that people grew up faster in those days. She wanted a husband, a baby, and a home, and thought she was ready for marriage.

After the two were married, Jerry Lee planned to take Myra along on a tour of England. Elvis had been drafted into the Army and Jerry Lee was positioned to become rock-n-roll's biggest name. The tour was supposed to

Jerry Lee Lewis and child bride, Myra

establish a fan base in England that would, hopefully, lead to a worldwide audience.

However, after arriving in London with his child bride, it became clear that the Brits were not keen on Jerry Lee. His managers had warned him that the British press delighted in tearing down American musicians, but Jerry Lee hadn't listened. When asked about Myra, Jerry Lee admitted they were married but claimed that she was 15, not 13. He added that, in America, it was quite all right to marry at age 15 – even 10 – as long as you could find a husband.

After a few shows in England, the tour was canceled. The British public, fueled by the tabloids that had branded Jerry Lee a "cradle robber" and a "baby snatcher," practically drove him out of the country.

And the reception at home wasn't much warmer. When they returned stateside, the newspapers not only publicized Myra's real age, but they also pointed out that Jerry Lee had married once again before his divorce was finalized. It also didn't help that his latest single was a song called "High School Confidential." It wasn't about his wife – who was actually still junior high school age – but it didn't help the situation.

Before he knew it, his booking prices dropped astronomically, from the $10,000 per night that he'd been getting to $250, if anyone would hire him. Despite re-marrying Myra, this time legally, and moving in with her parents afterward, Jerry Lee's rise to the level of fame that had been achieved by Elvis had come to a crashing halt. He never really recovered. Despite being recognized as one of the innovators of rock-n-roll, having plenty of hit records, and earning a place in music history, there will always be a dark cloud over the career of Jerry Lee Lewis.

But maybe that's a cloud conjured up by guilt. Not long after his aborted tour of England, the tape was rolling at Sun Records in Memphis during a recording session. Seven years after he had been expelled from the Assemblies of God Bible Institute in Waxahachie, Texas for playing a boogie-woogie version of "My God is Real," Jerry Lee was using his talent for sin – and he knew it.

He told Sun Records' founder Sam Phillips: "Music should not do the work of Satan. When it comes to worldly music, rock-n-roll, anything like that, you're in the world, and you haven't come from out of the world, and you're still a sinner... You got to walk and talk with God to go to heaven ... Mr. Phillips, I don't care ... it ain't what you believe. It's what's written in the Bible!"

Other stars from the early years of rock-n-roll – many of them with connections to Pentecostal churches – were equally consumed by guilt. Johnny Cash, who grew up in the Church of God, struggled with alcohol and pills.

Little Richard, too, was convinced that his stardom – and his homosexuality – would put him on the road to hell. When he was a young man, Richard said he liked the fiery Pentecostal services the most, where enthusiasts spoke in tongues and did the "holy dance." He had long lasting memories of the singing evangelist Brother Joe May and the Pentecostal guitarist Sister Rosetta Tharpe.

While on tour with Gene Vincent and Eddie Cochran in Australia in 1957, Richard decided to turn his life around and return to the Lord. He believed that the Russian launch of *Sputnik* in 1957 was

Little Richard

a clear sign of the impending apocalypse. When his bandmates doubted his sincerity, Richard tried to convince them by tossing $8,000 worth of his flashy jewelry into the ocean. He planned to enroll in a Seventh-day Adventist seminary, later saying "I wanted people to forget Little Richard as a rock-n-roller. I was soon to be qualified as an evangelist like Billy Graham."

Soon after, he left his label and signed with Mercury Records, releasing a gospel album, produced by Quincy Jones, in 1962. But it didn't last long. Richard returned to the "Devil's Music" following a tour of England with Sam Cooke as his opening act. Two years later, he'd recorded a new rock-n-roll album. But Richard struggled with recordings throughout the rest of his career, and it wouldn't be until his performances at rock-n-roll revivals that he would return to the mainstream, adopting a more flamboyant stage look.

And then he was gone again. Drug abuse and personal deaths led him to retire again and return to evangelism in 1977. He was back again by the 1980s, performing his rock-n-roll classics until a failed hip surgery forced him to retire from show business for good in 2013.

He never seemed able to give up God or rock-n-roll. He continued to say, "I believe this kind of music is demonic," but that never stopped him from performing or constantly anointing himself as the "real King of rock-n-roll."

I guess the Devil won out again.

Other, lesser-known rock-n-roll performers like Jimmie Rodgers left the stage for the Pentecostal pulpit. The son of county music legend Hank Snow, Jimmie signed a record contract with RCA, making minor hits like "How Do You Think I Feel?" and "The Rules of Love" and toured with Buddy Holly, Bill Haley and the Comets, and Elvis. Snow told Elvis that he was contemplating a Pentecostal preaching career the same year that Little Richard had his own epiphany. Of course, Elvis couldn't have known then that Snow would later target him – as well as other performers – as "emissaries of the Devil." The thin, slick rocker-turned-pastor, with hair swooped back and sporting sideburns, lashed out against rock-n-rollers and warned teenage fans against the wild new music.

In 1971, Johnny Cash underwent a second, public, conversion experience and became a regular at Snow's Pentecostal Evangel Temple in Nashville, Tennessee. By then, Cash had hooked up with a new religious movement that combined hippy, counterculture views with pop music and conservative Pentecostalism. The "Jesus People," as observers dubbed the Christian movement, played loud, guitar music, worshipped in house churches and non-denominational communities, and attracted crowds with a looser style of worship. Youth pastors and ministers in the movement wore sandals and fringed leather jackets to show how "cool" they were.

Billy Graham joined Johnny Cash on stage and grew his hair and sideburns a little longer in keeping with the times. America's pastor had made his peace with the style – although probably not the lyrical content – of rock-n-roll. Followers called the new sound "Jesus music" or "Christian rock."

Like Billy Graham, Christianity was starting to accept rock-n-roll. In the late 1960s and 1970s. Christian rockers sang about the gifts of the spirit, a need for spiritual revival, and the quickly approaching return of Jesus. New record labels like Myrrh, Maranatha, and Zondervan Records catered to a growing fan base. In an era when Americans elected their first "born again" evangelical president, Jimmy Carter, Christian rock bands and religious messages in pop music became commonplace.

By the late 1970s, artists including Donna Summer, Al Green, Van Morrison, Arlo Guthrie, and Bob Dylan had infused their songs with

Christian themes and evangelical messages. Dylan, in particular, was inspired by the Charismatic Movement, which, as an offshoot of the Pentecostals, emphasized speaking in tongues and an expressive style of worship. Many charismatics, Dylan included, thought that the world would soon come to an end. Soon, there were new charismatic denominations, along with charismatic factions within mainstream Protestant and Catholic churches.

Rock-n-roll and religion really could mix, right?

Nope. Prominent fundamentalists weren't having any of it. Some worried that the music smuggled Pentecostal beliefs into their churches. Even for some Pentecostals, the music was too secular and too untraditional and had no place in their churches.

"You cannot proclaim the message of the anointed with the music of the Devil!" Jimmy Swaggart shouted at his followers in 1987.

But Swaggart was about to veer a little too close to the Devil himself. Early in 1988, his face contorted in grief and tears streaming down his face, he admitted to the 8,000 congregants of his Baton Rouge Family Worship Center that he had sinned against them and against God. His affair with New Orleans prostitute Debra Murphee was now public knowledge. The national media focused its attention on the scandalous private life of the humiliated Swaggart.

Like his cousin Jerry Lee, he now knew what it felt like to be an outcast.

Despite holdouts – including the publicly shamed Jimmy Swaggart – Christian rock had become a powerful force by the 1990s. By the turn of the century, so-called contemporary Christian music – an umbrella category containing rock, rap, pop, worship, and related genres – had reached an astonishing $1 billion in annual sales, outselling jazz and classical music combined. Church services around the world still regularly feature wailing singers, heavy drums, electric guitars, and synthesizers in their "contemporary services."

As the church inspired early rock-n-rollers, now the influence has gone in the other direction. Rock music has worked its way into countless congregations. The driving beat and the interracial element that made fundamentalist Christians recoil in horror in the 1950s has now become mainstream.

They didn't even know it, but they'd invited the Devil into church and then invited him to take off his coat and stay awhile.

PART TWO:
THE MARK OF THE DEVIL

The Sordid and Strange Curses that Haunt the Music World

After already reading about the "Gloomy Sunday Curse" and the curse that was placed on Jellyroll Morton, it shouldn't be surprising to learn that there are dozens of stories of curses, superstitions, and creepy coincidences that have been interwoven into the fabric of the music industry. Some are silly and a bit of a stretch, some are eerie, and some – like the most famous music curse of the "27 Club" – are downright unnerving.

But the idea of music-related curses isn't new. Musicians are a superstitious bunch and they have been looking for supernatural reasons to explain their failures – and successes – for centuries.

In classical music, there is something called the "Curse of the Ninth," based on the fact that many composers who have written a Ninth Symphony died soon after finishing it. Beethoven is the curse's most famous victim but there have been others. Gustav Mahler thought he had the curse beaten when he began his Tenth Symphony – but died before it could be completed.

Even musical instruments can be cursed. The glass harmonica was created by Benjamin Franklin in 1761. The music that emerged from it had a disorienting quality and a haunting sound that has been compared to rubbing a wet finger around the rim of a wine glass. In the eighteenth century, strange rumors claimed that using the instrument caused both musicians and their audiences to go mad.

There are plenty of cursed songs, too. The Piano Sonata No. 6 was composed by Alexander Scriabin in 1911 but according to his biographer, "It is one of the few pieces Scriabin never played in public, because he felt it was nightmarish, murky, and unclean. He often started shuddering after playing a few measures for other people." The intricate piece has been dubbed the "Black Mass Sonata," which says a lot about the eeriness of it.

There are even stories of particular roles in bands that are cursed. Fleetwood Mac has been through so many guitarists that it's a wonder that anyone wants to play with them anymore. The group was founded by guitarist Peter Green, who left the band to deal with his declining mental health. Slide guitarist Jerry Spencer left soon after. In 1972, guitarist Danny Kirwin started acting strangely during a gig on the eve of a tour, smashing his head against a wall and then taunting the band from the audience. He later passed away after more issues with mental illness. More recently, in 2012, guitarist Bob Weston suffered a fatal aneurysm – the same year that guitarist Bob Welsh took his own life after receiving news that he would never walk again.

Curses and superstitions are not taken lightly in the music world, as you'll soon see, but I'll leave it up to you to decide if the frightening things that occurred were instances of the supernatural at work, mere coincidence, or the result of "living fast and leaving a good-looking corpse behind."

THE BUDDY HOLLY CURSE

February 3, 1959 will always be remembered as the "Day the Music Died." It was during those early morning hours that a small plane crashed to the earth in Iowa and took the lives of three of the biggest rock-n-roll stars of the time: Buddy Holly, Ritchie Valens, and J.P. "Big Bopper" Richardson.

The plane crash occurred in the midst of Buddy Holly's "Winter Dance Party" Tour, which he started after going solo from his original band, the Crickets. For the start of the tour, he assembled a new band consisting of Waylon Jennings (bass), Tommy Allsup (guitar), and Carl Bunch (drums). The tour was set to cover 24 Midwestern cities in as many days. Ritchie Valens, who was climbing the charts with songs like "La Bamba" and "Donna," joined the line-up, along with J. P. "The Big Bopper" Richardson, who had a huge hit with "Chantilly Lace." Another tour member was Dion DiMucci, who performed under only his first name and had hits like "The Wanderer" and "Runaround Sue."

The tour began in Milwaukee, Wisconsin, on January 23, 1959. The amount of travel created a logistical problem nightmare for the tour. The distance between venues had not been considered when scheduling each performance. Adding to the disarray, the tour bus was not equipped for the weather. Its heating system broke shortly after the tour began, in Appleton, Wisconsin. While flu spread among the rest of the performers, Buddy's drummer, Carl Bunch, was hospitalized in Ironwood, Michigan for severely frostbitten feet. The musicians replaced the broken-down bus with a school bus and kept traveling. As Buddy's group had been the backing band for all the acts, Buddy, Ritchie, and Dion took turns playing drums for each other at the Green Bay, Wisconsin, and Clear Lake, Iowa, performances.

On Monday, February 2, the tour arrived in Clear Lake, where they were set to play the Surf Ballroom. The venue had not been a scheduled stop, but the tour promoters, hoping to fill an open date, called Surf Ballroom manager Carroll Anderson and offered him the show. He had accepted and began a flurry of advertising.

By the time Buddy arrived at the venue that Monday evening, he'd had his fill of traveling by school bus. He decided to charter a plane to take him to the next stop in Moorhead, Minnesota. Not only could he skip the cramped seats on the bus, but he'd arrive in Minnesota in enough time to do some laundry.

Surf Ballroom manager Carroll Anderson called Hubert Dwyer, owner of the Dwyer Flying Service in nearby Mason City, and chartered a plane to

The plane crash that killed Buddy Holly, Ritchie Valens, and the Big Bopper

Fargo, North Dakota. Flight arrangements were made with Roger Peterson, a 21-year-old local pilot. The flying service charged a fee of $36 per passenger for the single-engine 1947 Beechcraft Bonanza. The plane would hold three passengers and a pilot. J.P. Richardson had contracted the flu during the tour and asked Waylon Jennings for his seat on the plane.

When Holly learned that Jennings was not going to fly, he said in jest, "I hope your ol' bus freezes up."

Jennings responded, "Well, I hope your ol' plane crashes." It was a humorous but ill-fated response that haunted Jennings for the rest of his life.

Ritchie Valens, who had a fear of flying but was already suffering from a cold after being stuck on the tour bus, asked Tommy Allsup for his seat on the plane. Tommy and Ritchie decided to toss a coin to decide. Ritchie won the coin toss for the seat on the flight. Dion didn't take the flight because he thought it was too expensive. It was same amount of money that his parents paid in rent for his childhood apartment -- he just couldn't justify the indulgence.

When the show ended, Carroll Anderson drove Buddy, Ritchie, and J.P. to the airport. The plane departed from the ramp and taxied toward the runway. The weather report indicated light snow and 20- to 37-mph winds. Though there were indications of deteriorating weather along the route, the weather briefings Peterson received failed to relay the information. According to the investigation that followed the crash, Peterson became disoriented due to the unfamiliar way the altitude indicator in the aircraft functioned, combined with an inability to find a point of visual reference on a starless night with no visible lights on the ground. He lost control of the plane when the tip of the right wing hit the ground. The aircraft tumbled across a field and banked heavily to the right when it struck the ground at around 170-mph. The plane tumbled and skidded another 570 feet across the frozen landscape before the crumpled wreckage came to rest against a wire fence.

Unfortunately, no one had seen the crash.

The next morning, when Hector Airport in Fargo, North Dakota, had not heard from Peterson, Hubert Dwyer contacted authorities and reported the aircraft missing. Dwyer took off in his Cessna 180 and flew Peterson's intended route. Within minutes, he spotted the wreckage less than six miles northwest of the airport. The Sheriff's office dispatched Deputy Bill McGill, who drove to the wreck site. The bodies of Buddy and Ritchie lay near the plane. J.P.'s body was thrown over the fence and into a nearby cornfield. Peterson's body was entangled in the plane's wreckage. With the other participants on "The Winter Dance Party" en route to Moorhead, it fell to Surf Ballroom manager Carroll Anderson to make positive identifications of the musicians. The county coroner Ralph Smiley declared that all four had died instantly in the crash.

J.P. "Big Bopper" Richardson

And as Don McLean immortalized it as the "Day the Music Died," it became a loss of innocence for the early rock-n-roll generation – and a calamitous event that sent out ripples of trauma that echoed for decades to come.

There was something strange about all of it from the very beginning.

Several documented reports appeared that stated that all three performers had some sort of premonition of their deaths. The Big Bopper served as a DJ for a radio station in Beaumont, Texas, while he developed his career as a singer and songwriter. One of his zany antics was the "Disc-A-Thon," which kept him on the air for as long as he could stay awake, playing record after record. In 1957, he broke his own record – 122 hours and 8 minutes, or just over 5 days. He was carried out of the station in an ambulance. He later said that during his marathon, he began to hallucinate. In one hallucination, he told of foreseeing his own death, but said the "other side doesn't seem so bad."

Ritchie Valens

For Ritchie Valens, the very thought of flying was terrifying. His terror began on January 31, 1957, when Ritchie missed school to attend the funeral of his grandfather. Shortly after returning home, a tremendous explosion shook the ground. Ritchie and his brother, Bob, saw an airplane, engulfed in flames, falling from the sky. The plane fell onto Ritchie's school – where he was supposed to be that day. There were 90 students injured and 3 were killed, including Ritchie's best friend. He spent the rest of his life convinced that he would have died that day if he had not been at the funeral.

He swore that he would never fly in an airplane, but once his music career took off, he had no choice. Even so, Ritchie often said that he would die in a plane a crash, a morbid premonition of what happened to him two years after the accident that killed his best friend.

The biggest star to die that day, though, had been Buddy Holly, who was determined to make the Winter Dance Party a success. Buddy's career was struggling. His last two records, "Heartbeat" and "It's So Easy," hadn't made much of a splash on the charts. He was determined to get back on top as a solo artist after splitting with the Crickets. In a deal worked out with his producer Norman Petty, the Crickets – Jerry Allison and Joe B. Maudlin – would retain the rights to the band's name and continue to perform without Buddy. They were on good terms, though, and ironically, both Jerry and Joe had tried to contact Buddy on the night of the plane crash in hopes of reuniting the band. Sadly, they never reached him.

Despite hoping to revive his career, Buddy hadn't wanted to do the Winter Dance Party Tour. But he did need to make some money – he was

Buddy Holly

expecting his first child, after all. The income was also to help support Buddy's new publishing company. Though he hated to travel in the middle of a brutal, midwestern winter, he had no choice. Maria Elena was heartbroken.

To make matters worse, shortly before he left on tour, both of them reportedly had disturbing dreams about Buddy's death. In Maria Elena's dream, she saw a burning object hurtling out of the sky and crashing to the ground. Buddy's strange dream was even more to the point – he got into a small airplane with his brother and left his wife behind. A few weeks later, these dreams would come back to haunt Maria Elena.

But something even more chilling had happened to Buddy in 1958 that seemed to predict his death.

While touring in England, Buddy was startled when a note was delivered to him personally by legendary engineer and producer, Joe Meek, who was also a student of the occult and fascinated with Ouija boards and tarot card readings. One night in January, Joe and several friends, including Jimmy Miller of Jimmy Miller and the Barbecues, were attempting to contact the spirits. Miller was a big fan of Ouija boards – he used them to pick up girls, who found the spooky messages to be fascinating – and was happy to play along.

According to Miller, they were using the board when an eerie message came through. It started with a date: February 3. That was followed by three words: Buddy Holly dies.

Joe was terrified by the message. Not only was he a fan of Buddy's, but he had little time to get the musician a message. He urgently tried to get in touch with Buddy through record companies, music publishers, and inside sources, but couldn't track him down.

Luckily, February 3, 1958, came and went and Buddy didn't die. Joe was relived and when he finally met up with Buddy in England a few weeks after the deadline, he told him the story. Buddy wasn't impressed but he liked Joe, so he listened and then politely told him that he'd be sure to be careful every year when February 3 rolled around.

Too bad he forgot his promise the following year when he boarded that airplane in Iowa.

Of course, there's a lot more to the story of that fateful flight, like Waylon Jennings's haunting joke to Buddy in which he "hoped the ol' plane would crash." And then there was the coin toss that Ritchie Valens won, forcing Tommy Allsup to ride on the cold tour bus. It's said that Ritchie quipped that it was the first time in his life that he'd ever won at anything.

Tommy then told Buddy that Ritchie was going to take his seat on the plane and handed his wallet to Buddy so that he could pick up a registered letter for him at the tour's next stop. Shortly after the crash, for a few anxious hours, the authorities believed there were five victims in the wreckage and looked everywhere for the fifth body – the one with the name Tommy Allsup in his wallet. Luckily, Tommy had called home just a few minutes before the official call came to notify his parents that their son had been killed in the accident.

Tommy was given a second chance.

To celebrate his good fortune, he opened his own saloon when he returned home to Austin, Texas. He called it the "Head's Up" – a reminder of the time when a simple coin toss saved his life.

But other musicians connected to Buddy would not fare so well.

Eddie Cochran – the groundbreaking guitarist most famous for "Summertime Blues" – was a close friend of both Buddy and Ritchie. They often toured together, and, in fact, Eddie was supposed to be on the Winter Dance Party Tour but couldn't make it to Iowa because he had a scheduled appearance on the Ed Sullivan Show. Eddie always believed that he cheated death that night in 1959 – but death caught up with him just over a year later.

Eddie had been born on October 3, 1938, in Albert Lea, Minnesota. His parents were originally from California and his earliest influences were in country music. He was a schoolboy when he started playing drums and then taught himself to play both guitar and piano. In 1950, the Cochran family returned to California and Eddie formed his first band in junior high, playing hillbilly songs with his friends. After a year of high school, he dropped out and became a professional musician. In 1954, he started working with a fellow county musician named Hank Cochran. They weren't related but started calling themselves the Cochran Brothers anyway. They were moderately

Eddie Cochran

successful with their country-rockabilly act but as rock-n-roll began to emerge as a new music form, Eddie fell under the spell of Bill Haley, Little Richard, Carl Perkins and other early rock musicians.

Eddie found a manager and collaborator in songwriter Jerry Capehart and cut his first rock record, "Skinny Jim," for the Crest label in 1956. His big break came when a movie producer approached him to appear in the film *The Girl Can't Help It* (1956), which also featured Fats Domino, Gene Vincent, Little Richard, and Jayne Mansfield. That same year, Eddie signed with Liberty Records, where he perfected his sound on "Summertime Blues" and "C'mon Everybody" that featured driving acoustic and electric guitars, handclaps and tambourines, and lyrics that spoke in volumes to the rebellious teen audience that had emerged in the late 1950s.

A flashy dresser with a tough-sounding voice, Eddie epitomized the sound of the era. But he was also a virtuoso guitarist, overdubbing parts like Les Paul even on his earliest singles and playing with an authority has led many music critics to claim he was a forerunner to guitar greats like Jimmy Page and Jimi Hendrix.

Eddie recorded a lot of records for Liberty, but with mixed results. The label tried turning him into a crooner and his debut album, "Singing to my Baby (1957), was full of schmaltzy ballads that had been foisted upon him. Eddie wanted a leaner rock sound and it's that part of his catalog – hard-rocking tracks like "Jeannie, Jeannie, Jeannie," "Something Else," and "Nervous Breakdown"— that he's remembered for today.

Seriously, go look them up. These don't sound like 1950s oldies. They're tough songs and can hold their own with modern rock-n-roll.

After the accident that killed his friends, Eddie's star continued to rise. However, his friends and family all later said that he was badly shaken by their deaths and he developed a morbid premonition that he would also die young. He recorded a song called "Three Stars," as a tribute to Buddy, Ritchie, and the Big Bopper. The session proved to be so overwhelming to him that he told his producer that if it was ever released, he would never cut another record. It wasn't released until 1964 – four years after Eddie had followed Buddy to the grave.

Gene Vincent

Eddie was anxious to give up life on the road and spend his time in the studio making music – thereby reducing the chance that he might suffer a fatal accident while touring. He had financial responsibilities, though, and it turned out that giving up the road just wasn't possible. He had to keep doing live shows, and in 1960, he accepted an offer to tour England with fellow guitarist Gene Vincent, who was climbing the charts with his song "Be Bop a Lula."

The English crowds loved Eddie. In fact, he is still revered there to this day. One young man followed Eddie from city to city, carefully studying where he placed his fingers on the guitar. That teenager's name was George Harrison.

A few days before her twentieth birthday, Sharon Sheeley joined them on the tour. She was the youngest songwriter to ever score a number-one hit with "Poor Little Fool," which had been performed by teen idol Ricky Nelson. Sharon had fallen in love with Eddie the moment she was introduced to him by Phil Everly, so when she got the chance to join him on tour, she flew to England. Sharon also had a link to Ritchie Valens. She had met Ritchie through Eddie and he had recorded Sharon's song "Hurry Up."

When Sharon arrived, she found that Eddie was deeply depressed. He was taking tranquilizers and had convinced himself that he was doomed to die violently, just like Buddy and Ritchie did. One night, he asked Sharon to buy all the Buddy Holly records she could find. He then sat in his room and played them over and over again. When Sharon asked him if it upset him to listen to Buddy that way, Eddie replied, "Oh no, because I'll be seeing him soon."

It turns out, he was right.

On April 17, 1960, Eddie, Sharon, and Gene were on their way to London's Heathrow Airport to fly back to California. Eddie still had more British performances scheduled but he wanted to return home for a visit before continuing the tour. On the way to the airport, their chauffeur-driven Ford sedan blew a tire, went out of control, and smashed into a light post. Eddie and Sharon were thrown from the car. Sharon suffered a broken neck and back. Gene's leg was badly injured, and he'd limp for the rest of his life.

All three were rushed by ambulance to St. Martin's Hospital. Ironically, Buddy Holly's old band, the Crickets, were in England at the time, finishing up an Everly Brothers tour. As soon as he heard the news, Sonny Curtis, a former member who had rejoined the Crickets, rushed to the hospital with Jerry Allison to see Eddie. The third Cricket, Joe Maudlin, feared there would be too many visitors and planned to go and see Eddie the next day. He was sure that he'd recover from the crash.

But Joe was wrong. Eddie died the next morning from massive head injuries. His signature orange Gretsch guitar was later found in the grass next to where he had been thrown. There wasn't a scratch on it. He was only 21-years-old when he died but he left a lasting mark as rock-n-roll pioneer.

Buddy's former band, the Crickets – who ironically acted as Eddie Cochran's backup band for his last single "Three Steps to Heaven" -- soon found themselves plagued by tragedy. Bad luck seemed to follow anyone associated with the band.

The next victim of what some were calling the "Buddy Holly Curse" was Ronnie Smith. In February 1959, he had been hired to replace Buddy on the Winter Dance Party Tour, backed by Waylon Jennings, Tommy Allsup, and drummer Carl Bunch. When the tour ended, he formed a new band that he called the Jitters -- the Crickets name was tied up in a legal mess – but not for long. In 1962, Ronnie was committed to a Texas state hospital after a drug overdose. He hanged himself in a hospital bathroom on October 25 of that same year.

The original Crickets – Jerry Allison, Joe Maudlin, and Sonny Curtis – continued as a group and brought in 17-year-old David Box to replace Buddy. David was born in Sulphur Springs, Texas, but moved to Lubbock with his family when he was only three-years-old. He was raised there and was greatly influenced by his father, Harold, a self-taught Western Swing fiddle player. David began making public appearances with his father and received his first guitar as a present when he was eight. His next great influence was Buddy Holly, who he first saw perform in 1954. He started his own band, the Ravens, in 1958.

When David learned that the Crickets were looking for a guitarist and vocalist, he sent in an audition tape and won the spot in the band. He traveled to Los Angeles to cut the Crickets' next single. The song "Don't Cha Know" was used as the A-side, while a Buddy Holly composition, "Peggy Sue Got Married," was used as the B-side. He stayed with the band on tour for the next three weeks before returning home to complete his schooling.

Neither recording turned out to be successful on the charts, but the band continued to tour with David as lead vocalist and guitarist for the next couple of years. Eventually, he left the Crickets and began a solo career. He became a regional success with one single, "Summer Girl," which did well in local Texas markets.

On October 23, 1964, David was flying to a show in Harris County, Texas, with his band. Soon after takeoff, the Cessna Skyhawk 172 that he'd rented nosedived into the ground, killing all the passengers. Sadly, David was supposed to be in Nashville the next day to record a new single that just might have put him on the national stage, but we'll never know.

David's parents met with Buddy Holly's parents a few days after the crash. Buddy's father remarked, "People will tell you that the pain eventually goes away, but I can tell you now that it never does."

Besides dying in a plane crash, there was one more similarity to Buddy Holly in David's death. He was 22-years-old when he died – the exact same age as Buddy when he met his own untimely end.

Fate continued to play a dark role in the lives of others connected to Buddy Holly. Bobby Fuller was another young Texas musician who modeled his sound after Buddy and the Crickets. Buddy's parents had been instrumental in getting Bobby his first big break, sending his demo tape to Buddy's former producer, Norman Petty.

At the time of Buddy's death, he and Petty had dissolved their business connections, but there were many stories of Petty hiding vast amounts of Buddy's money. Some of Buddy's friends even went so far as to blame Petty for Buddy's death. If he had paid Buddy the money that he had coming, then Buddy would not have been forced to go on the Winter Dance Party tour.

Petty ended up producing two tracks for Bobby Fuller – "Gently My Love" and "My Heart Jumped." They became regional hits and Bobby became a hometown hero in El Paso long before he hit the national charts.

In 1961, when he was 19, he built his own studio in the den of his parents' three-bedroom home, recording initially on a Viking reel-to-reel tape deck before gradually buying more and better equipment. He built his own control booth and echo chamber and started two labels – Eastwood and Exeter – to release his music. A short time later, inspired by what he saw and heard at

Bobby Fuller

surf music pioneer Dick Dale's Rendezvous Ballroom on a trip to California, Bobby opened his own teen club in El Paso, which he dubbed the Rendezvous. His group, then known as the Fanatics, were the house band. Texas desert kids dressed as surfers and beach bums flocked to the club.

Bobby was working hard during the early 1960s. He was a songwriter, performer, producer, label-owner, and impresario, and managed to carve out a unique sound that blended southern styles with the stripped-down, raw, rock-n-roll of Buddy Holly, Ritchie Valens, and Eddie Cochran. To those elements, he added vocal elements styled after the Everly Brothers and hot blasts of surf guitar and garage rock.

But Bobby was never going to become a national sensation in El Paso. By the end of 1964, he and his band – now known as the Bobby Fuller Four – packed up and moved to California, where they looked up Bob Keane, owner of Del-Fi Records, who had discovered and produced Ritchie Valens. Keane had expressed an interest in the band after seeing them perform live at a local club. He quickly signed the band and became their manager, booker, producer, label boss, and publisher. Years of playing across the southwest had honed the boys into a formidable live group who wowed the Hollywood music scene.

But it was Bobby's best-remembered song that turned them into teen idols almost overnight. In 1965, Crickets guitarist Sonny Curtis provided Bobby with the song that would change everything – "I Fought the Law." The Crickets had tried a recording of the song earlier, but it was lackluster compared to the fiery treatment that Bobby put to vinyl. By channeling his roots of Buddy Holly and Eddie Cochran, Bobby finally had his hit song.

"I Fought the Law" has become the archetypal outlaw rock-n-roll anthem. It's been covered more than 50 times, by the likes of Bruce Springsteen, the Stray Cats, Tom Petty, and, most famously, the Clash. Bobby's version captures the intense, frenetic energy of it in its purest state and has managed to draw generations of rockers and punks to it.

Bobby was on top – for a little while, at least. Things quickly soured. Bob Keane's attempts to turn Bobby into a Valens-style star alienated the rest of the band, and Bobby himself became unhappy with the direction that Keane was pushing the group and with the punishing tour scheduled that kept them out of the studio. Keane also came up with a succession of gimmicky marketing stunts that Bobby felt stifled his career – like releasing a single as the "Shindigs" so they could secure a slot on the music TV show *Shindig* or doing a drag-racing themed song that was branded with the name of the Los Angeles radio station KRLA. Bobby also did a cameo in *The Ghost in the Invisible Bikini* – a goofy beach party movie starring Boris Karloff, in which he lip-synched songs behind Nancy Sinatra.

And then there were the tragic comparisons to Buddy Holly that plagued his short career. It took a song by the Crickets to put Bobby on the national stage. The last song he recorded was "Love's Made a Food of You," which was written by Buddy Holly. As his career floundered, Bobby was contacted by Norman Petty, asking him to make him his manager again, much in the same way that Buddy Holly had been contacted by Petty to ask if they could work out their differences. And, also like Buddy, Bobby split with his backing band so that he could put together a solo career.

There was also the final comparison – both men died far too young and under violent circumstances.

On the afternoon of July 18, 1966, Bobby was found dead by his mother in her blue Oldsmobile. The initial reports suggested suicide: "Musician Robert Fuller, 23, was found dead on the parking lot at his Hollywood apartment house with a plastic hose in his hands leading to a gasoline can," the *Los Angeles Times* reported. That's how the police saw it, too, closing the case without even brushing for fingerprints or interviewing anyone. The details told a different story. The car had not been in the lot 30 minutes before his mother found it, yet Fuller's body was in an advanced state of rigor mortis, suggesting he had died elsewhere.

How had this happened?

Bobby had received a telephone call around 1:00 AM that morning at the Hollywood apartment that he shared with his mother. He left after the call and told his mother that he'd be right back. He had just bought a new Corvette but on this night, he drove his mother's Oldsmobile.

When Bobby didn't return home by the following morning, his worried mother called Bob Keane and asked him to look for the car. Then, around 5:00 PM, the car mysteriously appeared in the driveway. When she went to check on the car, she found Bobby lying dead across the seat. He was badly beaten and covered with blood. He had also been soaked in gasoline. Gasoline was also found in his stomach. Bob Keane was at the scene when the police arrived, and he witnessed an officer take a gasoline can from the backseat of the Oldsmobile and toss it into a dumpster. They dismissed the whole thing as a drug overdose. No fingerprints were taken, and the car was not impounded. There was, the authorities said, no signs of foul play. It was officially listed as suicide.

Of course, rumors circulated about Bobby's death. One story claimed that Bobby had become romantically involved with a young woman who was also dating a major Los Angeles underworld figure. His death was in retaliation for the relationship. Other theories – even more wildly implausible – suggested an accident following a bad reaction to LSD or that he was knocked off by the Manson family. One rumor even implicated Bob Keane, noting that Bobby was the third artist he'd managed – after Ritchie Valens and Sam Cooke – to die under mysterious circumstances.

Recently, a book about Bobby Fuller points the finger at Morris Levy, the owner of Roulette Records and a notorious figure once described as the "Godfather of the American Music Business." Levy's business partners and associates included members of the Gambino, Genovese, and DeCavalcante crime families and there was a long line of beatings, threats, and deaths, connected to Levy. Shortly before Bobby's death, Keane's label had signed an exclusive distribution deal with Roulette Records, and the Bobby Fuller Four's last single, "The Magic Touch," a Motown-style soul number, was penned by a songwriter associated with Roulette. It's been suggested that Bobby's death was connected to a business deal that he wanted to back out of.

But, as they say, once you're in that "family," there's no getting out.

In the years that followed Bobby Fuller's death, other artists fell victim to the so-called "Buddy Holy Curse." In 1977, a film based on his life and career, *The Buddy Holly Story*, was released. It starred Gary Busey, and while well-received, contained a lot of errors. First, there was no mention of Norman Petty, nor of the original Crickets, Jerry Allison and Joe B. Mauldin. In the movie, Buddy's parents discouraged his desire to play rock-n-roll, which couldn't have been further from the truth. Buddy's parents had encouraged every part of his career.

Other inaccuracies suggested that Buddy could read and write music charts, that his recordings were made in New York and not in New Mexico, where Norman Petty lived, and that on the Winter Dance Party tour, Buddy was backed up by an orchestra. The roles of Waylon Jennings and Tommy Allsup were left out of the film altogether. Gary Busey did his own singing in the film, refusing to lip sync to Buddy's actual recordings. A soundtrack album was released following the film's debut and while it didn't sell well, Buddy's original music became popular again as a new audience discovered his music.

Busey's performance was pretty amazing and the actor was nominated for an Academy Award – but the film was not exempt from the curse. Soon after its release, Robert Gittler, who wrote the screenplay, committed suicide. And then there was Busey's accident.

After several other well-received roles, Busey was involved in a serious motorcycle accident on December 4, 1988. He was not wearing a helmet and his skull was fractured, causing permanent brain damage. Following the accident, Busey suffered from personality disorders and drug addiction, as well as a cocaine overdose in 1995. In 2008, after a psychiatric evaluation, doctors began to suspect that Busey's brain injury had a greater effect on him than realized. They described it as essentially weakening his mental "filters" and causing him to speak and act impulsively. Needless to say, this has been detrimental to his career. Busey still appears in the occasional film but his career has never recovered from the 1988 accident.

In the late 1970s – during a time when interest in Buddy Holly was seeing a resurgence – there were two instances of the alleged curse across the Atlantic in England. The death of T. Rex founder Marc Bolan contained a Holly connection. Bolan died in a terrible car crash on September 16, 1977. As investigators searched through the rubble, they discovered a peculiar pin.

It's message? "Everyday is a Holly Day."

Eerily, it's been said that Bolan had premonitions of his death. Because of this, he never learned to drive. He was convinced that he would die young – which he did, at age 29 – once saying, "The thing about success, certainly in the rock-n-roll business, is that it gives you an incredible amount, but what it takes away is irreplaceable and sometimes I get a funny feeling that I shan't be here very long. And I'm not talking in terms of things like success. It frightens me sometimes."

English record producer and writer Simon Napier-Bell noted about Marc: "Chet Baker was a hero of his, and James Dean. And I said, 'Well, be careful having James Dean as a hero, because you might end up dying in a Porsche. And he said, 'Oh, I'm just tiny, I'd like to die in a Mini.'"

It was in a Mini that he was killed on that night in 1977.

The curse also allegedly claimed the life of rock-n-roll's original madman, Keith Moon. Keith grew up in Alperton, a suburb of Wembley, in Middlesex, and began playing drums in the early 1960s. After playing in local bands, he joined the Who in 1964, before they recorded their first single. He remained with the band during their rise to fame and was quickly recognized for his drumming style. He occasionally collaborated with other musicians and later appeared in films, but always considered his role in the Who as his real job.

And he did it very well, earning a reputation not only as an exemplary drummer but as a crazed musician who smashed his kit on stage and destroyed hotel rooms while on tour. He especially loved smashing television sets and blowing up toilets with cherry bombs and dynamite.

Perhaps his most infamous tour incident occurred in Flint, Michigan in August 1967. Keith was celebrating what he said was his 21st birthday – it was actually his 20th but he decided that if he publicized that it was his 21st he could legally drink – and began drinking as soon as the band arrived in town. The Who spent the afternoon visiting local radio stations and Keith was quite drunk by the time the band went onstage at Atwood Stadium.

After the show, the band returned to the Holiday Inn where they were staying. Keith started a food fight and somehow managed to knock out part of his front tooth. At the hospital, doctors were unable to give him an anesthetic, because he was so drunk, while they removed the remainder of the tooth. Back at the hotel, chaos erupted – fire extinguishers were set off, guests, patio furniture, and other items were thrown into the swimming pool, and a piano was reportedly destroyed. The melee only ended when the police arrived with guns drawn.

The furious Holiday Inn management presented the Who – and Herman's Hermits, who they were touring with – with a bill for $24,000. For the rest of his life, Keith claimed that he had driven a Lincoln Continental into the hotel's swimming pool. He didn't, but it really wouldn't have been much of a surprise if he had.

Keith suffered a number of setbacks during the 1970s, most notably the accidental death of chauffeur Neil Boland and the collapse of his marriage. He became addicted to alcohol, particularly brandy and champagne, and even his closest friends became concerned about his health and stability.

After moving to Los Angeles with personal assistant Peter 'Dougal' Butler during the mid-1970s, Keith recorded his only solo album, the poorly received "Two Sides of the Moon." He continued to tour with the Who, but

Keith Moon

his drinking had become so bad that it became uncertain whether he could finish a show without incident.

At the Cow Palace in Daly City, California, during the Who's 1973 Quadrophenia tour, Keith ingested a mixture of tranquilizers and brandy. During the show, he passed out on his drum kit during "Won't Get Fooled Again." As important as the role of the drums are in the song, people noticed. The band stopped playing and a group of roadies carried Keith offstage. They put him in a shower, gave him an injection of cortisone, and sent him back onstage after a 30-minute delay. He passed out again during "Magic Bus" and was again removed from the stage. This time, he didn't come back. The band continued on without him for several songs before Pete Townshend called out into the audience, "Can anyone play the drums? I mean somebody good?" A drummer named Scot Halpin came onstage and played the rest of the show.

On opening night of the band's March 1976 tour at the Boston Garden, Keith passed out on his drum kit after just two songs. The show had to be rescheduled. The next evening, he systematically destroyed everything in his hotel room – badly cutting himself in the process – and passed out. He was discovered by manager Bill Curbishley, who took him to the hospital and told him, "I'm gonna get the doctor to get you nice and fit, so you're back within two days. Because I want to break your fucking jaw ... You have fucked this band around so many times and I'm not having it anymore." Doctors told Curbishley that if he had not intervened, Keith would have bled to death in his hotel room.

At this point, Roger Daltrey and John Entwistle seriously considered kicking Keith out of the band but, in the end, decided against it. They feared that doing so would make his life even worse. It would, they believed, literally kill him.

But Keith didn't get better. At the end of the 1976 tour, in Miami that August, Keith, delirious, was treated at Hollywood Memorial Hospital for eight days. The rest of the band was worried that he wouldn't be able to complete the last leg of the tour, which ended at Maple Leaf Gardens in Toronto on October 21. He managed to get it together for two more months, and October 21, in Toronto, turned out to be Keith's last public show.

Over the next two years, the Who was on a recording sabbatical, during which Keith's health continued to deteriorate. By the time of the band's invitation-only show at the Gaumont State Cinema on December 15, 1977, for *The Kids are Alright,* Keith was visibly overweight and had difficulty getting through their performance.

The rest of the band was fed up by this time. After recording "Who Are You," Pete Townshend refused to follow the album with a tour unless Keith stopped drinking. If things didn't change, he'd be fired. Roger Daltrey later denied threatening to fire him, but said that by this time, Keith was completely out of control.

By mid-1978, Keith was making an attempt to get clean. He moved into a flat in Shepherd Market, Mayfair, London, that he rented from musician Harry Nilsson. It was the same apartment in which "Mama" Cass Elliot had died four years earlier. Nilsson was worried about renting the place to Keith because he believed it was cursed.

But Pete Townshend assured him "lighting wouldn't strike the same place twice."

After moving in, Keith was prescribed a sedative called clomethiazole to alleviate his alcohol withdrawal symptoms. He wanted to get sober but was terrified of psychiatric hospitals, so he wanted to do it at home. The use of the drug was discouraged by doctors for unsupervised detox because it was very addictive – and could be deadly when mixed with alcohol. Keith was supposed to take one pill whenever he had a craving for booze but was told not to take more than three pills in a single day.

On September 6, Keith and his girlfriend, Annette Walter-Lax, went to the movies with Paul and Linda McCartney – an early screening of *The Buddy Holly Story.*

After the film, they dined at Peppermint Park in Covent Garden and then Keith and Annette returned to their flat. Keith watched a film – *The Abominable Dr. Phibes*, starring Vincent Price – and asked Annette to make him steak and eggs. When she objected, Keith replied, "If you don't like it, you can fuck off!" Those were his last words.

At some point during the early morning hours, Keith took 32 clomethiazole tablets. Doctors later found that six were digested in his system, enough to cause his death. The other 26 were undigested when he died.

Bill Curbishley called the flat that afternoon, looking for Keith and was given the news. He called Pete Townshend, who called the rest of the band. John Entwistle was giving an interview to French journalists when he was interrupted by a phone call with the news of Keith's death. Trying to quickly end the interview, he broke down and wept when the journalist asked him about the Who's future plans.

Keith's last public appearance had been at a film about Buddy Holly and September 7, the date of his death, was Buddy Holly's birthday.

It's a tenuous connection but when it comes to musical curses, I've seen some that are even harder to swallow. But musicians, as we've already discussed, are even more superstitious than athletes – and the Buddy Holly curse still wasn't finished.

There were two other American musicians associated with the curse, both of whom also gained their fame at the same time that Buddy Holly was raving on.

The first was Rick Nelson, who became a star at the same time as Buddy and later, recorded two of his songs. As a rock-n-rolling teenager on *The Adventures of Ozzie and Harriet*, Ricky practically grew up in America's living rooms. He and his brother, David, played themselves on the show – the real-life sons of Ozzie and Harriet Nelson. Both the family and the television show were loved by practically everyone. Starting in 1957, the show concluded each episode with a song from Ricky Nelson and his band. Many teenagers tuned into the show because of him, and these performances helped keep Ozzie and Harriet on the air until 1966.

Ricky became a teen idol, who wore his hair in a fashionable flat-top with a ducktail. He was a rock-n-roller, everything about him said, but he wasn't too threatening. His principal influences were Elvis Presley, Carl Perkins, and Buddy Holly. For his first recording, he cut a double-sided smash – "A Teenager's Romance" and "I'm Walkin'" by Fats Domino. Both songs ended up in the Top Five in April 1957 and instantly launched Rickey's career.

Rick Nelson

He was only 16-years-old but that was just the beginning. He'd eventually go on to score three dozen hits, making him one of the most successfully prolific artists in the business.

Even though his role on television started his career, he was the real thing – a mellow-voiced singer and guitarist with an instinctive feel for country-tinged rockabilly. His less frantic, more pop-sounding brand of rock-n-roll went down easily with America's suburban teenagers and, probably more importantly, with their parents, who paid for the records.

In 1958, Ricky reached Number One with "Poor Little Fool," which was written by Sharon Sheeley, making a link between Nelson and Buddy Holly, through Sharon, who was Eddie Cochran's girlfriend at the time.

His discerning taste in material also led him to "Hello, Mary Lou," which became his signature song, and "Travelin' Man," both of which topped the charts. During a three-year period from 1957 to 1959, Ricky placed 18 songs in the Top 40 for nearly 200 combined weeks.

For his sixth album – released in 1961 when he was 21 – he dropped the "y" from his name. As he got older, his appeal to the teen audience waned and his career stumbled in the mid-1960s, finally getting back on track later in the decade with a more country-flavored sound. He scored big in the early 1970s with "Garden Party," in which he pointedly resisted the idea of becoming a nostalgia act, as some other musicians from the 1950s were starting to become.

Rick formed the Stone Canyon Band, whose mellow, California-based country-rock sound anticipated the laid-back likes of the Eagles and Linda Ronstadt. One of his band members, in fact, was bassist Randy Meisner, a founding member of Poco, who would later find fame with the Eagles.

Although Rick stopped having hits in the late 1970s, he remained a hard-working musician who performed up to 200 dates a year – largely for audiences who wanted to hear the oldies. The decade wasn't entirely kind to him, as personal problems --including cocaine addiction -- began to mount and his popularity waned. It was in 1979, though, that Rick recorded "Rave On" and "True Love Ways," both written by Buddy Holly. He had only met Buddy once but respected, and was influenced by, his music.

Rick Nelson's last performance was in Guntersville, Alabama, on December 30, 1985, and his death would have another Buddy Holly connection.

Though Rick had changed his musical style over the years – and vowed to never become a novelty act – he found himself more and more having to play oldies from the 1950s. He had to give the audience what they wanted and the majority of them were baby boomers who had grown up watching him on his parents' television show. Rick didn't want to disappoint them, so he generously sprinkled the old tunes in between his more recent recordings.

For an encore on the night of December 30, Rick chose to do Buddy Holly's "Rave On." It brought down the house. After the show, Rick and his band flew off in a reconditioned DC-3 aircraft. It caught on fire during the flight and crashed near a highway outside of Dekalb, Texas. Rick and his band were killed, although the pilot and co-pilot survived.

Like Buddy Holly, Rick Nelson perished in a plane crash. But wait, there's more...

Ironically, the plane had been purchased from Jerry Lee Lewis, who sold it because he'd had a premonition that he would die in the plane during a terrible crash.

Del Shannon was another rocker who hit the charts in the early 1960s, providing a key transition in American music between the sound of Elvis Presley and the Beatles. He was one of the few self-reliant acts of the "Teen Idol" era. He wrote his own material, played guitar, and sang without projecting a manufactured image. Del produced a solid run of hits during the first half of the 1960s, including a bonified classic with "Runaway" and seven more Top 40 singles. He also influenced a number of up-and-coming British Invasion bands, including the Beatles.

Del was born as Charles Westover in Coopersville, Michigan. He was an early fan of Hank Williams and first picked up a guitar in his childhood years. By age 14, he was playing at school shows. His high school principal later recalled that he played his guitar everywhere he went, at football games, in the hallways at lunch, everywhere.

After high school, Del served in the army in Germany. When he returned home, he formed his first band, the Midnight Ramblers. He took his stage name from a friend – March Shannon – and from his boss' car, a Cadillac

Del Shannon

Coupe de Ville. The Midnight Ramblers became regulars at the Hi-Lo Club in Battle Creek, Michigan, and in early 1960, a deejay from a local station caught one of their shows and arranged for an audition with Big Top Records in Detroit. Del was signed to the label and sent to New York to record some songs. Everything he tried fell apart and he was sent home. He tried once more, though, and ended up recording his most famous hit, "Runaway."

This classic – which occupied the Number One spot for four weeks and has since been covered by 200 other artists – had two distinctive qualities that became signatures of Del's sound: his use of a strong falsetto voice and bandmate and co-writer Max Crook's solo on the "musitron," a high-pitched electric organ. "Runaway" turned Del into an overnight star and he soon found himself performing on package tours with performers like Dion and Jackie Wilson.

He followed "Runaway" with pop-rockers like "Hats Off to Larry," "So Long Baby," "Hey! Little Girl," "Little Town Flirt," and covers like "Do You Wanna Dance." Del did his first tour of England in 1962, and he returned the following year. On that second trip, he met the Beatles and shared a bill with them at London's Royal Albert Hall on April 18, 1963.

Two more chart singles—"Keep Searchin' (We'll Follow the Sun)" and "Stranger in Town"—came in 1964. Each bore a haunted, minor-key aura that was Del's unmistakable signature and a likely symptom of the depression that plagued him throughout his life.

Shannon's career cooled off as musical tastes changed in the latter half of the 1960s. He continued to record, though, and began focusing more of his attention on production, setting up his own independent company. He toured mostly in England, where he remained very popular.

As time moved on, Del's popularity continued to fade and he began suffering from bouts of alcoholism. In 1981, however, he first teamed up with Tom Petty, who produced Del's first Top Ten hit since 1965, a cover of Phil

Phillips "Sea of Love." In 1986, NBC-TV began airing the first of two seasons of the drama *Crime Story*, starring police officer turned actor Dennis Farina. Set in Chicago in the early 1960s, the series used "Runaway" as the theme song, introducing Del Shannon to a new generation of fans.

He began working on his comeback – with Tom Petty's help – throughout the remainder of the 1980s. He began working steadily on the oldies circuit, and in 1990, recorded a new album, *Rock On!*, with musical accompaniment by Petty, among others.

His career was on the rise again but Del had never been able to shake off the depression that he'd suffered from for so long. It soon claimed his life.

Del Shannon's last performance took place at the Surf Ballroom on February 3, 1990. It was the anniversary of Buddy Holly's death and the same place where he, Ritchie, and the Big Bopper played their final songs. His backing band that night? The reunited Crickets.

Six days later, Del committed suicide with a shotgun.

He was unaware of the fact that he had just been selected to take the place of the late Roy Orbison in the superstar band the Traveling Wilburys.

Some medical experts believe that the antidepressants that Del was taking might have contributed to his death, while others simply point to a night 31 years earlier when a young man named Buddy Holly gained rock-n-roll immortality.

It was the curse, they said, it gets them all in the end.

THE "CROSS ROADS BLUES" CURSE

If I had to pick a favorite version of this song, it has to be the one that Eric Clapton did with Cream. Clapton's guitar solo is unbelievable, and the live version has so much energy that it makes it come alive in ways that Robert Johnson never would have dreamed of.

That's right, "Cross Roads Blues" is a Robert Johnson tune. I'm sure you remember Robert – the enigmatic bluesman that allegedly made a deal with the Devil at the crossroads one night to achieve fame and fortune. Robert went on to become the founding member of the sinister "27 Club" – which we'll be getting to soon, don't worry – but that wasn't the only curse that began with the young guitar player.

There's also the "Cross Roads Blues Curse."

I'm sure you remember the story of Robert Johnson, but you may not realize that his song is believed to be cursed. According to legend – crossroads deal or not – Robert became its first victim. He died a horrible death after likely being poisoned by a jealous husband and was buried in a grave that went unmarked for decades.

He would not be the last victim.

In the early 1970s, a southern rock band from Macon, Georgia, emerged on the music scene. Duane and Gregg Allman assembled a group of musicians they called the Allman Brothers, who relied on the guitars of Duane Allman

Duane Allman

and Richard "Dickey" Betts to establish their place in history. Duane was a disciple of the blues and the band loved to go into extended jams of classics by bluesmen like Sonny Boy Williamson, T-Bone Walker – and Robert Johnson. In fact, "Cross Roads Blues" was a particular favorite and the band played it many times in concert.

And some say that this had dire results.

Duane Allman had already established himself as an extraordinary guitarist, well before the founding of the band. He was a session player whose incredible skills had already earned him international fame. His fans included Eric Clapton, who invited him to record with Derek and the Dominos. The opening guitar riff in "Layla?" That's Duane Allman. Give it another listen, and you can hear Duane playing throughout the song. His soaring guitar lines add emphasis to one of the greatest rock-n-roll songs ever recorded by pushing Eric Clapton's playing to another level.

The two guitar greats fed off each other's energy and became good friends. Clapton was first introduced to Duane's playing when he heard Wilson Pickett's version of the Beatles' song, "Hey Jude." The story goes that Duane suggested to Pickett that he do the song and when Wilson hesitated, he asked him, "What's the matter? You haven't got any balls?" Pickett answered the challenge by laying down a scorching rendition of the song like nothing the Beatles had ever imagined. Pickett's raspy, rhythm and blues voice does something that sets it apart from other covers. He knew he had Duane to thank for that, and in appreciation, awarded him with the nickname of "Sky Dog" – a reference to the southern hippie guitarist with long, blond hair and an affinity for getting high.

By the way, since you're looking up Wilson Pickett's cover of "Hey Jude," go ahead and give a listen to some of his other hits, like "Mustang Sally," "Land of a 1000 Dances," and "In the Midnight Hour." Man, that guy could really sing.

Returning to the Allman Brothers and the curse, legend has it that the band often took their guitars into Rose Hill Cemetery and jammed late into the night – just like Robert Johnson did. The graveyard turned out to be the inspiration for some of the Allman Brothers' classic tunes. The haunting "In Memory of Elizabeth Reed" was said to have been composed by Dickey Betts while he was making love to a girl in the cemetery. The melody was running through his head and when he looked up, he found that they were lying on the grave of a woman named Elizabeth Reed. I'm guessing that he didn't stop everything he was doing to write the music at that very moment, but, according to Duane Allman, the location definitely inspired the song.

Duane's beautiful instrumental "Little Martha" took its name from another resident of Rose Hill Cemetery. Ironically, that song turned out to be one of his last recordings.

The Allman Brothers' connections to Robert Johnson went beyond just jamming to great blues songs in old graveyards at night. At the very peak of his career, tragedy claimed Duane Allman. On October 29, 1971, on his way to a birthday party, he was killed in a horrific motorcycle accident. He was riding a Harley-Davidson Sportster with long fork legs like Peter Fonda's bike in *Easy Rider*. The chopper-style motorcycle may have looked cool, but the long legs made it harder to handle. Shortly after 5:30 PM, Duane shot through the intersection of Inverness Avenue. As he approached Bartlett Avenue, a large Chevy flatbed truck stopped down in front of him. Duane tried to miss the truck by swerving to the left, but he clipped the corner of the truck's bumper. His helmet was ripped from his head when he went down and the heavy chopper ended up on top of him, causing serious internal damage, including a ruptured coronary artery and major liver damage.

Duane was rushed to the hospital, but it was too late to save him. He died three hours after the accident at the age of only 24. The terrible news of Duane's death shattered the other band members. Close friend and bassist

Berry Oakley totaled his car on the way home from the hospital after learning of Duane's death.

But this was not the only odd story connecting Duane, Berry, and death.

One night in 1970, the band had been in Nashville, Tennessee, for a show. Duane was rushed to the hospital after a drug overdose. Doctors didn't give him much hope for survival. But Berry Oakley wasn't ready to give up. He pleaded with God to give Duane just one more year of life – one more year of playing his music and living his dreams. Amazingly – and some said, against all medical odds, Duane pulled through and survived the overdose.

The overdose had occurred on October 29, 1970.

It was exactly one year later that Duane was killed in that motorcycle accident in Macon, Georgia.

Berry Oakley

It was not the last tragedy for the surviving band members. A little over a year later – on November 11, 1972 – Berry Oakley was preparing for a jam session at a club that he had booked for the night in downtown Macon. He was driving his 1967 blue Triumph motorcycle along Bartlett Avenue when he crashed into the side of a city bus. The accident occurred at the intersection of Inverness Avenue as the bus driver tried to avoid the approaching motorcycle. At the time of the crash, Berry was thrown from his bike and the heavy Triumph fell on top of him. Unlike his friend, Duane Allman, Berry climbed to his feet after the accident. He walked around and surveyed the crash site, refusing medical attention when an ambulance arrived. It seemed the Allman Brothers had narrowly avoided a second tragedy.

Berry went back to the band's headquarters, the Big House, in Macon and it seemed as though he was fine until someone noticed the trickle of blood that was running from his nostril. He collapsed a few hours later with a head injury. He was rushed to the hospital, where he died at 3:40 PM. The cause of death was listed as complications from hemorrhaging that was caused by a fractured skull.

Even the most casual reader must find it hard to miss the chilling coincidences in the deaths of Duane Allman and Berry Oakley. Both men were killed at the same intersections – or crossroads, if you will. Duane had crossed Inverness Avenue and was killed at Bartlett, while Berry, traveling from the opposite direction, had just crossed Bartlett and was killed at Inverness. The two accidents occurred within 90 yards of each other.

It's even stranger when we think about Robert Johnson and his legendary pact at the crossroads. Like Duane Allman, Robert was without equal as a blues guitarist. One of Duane's favorite songs was "Melissa," a ballad that was written and sung by his brother, Gregg. The eerie lyrics ask two questions: "Crossroads, will you ever let him go?" and "Who will hide the dead man's soul?" You can't help but find that spooky.

Duane and Berry were both 24-years-old when they died. The drivers of the truck and the bus – the other vehicles in the accidents – were also both 24.

According to author Scott Freeman, there is a legend that claims that Duane Allman's body was still in cold storage at the time of Berry's death. Because of this, the families decided to bury the two friends side-by-side at Rose Hill Cemetery. But here's the weird part – the first Allman Brothers album features a photo of the band that was taken in the cemetery. In one photo, Berry stands in what appears to be a chapel window, dressed in angelic robes, with his arms held wide open; standing in front of him is Duane Allman. They're forever immortalized, side-by-side in eternity – just as they were laid to rest.

The Allman Brothers survived member changes, internal feuds, and battles with their own excesses. Strangely enough, the coincidences of tragedy did not end with the deaths of Duane and Berry.

Twiggs Lyndon was the band's longtime friend and road manager – and a very interesting dude. He had signed the Allman Brothers to their first managerial contract in 1969 and was fiercely devoted to them. When the Allman Brothers Band moved to Macon, Georgia, they moved into Twiggs' apartment, turning the one-bedroom flat into a den of iniquity known to all as the "Hippie Crash Pad." Twiggs quickly became an indispensable part of the operation, finding gear, rehearsal space, and transportation once the band started touring. The group appreciated his attention to all details -- including a carefully curated list of the age of legal consent for sexual activities in each state. He was sharp-minded and creative, as well as being an obsessive-compulsive perfectionist with a violent temper that could flare up suddenly and unexpectedly.

On April 30, 1970, Twiggs stabbed club owner Angel Aliotta to death in Buffalo, New York, in a dispute over $500 owed to the band. He was eventually found not guilty by reason of temporary insanity. His lawyer, John

Condon, essentially argued that life on the road with the Allman Brothers had driven him crazy.

Twiggs's trial was delayed until September 1971, and he was still serving mandated time in a Buffalo mental hospital when Duane was killed in a motorcycle accident on October 29.

After the Allman Brothers split up in 1976, Twiggs discovered the Dixie Dregs -- a mostly instrumental band that fused hard rock, southern rock, and progressive metal -- in Nashville and helped get them signed to Capricorn Records. Lyndon had bought the Allman Brothers' smaller equipment truck, known as "Black Hearted Woman," and turned it into a mini tour bus. He offered it, and his services, to the Dixie Dregs.

While the band was in upstate New York in 1979, Twiggs met up with a group of skydivers to participate in a choreographed formation dive. He jumped from a plane and plunged 8,000 feet to his death.

Some of his friends hinted that Twiggs had never come to terms with the deaths of Duane and Berry and that his accidental death – caused when his chute didn't deploy – was actually suicide. He had often discussed killing himself and it was unthinkable to many who knew Twiggs that such a perfectionist would have made an error packing his chute.

Ironically, the name of the town where the plane had taken off was Duanesburg.

After Berry Oakley was killed, the band replaced him as bassist with Lamar Williams. He later left the band with keyboardist Chuck Leavell to form Sea Level, an obvious pun on the name C. Leavell. By the early 1980s, Sea Level had broken up and Lamar had fallen on hard times. He was diagnosed with lung cancer, thought to be caused by his exposure to Agent Orange during the Vietnam War. An exploratory surgery was scheduled for October 29, 1981 – the tenth anniversary of Duane Allman's death. Over one-third of his lung was removed, but it was to no avail. He died on January 21, 1983 at the age of 36.

Bassist Allen Woody joined The Allman Brothers Band, along with guitarist Warren Haynes, when the group reunited in 1989. Woody and Haynes formed side project Gov't Mule in 1994 with former Dickey Betts drummer Matt Abts. Haynes and Woody decided to leave The Allman Brothers Band in 1997 to put a full-time effort into Gov't Mule. But even getting away from the Allman Brothers didn't keep him clear of the alleged curse.

Allen was found dead on the morning of August 26, 2000 at the Marriott Courtyard Hotel in Queens, New York. A preliminary autopsy performed was inconclusive and showed no immediate cause of death.

The other surviving members of the Allman Brothers struggled with an assortment of personal demons, illnesses, substance abuse, divorce, the threat of prison terms, and in some cases, poverty. The band – with a number of new members coming and going – continued to record and perform until October 2014. In May 2017, the other founding brother, Gregg Allman, died from complications arising from liver cancer at the age of 69.

The band had reformed in 1989 and released their first new album, *Seven Turns*, a year later. For the cover, the band was photographed standing in the middle of a deserted country crossroads.

Robert Johnson would have been proud.

Eric Clapton, who, as mentioned, performed my favorite version of "Cross Roads Blues" with Cream – reportedly also fell under the curse. Although he managed to come out of it alive, not everyone around him was able to do so.

Eric grew up in England believing that his grandparents were his parents and his 16-year-old mother was his older sister. She'd gotten pregnant by a soldier from Canada near the end of the war and he left her behind in England. Years later, his mother married another Canadian soldier and moved to Germany, leaving young Eric with his grandparents in Surrey.

When Eric was 13, he received an acoustic guitar as a birthday present, but the cheap, steel-stringed instrument was difficult to play and he lost interest in it – although, thankfully, not for long. Two years later, he picked it back up and began playing every day, spending hours learning the chords of blues music by playing along to records. He recorded his sessions, listening to them over and over until he was satisfied it sounded right.

In 1961, Eric enrolled at Kingston College of Art, but he was dismissed at the end of the year because his focus was on music, not art. His guitar playing was so advanced that he was attracting a lot of attention. Around this time, he began busking in London's West End and formed a duo that played in pubs. When he was 17, he joined his first band, an early British R&B group called The Roosters. He stayed with them for about eight months before doing a series of gigs with Casey Jones and the Engineers.

In October 1963, Eric joined the Yardbirds, a blues-influenced rock-n-roll band and stayed with them until March 1965. He was making a name for himself by taking Chicago blues influences like Buddy Guy, Freddie King, and B.B. King and turning them into his own distinctive style. He became the most talked-about guitarist in the British music scene and developed a cult following.

The rhythm guitarist for the Yardbirds, Chris Dreja, recalled that whenever Eric broke a guitar string during a concert, he would stay on stage and replace it. British audiences waited out the delay by doing what was called a "slow handclap." Soon, Eric's nickname of "Slowhand" was born.

In March 1965, the Yardbirds had their first major hit, "For Your Love." In part because of its success, the band elected to move toward a more pop-oriented sound, much to Eric's annoyance. He was devoted to the blues, not commercial success. He left the Yardbirds on the day "For Your Love" was released, leaving the band without a lead guitarist and most accomplished member.

He soon joined John Mayall and the Bluesbreakers but quit just a few months later. Over the course of the next year, he worked on projects with musicians like Jimmy Page, Jack Bruce, Steve Winwood, and traveled in Greece with a band called the Glands. By this time, he had gained a reputation as the best blues guitarist on the club circuit. His immediately recognizable sound and electric talent inspired the famous slogan "Clapton is God," which was spray-painted by an unknown admirer on a wall in Islington in 1967. The graffiti was captured in a now-famous photograph, in which a dog was urinating on the wall.

In the summer of 1966, Eric was invited by drummer Ginger Baker to play in his newly formed band Cream. During his time with Cream, Eric began to develop as a singer, songwriter, and guitarist, though Jack Bruce took most of the lead vocals and wrote most of the band's material. Cream's first gig was an unofficial performance at the Twisted Wheel Club in Manchester, two nights before their full debut at the National Jazz and Blues Festival. Cream established its enduring legend with high-volume blues jamming and extended solos at their live shows.

By early 1967, fans of the emerging blues-rock sound in England had anointed Eric as Britain's top guitarist. He was soon rivalled by the emergence of Jimi Hendrix, the acid rock-infused guitarist who used wailing feedback and effects pedals to create sounds that had never been heard before. Jimi attended a performance of the newly formed Cream in October 1966, during which he sat in on a double-timed version of the song "Killing Floor." Eric and Jimi became friends and Eric attended many of Hendrix's early club performances.

Before playing with Cream, Eric was relatively unknown in the United States. That was all about to change. In March 1967, Cream performed a nine-show stand at the RKO Theater in New York. They recorded the album *Disraeli Gears* in New York two months later. It ran the gamut from hard rock to lengthy blues-based instrumental jams and featured Clapton's searing guitar, Bruce's soaring vocals, and Baker's jazz-influenced drumming.

They became one of rock's most influential power trios and over the course of 28 months, Cream became a commercial success, selling millions of records while touring the U.S. and Europe. Their biggest singles were "Sunshine of Your Love," "White Room" – and "Crossroads," the live version of Robert Johnson's song, "Cross Roads Blues."

And that's where the trouble began.

Though Cream was hailed as one of the greatest groups of

Eric Clapton

its day – and the adulation of Eric Clapton as a guitar legend reached new heights – it didn't last long. Drug and alcohol use escalated the tensions between the three members and conflicts between Bruce and Baker soon led to Cream's demise.

A new band was put together – Blind Faith – with Ginger Baker, Steve Winwood, and Ric Grech, and while they toured the U.S. and Europe, they only released one album with six songs on it. The album's jacket image of a topless pubescent girl was deemed too controversial in the states and had to be replaced by a photo of the band. Blind Faith dissolved in less than seven months.

Clapton toured as a sideman for a time, performed at the Toronto Rock and Roll Revival in September 1969, and played lead guitar on John Lennon's second solo single. In December, he performed with Lennon, George Harrison, and others at a fundraiser for UNICEF IN London.

He'd used his time away from groups to work on his singing and writing and so, using an all-star cast of session players (including Leon Russell and Stephen Stills), Eric recorded his first solo album, titled *Eric Clapton.* The album produced an unexpected U.S. hit, J.J. Cale's "After Midnight."

In the spring of 1970, he played on George Harrison's album, *All Things Must Pass*, and recorded with a string of other artists like Dr. John, Leon Russell, Billy Preston, Ringo Starr, and Dave Mason. With Chicago blues artist Howlin' Wolf, he recorded the *London Howlin' Wolf Sessions*, that also included members of the Rolling Stones, Steve Winwood, and others.

With the intention of playing down the "superstar" status that had started to bother him, Eric assembled a new band that included Bobby Whitlock, Carl Radle, and Jim Gordon. It was his intention to show that he did not need to fill the starring role – the band was meant to be an ensemble. The band was originally called "Eric Clapton and Friends" but soon became "Del and the Dominos." The name was misread, though, and Derek and the Dominos was born.

"Layla" was certainly not the only hit song that was recorded for the band's 1970 album, but it's certainly the most memorable. Like any great rock-n-roll song, it was written about a woman.

There are women who marry rock stars, and then there's the woman who married two.

Pattie Boyd was a blond knockout from South West England. She was a successful model who was cast in the 1964 Beatles film, *A Hard Day's Night*. She only had one line in the movie but more importantly, her role led to her meeting George Harrison, whom she went on to marry.

And thanks to his friendship with Harrison, she also met Eric Clapton.

Pattie and George had been an iconic couple. Their marriage was marked by several milestones. The Beatles song "Something" was written for Pattie by Harrison. It was Harrison who introduced the formerly innocent Pattie to LSD, as well. She claimed that she was the one who introduced George to meditation, leading to the Beatles' highly-publicized trip to India in 1968. And in 1969, Pattie and George were arrested for marijuana possession after a police raid. Despite the excitement, Pattie claimed that after returning from India, George's newfound spiritualist made him increasingly isolated. He would spend hours alone, chanting and meditating.

While Pattie was feeling neglected by Harrison, Eric was showering her with attention. Clapton and Harrison had become close friends and Eric visited the Harrisons' home on a daily basis. Pattie knew that Eric was interested in her and it wasn't just light-hearted flirting – he was falling in love. But Pattie good-naturedly brushed off his advances.

Then, one night he invited her over to his London apartment so that he could play her a song that he had been working on – a song about a man completely captivated by a woman, begging her to be his. The song was "Layla" and it was written about Pattie Boyd.

Pattie Boyd and husband, George Harrison

There was a party that same evening and Pattie, George, and Eric were all in attendance. At one point – and you have to give him credit for having nerve – Eric casually walked over to his friend and said, "I have to tell you something. I'm in love with your wife."

Harrison was furious. A shouting match followed in which he told Pattie to just go off with Clapton. She didn't. Instead, she stayed with Harrison for another three years. What ultimately made her leave was when she discovered an affair that George had been having – ironically, with Maureen Starr, Ringo's wife.

Pattie and Eric moved in together and married in 1979, which could be considered a happy ending – if this was another story. Their relationship was ultimately doomed, thanks to affairs on both sides, Clapton's alcoholism, and finally a baby by another woman. They divorced in 1989.

As dramatic as the situation must have been, Eric's friendship with George survived. Harrison even once said, "I'd rather she be with him than with some dope." When Harrison died in 2001, after a battle with cancer, Eric was the musical director for the "Concert for George" tribute show.

That's the story behind "Layla" but the recording of the song is something else altogether, thanks to the unforeseen inclusion of guitarist Duane Allman – another doomed Clapton friend. The two guitarists first met on stage -- at an Allman Brothers show in Miami -- then played all night in the studio and became friends. Duane played on a number of tracks for *Layla and Other Assorted Love Songs*, including a cover of Jimi Hendrix's "Little Wing."

And then eight days after they recorded it, Jimi died. Just one day before his death, Eric had purchased a left-handed Fender Stratocaster that he planned to give Hendrix as a birthday gift. He was heartbroken. To add to Clapton's woes, the Layla album received only lukewarm reviews when it was released. The shaken group started a U.S. tour without Duane Allman, who had returned to the Allman Brothers band. Eric later admitted that the tour took place amidst a "veritable blizzard of drugs and alcohol."

But things got worse.

On October 29, 1971, Duane was killed in a motorcycle accident. Eric later wrote that he and Duane had become inseparable during the sessions in Florida and that Allman was the "musical brother I'd never had but wished I did."

That was not the end of the tragedies. Although Carl Radle remained Eric's bass player until the summer of 1979 – he died in 1980 from the effects of alcohol and drugs – it would not be until 2003 that he and Bobby Whitlock would appear together again.

Things were even worse for Dominos' drummer Jim Gordon. He developed schizophrenia and he began to hear voices, including those of his mother, which compelled him to starve himself and prevented him from sleeping or playing music. His doctors misdiagnosed the problem and instead, treated him for alcohol abuse. Gordon rapidly declined and while on tour with Joe Cocker in the early 1970s, he reportedly beat up his then girlfriend, Rita Coolidge, in a hotel hallway, ending their relationship.

On June 3, 1983, he attacked his 72-year-old mother, Osa Marie Gordon, with a hammer before fatally stabbing her with a butcher's knife. He claimed that voices told him to kill her. Only after his arrest was he properly diagnosed as a schizophrenic. At his trial, the court accepted that he was mentally ill, but he was not allowed to use an insanity defense because of recent changes to California law. He was sentenced to 16 years to life in prison.

He was first eligible for parole in 1991, but parole has been denied many times. At a 2005 hearing, he claimed that his mother was still alive. In 2014, he declined to attend his hearing and was denied parole for at least four more years. A Los Angeles deputy district attorney stated at the hearing that he was still "seriously psychologically incapacitated" and "a danger when he is not taking his medication." He was re-diagnosed with schizophrenia in 2017 and was denied parole for the tenth time in 2018. As of this writing, he is serving his sentence at the California Medical Facility, a medical and psychiatric prison in Vacaville.

It's unlikely that he will ever be released.

Meanwhile, Eric Clapton was descending into his own turbulent world of drugs and alcohol. His career successes were in stark contrast with the struggles he was facing in his personal life, which was filled with the drama of the love triangle between himself, George Harrison, and Pattie Boyd. He withdrew from recording and went into seclusion. A second Derek and the Dominos album was begun but never completed as he became more reclusive. Alone, he nursed a heroin addiction, which resulted in a lengthy career hiatus, interrupted only by the *Concert for Bangladesh* in August 1971, during which he passed out on stage, was revived, and managed to finish his performance.

A January 1973 comeback concert at London's Rainbow Theatre re-introduced him to public performing, but his solo career really commenced in earnest a year later with *461 Ocean Boulevard*. Recorded in Miami, it was influenced by mellower sounds from J.J. Cale and Bob Marley. The album struck a chord with the public and topped the charts in 1974. Meanwhile, Clapton's cover of "I Shot the Sheriff," originally by Bob Marley and the Wailers, helped introduce reggae to a mass audience. His output in the 1970s included albums like *There's One in Every Crowd* and *No Reason to Cry* but he really struck commercial pay dirt in 1977 with *Slowhand*, which included Clapton's definitive version of J.J. Cale's "Cocaine" and "Lay Down Sally."

His personal life was still a mess. In 1974, he moved in with Pattie Boyd and stopped using heroin. He started drinking heavily instead. He tried out Christianity, too, and while it didn't stick, it did help him to kick his heroin habit. Finally, after calling his manager and admitting that he was an alcoholic, Eric flew to Minneapolis in January 1982 and checked in at the Hazelden Treatment Center. On the flight over, he consumed copious amounts of alcohol, fearing that he would never be able to drink again. He later wrote, "In the lowest moments of my life, the only reason I didn't commit suicide was that I knew I wouldn't be able to drink any more if I was dead. It was the only thing I thought was worth living for, and the idea that people were about to try and remove me from alcohol was so terrible that I drank and drank and drank, and they had to practically carry me into the clinic."

When he was released from the clinic, he was told that he should not partake in any activities that might cause stress and trigger his alcoholism but – against doctor's orders – he began working on his next album. He called it *Money and Cigarettes* because "that's all I saw myself having left" after his first rehabilitation from alcoholism.

Eric threw himself back into music. He played with Roger Waters for his solo album and he performed at the Live Aid Concert in 1985. As Clapton recovered from his addictions, his album output continued in the 1980s, including two produced with Phil Collins that featured songs like "Forever Man" and "She's Waiting." His song "It's in the Way that You Use It" was featured in the Tom Cruise – Paul Newman movie *The Color of Money*. Clapton later remade "After Midnight" as a single and a promotional track for Michelob beer, which had also used earlier songs by Collins and Steve Winwood. In 1989, Eric released *Journeyman*, an album that covered a wide range of styles, including blues, jazz, soul, and pop. Collaborators included George Harrison, Phil Collins, Daryl Hall, Chaka Khan, Mick Jones, David Sanborn, and Robert Cray.

But there was still more tragedy to come.

In August 1990, Eric was touring with Buddy Guy, Robert Cray, Jimmie Vaughn of the Fabulous Thunderbirds, and Jimmie's brother, Texas bluesman Stevie Ray Vaughn, who had risen to fame in the 1980s with a fiery style of blues that had appealed to Clapton. They had just ended a performance at Alpine Valley, outside of East Troy, Wisconsin, and Stevie Ray took off in a chartered helicopter with three members of the road crew. It crashed and he was instantly killed. He was just 35 years old.

Then, on March 20, 1991, Eric's four-year-old son died after falling from the 53rd-floor window of his mother's friend's New York City apartment. It was supposed to be the start of a new beginning between father and son, but it ended in horror.

Just the day before, Eric had picked up Conor, who Clapton had with Italian actress Lory Del Santo, and had taken him to the circus on Long Island. It was the first time that he had taken his son out by himself. The relationship between Eric and the boy's mother had been strained. Conor had been fathered while Clapton was still married to Pattie Boyd, leading to divorce and fodder for the gossip columnists. Eric was determined to be a proper father to the boy and made plans to see him as often as possible in New York.

The next morning, as Eric was due to arrive to pick up Conor for another day out -- this time to the Bronx Zoo and lunch at an Italian restaurant -- tragedy struck. Conor was running around the apartment that belonged to Italian film producer Silvio Sardi, excited to see his father. A janitor had been working on the windows in the living room and one of them was still open. He called out to the nanny to watch the child, but before she could react,

Conor ran past her, jumped on the low window ledge – where he normally pressed his nose against the glass to look out – and disappeared.

The little boy fell 53 stories to his death.

The devastating event made headlines around the world and sent Eric into a tailspin. To make things even more heartbreaking, a few days after the funeral, he received a letter in the mail that had been written by Conor, telling him how much he loved him and missed him whenever he was away.

That year, Eric wrote "Tears In Heaven," a gut-wrenching ballad about the pain of losing Conor. It went on to become his best-selling single in the United States and one of the best-selling singles of the 1990s. He won six Grammys for the song and the *Unplugged* album that it appeared on.

But I'm going to say that he would have traded all the awards, acclaim, and money that he received for the song for just one more day with Conor.

Clapton's career received a major boost from MTV's *Unplugged* series and allowed him to return to his roots on the heels of that acoustic folk-blues set. His next album was his long-promised blues album, *From the Cradle*, and throughout the 1990s, he continued to rack up hits – no mean feat, given the shifting musical climate – including "Change the World," a collaboration with R&B artist/producer Babyface that won a Grammy for Record of the Year.

In 1998, Eric opened the Crossroads Centre, a medical facility for substance abusers, on Antigua. Since then, he has organized four Crossroads Guitar Festivals to benefit the center. He also continues to record and tour on a regular basis and remains a relevant and creative force in popular music.

In 2004, Eric released two albums of Robert Johnson songs – *Me and Mrs. Johnson* and *Sessions for Robert J*. The albums included many of Johnson's tunes, but there was one song that was noticeably absent – "Cross Roads Blues."

Perhaps by that time, he'd realized that he'd finally tempted fate enough.

Was the curse of the "Cross Roads Blues" behind the tragic events in the lives of Robert Johnson, the Allman Brothers, and Eric Clapton? Or were the events merely the result of coincidences in the lives of musicians who rightfully admired a great song by an innovative blues artist?

The so-called curse had allegedly claimed other lives. For instance, some blame the curse for the misfortunes that dogged Lynyrd Skynyrd, another popular southern rock band. They also loved to perform rowdy versions of Robert Johnson songs, including "Cross Roads Blues."

Like other bands linked to the song, their years were marred with a number of misfortunes. In the mid-1970s, the band became extremely popular, turning authentic-sounding southern rock and energetic live performances into multi-platinum albums and sold-out shows.

In 1977, at the height of their fame, the plane the band had chartered ran out of fuel on its way to Louisiana. The pilots attempted an emergency landing at a small airport, but they didn't make it. The plane crashed into a forest near Gillsburg, Mississippi. The pilots, assistant road manager Dean Kilpatrick, and three band members – Ronnie Van Zant, Steve Gaines, and Cassie Gaines – died in the crash.

Years later, the curse was said to have returned for another victim – Kurt Cobain, the lead signer of Nirvana, who will return to these pages very soon. Friends say that Cobain played "Cross Roads Blues" for his own entertainment for years. He liked to play it acoustically, just like Robert Johnson did. His plan was to rework the song and add it into the Nirvana playlist or cover it for an album.

But it wasn't meant to be. That plan ended when Kurt killed himself with a shotgun.

THE GRAND OLE OPRY CURSE

It seems that not all musical curses can be linked to performers or the songs they sing. Some of them are connected to the places where the music is played – like the Ryman Auditorium, located in downtown Nashville, which was the center of repeated tragedies for many years.

"When's it all going to end?" asked Herb Shucher, the national promotions director for Star Records, after one Grand Ole Opry death after another.

There were a lot of performers who played at the Ryman who were asking the same thing.

Between the 1940s and the 1970s, many of them had experienced personal tragedies and losses, and in a single decade, a dozen Opry stars were killed by violence. And when they died, they took others with them, including relatives, business associates, and friends. They burned to death, suffered beatings, robberies, murders, became victims of automobile and airplane accidents, and succumbed to deaths linked to alcohol and drugs.

It was no wonder that rumors spread of the "Opry Curse" that was stalking the performers who appeared under the Ryman's spotlights.

The building that became the Ryman Auditorium – mecca for country music performers and fans – was opened in 1892, when it was the Union

Nashville's Ryman Auditorium

Gospel Tabernacle. It was built by Captain Tom Ryman, steamboat skipper and a hellraiser who was known for drinking, fighting, and carousing along the Cumberland, Ohio, and Mississippi Rivers. One night, he stumbled his way into a tent revival meeting and found God. He gave up his sinful ways, banned liquor and gambling on his steamboats, and shut down the tavern that he owned in Nashville. He decided to spend his money building a place that was dedicated solely to religious revivals and events.

The Union Gospel Tabernacle opened – just a short distance from the city's notorious Black Bottom vice district – as a place where people of all faiths could join in worship. It was also used as a public meeting hall and, in 1897, hosted a large reunion of Confederate military veterans of the Civil War. The gathering was so large that a balcony had to be added to the hall to accommodate the crowd. Legend has it that one of the Confederates – a spectral man in gray – has remained behind to haunt the building. He is allegedly joined there by the ghost of Captain Ryman himself, who passed away in 1904. More than 4,000 people jammed the auditorium to say farewell and it was during that funeral that a name change was proposed for the place. It soon became the Ryman Auditorium.

Though the building was meant to be a house of worship – which it continued to be throughout most of its early existence – it was often leased to promoters for other kinds of events. This kept the doors open, the lights on, and the bills paid. In 1904, Lula C. Naff, a widow and mother who was trained as a stenographer, began booking speaking engagements, concerts, boxing matches, and other attractions at the Ryman in her free time. After her

Lula C. Naff

employer went out of business in 1914, she made the Ryman her full-time job and rose to the ranks of official manager in 1920. Using the name "L.C. Naff" – so that no one knew she was a woman in a male-dominated industry – she began booking big name acts in the Ryman. She also gained a reputation for battling local censors, who threatened to ban performances they deemed too risqué for Nashville. In 1939, she won a landmark lawsuit against the Nashville Board of Censors, who tried to arrest the star of the play *Tobacco Road* because they thought it was to provocative. The court declared that the law that had formed the censorship group was invalid, effectively shutting them down for good.

Lula's ability to book stage shows and world-renowned entertainers made the Ryman one of the greatest attractions in the city and enhanced Nashville's reputation as a cultural center for the performing arts. The Ryman attracted names like W.C. Fields, Will Rogers, Charlie Chaplin, Bob Hope, John Phillip Sousa, Harry Houdini, and many others, earning it the nickname of the "Carnegie Hall of the South." The Ryman hosted lectures by U.S. Presidents Theodore Roosevelt and William Howard Taft. World-famous opera singer Enrico Caruso appeared in concert there and the Ryman hosted inaugurations for three Tennessee governors.

The first event to ever sell out at the Ryman was a lecture by Helen Keller and Anne Sullivan in 1913. Lula Naff was a trailblazer for working women but also championed civil rights. The building was used as a regular venue for the Fisk Jubilee Singers from nearby Fisk University, a historically black college. "Jim Crow" laws often forced the Ryman to be segregated – with separate shows for "white" and "colored" audiences – but Lula openly flaunted the laws and photographs exist showing integrated performances. Lula eventually retired in 1955 and passed away five years later.

In 1943, the Ryman became home to the legendary Grand Ole Opry, which marked the beginning of the curse.

After it debuted in 1925, the local country music radio program known as the Grand Ole Opry – originally called the WSM Barn Dance – became a

Nashville institution. Broadcast on radio station WSM on the AM dial, it could be heard in 30 states. Although not originally a stage show, the Opry began to attract listeners from around the region who went to the WSM studio to see the live broadcast. In 1934, after crowds became too large for the studio, WSM began broadcasting the show from the Hillsboro Theatre. In 1936, it moved again, this time to East Nashville's Dixie Tabernacle, and then to the War Memorial Auditorium in 1939.

After four years – a lot of damage to the seats caused by rowdy crowds – the Opry was kicked out of War Memorial Auditorium to find a new home. Thanks to its wooden pews and central location, Lula Naff thought the Ryman would make a perfect venue for the show and began renting the place out to WSM.

The Grand Ole Opry was first broadcast from the Ryman on June 5, 1943 and continued every week for the next 31 years. Every show sold out and hundreds of fans were frequently turned away.

During its time at the Ryman Auditorium, the Opry hosted the biggest music – both kinds, country *and* western – stars of the day. The show became known around the world, thanks to frequent simulcasts on network radio and television. Playing off the building's origin as a house of worship, the Ryman earned the nickname of "The Mother Church of Country Music."

But not everyone was thrilled with the place.

Because of the period when it was built, it was never designed to be a performance venue. There was no true backstage area. It only had one dressing room for the men and female performers were forced to use the cramped ladies' restroom, which they shared with the customers. The shortage of space forced the performers to wait in the wings, narrow hallways, or out in the alley behind the Ryman's south wall. Since they were in such close proximity to Tootsie's Orchard Lounge and other taverns, they often wandered off for a drink – enhancing the notoriety and appeal of the honky-tonk bars nearby.

In September 1963, radio station WSM purchased the building from its board of governors and renamed it the Grand Ole Opry House -- although the Ryman name was hard to shake after 60 years. Buyer's remorse soon followed. The building was deteriorating, there was no air conditioning, the neighborhood was in rapid decline, and the show's continuing popularity often resulted in crowds that were too large for the aging venue. A few minor upgrades were made but in 1969, plans were announced to move the Opry to a larger, custom-built auditorium. A large tract of land was purchased in a rural area a few miles away with the new theater serving as the anchor for a grand entertainment complex. The development became known as Opryland

USA and eventually included the Opryland theme park and the Opryland Hotel. The park opened in May 1972, and the new venue – also called the Grand Ole Opry House – debuted on March 16, 1974.

The last Opry show at the Ryman had been broadcast the previous evening, March 15. It was an emotional night. Sarah Cannon, performing as Minnie Pearl, broke character and cried on stage.

It was the end of an era and, without fanfare, the building went back to using the Ryman Auditorium name to differentiate it from the new Grand Ole Opry House.

Over the next 20 years, the Ryman sat vacant and deteriorating. The surrounding neighborhood had gotten worse, but the building continued to stand, even with its future uncertain. The stage was dark, and no one performed there but it attracted so many visitors that it remained open for tours.

In 1983, the Ryman became an almost accidental addition to the sale of WSM and the Opryland properties to Gaylord Entertainment Company. The company's chief executive, Ed Gaylord, became acquainted with many of the Opry stars during his involvement with the long-running television series *Hee Haw*. His fondness of the Opry and friendships with its personalities – particularly Sarah Cannon – are often cited as the reason for the buyout. The Ryman's inclusion in the sale was an afterthought but Gaylord had no plans to demolish it. In fact, a few years later, he began work to beautify the Ryman's exterior. Bricks were replaced, broken windows were repaired, and a new roof was added, but the interior was untouched.

The abandoned building wasn't always empty, though. As part of the Grand Ole Opry's 60th-anniversary, CBS aired a special that featured some of the Opry's legendary stars performing at the Ryman. Movies and television shows often used it as a location. From April 30 to May 2, 1991, Emmylou Harris and the Nash Ramblers performed a series of acoustic concerts in the dilapidated building, during which no one was allowed to sit on or beneath the balcony due to safety concerns. The resulting album won two Grammy Awards and brought renewed interest to the Ryman.

In September 1993, renovations began to restore it into a world-class concert hall. In the renovations, the auditorium's original wooden pews were removed, refurbished, and returned to the building to continue to serve as the auditorium's seating, parts of the old balcony were removed, new backstage facilities were built inside the original building, and a new structure was added for a lobby, restrooms, concessions, and offices. In addition, the Ryman was finally air-conditioned for the first time.

The Ryman soon became a popular venue again. Even the Grand Ole Opry returned, first for benefit shows and then for three months of performances during the construction of the Opry Mills Shopping Mall, which replaced the Opryland USA theme park in 2000. The Opry returned in 2010 while the Grand Ole Opry House was undergoing repairs after a devastating flood.

Repairs and renovations have continued, as recent as 2015, when the original building was touched up and the addition expanded to include more lobby space and restrooms, a gift shop, and a restaurant called "Café Lula," in honor of Lula C. Naff.

Weekly stage shows still take place at the Ryman. In addition to Grand Ole Opry shows in the winter, the auditorium hosts a variety of acts throughout the year. It's also served as a gathering place for the memorial services of many prominent country music figures like Tammy Wynette, Chet Atkins, Skeeter Davis, Waylon Jennings, Johnny Cash, Earl Scruggs, and many others.

The Ryman may have faded away for a while, but it never truly died. Its revitalization has helped to turn Nashville's downtown district into a destination for locals and tourists alike.

But there was something about the place during its Grand Ole Opry years that had strange repercussions for those who walked the stage and played their music under the lights. Many called it a "curse," but others shrugged it off as bad luck – at first anyway.

But following one death after another, the tragedies became hard to ignore.

Most people don't realize that the Ryman Auditorium almost didn't survive the early 1970s.

When the plans for the Opryland USA amusement park were announced, WSM revealed that the company planned to tear down the Ryman and use its materials to construct a chapel called "The Little Church of Opryland" at the theme park. A consultant was brought in to evaluate the building and he concluded that the Ryman was "full of bad workmanship and contains nothing of value as a theater worth restoring." WSM had managed to justify its destruction but the station's plans were met with resounding resistance from the public, including many influential musicians of the time.

But Roy Acuff was not one of them.

Roy was a country singer, fiddler, and promoter who was known as the "King of Country Music." He started his musical career in the 1930s and after achieving regional fame, joined the Grand Ole Opry in 1938. After his popularity as a musician waned, he founded Nashville's first country music publishing company and signed artists like Hank Williams, Roy Orbison, and the Everly Brothers. In 1962, he became the first living inductee into the Country Music Hall of Fame.

But in addition to all that, Roy was also a major stakeholder of Opryland USA – and he hated the Ryman Auditorium. He told the *Washington Post* in 1974, "I never want another note of music played in that building. Most of my memories of the Ryman Auditorium are of misery, sweating out here on this stage, the audience suffering too... We've been shackled all of my career."

The building was saved, much to Roy Acuff's chagrin, but he never recovered from his dislike of the place. He'd simply seen too much death associated with it.

If you can say that a curse "began," then the Opry Curse apparently started on January 1, 1953, when the body of Hank Williams, 29, was discovered dead in the back seat of his car during a stop in Oak Hill, West Virginia. He was being driven to a concert date in Canton, Ohio.

Hank was born in Mount Olive, Alabama, and while still a very young man, moved to Georgiana. There, he met bluesman Rufus Payne, who gave him guitar lessons in exchange for meals or money and greatly influenced

Hank Williams

Hank's later style. After moving to Montgomery in 1937, his music career began when he was hired by radio station WSFA to host and perform a recurring 15-minute program. Hank formed the Drifting Cowboys Band – managed by his mother – and dropped out of school to devote all his time to his career.

After recording "Never Again" and "Honky Tonkin'" with Sterling Records, he signed a contract with MGM. In 1948, he released "Move it on Over," which became a hit, and also joined the Louisiana Hayride radio program. One year later, he released a cover of "Lovesick Blues," which launched him into the mainstream. Between 1948 and 1953, he had 11 number one songs, despite the fact that he was unable to read music. Among his hits were "Your Cheatin' Heart," "Hey, Good Lookin'," and "I'm So Lonesome I Could Cry."

Despite his short life, Williams has had a major influence on decades of popular music. The songs he wrote and recorded have been covered by numerous artists, and have been hits in various genres including pop, gospel, and blues. He has been inducted into multiple music halls of fame and remains a music legend today.

He was also an integral part of the Grand Ole Opry during its heyday. He almost didn't get in. Initially, he was rejected, but as he became more popular, WSM reconsidered and added him to the roster. Producers probably felt like they'd been right in the first place when they kicked him out a few years later, though, citing unreliability and drunkenness.

Hank's career was at its peak when he joined the Opry, but it soon began to fall apart.

Hank married Audrey Sheppard on December 15, 1944. It was her second marriage and his first. Their son, Randall Hank Williams – who later achieved his own fame as Hank Williams, Jr. – was born on May 26, 1949. The marriage, always turbulent, rapidly disintegrated, and Hank developed serious problems with alcohol, morphine, and other painkillers that had been prescribed to him for severe back pain. By May 1952, Audrey couldn't take any more, and the couple divorced.

In the middle of the divorce, Hank moved in with his mother – at the same time that he was releasing hit songs like "Half as Much," "Jambalaya (On the Bayou)," and "I'll Never Get Out of this World Alive."

His substance abuse problems continued to spiral out of control and Hank made a lot of bad decisions, including marrying a woman named Billie Jean Jones Eshlimar in October 1952. It was a second marriage for both and maybe that's why they had two ceremonies. The first was in front of a justice of the peace, but the second was at the New Orleans Civic Auditorium, in front of 14,000 paying guests. The marriage – both of them – turned out not to be legal since Billie's divorce wasn't final until 11 days after she married Hank.

Two months passed in a haze of booze and drugs. He likely had no idea that he'd be dead by the end of the year – or did he? Some say that he saw it coming. On the night of December 30, 1952, Hank spent the hours tossing and turning in bed at his home in Montgomery, Alabama. When new wife Billie Jean asked what was wrong, she later claimed he replied, "I think I see God comin' down the road."

Just 48 hours later, Hank met his maker, but the circumstances surrounding how he died continue to provide a mystery to this day.

On December 31, 1952, Hank was scheduled to perform at the Municipal Auditorium in Charleston, West Virginia. He was supposed to fly but an ice storm in the area closed the airport. Hank hired a college student, Charles Carr, to drive him to his upcoming shows. They ran late because of the storm and missed the Charleston performance so Carr was ordered to drive Hank to Canton, Ohio, for a New Year's Day concert there.

They made it as far as Knoxville, Tennessee, and checked into the Andrew Johnson Hotel. When they arrived, Carr requested a doctor for Hank. On the way, he had consumed alcohol -- and, it was later alleged, chloral hydrate -- and was feeling the effects. The doctor injected Hank with two shots of vitamin B12 that also contained a quarter-grain of morphine. Hotel porters had to carry Hank to the car when they checked out.

Just after midnight on January 1, 1953, when they crossed the Tennessee line and arrived in Bristol, Virginia, Carr pulled into a small all-night diner for a break. He asked Hank if he wanted to eat and Hank replied that he did not.

Those are believed to be his last words.

Carr later drove on and stopped for gas at a station on Oak Hill, Virginia. Hank had been silent for the entire ride and Carr assumed he was sleeping. He tried to rouse him at the gas station and realized that he was dead – and had been for some time. Rigor mortis was already starting to set in. The service station's owner called the police. When they arrived, they found some empty beer cans and some unfinished, handwritten lyrics with Hank in the backseat of his Cadillac.

Dr. Ivan Malinin performed the autopsy at the Tyree Funeral House. Malinin found hemorrhages in the heart and neck and pronounced the cause of death as "insufficiency of the right ventricle of the heart." It seemed straightforward enough – Hank Williams had abused his body to the point that it caused his death.

That evening, when the announcer at the Canton show where Hank was supposed to have performed announced his death instead of introducing him, people in the audience started to laugh. They assumed it was simply an excuse for the fact that he wasn't there. But when Hawkshaw Hawkins and other performers started singing "I Saw the Light" as a tribute to Williams, the crowd, now that he was indeed dead, sang along.

It seemed a fitting farewell to a musical legend.

The next day, though, the story took a strange turn.

Apparently, Charles Carr hadn't just discovered Hank's body in the backseat at a gas station in Tennessee. There seemed to be a little more to it than that. Tennessee Highway Patrol Corporal Sawn Kitts reported that he had stopped Williams' Cadillac just outside Knox County around 1:00 AM on January 1. Hank was prone in the backseat and already "looked dead." But

Carr insisted that he was just sleeping. He'd been given a sedative by a doctor in Knoxville.

Investigations ensued. The Highway Patrol found no sign of foul play but at the autopsy, Dr. Malinin wrote that it looked as though Hank had been severely beaten and kicked in the groin recently. Local magistrate Virgil F. Lyons ordered an inquest into Williams' death concerning a welt that was visible on his head. The coroner's jury determined that Williams died of a "severe heart condition." Alcohol was in his bloodstream, but, supposedly, no drugs.

In March, though, a paroled convict with phony medical credentials named Horace "Toby" Marshall told investigators in an unrelated case that Hank Williams had been paying him $300 a week plus expenses to treat him for alcoholism and help him "sober up" for appearances. The phony physician had prescribed a powerful sedative, chloral hydrate, in the last months of 1952.

Marshall insisted that Hank had committed suicide. He said that Williams had told him that he had decided to "destroy the Hank Williams that was making the money they were getting." He attributed this to Hank's declining career, telling investigators, "Most of his bookings were of the honky-tonk beer joint variety that he simply hated." Marshall added that if Hank killed himself now, he still had enough prestige left as a star to make a first-class production of it.

He insisted that Williams was depressed and committed suicide by taking a lethal dose of the chloral hydrate that he prescribed for him.

Billie Jean Jones told investigators that, after Hank's death, she had received a bill for $800 from Marshall for Hank's treatment. She refused to pay, and further stated that Marshall later intended to convince her to pay him by assuring that he would "pave the way to collect her husband's estate." Billie Jean stated, "I have never accepted the report that my husband died of a heart attack."

For some conspiracy theorists, Marshall was the main suspect in Hank's death. They refused to believe the legendary musician would have taken his own life. Others still pointed the finger at college student Charles Carr, who, according to police reports, was nervous enough when interviewed by investigators to invite suspicion that foul play had occurred in Hank's death.

Others suspected the doctor in Knoxville. In fact, public outcry was so strong that he eventually was forced to come forward. The doctor -- "who asked that his name be withheld," but later was discovered to be Dr. P.H. Cardwell -- told a newspaper reporter that he had given Williams two shots just hours before he died. Williams had been drinking, but the doctor denied the injections were the "final blow" that did him in. "The shots I gave

Williams had absolutely nothing to do with his death," Dr. Cardwell said, and "it is ridiculous to think that they did."

The theories eventually cooled, and the news tapered off in the months that followed, but books and articles about Hank's death have continued to appear throughout the years. It's been suggested that Hank was already dead when Carr took him to the Andrew Johnson Hotel, or that he was badly beaten and killed while he was there. His body was then driven away to look as though he died somewhere else.

Is there any truth to these theories? Who knows?

Hank's body was taken back to Montgomery on January 2. It was placed in a silver coffin and he lay in state at his mother's boarding house for the next two days. His funeral took place on January 4, at the Montgomery Auditorium and included performances by Roy Acuff, Ernest Tubb, and Red Foley. An estimated 15,000 to 25,000 passed by the silver casket. Four women fainted during the funeral and a fifth had to be carried out of the auditorium in hysterics.

He was buried in Montgomery – with more than two tons of flowers at his grave – and laid to rest as the first victim of what would become the so-called "Grand Ole Opry Curse."

And there's a little more to this story – a sort-of "curse by extension" addendum that's pretty eerie by itself.

Johnny Horton

Later in 1953, Hank's widow – if that's what she was since the marriage was such a mess – married a young country singer named Johnny Horton. He was kind of a reluctant performer whose greatest hit was "The Battle of New Orleans." His new wife, Billie Jean, had received a lump-sum payment from Hank's first wife, Audra, in return for the opportunistic Billie Jean not performing under the stage name of Mrs. Hank Williams.

In the years after they got married, Johnny Horton began having recurring dreams and visions of being in an accident and being killed by a drunk driver. His mental state became so bad that he began to fear playing on the road, turning down lucrative shows in the wake of his hit song because he simply didn't want to travel. Finally, he agreed to play at the Skyline Club in Austin, Texas – the same place where Hank Williams had played his final show in 1952.

After playing two sets on the night of November 5, 1960, he was driving back to Shreveport, Louisiana with his band when a drunk driver in a truck collided head-on with his car while crossing a bridge. Johnny died en route the hospital.

The next victim of the "jinx" was another of the most influential women in country music – or really in any kind of music. Her name was Patsy Cline and she died at the height of her career in a private plane crash. Patsy became a part of the Nashville Sound – created by Jim Reeves, the next victim of the curse – and successfully "crossed over" to pop music, making her one of the most successful and acclaimed female vocalists of the twentieth century. Patsy was known for her rich tone and emotionally expressive voice that "could make grown men weep." Along with Kitty Wells, she helped pave the way for women as headline performers in the country music world and, without a doubt, inspired legions of performers who followed in her wake.

Patsy Cline was born Virginia Patterson Hensley in Winchester, Virginia, in 1932. Her mother was a 16-year-old seamstress and her father was a 43-year-old blacksmith. The family moved often, and Patsy always admitted that she grew up "on the wrong side of the tracks." Her father deserted the family in 1947, but the children (she had a brother and a sister, Samuel and Sylvia) had a happy life.

Patsy got her start singing in church and had a love for musicians like Kay Starr, Jo Stafford, Hank Williams, Judy Garland, and Shirley Temple. She had perfect pitch but was self-taught and couldn't read music. When she was 13, Patsy was hospitalized with a throat infection and rheumatic fever. Her throat was affected for the better, and from that point on, she had a booming voice "like Kate Smith," she said.

After her father abandoned the family, Patsy dropped out of high school to work. She performed various jobs, from soda jerk to waitress, but spent much of her free time watching performers through the window at the local radio station, WINC-AM. She eventually got up the nerve to ask if she could perform. Her first number was such a success that she was asked back. This led to performances at local nightclubs, wearing fringed Western outfits that her mother made from Patsy's designs. She appeared in variety and talent shows around the region and with more radio shows, she developed a large following. In 1954, Jimmy Dean, a young country star in his own right, learned of her and she became a regular with Dean on Connie B. Gay's Town and

Legendary singer Patsy Cline

Country Jamboree radio show, which aired on weekday afternoons live on WARL-AM in Arlington, Virginia.

In September 1953, she married a contractor named Gerald Cline, but they divorced four years later. It was a stormy marriage. Gerald wanted her to be a housewife and Patsy wanted to sing. It was destined to fail, and it did, producing no children.

Bill Peer, her second manager, gave her the name Patsy, from her middle name and her mother's maiden name, Patterson. In 1955, he got her a contract at Four Star Records, a small label that didn't offer much money. The contract forced her to record compositions by Four Star writers only, which Patsy found limiting. She later expressed regret over signing with the label, but thinking that nobody else would have her, she took the deal.

Her first record – "A Church, A Courtroom, and Then Good-Bye" – attracted little attention with the public, but it did get a listen from promoters. Her records soon began to sell – a little.

Between 1955 and 1957, Patsy recorded for Four Star Records. Unfortunately, nothing really seemed to take off for her. She recorded honky-tonk tunes – some of which she co-wrote – and even experimented with rockabilly, but nothing she did gained any notable success. Record producer Owen Bradley, said that the Four Star compositions only hinted at Patsy's potential. Bradley thought that her voice was best-suited for pop music, but Patsy only wanted to perform country music. Every time Bradley tried to get her to sing the torch songs that would become her signature, she would panic, missing her familiar banjo and steel guitar. She recorded 51 songs with Four Star.

On July 1, 1955, Patsy made her network television debut on the short-lived television version of the Grand Ole Opry on ABC television. This was followed by an appearance on the network's *Ozark Jubilee* later that month. Later that year, while looking for material for her first album, a song called "Walkin' After Midnight" appeared, written by Donn Hecht and Alan Block. Patsy initially didn't like it – it was "a little old pop song," she said – but the record label insisted that she record it.

In the late fall of 1956, she auditioned for Arthur Godfrey's *Talent Scouts* in New York, and was accepted to sing on the CBS show on January 21, 1957. Patsy was initially supposed to sing "A Poor Man's Roses (Or a Rich Man's Gold)," but the show's producers insisted she sing "Walkin' After Midnight" instead. Even though Patsy had turned it into a country song --and recorded it in Nashville -- Godfrey's staff insisted that Patsy appear in a cocktail dress rather than in one of her mother's hand-crafted cowgirl outfits. The audience's enthusiastic reaction -- talent was measured on an "applause meter" -- won her the competition. After the Godfrey show, listeners began calling their local radio stations to request the song. Although Patsy had been performing for almost a decade and had appeared on national TV three times, it took the Arthur Godfrey show to make her a star. For a couple of months thereafter, Patsy appeared regularly on Godfrey's radio program.

"Walkin' After Midnight" reached No. 2 on the country chart and No. 12 on the pop chart, making Patsy one of the first country singers to have a crossover pop hit. For the next year, the song continued to help Patsy's career rise. She stayed visible by making personal appearances and performing regularly on Godfrey's show, as well as performing for several years on *Ozark Jubilee*.

A month after her recording session, she met Charlie Dick, a good-looking ladies' man who frequented the local club circuit Patsy played on weekends. His charisma and admiration of Patsy's talents captured her attention, and their relationship resulted in a marriage that lasted until her death. Patsy regarded Dick as "the love of her life." After the birth of their daughter, Julie, in 1958, they moved to Nashville, Tennessee. They also had a second child, a son named Randy.

In 1959, Patsy met Randy Hughes, a session guitarist and promotion man. Hughes became her manager and helped her change labels. When her Four Star contract expired in 1960, she signed with Decca Records-Nashville, directly under the direction of legendary female-singer country music producer Owen Bradley. He was responsible for much of Patsy's success and positively influenced the careers of both Brenda Lee and Loretta Lynn. Even though she was still scared of the lush Nashville Sound arrangements, Bradley considered Patsy's voice best-suited for country pop-crossover songs. Bradley's direction and arrangements helped smooth her voice into the silky, torch song style for which she remains known today.

Patsy's first release for Decca was a ballad "I Fall to Pieces," written by Hank Cochran and Harlan Howard. The song was well-promoted and won success on both country and pop music stations. On the country charts, the song slowly climbed to the top, garnering her first Number One ranking. In a major feat for country singers at the time, the song hit No. 12 on the pop and No. 6 on the adult contemporary charts, making her a household name and demonstrating that women could achieve as much crossover success as men.

In 1960, Patsy realized a lifelong dream when the Grand Ole Opry accepted her request to join the cast, making her the only person to achieve membership in such a fashion. She became one of the Opry's biggest stars. Even before that time, Patsy, confident of her abilities and appeal, embraced, encouraged, and befriended many women starting out in the country music field, including Loretta Lynn, Dottie West, Jan Howard, Brenda Lee, and a 13-year-old steel-guitar player named Barbara Mandrell. All of these women cited Patsy as a major influence in their careers.

According to both Lynn and West, Patsy always gave herself to friends, buying them groceries and furniture and even hiring them as wardrobe assistants. On occasion, she paid their rent, enabling them to stay in Nashville and continue pursuing their dreams. Honky-tonk pianist and Opry star Del Wood said, "Even when she didn't have it, she'd spend it—and not always on herself. She'd give anyone the skirt off her backside if they needed it."

But Patsy wasn't only accepted by the women. She cultivated a brash personality that allowed her to be considered "one of the boys." This allowed her to befriend male artists like Roger Miller, Hank Cochran, Faron Young, Ferlin Husky, Harlan Howard, and Carl Perkins all of whom she drank and socialized with at famed Nashville establishment Tootsie's Orchid Lounge, next door to the Opry.

Patsy used the term of endearment "Hoss" to refer to her friends, both male as well as female, and referred to herself as "The Cline." Patsy met Elvis Presley in 1962 at a fundraiser for St. Jude Children's Research Hospital and they exchanged phone numbers. Having seen him perform during a rare Grand Ole Opry appearance, she admired his music, called him "The Big Hoss." She often recorded with his backup group, The Jordanaires.

By this time, Patsy controlled her own career. In an era when concert promoters often cheated stars by promising to pay them after the show but skipping out with the money before the concert ended, Patsy demanded her money before she took the stage by proclaiming: "No dough, no show," a practice that became the rule.

On June 14, 1961, Patsy had her first brush with death. That afternoon, she and her brother, Sam, were involved in a head-on collision on Old Hickory Boulevard in Nashville. The impact threw Patsy into the windshield, nearly killing her. Upon arriving at the scene, Dottie West picked glass from Patsy's hair, and went with her in the ambulance. When help arrived, Patsy insisted that the other car's driver be treated first -- an event which had a long-term detrimental effect on Dottie. In 1991, she was involved in a terrible car accident. When first responders arrived at the scene, she, like Patsy, insisted that the driver be treated first, leading to her own death.

Patsy was haunted by the crash. She later recalled seeing the young women who had been driving the other car die before her eyes. She spoke of it frequently and said that she often dreamed that terrible moment over and over again.

She was mentally and physically changed by the accident. Patsy spent a month in the hospital, suffering from a jagged cut across her forehead that required stitches, a broken wrist, and a dislocated hip. When she left the hospital, her forehead was visibly scarred. For the remainder of her career, she wore wigs and makeup to hide the scars, along with headbands to relieve the forehead pressure that caused horrific migraines. Regardless of her injuries, six weeks later, she returned to the road on crutches.

Unable to capitalize on the success of "I Fall to Pieces" due to her hospital stay, Patsy sought another recording to re-establish herself. When introduced to "Crazy," a song written by Willie Nelson, Patsy hated it at first and the first recording session was unsuccessful. Patsy claimed that the song was too difficult for her; not only because of the odd style in which Nelson wrote it, but also because her ribs, injured in the crash, made it difficult for her to reach the high notes. It was eventually decided that Patsy would overdub her vocals over an instrumental recording of the track.

A week later, Patsy's ribs felt better, and she returned to the studio. With the high notes no longer a problem, she recorded her part in a single take. By late 1961, "Crazy" was a crossover success, straddling the country and pop genres, and reached the Top 10 on the charts. It became Patsy's biggest pop hit and "Crazy" ultimately became Patsy's signature song.

Patsy's influence on the music world continued. She was so respected by men in the industry that rather than being introduced to audiences as "Pretty Miss Patsy Cline" as her female contemporaries often were, she was given a more formal introduction, such as the one given by Johnny Cash during their 1962 tour: "Ladies and Gentlemen, The One and Only – Patsy

Cline." Patsy became a favorite among fans, too. She treated them wonderfully and many of them became close friends. She often stayed for hours after concerts to chat and sign autographs.

Patsy was the first woman in country music to perform at New York's Carnegie Hall, sharing the bill with fellow Opry members. She headlined the famous Hollywood Bowl with Johnny Cash. Later in 1962, she became the first woman in country music to headline her own show in Las Vegas appearing at the Mint Casino.

Her massive success enabled Patsy to buy her dream home in the Goodlettsville suburb of Nashville, decorating it in her own style. There was gold dust sprinkled in the bathroom tiles and a music room with the finest sound equipment. Patsy called it "the house that Vegas built" since the money from the Mint covered its cost. After her death in 1963, Patsy's home was sold to singer Wilma Burgess who later reported that "strange occurrences" took place while she was living there. She believed that she shared the house with Patsy's ghost.

Success brought Patsy more money. She was paid at least $1,000 for appearances, an unheard-of sum for women in country music, whose average fee at the time was less than $200. During her career, Patsy received a dozen awards for her achievements, and three more following her death from the Music Reporter, Billboard Awards and Cashbox.

In the fall of 1961, Patsy was back in the studio again to record songs for an upcoming album which was to be released in early 1962. One of the first songs was "She's Got You," written by Hank Cochran. Cochran pitched the song over the phone to Patsy and she fell in love with it at first listen. It became one of the few songs that she enjoyed recording. It was released as a single in January 1962, and soon crossed over, becoming a hit on all of the charts. In late 1962, Patsy appeared on *Dick Clark's American Bandstand* and released her third album, *Sentimentally Yours,* in August of that year.

A month before her death, Patsy was back in the studio to record her fourth album, originally entitled *Faded Love.* She recorded a mix of country standards and vintage pop classics like Irving Berlin's "Always" and "Does Your Heart Beat for Me." Patsy became so wrapped up in the stories told by the lyrics in the songs that she reportedly cried through most of her final sessions.

At the playback party, according to singer Jan Howard, Patsy held up a copy of her first record and a copy of her newest tracks and stated, "Well, here it is...the first and the last."

It was around this time that Patsy began to tell her friends about a sense of impending doom that she was feeling. Dottie West, June Carter Cash, and

Loretta Lynn all three recalled that Patsy told them that she did not expect to live much longer. Patsy, already known for her generosity, had begun giving away personal items to friends. While traveling, she wrote out her will on Delta Air Lines stationery and asked close friends to care for her children should anything happen to her. As she was walking out of the Ryman Auditorium -- after a Grand Ole Opry show that was recorded a week before her death – she told Jordanaires back-up singer Ray Walker, "Honey, I've had two bad ones [accidents]. The third one will either be a charm, or it'll kill me."

On March 3, 1963 Patsy performed at a benefit at the Soldiers and Sailors Memorial Hall in Kansas City, Kansas, for the family of disc jockey "Cactus" Jack Call. He had died in an automobile crash a little over a month earlier. She was joined at the show by George Jones, George Riddle and The Jones Boys, Billy Walker, Dottie West, Wilma Lee and Stoney Cooper, George McCormick, the Clinch Mountain Boys, Cowboy Copas, and Hawkshaw Hawkins.

Reports vary as to whether Patsy, ill with the flu, gave two or three performances. Regardless, she was miserable. She had spent the night at the Town House Motor Hotel and was unable to fly out the day after the concert because Fairfax Airport was fogged in. Dottie West asked Patsy to ride in the car with her and husband, Bill, back to Nashville. It was going to be a 16-hour drive and Patsy just couldn't do it. She was too sick to be closed up in the car for that long.

On March 5, she called her mother from the hotel and then checked out at 12:30 p.m. It was a short drive to the airport. She boarded a Piper Comanche aircraft with fellow performers Hawkshaw Hawkins – who took Billy Walker's seat after Walker left on a commercial flight to get home faster – and Cowboy Copas. The pilot, Randy Hughes, was an experienced flyer, but he was not trained in instrument flying – which would turn out to be fatal for everyone on board.

After take-off, the plane stopped once in Missouri to refuel and next landed at Dyersburg Municipal Airport in Dyersburg, Tennessee, at 5:00 p.m. Weather was bad in Tennessee. The airfield manager at Dyersburg suggested that the party stay the night in a local hotel after advising them of high winds and bad weather. He even offered them free rooms and meals, but Hughes responded that he was confident about the short flight ahead of them. The plane took off at 6:07 p.m.

According to Patsy's stopped wristwatch, the plane went down 13 minutes later.

An alert went out about the missing plane and a search was started almost immediately. Family and friends were hopeful throughout the night, but the crash was found just after sunrise. The wreckage was discovered about 90 miles from Nashville in a forest outside of Camden, Tennessee. Investigators believed that everyone on the plane died instantly when it crashed.

Singer Roger Miller was among those searching for the downed plane – or hopefully, for survivors. He later said, "As fast as I could, I ran through the woods screaming their names—through the brush and the trees, and I came up over this little rise, oh, my God, there they were. It was ghastly. The plane had crashed nose down."

Shortly after the bodies were removed, looters scavenged the area. Some of the items which were recovered were eventually donated to The Country Music Hall of Fame – Patsy's watch, her cigarette lighter, a studded belt, and three pairs of gold slippers.

Patsy was taken home to Virginia for her funeral. Thousands attended her visitation and her burial at Shenandoah Memorial Park in her hometown of Winchester, Virginia. Her grave is marked with a bronze plaque, which reads: "Virginia H, (Patsy) Cline 'Death Cannot Kill What Never Dies: Love." With the help of Loretta Lynn and Dottie West, a bell tower was erected at the cemetery in her memory. Another memorial marks the exact place off Fire Tower Road in Fatty Bottom, Tennessee, where the plane crashed in the still-remote forest outside of Camden.

If you ever get the chance to visit either site, shed a tear while you're there for a life loss too soon and a talent that fell from the heavens – perhaps because of the "Grand Ole Opry Curse."

Tragically, another Grand Ole Opry performer, Jack Anglin, was killed on the way to Patsy's funeral.

Jack was born on May 13, 1916, on a farm in Franklin, Tennessee. His father, John, taught him to play guitar at a young age. He never learned to read music, but by age 14, was singing and playing guitar on local radio stations. In 1930, Jack left the family farm for the bright lights of Nashville with dreams of becoming a musician. He brought along his brothers, Van and Jim, and they started performing at the Anglin Twins and Red. They played together until 1939 without much success.

To make ends meet, Jack worked at a local hosiery mill, where he met his future wife, Louise, and, through her, her brother, Johnnie Wright. At that time, Johnnie, his wife, Murial – who performed as Kitty Wells – and Louise were regulars on radio station WSIX as Johnnie Wright and the Harmony Girls. Soon, Johnnie and Jack – who shared the same birthdate – began performing together. They made their partnership official and became Johnnie and Jack, the duo that would become famous for somber lyrics, homespun harmonies, and rhythm of the deep south. Jack played the rhythm guitar and sang tenor vocals, while Johnnie took the lead.

They got off to a bumpy start. The duo toured locally around Nashville until 1940, when they decided to hook up with a concert promoter and take the show on the road. To pay for their travel, Johnnie sold his carpentry tools to raise money. There was no turning back after that.

They stayed together for the next two years and then, ironically, broke up over a dispute about gas money.

Jack returned to Nashville and began performing at the Grand Ole Opry as part of Roy Acuff's Smoky Mountain Boys band. He played with the band for six months before World War II began. Jack decided to enlist in the army and served in the medical corps in Europe for the next four years.

After returning to Nashville, he and Johnnie patched up their differences and began touring together again. Hoping to solidify their position in the country music scene, they founded the Louisiana Hayride show in 1947. This led to them becoming permanent residents of the Grand Ole Opry in 1952.

Johnnie and Jack performed together over 3,000 times throughout five countries, traveled 100,000 miles a year, and wrote over 100 songs. Known for their "fast-moving and fun" routines, audiences clamored to hear the brotherly folk and country duet sing some of their "love gone wrong hits" like "Poison Love," "Crying Heart Blues," "Ashes of Love," and "Hummingbird."

Jack's career was still going strong when he was killed. Like the other members of the Grand Ole Opry, he had been stunned by the deaths of Patsy Cline, Randy Hughes, Cowboy Copas, and Hawkshaw Hawkins. On the morning of March 8, he first attended the joint services of Copas and Hughes, followed by a memorial for Hawkins, and then went to the barbershop before going to the service for Patsy.

It was the haircut that made him late and put him in a rush to get to Patsy's memorial on time. While speeding, he lost control of his car, veered off New Due West Avenue in Madison, Tennessee, plunged into a 12-foot ditch, and slammed into a tree. Jack died on impact from a fractured skull.

Jack Anglin would not be the last Grand Ole Opry performer to die in March 1963. The next was Ruby Agnes Owen, who was better known to country music fans as "Texas Ruby." She never headlined a major tour or had any huge hit records during her too-short career, but she remains one of the most memorable country music stars of all time. Almost always accompanied by her husband Curly's fiddle, her deep singing voice and distinctive performing style helped make her special, but her personality was what everyone remembered. She was sassy, tempestuous, and a hard-living, highly-spirited force of nature.

"Texas Ruby" Agnes Owen

Born on a Texas ranch on June 4, 1908, Ruby Agnes Owens often sang with her brothers while growing up and it's been said that she was discovered when a radio station owner in Fort Worth heard her singing on the back of the wagon during a trip to the city in 1930. She soon began appearing on the air and building a career from there, spending the early part of the 1930s working all over the country and appearing with outfits like Zeke Clements and his Bronco Busters. She also built a reputation for being tough-talking and feisty. She drank hard and played hard with a "rowdy laugh and a heart of pure gold."

Beneath Ruby's "heart of gold," though, was a fierce temper – as evidenced by the time she spent with the barn dance radio show at WHO in Des Moines, Iowa. The story goes that a young announcer named Ronald 'Dutch' Reagan felt the force of her temper and subsequently left for Hollywood fame.

Ruby's temper and hard-living lifestyle also had repercussions on her music career. WBAP wanted to hire Texas Ruby and Zeke Clements, but she arrived at a meeting with potential sponsors drunk. In 1937, Ruby, suffering from a hangover, also missed auditions for *Snow White and the Seven Dwarfs* (Clements yodeled for Bashful). After this, Ruby and Zeke went their separate ways.

In any case, Ruby ended up at the Grand Ole Opry, where she eventually met up with a tall and talented Tennessee fiddler named Curly Fox. The twosome formed a duo in 1937 and married a couple of years later. Their act became a favorite at the Opry and on the road. The decade of the 1940s was especially good to them as they headlined on the Opry and starred on tour while also making records.

In the 1950s, they moved to Ruby's home state of Texas and continued to enjoy some success, even appearing on regional TV for a while. But as things slowed down for them, they eventually moved back to Nashville and returned to the Opry.

That might have been a fatal mistake.

On the night of March 29, Curly was performing as a side musician at the Opry when Ruby fell asleep in the trailer they were living in. Always a heavy smoker, she had a cigarette in her hand when she drifted off. The trailer was engulfed in flames and Ruby died in the fire.

"Gentleman" Jim Reeves

The next to perish under the cloud of the "curse" was James "Gentleman Jim" Reeves, who created what became known as the Nashville Sound – a mixture of older country-style music with elements of popular music.

Jim was born at home in Galloway, Texas, a small town near Carthage. He was the youngest of eight children and was raised by his parents, Thomas and Mary. After winning a baseball scholarship to the University of Texas, he enrolled to study speech and drama but quit after only six weeks to work in the shipyards in Houston.

He decided that college just wasn't for him – perhaps because of his uncertainty about whether he'd be drafted to serve in World War II. In March 1943, he reported to the Army Induction Center in Tyler for his preliminary physical exam. He had a heart irregularity, though, which exempted him from the military.

He soon returned to his first love – baseball. Jim played in semi-professional leagues before signing a pitching contract with the St. Louis Cardinals' farm team in 1944. He played in the minor leagues for three years before damaging his sciatic nerve. That ended his baseball career.

Jim next began work as a radio announcer. He had the voice for it and he also liked to sing live on the air between records. He got attention for his singing abilities, and during the late 1940s, he was contracted with a couple of local recording companies. Their reach was too small, though, and he didn't find much success. Jim joined up with Moon Mullican's band, which was part of the Western Swing movement, and made a few Jimmie Rodgers-style swing recordings in the late 1940s and early 1950s.

As most musicians know, playing music doesn't always pay the bills, so Jim got a job as an announcer on KWKH radio in Shreveport, Louisiana, which was home to the popular radio show, Louisiana Hayride, which was the Louisiana version of the Grand Ole Opry. According to Hayride host Frank Page – who introduced Elvis Presley for the first time on the program in 1954 – singer Sleepy LaBeef was late for the show one night and Jim Reeves was asked to fill in. It turned into his first big break.

By the early 1950s, Jim was on his way. He recorded several songs for Fabor Records and Abbot Records, including "Bimbo" in 1954, featuring performer Little Joe Hunt. They had met at the Louisiana Hayride and after the record went to number one, they began traveling and performing together at dance halls and clubs in East Texas and rural Arkansas with Jim as the headliner and Hunt as the opening performer.

Jim's popularity grew. He released his first album in 1955 and signed a 10-year recording contract with RCA Victor. That same year, he joined the Grand Ole Opry.

As his popularity grew, Jim began taking risks – risks that would turn him into a country music innovator. From his earliest recordings, he had relied on the loud, Texas style that was considered standard for country and western singers at the time. But he began to develop a new style, telling one interviewer, "One of these days, I'm going to sing like I want to sing." He lowered his volume and used the lowest registers of his voice, with his lips nearly touching the microphone. Executives at RCA lost their minds, demanding that he return to his old style, but Chet Atkins stuck up for him, convincing his critics to give Jim's new style a try. Needless to say, it worked. He became instrumental in creating a new kind of country music, using violins and lush background arrangements to create the "Nashville Sound." The new style crossed genres, which made Jim an even bigger star. In the early 1960s, he began scoring hits on European charts, helping to give country music an international market for the first time.

Jim Reeves recorded his last song for RCA Victor in June 1964. A few weeks later, he'd be dead.

On Friday, July 31, 1964, Jim and his business partner and manager, Dean Manuel – who also played piano in the Blue Boys, Jim's backup group – left Batesville, Arkansas, en route to Nashville in a single-engine Beechcraft Debonair aircraft, with Jim at the controls. They had been in Arkansas for a real estate deal.

While flying over Brentwood, Tennessee, they encountered a violent thunderstorm. A subsequent investigation showed that the small aircraft was caught in the storm and Jim became disoriented. According to tower tapes and accident reports, it's believed that instead of making a right turn to avoid the storm – as he'd been advised by the approach controller to do – Jim turned left, trying to follow Franklin Road to the airport. This caused him to fly further into the rain. While preoccupied with trying to figure out where he was from the landscape below, Jim let his airspeed get too low and the aircraft stalled. He instinctively applied full power and pulled back on the yoke before leveling his wings – a fatal, but not uncommon mistake. The plane went into a spin. Jim was too low to recover from it and the plane crashed to the ground. It struck the earth with such force that the aircraft's nose and engine were buried in the mud.

It took 42 hours to find the wreckage. On the morning of August 2, after an intense search – joined by friends like Ernest Tubb and Marty Robbins – the wrecked plane was found in a wooded area northeast of Brentwood, southwest of the Nashville airport, where Jim planned to land. The bodies of the singer and Dean Manuel were found twisted in the smoldering wreckage. Word went out to radio stations around the country at 1:00 PM that afternoon – Jim Reeves was dead.

Thousands of fans traveled to Tennessee to pay their last respects at his funeral two days later. The coffin, draped in flowers from admirers, was driven through the streets of Nashville and then to Reeves' final resting place near Carthage, Texas.

Whatever "jinx" haunted the Ryman Auditorium had claimed another victim.

If a psychic premonition had not warned Jack Greene of an impending disaster, he always believed that he, Ernest Tubb, and a busload of Opry musicians would have fallen victim to the infamous Grand Ole Opry "curse."

Jack Henry Greene – nicknamed the "Jolly Greene Giant" due to his height and deep voice – was born on January 7, 1930, in Maryville, Tennessee. He learned to play guitar when he was 10 and first became involved in the music industry when he was a teenager, working as a disc jockey at radio station WGAP.

By 18, Jack was a regular on the Tennessee Barn Dance show on WNOX in Knoxville. He moved to Atlanta in the early 1950s and formed a band, the Peach Tree Boys. He was lead vocalist, drummer, and guitarist for the group for eight years before moving back to Tennessee and settling in Nashville. He started a new band – the Tennessee Mountain Boys – and got his first real break in 1961 when the band opened for Ernest Tubb. Impressed, Tubb asked Jack to become a part of his backing band, the Texas Troubadours, in 1962.

For the next few years, Jack was the drummer, guitarist, vocalist, and master of ceremonies for the Troubadours appearances. He was a regular solo opening act for Ernest Tubb, who convinced him to release a solo album in 1964. They often played together at the Grand Ole Opry.

It was during this time that Jack narrowly avoided death. While traveling on the road with Ernest Tubb, Jack often filled in as a relief bus driver. He was relaxing in back one afternoon while Johnny Wiggins had the wheel but was suddenly overcome with a feeling of uneasiness. Cold chills swept through his body and he felt compelled to take over the driving. Less than five minutes later, as the bus ascended a steep hill, two semi-trailers appeared before them on the two-lane highway. They were running side-by-side, full throttle, and coming right at the bus.

They should have all been killed but, unable to shake the bad feeling, Jack had pulled the bus off the road seconds before meeting the trucks. Everyone on board the tour bus owed their lives to Jack and his premonition.

Two years later, Jack released his signature song, "There Goes My Everything." The song reached number one and stayed on the country charts for seven weeks. The album stayed at number one for an entire year. He went on to release scores of hits, received numerous awards, and became a mainstay at the Grand Ole Opry. After his health began to decline, he retired from performing in 2011. He passed away in 2013 from complications of Alzheimer's disease, having long outlived the infamous "curse."

But not everyone was so lucky. In 1965, Ira Louvin was killed in a fatal, head-on automobile crash, along with his wife, two friends, and the occupants of the other car. Ira had once been shot multiple times by his third wife and survived, but many believed that it was the "curse" that finally killed him.

Ira Louvin – whose real name was Ira Lonnie Loudermilk -- was born in Section, Alabama, and with his brother, Charlie, began his career singing gospel songs in church. Their childhood was literally hell on earth. Their father, himself the son of a cruel drunk, turned his violence on his sons. Ira, being the oldest, received the worst of the beatings that used fists, feet, switches, pieces of furniture, logs -- anything within reach if their father was angry enough – and he almost died more than once.

But their father also loved music, and Charlie and Ira could always sing. Despite their impoverished life and their humble beginnings – as shy children, they'd sing from under a bed when their father demanded they perform for company – they managed to pursue a music career. Ira played the mandolin and Charlie played guitar. They managed to bring their music to the airwaves on a small Chattanooga radio show. When Charlie entered the Army in the early 1940s, Ira continued to play with local acts until his brother came home. After that, they moved to Knoxville, where they played the radio circuit and changed their last name of Loudermilk to their stage name of Louvin.

In 1951, the brothers signed a contract with MGM records and recorded 12 songs, all of which were only moderate hits. After the MGM contract expired, the two headed to Memphis, where they played concert and radio shows. Capitol Records later signed them, and they became famous for their gospel standard, "The Family Who Prays." The Louvins, greatly influenced by their Baptist upbringing, often used their music to warn against sin – especially in their 1958 release "Satan is Real," which we'll come back to in a minute.

Almost as soon as they signed the contract, Charlie was once again called to the

Charlie and Ira Louvin

Army to serve in the Korean War. The Louvin Brothers' career came to a sudden halt. Soon after he returned, though, they began performing for the Grand Ole Opry and also broadened their style to include pop and hillbilly music. Their song "When I Stop Dreaming" became a Top Ten hit as well as "I Don't Believe You've Met My Baby." In 1956, the two released two albums – one a country pop release and the other, gospel songs. The brothers often struggled with their faith and the commercial success they were experiencing in country music, finding it hard to reconcile their Baptist beliefs with the secular songs they were recording.

This was the first time they recorded two different albums in two very different genres – but it would not be the last.

In 1958, the duo's producer, Ken Nelson, set them up in a studio for their next pair of album recordings. One of them was to be called *Country Love Ballads*, but the other was a bizarre album that was called *Satan is Real*.

It's hard to know where to start when describing this album, especially the cover. In fact, *Satan is Real* is perhaps more infamous for its weird cover art than for the songs recorded for it. The cover shows the two Louvin brothers

Satan is Real – the mind-boggling album by the Louvin Brothers

standing in front of a gigantic cutout of Satan and surrounded by fire. It's a strange combination of corny and terrifying – with the Louvins dressed in white and posing in front of a background that is literally fire and brimstone. The crude replica of Satan looms behind them.

But there was a reason for what seemed to be insanity.

Ira was reportedly known for falling into "fits of faith" and during these times, he often painted portraits of the Devil. The Satan that is in the photo was actually constructed by Ira and he created the hellscape that surrounded them. Charlie Louvin later recalled the set they built to capture the cover image. He explained, "Ira built that set. The devil was 12-feet-tall, built out of plywood. We went to this rock quarry and then took old tires and soaked them in kerosene, got them to burn good. It had just started to sprinkle rain when we got that picture taken."

The rocks behind them nearly injured the brothers. They had doused them with kerosene, and they exploded while the photos were being taken.

While the sound of *Satan is Real* was similar to the standard country pop that the brothers had been producing, the lyrical themes were extremely dark and spoke of evil and death. On "Satan's Jeweled Crown," the duo sings:

> *This life that I've lived so sinful and evil*
> *Drinking and running around*
> *All the things that I do, for the love of the devil*
> *I know my reward is Satan's jeweled crown*

The brothers believed that the cover art was a way to preach a particular message, something that Ira always struggled with. "Ira never would preach to an audience," Charlie later recalled, "but he could get through the most sentimental recitation and never lose it, always keep a straight face."

It was not long after the recording of *Satan is Real* that the duo began falling apart. Ira's increasingly worrying behavior, centered around a severe alcohol problem, prompted Charlie to abandon their career and effectively end the Louvin Brothers in 1963. It was a sad end to an act that had been an important part of country music in that era. This was evident in their final recordings. On record, the Louvins always sounded like their better selves, as if their deepest conflicts – with each other, their inner and outer lives, God and a Devil that was painfully real for both – could be set aside and forgotten only when they sang together. Their voices were pure, guileless, and clean as well water – but there was something dark under the surface of that water.

The end had been coming for years. The alcoholism and self-destructiveness that defined Ira seemed inevitable, given his grandfather's drunkenness, his father's cruelty, and Ira's mix of insecurity and rebellion. Even after they found their fame, Ira's addiction and behavior made the Louvin Brothers a risky act to book. He had a tendency to sabotage the duo's success, even costing them several million dollars – by Charlie's estimate – by insulting Elvis Presley, who until then had a habit of including Louvin Brothers songs on his albums. By 1963, Charlie just couldn't take it anymore. He loved his brother, but he couldn't perform with him.

Ira didn't handle the break-up well. He began acting out and even tried to strangle his third wife with a telephone cord. She shot him six times in response. She famously told the police that she'd do it again if she needed to. "If that sonofabitch don't die, I'll shoot him again," she said.

Ira's alcoholism had destroyed his career but ironically, he was sober when he and his fourth wife, Anne, died in a traffic accident in 1965 – a head-on collision in a Missouri construction zone. Compounding the irony, the other driver was drunk and Ira, when he died, had an outstanding warrant for driving under the influence. A wretched alcoholic – amiable when sober, violent when drunk – Ira Louvin died at 41.

Bullets and booze couldn't do to Ira what the infamous "curse" allegedly did.

Even though the death of Dave "Stringbean" Akeman was one of the last tragedies associated with the "Grand Ole Opry Curse," I honestly don't believe that the legend of the "Opry jinx" would have ever gotten started if he hadn't died the way that he had. It was after the death of the beloved musician that people began to realize just how many county music stars affiliated with the Opry had met with tragic ends.

But the murder of Stringbean Akeman went beyond just the "curse." It shattered the sense of security that so many Nashville artists had in those days and, in a way, forever closed the door on a unique way of American life.

Dave Akeman grew up poor on his family's farm in Annville, Kentucky. He came from a musical family, and they encouraged his early enthusiasm for making tuneful noise -- like when he fashioned his first banjo at age 7, using a shoebox and some borrowed thread. When he was 12, he traded a pair of chickens for a real banjo and began making a little extra money by playing gigs around town. He also spent a few years of the Great Depression working for the New Deal-era Civilian Conservation Corps, building roads and planting trees.

His passion and talent eventually landed him in a talent show judged by Asa Martin, a country music original of the 1920s. Martin was so impressed with the young man that he invited him to play some shows with his band. It was there that he earned his iconic nickname, mostly thanks to a forgetful band leader. Stumbling over Akeman's name, the band leader called out for "Stringbean," a comical nod to his lanky, 6-foot, five-inch frame. Dave loved it and he was billed as Stringbean for the rest of his life.

Stringbean's biggest musical break came about because of semi-professional baseball – a favorite career path of several country musicians of the era. Bluegrass player Bill Monroe owned a rival baseball club. After seeing Stringbean hurling fastballs on the field, he inquired about the pitcher, only to discover that he was a musician. Stringbean left baseball behind and honed his skills with Bill Monroe from 1943 to 1945.

In 1945, Stringbean married Estelle Stanfill, and that same year, Stringbean also started working on a comedy routine, joining up with Willie

Dave "Stringbean" Akeman

Egbert Westbrook to form "String Beans and Cousin Wilbur," which got audiences laughing during the mid-show break of Monroe's set.

It was during this banjo comedy show that he put together his signature outfit, a look inspired by one of his heroes – and fellow banjo player – Slim Miller. Stringbean tucked an extra long shirt into a particularly small pair of pants. He fastened them around his knees, making his long, lean body look comically elongated.

The show was a hit and Stringbean received his first invitation to perform at the Grand Ole Opry. By then, he had parted ways with Bill Monroe – who replaced him with a young man named Earl Scruggs – and started working with Louis Marshall "Grandpa" Jones, another old-time banjo player and comedian.

Stringbean formed a strong bond with one of the Opry's leading stars, "Uncle" Dave Macon. They shared a connection with their playing styles, love for the old style of clawhammer banjos, a simple, rural way of life. It was Uncle Dave who brought Stringbean into the Opry and took him under his wing. When the older man passed away in 1952, Stringbean was the obvious choice to take his place. He became a Grand Ole Opry favorite. Though he wouldn't record his own solo material until a decade later, Stringbean played with and recorded for countless country stars.

Stringbean built a loyal audience with his traditional playing and his mixture of comedy and song. He scored country-chart hits with tunes like "Chewing Gum" and "I Wonder Where Wanda Went" and his first album, *Old Time Pickin' & Grinnin' with Stringbean*, included folk songs, tall tales, and country jokes.

In 1969, he and Grandpa Jones became cast members of a new television show called *Hee Haw*. Created by two Canadian writers, Frank Peppiatt and John Aylesworth, the show only lasted two seasons on CBS. The network canceled it in 1971 as part of its "rural purge," which ended *The Beverly Hillbillies*, *Mayberry R.F.D.*, and *Green Acres*. But *Hee Haw* continued in first-run syndication through 1993 and was revived by the Nashville Network from 1996-97. Roy Clark and Buck Owens, already country legends, were the hosts, and cast members included Stringbean and Grandpa, as well as Minnie Pearl, Junior Samples, Gordie Tapp, Lulu Roman and the Hagar Twins. Guest stars were a who's who from entertainment and sports—from Loretta Lynn and Johnny Cash to Terry Bradshaw and Sammy Davis, Jr. The show gave some viewers – including myself – their first exposure to country, old-time, and bluegrass music. The show was corny but funny and was never mean-spirited.

One of Stringbean's regular routines was reading a "letter from home" to his friends. Asked about the latest letter, Stringbean would take it out, saying he carried it "right next to my heart." Not finding it in his overalls pocket, he would check all his other pockets by patting them with his hands until he found the letter, usually in his hip pocket. He was also the scarecrow in a cornfield who would say one-liners before being shouted down by the crow on his shoulder.

There was no question that Stringbean was a star, but despite his success, he was still a simple man. Stringbean and his wife, Estelle, lived in a rural cottage away from the hustle and bustle of Nashville. They spent little of the money that Stringbean earned, opting for simpler pleasures. Stringbean's only luxury was the newest model of Cadillac that he purchased every year. It was a peculiar thing to spend money on, though – Stringbean never learned to drive. But Estelle loved it and she drove her husband to the Ryman Auditorium every Saturday night for the Grand Ole Opry show.

Aside from buying a new car every year, what did Stringbean do with all this money? Growing up during the Depression, he had a deep distrust of banks. Throughout his life, he'd always kept his cash in his overalls. By 1973, his money – sometimes rolled up in thousands of dollars in a tight wad – was still kept in the front of his overalls.

It was a habit that eventually led to his death.

A woman who worked for Stringbean's booking agency casually mentioned to her husband, Charlie Brown, that there was a rumor going around about where the musician kept his money. He told his brother, Doug, and a cousin, John, and they came up with a plan to steal his cash.

On Saturday, November 10, 1973, Stringbean made his usual appearance at the Opry show. He didn't know it, but Doug and John Brown were rummaging through his house at the very moment that Stringbean was performing his last song. They were listening to the broadcast live on the radio – everyone knew where Stringbean was on Saturday night.

They ransacked the house but found nothing. Stringbean didn't trust banks, but he hadn't hidden the money at home. They assumed the rumor over his overalls was true. Although upset, John convinced Doug to wait until Stringbean and Estelle returned.

Later that night, Cadillac headlights flashed across the front windows of the house – Stringbean and Estelle were back. When Stringbean got out of the car, though, he noticed that something looked wrong. He placed his banjo on the porch and approached the front door with his own pistol drawn, surprising Doug Brown, who was inside. But before he could act, John Brown approached and shot Stringbean at point-blank range.

Hearing the gunshots, Estelle fled from the car to get help. But she was not fast enough. John ran her down and fired three shots into her back. She was later found lying facedown in the grass.

The killers fled the scene in a panic, failing to find the $2,200 that Estelle had attached to her bra in a tobacco sack and the $3,500 that Stringbean had hidden in a secret pocket in his bib overalls.

Stringbean and Estelle had literally been murdered for nothing.

The following morning, November 11, Grandpa Jones drove to the Akeman home from Nashville. He intended to pick up his friend for a hunting trip to Virginia. When he arrived, he discovered the horrific, bloody scene and called the police.

The entire country music scene was in shock. After hundreds of tips, it didn't take long to find the killers, but the damage to the Nashville music community was done. The city suddenly didn't feel so neighborly anymore. Country stars no longer felt safe chumming around and drinking with tourists and locals. Over the next few years, private estates and security guards became commonplace, replacing the old-fashioned life that Stringbean and so many other Opry stars had always loved.

And people began talking about the possibility of a "curse."

Stringbean's legacy lived on after his death with airings of *Hee Haw*. An entire season featuring Stringbean had already been taped, so he appeared alongside the rest of the cast for almost a year after his murder. Finally, Grandpa Jones addressed the tragic loss in a moving tribute to his friend on the show.

The Browns were sentenced to two consecutive 99-year sentences. Doug died in prison in 2003, but John was paroled in 2014. Every year on the anniversary of the murders, John had fasted and prayed, begging for forgiveness. Fellow inmates and correctional officers said that he became a positive influence on other prisoners and expressed a profound sense of guilt for what he did. After 41 years, the parole board agreed.

But that couldn't bring back Stringbean Akeman. He represented a forgotten way of life in his person and his playing. His death ushered in the first wave of a new country sound that changed Nashville forever. His story has now become a part of country music folklore, but it's important to remember what he achieved through his talent and his humor. Like Stringbean himself, his place in country music is truly unique.

Just 17 days after the murders of Stringbean and Estelle, the "curse" reached out one last time and claimed the life of another Opry star – Jimmy Widener.

On the night of November 27, police were called to Milson Alley, near the intersection of Jo Johnston and 12th Avenues in North Nashville. The body of Jimmy Widener was sprawled out in the weeds near the alleyway. Sprawled across his legs was the body of a woman named Mildred Hazelwood. Both had been beaten up and shot twice from behind, execution-style.

Mildred was the widow of performer and songwriter Eddie Hazelwood. She lived in Laguna Hills, California – which made Nashville a long way to travel to end up dead atop Jimmy Widener's legs.

Jimmy was a well-known rhythm guitar player in the Nashville scene. He'd lived in California, too, back when he was playing with cowboy stars like Gene Autrey and Roy Rogers. He had been born and raised in Seminole, Oklahoma, but had been in Nashville since the 1940s. For the past 10 years or so, he had been playing guitar with the Rainbow Ranch Boys, the backup band for country star and Opry regular Hank Snow. The two musicians were close friends.

Jimmy didn't know Mildred well. He had been friends with her late husband, and she had contacted him while in town to try and sell him some songs and unreleased recordings that Eddie had left behind. Jimmy was thinking of trying his hand at a solo career and thought that his old pal's songs might be just the thing for a possible angle.

They were walking to the Holiday Inn, where Mildred was registered, when they were killed. No wallet or purse was found with the victims, so police assumed they'd been killed during a robbery.

Bud Wendell, manager of the Ryman Auditorium at the time, was spooked. "Killed? I can't believe it!" Wendell said that he'd seen Jimmy on his

Jimmy Widener

last day on earth, "right here at the Opry, meeting with artists, promoters, and bookers."

"First it was Stringbean – a good guy. Now it's Jimmy Widener – a good guy," Hank Snow said. "I wonder when it's going to stop."

On Thursday, November 29, two nights after the bodies were found, Lieutenant Harold Woods and three Nashville Metro detectives led a raid on the Cayce Motel in South Memphis. They nabbed two suspects – Richard Dunn and Phillip Mason -- outside the motel, but when they went inside to arrest a third man, he started shooting. Detectives returned fire and managed to clip Maurice Taylor in the chest as he tried to flush credit cards and jewelry down the toilet.

The three men were charged with the murders of Jimmy Widener and Mildred Hazelwood. It turned out that they had accosted the pair at the Holiday Inn. After beating and robbing them, they put them in the trunk of Jimmy's car and dumped them in the alley where their bodies were found. They executed them while they were lying on the ground. Jimmy's Lincoln Continental was found at the Memphis motel. The killers had paid for their room with his stolen credit card. The police recovered seven pieces of evidence from the room, including jewelry, credit cards, a 9mm pistol that was likely the murder weapon, and the keys to Jimmy's car.

Their trial began at the same time the Browns were being tried for the murder of Stringbean and Estelle Akeman in a neighboring courtroom. Dunn and Mason – originally charged with two counts of murder – were allowed to plead guilty to being accessories after the fact and given four-to-seven-year prison terms. That left Maurice Taylor to face murder charges alone.

Hank Snow was the first person to take the stand for the prosecution. He testified that he had paid Jimmy $400 a few days before he was murdered. A waitress at the Pitt Grill – where Jimmy and Mildred had supper – testified that Taylor had entered the place while the couple was dining there. He left the eatery at 9:40 PM and walked south. Jimmy and Mildred left 10 minutes later. A civilian identification technician in the Nashville Police Department testified that Taylor's thumbprint was found on a drinking glass in Mildred's room at the Holiday Inn.

That thumbprint, Assistant District Attorney John Rodgers said in his closing summation, proved that the suspect approached the couple as they were about to enter Mildred's room, and followed them inside. "This man was so callous that not only did he rob them, but he had a drink in that room!" he told the jury. He then forced them into Jimmy's car, drove them five blocks away, and killed them.

The case against Taylor went to the jury on Thursday, October 31. They didn't take long to decide his fate – two life terms in prison, to be served concurrently.

The so-called "Grand Ole Opry Curse" apparently died with Jimmy Widener. Less than a year after Jimmy's death, the lights went out at the Ryman Auditorium as the Grand Ole Opry moved to its new location at the Opryland theme park. Was this the reason why the string of tragedies finally came to an end?

It's impossible to say, especially because there were certainly some near-miss brushes with death involving Opry stars in the years that followed.

In 1975, Hank Williams, Jr., who had become a celebrity following in his father's footsteps, fell over 500 feet while mountain climbing in Montana. His injuries were gruesome – his skull was shattered, and he lost several teeth and a good part of his nose. He was on the critical list for three days and was in horrible pain for years afterward. To make matters worse, his mother died three months later. Most importantly, though, he survived – unlike the many other stars with Opry connections who didn't.

Tammy Wynette survived two abusive marriages, the burning of her Nashville home in 1976, a hysterectomy, gall bladder surgery, a kidney operation, and an abduction in 1978. The medical problems eventually caught up with her and she died in her sleep in 1998. Despite her persistent illnesses, she continued to perform until shortly before her death and had other performances scheduled. She persevered through any kind of "jinx" that might have plagued her career – and even had the last laugh.

Her memorial service was held on the stage of the Ryman Auditorium.

The "Opry Curse" rarely gets mentioned anymore and perhaps, as has been suggested, it was nothing more than a series of coincidences and plain old bad luck. As one country star put it in the early 1970s: "Take a guy who's a comedian. Something funny happens to him and everybody thinks it's natural. He's a funny guy and funny things happen to him, and so the comedian lives up to his role. Why then are fans surprised when the sad things we sing about happen to us more often than normal?"

Bad luck and hard times, right? That's a country song – like the one about the guy whose mama gets hit by a train on the day she gets out of prison, his dog dies, and his truck won't start.

But what if it wasn't just a bad luck? What if that string of deaths really was tied to the years that the Opry was broadcast from the Ryman Auditorium? Look at the dates, where the deaths began and where they ended – kind of spooky, isn't it?

THE CURSE OF THE "27 CLUB"

Buddy Holly, "Cross Roads Blues," and the Grand Ole Opry aside, there is a much greater curse in rock-n-roll history. Or perhaps I should say that it's a club – one that few musicians want to join. Entry in this club is simple – all you need to do is die at age 27.

The club has it roots centuries ago, and then, you didn't have to be a musician and you didn't even have to be 27. You just needed to flame out at a young age.

In ancient Greek history, it was said that Alexander the Great made a pact with the god Zeus that allowed him to choose between living to old age and never achieving glory or gaining everlasting fame and glory but dying as a young man. Alexander chose a short life and he conquered the entire known world before dying at the age of 33. His body was encased in solid gold and carried through the provinces so that his subjects could pay homage to their fallen leader. The Egyptians worshipped Alexander as a living god in the same manner as they did the ancient pharaohs. He was buried in secret and to this day, his tomb has not been discovered.

Did he make the right choice? In the words of James Dean, Alexander planned to "live fast, die young and leave a good-looking corpse."

Sadly, throughout literary history a great number of the most creative writers may as well have entered into Alexander's pact. The English Romantic poets are a prime example: John Keats died at age 25, Percy Shelley died at 29, Lord Byron met his death at 36, each dying at the height of his poetic talents.

When it comes to rock-n-roll, though, you achieve infamy not just by dying young – it's got to be at 27. Seems hard to believe? I think you might be surprised by the number of music greats who didn't make it past that magic number.

The "founder" of the 27 Club was bluesman Robert Johnson – who just keeps popping up in this book. He was the guitarist who made a deal with the Devil at the Mississippi crossroads, giving him fame and fortune, although not for long. He died under mysterious circumstances and started the "cursed club" that few want to become a member of.

Jesse Belvin

The first new member to join Robert Johnson in the club was rhythm and blues singer Jesse Belvin. Just three days after the first anniversary of the plane crash that killed Buddy Holly and Ritchie Valens, an automobile accident in Hope, Arkansas, ended the life and career of a major figure in the fusion of black soul and white folk music.

Belvin was a golden-voiced crooner who co-wrote some of the biggest hits of the 1950s, like "Earth Angel," a hit for the Penguins in 1955, and his own recording of "Goodnight My Love," which was used by Dick Clark as the closing theme of *American Bandstand* for several years. He had an impressive career, producing tunes in the style of both Nat King Cole and Elvis Presley.

In fact, it was his talent for emulating Elvis that caused RCA Records to sign Jesse and begin a unique promotion in 1959. It would be a few years before the civil rights movement built up momentum, but RCA badly wanted to tap into markets in the South, so they offered Jess as the new "Black Elvis."

Jesse's fatal car crash occurred on February 6, 1960, less than four hours after he had performed his first concert for an integrated audience in Little Rock. It had been an ugly scene – white protestors managed to stop the show twice, shouting racial slurs, and urging white teenagers who were in attendance to leave the show at once.

In the brief time that he was in town, Jesse had received six death threats, so speeding away from Little Rock in Jesse's 1959 Cadillac was a relief. But the escape was tragically cut short. Jesse's wife, JoAnn, died from her injuries at the Hope Hospital, while his drive – like Jesse – died at the scene.

As word reached the black community in Jesse's hometown of Los Angeles, there were immediately rumors of foul play. One of the first state troopers at the accident scene stated that both rear tires on the Cadillac had been "obviously tampered with." He offered no more details, fueling more speculation. The fact that Jesse had telephoned his mother twice in three days – he rarely called from the road -- every time telling her about the hostile reception that he received, made suspicions even stronger. In the end, though, nothing was proven, and no investigation was ever launched into the crash.

With his death at age 27, Jesse left behind a legacy of brilliant songwriting and a golden voice, as well as many questions about how he died.

On May 21, 1964, Rudy Lewis – the lead singer of the Drifters – was found dead in a Harlem hotel room on the day that group was set to record their classic song "Under the Boardwalk." He was also 27 years old.

Rudy Lewis

Rudy was sort of the "odd-man-out" in the history of the Drifters. He was the lead singer from late 1960 until 1964, occasionally sharing the role with Johnny Moore toward the end. Rudy was featured on such hits as "Some Kind of Wonderful," "Please Stay," "On Broadway," and "Up on the Roof."

He had the bad luck, though, to come in after Ben E. King redefined the group's sound and he never got the recognition that King did, despite the fact that he ended up performing most of King's songs in concert. Like King, he had a rich, silky voice that was filled with passion. There is a large contingent of Drifters fans that hold him in just as high of regard as they do King.

Born in Philadelphia, Rudy had started out in gospel music and had sung with the Clara Ward Singers until immediately prior to the day, late in 1960, when he auditioned for the Drifters' manager, George Treadwell, at

Philadelphia's Uptown Theater. At the time, the group had been reduced to a trio with Charlie Thomas taking the lead role. After hearing him sing, Treadwell hired him on the spot.

Tragically, though, his time with the band ended during the early morning hours of May 21. He was found later that morning, dead in his bed. Some accounts say that the cause of death was a drug overdose, while others who knew him said that Rudy, who a binge eater, choked to death in his sleep.

Johnny Moore – the group's other lead singer – stepped in that same day for the band's scheduled session for "Under the Boardwalk," reducing Rudy Lewis to a footnote in rock-n-roll history.

The next member of the 27 Club was Rolling Stones founder Brian Jones – who drowned in his own swimming pool on July 3, 1969.

Lewis Brian Hopkin Jones was born in Cheltenham, Gloucestershire, England on February 28, 1942. His middle-class family, made up of his father, Lewis, mother, Louisa, and younger sisters, Pamela – who died of leukemia in 1945 – and Barbara, were of Welsh descent. Both of Brian's parents were interested in music and encouraged a love for it in their son. His initial passion was jazz but that changed when he received his first guitar for his 17th birthday.

Brian had little interest in school – mostly because he was so smart that he was often bored. He put little effort into it but did well on all his exams. He found school to be too regimented and he disliked the uniforms and having to conform to behavior that was expected from him. He angered his teachers – and was suspended twice – but was popular with his classmates.

In late summer 1959, Brian's 17-year-old girlfriend, Valerie Corbett, became pregnant. Although Brian is said to have encouraged an abortion, she carried the child to term and later placed the boy for adoption.

Brian quit school in disgrace and left home, traveling for the rest of the year through Northern Europe and Scandinavia. He lived a Bohemian lifestyle, busking with his guitar on the streets for money, and living off the charity of others for as long as he could. When he finally ran out of money, he returned to England.

At some point as a teenager, Brian had become fascinated with the blues – particularly the works of Robert Johnson. After he returned home, he began performing at local blues and jazz clubs while he worked odd jobs to make ends meet. He applied for a scholarship to Cheltenham Art College and was initially accepted, only to have the offer withdrawn two days later. Someone had written to the college and called Brian an "irresponsible drifter." At the time, the anonymous letter writer wasn't that far off the mark.

In October 1961, Brian's girlfriend, Pat Andrews, gave birth to a child. It was actually Brian's third. He had earlier met a young married woman in a club, and she had gotten pregnant after a night they spent together. She ended up raising the baby with her husband and Brian never knew about it. This time around, Brian sold off his record collection to buy flowers for Pat and clothes for the baby. He lived with them for a while but didn't settle for long.

Brian left Cheltenham and moved to London, where he became friends with fellow musicians like Alexis Korner, future Manfred Mann singer Paul Jones, future Cream bassist Jack Bruce, and others who made up the small

Rolling Stones founder Brian Jones

rhythm and blues and jazz scene at the time. He played the blues in various clubs and played with Paul Jones in a band called the Roosters. After Brian and Paul left the group, Eric Clapton took over Brian's role as guitarist.

In May 1962, Brian decided to start a new band and placed an ad in a local music paper, inviting musicians to audition at the Bricklayer's Arms pub. Two young men showed up, both of whom Brian had met before – Mick Jagger and his childhood friend, Keith Richards. As Keith later told it, Brian came up with the name the "Rolling Stones" while on the phone with a venue owner who wanted to know the name of the band he'd just booked. They didn't have one, so Brian looked around and saw an album, *The Best of Muddy Waters*. Track five on side one was called "Rollin' Stone Blues." The rest was history.

From September 1962 to September 1963, Brian, Mick, and Keith shared a flat in Chelsea with photographer James Phelge. Brian and Keith spent most of the day playing guitar while listening to blues records and during this time Brian also taught Mick how to play harmonica. They were looking for a bassist and drummer and finally settled on Billy Wyman on bass because he had a spare amplifier and always had cigarettes.

In January 1963, they finally talked Charlie Watts into joining them. Charlie was more into jazz than rhythm and blues and most musicians considered him the best drummer in London. He described Brian's role in those early days: "Brian was very instrumental in pushing the band at the beginning. Keith and I would look at him and say he was barmy. It was a crusade to him to get us on the stage in a club and be paid half-a-crown and to be billed as an R&B band."

Brian was always erratic; there was no question about that. Almost from the beginning, he rubbed the other band members the wrong way, nominating himself as the band's business manager and paying himself more than the others for the extra work.

Resentment grew, especially after Andrew Loog Oldham took over as the band's manager. Oldham recognized the financial advantages of the band members writing their own songs. He insisted that playing covers would not keep them in the spotlight for long. Further, Oldham wanted to make Mick's flamboyance and charisma the focus of live performances. Brian saw his influence over the Stones' direction begin to disappear as their show sets began to be made up of more Jagger/Richards originals and fewer of the classic blues covers that he preferred. There was no question about it – Brian's concept of what the band was all about had been forgotten.

But a lot of that was Brian's fault and he knew it. He was always an outsider, even in his own band. When the first tours were arranged in 1963, he traveled separately from the band, stayed at different hotels, and demanded extra pay. He was also bothered by the fact that, while an exceptional musician, he was not a prolific songwriter. He was emotional about the fact that one role that he felt he did well – business manager – had been taken away.

The toll from days on the road, the money and fame, and the feeling of being alienated from the group resulted in Brian's overindulgence in alcohol and other drugs. His excesses had a terrible effect on his physical and mental health. Brian became reckless and self-destructive.

In July 1964, another woman, Linda Lawrence – who later married the singer Donovan – gave birth to Brian's fourth child. Three months later, an occasional girlfriend of Brian's, Dawn Molloy, announced to Brian and the band's management that she was pregnant. She received a check for £700 from manager Oldham. In return, she signed an agreement that the matter was now closed and that she would make no statement about Brian Jones or the child to the public or the press.

Hostility continued to grow between Brian, Keith, and Mick, pushing Brian further from the group. Although many noted that Brian could be friendly and outgoing, Bill, Keith, and Charlie all claimed that he could be cruel and difficult. His personality frequently changed – one minute, kind and generous and the next, trying to get everyone pissed off at him. Bill Wyman said, "There were at least two sides to Brian's personality. One Brian was introverted, shy, sensitive, deep-thinking. The other was a preening peacock, gregarious, artistic, desperately needing assurance from his peers... He pushed every friendship to the limit and way beyond."

By early 1967, the authorities were creating a lot of problems for the Stones, with the police conducting a dramatic drug raid on the country home of Keith Richards in February. This resulted in drug charges against Keith, Mick, and their friend, Robert Fraser. As the dust was settling from the raid, Keith decided to take a road trip to Morocco with Brian and Brian's current girlfriend, Anita Pallenberg.

They traveled in Keith's Bentley, driven by Stones employee, Tom Keylock. While in the south of France, Brian became ill and checked into a hospital near Toulouse. Keith and Anita traveled on without him to Spain. Somewhere along the way, Keith and Anita's platonic relationship turned into a torrid affair. According to Keith, he'd fallen in love with her. Both of them were now worried about the effect this would have on the band – and especially on Brian. Anita flew back to France and picked up Brian, taking him to London for medical tests. After that, they both flew to Morocco to meet up with Keith, Mick, and other friends in Marrakesh.

It all broke bad in Morocco. A jealous Brian attacked Anita at the Es Saadi Hotel in Marrakesh. Keith heard the fight. Brian tried to get Anita to have a four-way with two Moroccan prostitutes and when she refused, he threw a room service tray at her. She fled to safety in Keith's room and they began planning an escape.

Keith arranged for Brian to take a trip to the Square of the Dead to record local musicians and while he was occupied, Keith an Anita left for Tangier. When Brian discovered that Anita had left him for Keith, he was crushed. Not only had Keith and Mick taken over his band, Keith had stolen his girlfriend – the only woman, he claimed, he'd ever loved.

Brian returned to England and invited a French playboy friend named Prince Stanislas Klosswoski de Rola – dubbed "Prince Stash" – to come and stay with him in London. Brian cried over losing Anita, whom he tried but failed to win back, and consoled himself by taking inordinate amounts of drugs. As the Stones had already discovered, Scotland Yard was currently targeting celebrity drug users and Brian was next on their list. On May 10, 1967, detectives called at his London flat, searched it, and charged Brian and Stash with possession of cocaine and cannabis. Brian was also charged with possession of methedrine.

All his friends agreed that Brian was never the same after the drug bust. Stones employee Ron Schneider said that Brian was so freaked out that he had to hold his hand to comfort him when he tried to sleep. He wasn't the same after the bust, Schneider recalled, "That's when he started going into real depressions."

As tensions between Brian and the rest of the band – along with his dependency on narcotics – increased, his musical contributions became sporadic. He became bored with the guitar and sought exotic instruments to play, and he was increasingly absent from recording sessions. His last substantial sessions with the Stones occurred in the spring and summer of 1968, when they produced "Jumpin' Jack Flash" and the *Beggars Banquet* album.

Where once Brian played multiple instruments on many tracks, he now played only minor roles on a few pieces. Brian's last formal appearance with the band was in the December 1968 *The Rolling Stones Rock and Roll Circus* – which we'll be discussing further later in the book. It went unreleased for more than 25 years, but later bonus material interviews indicated that nearly everyone there thought Brian's time with the Stones was coming to an end. Roger Daltrey and Pete Townshend of the Who thought it would be Brian's last live musical performance.

Brian was arrested a second time on May 21, 1968, again for possession of cannabis. Since he was on probation, he was facing a long jail sentence if found guilty. His defense was that the weed had been left behind by previous tenants of the flat. The jury didn't believe him and found him guilty. The judge, though, felt sorry for him and fined him instead of locking him up. He even told Brian, "For goodness sake, don't get into trouble again or it really will be serious."

Brian's legal troubles, conflicts with other band members, substance abuse, and mood swings, became too much of an obstacle to his active participation in the band. The Rolling Stones wanted to tour the United States in 1969, for the first time in three years, but Brian was not in any kind of condition to go on tour. Plus, his second arrest had created problems with getting him a U.S. work visa. In addition, Brian's attendance at rehearsals and recording sessions had become erratic. When he did bother to show up, he either rarely contributed anything musically, or, when he did, his bandmates switched off his amplifier, leaving Keith to play nearly all the guitars. He was literally incapable of making music.

Brian's behavior had worsened by the time the band started recording *Let it Bleed*. In March 1969, Brian borrowed the group's Jaguar and went shopping – only to have the car towed away by the police. In May, he crashed his motorcycle into a shop window and was secretly taken to the hospital under an assumed name.

Brian was still attending some of the recording sessions, but he was no longer a major contributor to the band's music. Finally, Mick informed him that he would be fired from the band if he did not turn up at a photo session. Looking frail, Brian did show up. The photos wouldn't be published until September – more than two months after Brian died.

A decision was made about the North American tour – it would be scheduled for November 1969. The group's management was informed that Brian would not receive a work permit, thanks to this drug convictions. A new guitarist had to be hired. There was no other choice but to let Brian go. On June 8, 1969, Mick, Keith, and Charlie Watts visited Brian and told him that the group that he had formed was going to continue on without him.

The public believed that Brian left the group voluntarily. He'd been kicked out, his bandmates, told him, but he could decide how to break it to fans. Brian issued a statement that pretty much said he'd split because of "creative differences" about the records the band was now making.

Brian had to have been hurt but in the days that were to precede his death, his friends recalled that he never seemed happier. They added that he was putting together a band to play his own music, which included Alexis Korner, Ian "Stu" Stewart, John Lennon, Mitch Mitchell, and Jimmy Miller.

During the period of Brian's decline, he had purchased Cotchford Farm in Sussex. The house had once belonged to author A.A. Milne and he had lived there during the years that he created Winnie-the-Pooh. Brian planned to build his own studio at the farm and start production with a new band as soon as possible.

Tragically, this was not to be.

On the night of Wednesday, July 2, 1969, Brian was entertaining a small number of guests at the country house, including his Swedish girlfriend Anna Wohlin; Frank Thorogood, a builder who was overseeing some renovations on the property; and Janet Lawson, a nurse and a friend of Thorogood. Around 10:30 PM, Brian announced that he was going for a swim and put on his swimming trunks. Janet Lawson warned him that it would be dangerous to get in the pool after drinking vodka and taking downers all evening, but Brian didn't listen. Anna, Janet, and Frank Thorogood went with him to the pool but only noticed that Brian seemed a little "sluggish." Brian turned up the water temperature and then got in the water. Janet stayed for a short time and then returned to the house. Shortly after they began swimming, Anna left the pool to answer the telephone. Approximately 10 minutes later, Frank came to the house, looking for a towel and a cigarette. It was then that Janet came back to the pool and found the submerged body of Brian Jones facedown in the deep end of the pool. Frantically, she and the others pulled him from the water and started artificial respiration, but it was too late. An ambulance was called, and Brian was pronounced dead just after midnight.

The founder of the Rolling Stones was dead at the age of 27.

The coroner's inquest ruled that Brian's cause of death was the result of "immersion in fresh water under the influence of drugs and alcohol" and recorded the tragedy as "death by misadventure." It was suggested that the warm water, combined with large amounts of alcohol and barbiturates, resulted in coma and death. But could it have happened in less than 10 minutes? It was also suggested that Brian could have had an asthma attack or seizure that led to his death. An inhaler was found next to the pool, but the autopsy ruled out the idea that asthma had played a part in his death.

No one knew what to think for sure, largely because it seemed unlikely that Brian's lungs could have filled so completely with water – and his body sink to the bottom of the pool – in such a short amount of time.

And then the rumors started.

One of the rumors suggested suicide. Some of his friends knew of the heartbreak he'd gone through after losing Anita to Keith. Some claimed that Mick Jagger had stolen yet another of Brian's lovers, forcing him to take his own life instead of dealing with another broken heart.

But some of Brian's closest friends disputed this story. They claimed they had never seen him happier. He had fallen in love with Anna Wohlin and was putting a new band together. Surely these were not the actions of a man who planned to commit suicide.

Another rumor claimed that Brian's death was a "satanic sacrifice," a terrible payment for the continued success of the Rolling Stones. Seems even harder to believe, but Brian was a believer in curses and the supernatural. During a recording of a native drum ceremony in Morocco, Brian was convinced that a voodoo curse had been put on him during the service.

It was estimated that over half a million people gathered along the roads to catch a glimpse of the hearse that carried Brian's body to the church in Cheltenham where the funeral was held. During the service, the Canon Hugh Evans Hopkins used the pulpit to condemn the lifestyle of Brian and the Rolling Stones: "He was a rebel. He had little patience with authority, convention, and tradition. In this he was typical of many of his generation who have come to see in the Rolling Stones an expression of their whole attitude to life. Much that this ancient church has stood for 900 years seems totally irrelevant to them and yet it is not humbug to come today to offer prayers on this tragic occasion."

Nice. Wouldn't some words of comfort to his loved ones be a little kinder?

But the Reverend Hopkins wasn't finished. He also blamed Brian for the suicide attempt of Marianne Faithfull, who had been in a drug-induced coma for two days and asked for prayers for her recovery. Brian's death had driven Marianne to total despair. She claimed that when she looked in a mirror, she saw Brian looking back. She cut her hair so that it resembled his. Her mental state suffered because of a heroin addiction that she was trying to kick. Her doctor had prescribed sodium amytal to help her sleep, but she decided to make her sleep permanent by swallowing 150 pills. Marianne recovered and claimed that, while in her coma, Brian had appeared to her, had taken her hand, and told her that she had to return. She could not come with him.

There was also a final indignity about Brian's burial. Hopkins refused to allow him to be buried in the parish churchyard because there was a rumor going around that he might have committed suicide. Brian was buried one mile away at Priors Road Cemetery.

Most fans and journalists readily accepted the idea that Brian's death was caused by either suicide or by accident, but others believed there could be only one logical answer – murder.

As Keith Richards recalled in a *Rolling Stone* interview, "Some very weird things happened on the night Brian died. And there were people there that suddenly disappeared. Some of them had a weird hold over Brian. It's the same feeling with who killed Kennedy. You can't get to the bottom of it."

One of the "weird things" that Keith mentioned was the disappearance of many of Brian's personal items a few days after his death. Whoever stole them had a key to the house. The items included his guitar collection, a large number of antiques and household items, and Brian's first retirement check from the Rolling Stones, made out in the sum of £100,000. The money and furnishings were never recovered.

Another "weird" happening on the night of the tragedy concerned the official statement made by the three witnesses – it appeared they were each telling different stories about the night. Each seemed to have a different recollection of what had actually happened. Their stories, along with others who claimed to be present, told a very different story than what the police based the results of their investigation on.

One man who claimed to have been present that night was one of the workers that Brian had hired to help with the renovations. His story mentioned a party in which he and his follow workmen returned to Brian's estate later that night. The workers were drinking and talking about their jealousy of Brian and his wealthy lifestyle. A few of their girlfriends, the story went, were attracted to Brian and watched him in the pool. It was then that two of the workmen decided that Brian needed to be taught a lesson. They attacked him in the pool, holding his head underwater. They kept bobbing his head up and down, paying no attention to his gasping or violent effort to breathe. When he stopped moving, the other partygoers fled the scene. Threats were reportedly made to keep the witnesses silent – but, of course, a few people talked.

Several people present that night corroborated the story – including a former member of the Walker Brothers band and Nicholas Fitzgerald, a longtime friend of Brian and a member of the Guinness family. Fitzgerald, along with his friend Richard Cadbury, went to Brian's house on July 2 to attend his party. Nicholas had run into Brian earlier that day and noticed that Brian seemed upset. Brian told him that there were a number of men hanging about his home and he was convinced they had bad intentions. Brian was upbeat about his future band plans and had recently contacted John Lennon and Jimi Hendrix about playing with him. Brian then invited him to come out to his house for a party that night.

At Nicholas approached the house from a wooded area, he noticed three men who were standing on the right side of the swimming pool. The man in the middle fell to his knees and pushed down on a struggling swimmer's head – a head of light blond hair like Brian's. At the opposite end of the patio, a man and woman were standing, staring at the pool. A moment later, a third man jumped into the pool and landed on the back of the swimmer.

It was then that Nicholas and Richard Cadbury were confronted by a "burly man, wearing glasses." He shouted at them and violently shoved them back the way they had come from, telling them to "get the hell out of here, or you'll be next."

The two men hurriedly left the area – and then things got even stranger.

When Nicholas tried to contact Richard a few days later, he was informed that his friend had moved and left no forwarding address. Stranger still, another of Brian's friends said that Anna Wohlin and her best friend, Linda Lawrence, were told that they had to leave England immediately. Anna also stated that Brian had not been using drugs that night and he was an excellent swimmer. Another friend, Ronni Money, told an interviewer: "I believe in ultimate evil now. I do, I've seen it, and I believe in it. And I don't think it's got anything to do with horned people, it's to do with people who can actually loathe you to death."

Over time, the theory about Brian's murder resurfaced – and never went away. In 1993, it was reported that Brian was murdered by contractor Frank Thorogood, who allegedly confessed the murder to the Rolling Stones' driver, Tom Keylock, who later denied it. After Thorogood's death, his family denied the claim, dismissing it as an attempted to sell a new book about Brian Jones. Those who buy into the theory say that, a few days before his death, Brian confided in a few friends that he intended to fire Thorogood, who didn't take it well. This was the motive, they claimed, for Brian's murder.

In August 2009, Sussex Police decided to review Brian's death for the first time since 1969. The decision was made after new evidence was given to them by Scott Jones, a British journalist. He had re-interviewed many of the people who were at Brian's house that night, plus he'd had a look at unseen police files held at the National Archives. According to Scott Jones, Frank Thorogood had killed Brian in a fight and senior police officers had covered up the true cause of death.

Following the review, though, the Sussex police force stated it would not be reopening the case. The department asserted "there is no new evidence to suggest that the coroner's original verdict of 'death by misadventure' was incorrect."

Was Brian Jones' death simply an accident, or did he allow himself to drown that night, taking his own life in despair? Or was he murdered by a man he had trusted? It's unlikely that we'll ever know and that this story will remain one of the great unsolved mysteries of rock-n-roll.

The next to be claimed by the "curse" of the 27 Club was Canned Heat guitarist Al "Blind Owl" Wilson on September 3, 1970.

Born on July 4, 1943, Alan Christie Wilson never fit the image of a "rock star." The man who would later earn the bluesy nickname of "Blind Owl," started out singing country blues in Cambridge, Massachusetts coffee houses and then moved to Los Angeles, where he met would-be disc jockey Bob "The Bear" Hite and made music history. They took the name of their band from a Tommy Johnson song, "Canned Heat Blues."

Al and Bob were the exact opposites of each other. Bob was a huge, larger than life kind of guy – hence the nickname – while Al was a slight, introverted young

Al "Blind Owl" Wilson

man whose poor eyesight and thick eyeglasses earned him his own moniker. But the two were united by their love of the blues.

The first incarnation of the band was in 1965, when Wilson and Hite were joined by Frank Cook and Henry Vestine. They went through a couple of bass players – including Mark Andes, who later founded the band, Spirit – until Larry Taylor came onboard. He had made a name for himself playing with Chuck Berry and Jerry Lee Lewis and also played on a few Monkees' hits.

In 1967, Canned Heat appeared at the Monterey Pop Festival, a relatively small event that was held at the Monterey County Fairgrounds, south of San Francisco. There were no big rock-n-roll names at the event, but it was a big success and set the stage for larger rock festivals that followed. It also started the careers of bands like Big Brother and the Holding Company and Canned Heat.

Al Wilson appeared out of place on the stage at the Monterey festival, with his glasses, short hair, sensible clothes, and low-key demeanor. But he was a superb musician and singer, blowing away other, more established acts.

Soon after Monterey Pop, Canned Heat signed with Liberty Records. In July of that year, they released a self-titled album, following it a year later with *Boogie with Canned Heat*, which spent three months on the Billboard charts. *Living the Blues*, a double album, came out in 1968 after which came *Hallelujah* in 1969, just before the band made an appearance at Woodstock.

Author's Note: Okay, we're going to stop right here and I'm going to suggest – no insist – that you go and find a copy of the *Woodstock* film, if you have never seen it before. It's essential viewing for pretty much the rest of this book. I promise that it's to make the stories come alive and it's a very cool time capsule of the period in which most of the rest of the book is set. Do it. You won't be sorry.

Okay, now you can keep reading.

It turned out to be a matter of luck that Canned Heat made the Woodstock stage – let alone that that their now classic song "Going Up the Country" was used to such great effect over the opening credits of the film.

Henry Vestine had quit Canned Heat just two days before Woodstock, following a fight with bass player Larry Taylor at the Fillmore West. Harvey Mandel was drafted into the band, only to find that drummer Adolfo de la Parra felt they didn't have enough time to rehearse before the festival –so, he quit, too. But their manager talked his way into the drummer's hotel room, which he had locked himself in, and talked him into changing his mind. They flew to Woodstock by helicopter, arriving just in time. It was only Harvey Mandel's third time playing with the band.

The band arrived just in time and as their set drug into the already-running late evening of the second day, they managed to secure a prime slot in the line-up.

Canned Heat got great exposure from Woodstock and exposed a huge audience to their unique blues sound. The use of "Going Up the Country" in the festival film – which the band began playing as an encore – catapulted them to greater recognition.

But not everything was great with the band. Al Wilson was a troubled young man. He was estranged from his family, lacked confidence, and suffered terrible bouts of depression. He even attempted suicide twice. But Al knew he had problems. He consulted a psychiatrist and took anti-depressants. He even dropped out of the band briefly, wondering if it was the cause of his problems, but returned quickly when he realized that it was the band he really loved.

One of his eccentric habits was sleeping outdoors when staying with friends and that's exactly what he was doing at Bob Hite's house on September 3, 1970. The band was leaving town to fly to Germany for a tour the next day. His body was found the next morning, still tucked in his sleeping bag. His hands were crossed over his chest and there was a bottle of sleeping pills in the sleeping bag with him. Though the official version of his death stated that his death was an accidental drug overdose, many of his closest friends believed that he committed suicide.

Only a year after their Woodstock appearance, Al Wilson was found dead in Bob Hite's Topanga Canyon garden. His death robbed the world of what bluesman John Lee Hooker called, "The most gifted harmonica player I've ever heard."

Later that same month, the rock world was stunned to learn that Jimi Hendrix had died in a girlfriend's apartment in London. Hendrix became known as a legendary guitar player in the late 1960s and some of his friends believed that he may have sensed his impending death. That July, before his death, he told some reporters, "I don't think I will live to see 28."

The headliner for Sunday night at the Woodstock festival – Jimi Hendrix – didn't take the stage until Monday morning at 9:00 AM. But even running more than 12 hours late, the guitarist closed out the festival in memorable style. During his two-hour set, he played plenty of his recognizable hits – "Hey Joe," "Purple Haze," Foxey Lady" – and then teased out a version of the "Star-Spangled Banner" like nothing anyone had heard before.

Although its melody was intact, Jimi applied his own style to everything else. He improvised distortion- and effect-filled detours that circled the

Jimi Hendrix

song's structure and gave it a psychedelic, blurry tone that was hypnotic. The instrument was mournful and angry – a reflection of the Woodstock generation's disillusionment with the country.

On this song especially, Jimi's unique style and technique was truly visible. A self-taught player who couldn't read or write music, he was a natural guitarist who performed by feel, emotion, and instinct. To Jimi, the sound quality and the emotional impact of the music mattered more than skill and textbook technique so, as a result, his music was fluid and immersive, and perfect for the psychedelic rock movement of the late 1960s.

Born in Seattle, Jimi was raised by his father, a U.S. Army veteran. As a child, he was shy and soft-spoken but was drawn to the music of bluesmen like B.B. King, Muddy Waters, and Robert Johnson. In fact, Jimi used to strum a broom and pretend it was a guitar, and even taught himself to play a one-string ukulele.

Jimi's father luckily encouraged his love of music and bought him a $5 used acoustic guitar in 1958 and then an electric one a year later. This second purchase inspired Jimi to join a band, although he wasn't thinking of music as a career choice just yet. Instead, he enlisted in the Army. While training to be a paratrooper, though, he injured himself during a jump and was honorably discharged in 1962.

Jimi's return home allowed Jimi to start working as a session guitarist. Using the stage name of Jimmy James, he played with Ike and Tina Turner, Sam Cooke, the Isley Brothers, and Little Richard – who fired Jimi because his flamboyant stage presence was outshining the main act.

In 1966, Jimi started out on his own with the band Jimmy James and the Blue Flames, which managed a Greenwich Village residence at the Café Wha? Former member of the Animals, Chas Chandler, was at one of his shows and he became Jimi's manager and encouraged him to move to London. It was there that Jimi formed the Jimi Hendrix Experience with British musicians Noel Redding on bass and Mitch Mitchell on drums.

Chandler's hunch had been correct – the U.K. embraced Jim and both "Hey Joe" and "Purple Haze" hit the tops of the singles charts. The group's 1967 album, *Are You Experienced*, remained on the charts for eight months. To increase his reputation as a can't-miss performer, Jimi set his guitar on fire during a March 1967 performance in London—a trick which drew the ire of the headlining band but plenty of press attention.

But it was a second round of the stunt at the Monterey Pop Festival that got even more attention. At the end of a cover of the Troggs' "Wild Thing," he torched and then smashed his Fender Stratocaster. People went crazy for Hendrix. *Are You Experienced* became a smash hit in the U.S. that summer and set the stage for *Bold as Love* in December.

The Jimi Hendrix Experience stayed on the road for much of 1968 but continued to release innovative sounds. *Electric Ladyland* was a double LP that included everything from zoned-out R&B, garage rock, and psychedelic rock, like the 15-minute "Voodoo Chile" and the evocative, soon-to-be-classic cover of Bob Dylan's "All Along the Watchtower" – my absolute favorite Jimi Hendrix song.

Less than a year later, though – at the height of their fame – the Jimi Hendrix Experience fell apart. Jimi performed with a variety of players throughout 1969 and 1970, including at Woodstock, but his exhausting lifestyle, chemical indulgences, and massive fame had started to catch up to him. In July 1970, he told a group of reporters during his last tour, "The next time I go back to Seattle, it'll be in a pine box."

In the late summer of 1970, Jimi was in London, where his life came to an end. On the morning of September 18, Jimi was found dead in his apartment by paramedics. The official story was that he had been partying the night before and had a little fight with his girlfriend, Monika Dannemann, who wanted to leave the party. He agreed and went to the apartment, where, according to Monika, he took some of her Vesperax, a sleeping pill, so that he could get some rest. A few hours later, she woke up and saw that Jimi was deeply asleep. She left the apartment to go buy some cigarettes but when she came back, Jimi still hadn't stirred. Concerned, she tried to wake him and saw that he had vomited in his sleep. In a panic, she called an ambulance. When paramedics arrived, they tried to revive him, but it was too late. Jimi was taken by ambulance to the hospital, where he was declared dead at 12:45 p.m. It was immediately assumed that Jimi had gone to sleep highly intoxicated and had choked to death on his own vomit.

But the story wasn't really that simple.

This was Monika Dannemann's version of events. According to paramedic Reg Jones, who was at the apartment that morning, the door was open when he and his partner arrived, but Monika was missing. They saw Jimi's body covered in vomit and he was not breathing. They tried everything to revive him, but he was already dead. He was pronounced dead at the hospital by Dr. Martin Seifert, but it was obvious that he had been dead for some time – long before an ambulance had been called.

In addition to the alcohol found in his body, the autopsy revealed that he had taken nine of Monika's sleeping pills – 18 times the normal dose. Eric Burdon -- lead singer of the Animals and a friend that Jimi had partied with that night -- surmised that Jimi had committed suicide, but this seems unlikely. Nothing in the autopsy pointed to suicide. Jimi took nine pills but there were 42 more in the bottle. Why wouldn't he have taken them all if he was trying to kill himself? Jimi suffered from chronic insomnia and knew a single pill would not help him fall asleep – but would he have taken nine?

The stories got wilder after that. Some friends – unable to believe that Jimi would commit suicide – suggested that he had been murdered. It was said that he had large amounts of wine in his stomach and lungs, but his blood levels didn't match the amount. In other words, he would have had to have died immediately after drinking all that wine. It was suggested that someone had forced the wine into his system to drown him with it and make it look like suicide or fatal intoxication. But who could've done something like that?

The first suspect was, of course, Monika Dannemann, who was found a short time later. Her statements about Jimi's death were contradictory and full of inconsistencies. She had no clear answers about where she had gone after she called for an ambulance and her recollections of Jimi's last hours were confused and made little sense. But there was no evidence against her – only rumors.

It was also said that, a few days before his death, Jimi told several friends that he had been forcibly kidnapped, forced into a car, and left in an abandoned building. He stated that he was now in fear for his life. Was this a true story, or another rumor?

There were also stories spread about Jimi's manager, Mike Jeffrey. It was a poorly-kept secret that Jeffrey manipulated Jimi and, some claimed, even stole money from him. In fact, it was Jeffrey's men who showed up to "rescue" Jimi from the abandoned building after he was allegedly kidnapped, prompting suspicion that Jeffrey was involved in the abduction.

It was also rumored that Jeffrey stood to make a lot of money if Jimi died, thanks to a huge insurance policy and the rights to Jimi's unreleased works. This rumor turned out to be true. In fact, Jeffrey built a financial empire based on Jimi's posthumous releases.

However, there was nothing to link Jeffrey physically to Jimi's "murder," if that's what it was. When Jimi died, Jeffrey was in Spain, far away from the "crime scene." Strangely, though, Jeffrey was killed in a plane crash on March 5, 1973. He was flying from Spain to England to answer questions about his financial dealings – but never made it. Not surprisingly, there was a conspiracy about Jeffrey's death, too. Some believe that he faked his death by using his many contacts to add his name to the plane's passenger list, while he safely disappeared.

Wild? Yes, but not the wildest conspiracy. The winner blames the U.S. government for Jimi's death. COINTELPRO – a real-life counter intelligence program created by the F.B.I. – allegedly had a scheme to get rid of the subversive characters in the country. According to this theory, many musicians were investigated for being dangerous influences for young people. Hendrix's ability to move and inspire the masses was a threat since the musician had allegedly made a public statement asking the Black Panthers to go to Washington and shoot members of the government. Because of this, some people believe it was the government who decided to eradicate the "threat" of Jimi Hendrix.

With Jimi's death, the conspiracies are pretty far-fetched. As Jimi's friends and fellow musicians knew, Jimi was a hard-partying young man who suffered from depression. At the time of his death, it was widely known among his friends that Jimi was very disappointed with his last several shows. One night, after only playing a few songs, he apologized to the audience, saying "he just couldn't get it together." He was unhappy with his financial affairs and complained about feeling restrained by the public's demand on his time and talents.

He drank hard and he did a lot of drugs, as did a lot of people, especially musicians, in that era. His death was probably as simple as taking too many pills. Friends recalled him often swallowing handfuls of pills at backstage parties, never knowing what he had been given. It's possible that he did that exact same thing that night when he came home from the party, but we'll never know for sure.

All that we do know is that the world lost an incredibly talented guitarist and musician on that night in September 1970 and we're never going to see another one like him again.

Two weeks after the death of Jimi Hendrix, Janis Joplin died from a heroin overdose at the Landmark Hotel in Hollywood. Joplin escaped a lifetime of pain through music, alcohol, and drugs and became one of the greatest rock and blues singers of all time. Her body was discovered in her hotel room after she failed to show up for a recording session. Her friends had

Janis Joplin

often begged her to stop using drugs, but Janis always had a bitter answer for them, "Let's face it, I'll never see 30."

And she was right. She only made it to 27.

Janis Lyn Joplin – "the greatest white urban blues and soul singer of her generation" -- was born in 1943 in Port Arthur, Texas, an oil-refining town on the coast. Growing up, she was a social outcast who found an outlet in music. She was drawn to the blues and soon found she had a talent for it. She performed folk blues on the coffeehouse circuit in Texas, sharing her real-life pain through her songs.

Janis had a brutal childhood. In high school, she was overweight and had a bad case of acne. Classmates referred to her as "pig face." During her short college career, there were stories that fellow students nominated her for "Ugliest Man on Campus." She escaped her pain through music and by dulling her senses with alcohol. She even made her drinking part of the show. Southern Comfort even bought her a fur coat, thanks to her ringing endorsement of their product. Eventually, she needed more than hard liquor and pills and turned to heroin.

Janis's music eventually took her to San Francisco, but she returned home the next year. Back in Port Arthur, she waited for a marriage that never took place. When she tired of waiting, she took her broken heart back to San Francisco, where she hooked up with Big Brother and the Holding Company -- guitarists James Gurley and Sam Andrew, bassist Peter Albin, and drummer David Getz – at the suggestion of entrepreneur and fellow Texan, Chet Helms. The chemistry came as a revelation to Janis. "All of a sudden, someone threw me in front of this rock and roll band," she said. "And I decided then and there that was it. I never wanted to do anything else."

Big Brother was a loud, explosive, and volatile mix of blues and psychedelia. Chet Helms booked the group on some of the venues that became integral to the San Francisco scene. They became regulars at Helm's Avalon Ballroom in the mid-to-late Sixties. It was at the Avalon where much of *Cheap Thrills*—an album that topped the album charts for eight weeks in 1968—was recorded. That explosive showcase of psychedelic soul featured Joplin's raw, impassioned readings of Willie Mae Thornton's "Ball and Chain" and "Piece of My Heart."

Janis became a sensation at the 1967 Monterey Pop Festival. Her powerful voice sent chills through the crowd as she belted out song after song. Everyone in attendance knew that a star had been born at the festival.

Joplin left Big Brother in December 1968, taking guitarist Sam Andrew with her. Her first solo album, *I've Got Dem Ol' Kozmic Blues Again Mama!*, appeared in 1969, and she toured extensively with her Kozmic Blues Band. By mid-1970, however, she dissolved that outfit and formed a superb new one, Full-Tilt Boogie. They gelled over the course of several months of touring and entered the studio to record what would turn out to be Janis's swan song.

On Sunday afternoon, October 4, 1970, producer Paul Rothchild became concerned when Janis failed to show up at Sunset Sound Recorders for a recording session in which she was scheduled to provide the vocal track for the already-existing instrumental track of the song "Buried Alive in the Blues." In the evening, Full Tilt Boogie's road manager, John Cooke, drove to the Landmark Motor Hotel in Hollywood, where Janis was staying. Her psychedelically-painted Porsche was parked outside of Room 105, and he knew that something was wrong.

When Cooke entered the room, he found her dead on the floor next to the bed. The official cause of death was an accidental heroin overdose, possibly compounded by alcohol. A hotel clerk remembered Janis asking for some change for the cigarette machine on Saturday night. That was the last time she had been seen alive. John Cooke later stated that he believed Janis had been sold a higher quality of heroin than she was used to and simply used too much.

The posthumously released album, *Pearl* —the title was her nickname— comprised nine finished tracks and one instrumental to which she was supposed to have added vocals on the day she died. It was left unfinished.

Pearl became Janis's biggest seller, holding the Number One spot for nine weeks in 1971. It included "Me and Bobby McGee," a song written for her by ex-lover Kris Kristofferson. The tune was a quirky portrait of a hippie love affair, sung by Janis as an affectionate, road-weary country blues song that perfectly captured the bohemian spirit of the times. The entire album remains as a hint of what might have been if Janis had not died at 27.

But she did. Janis Joplin passed into the realm of legend – an outwardly brash yet inwardly vulnerable woman who possessed one of the most passionate voices in rock-n-roll history.

On March 8, 1973, the "curse" claimed another member for the Club – Grateful Dead founding member, Ron "Pigpen" McKernan. Pigpen was a leading member of the band, contributing harmonica, percussion, organ, vocals, and guitar until congenital cirrhosis prompted doctors to make him stop touring in 1971. Two years later, he was dead.

Ronald Charles McKernan was born on September 8, 1945, in San Bruno, California. His father, Phil McKernan, was one of the first white R&B and blues disc jockeys in the country. Thanks to this, Ron grew up with African-American friends and enjoyed black music and culture. When he was growing up, he taught himself blues piano, guitar, and harmonica. When he was 14, Ron and his family moved to Palo Alton, where he became friends with another aspiring musician, Jerry Garcia.

Ron began spending his time in the local coffeehouses and even got a job at Dana Morgan's Music Store so that he could be close to the scene. One night, Jerry invited Ron on stage with him to play harmonic and sing the blues. He was never the same after that. Soon, he was haunting every jam session that he could find, singing the blues. He was given the nickname "Pigpen," thanks to his untidy habits and similarity to the permanently dirty character in the comic-strip *Peanuts*.

Along with Jerry and guitarist Bob Weir, Ron got involved in several groups before the founding of the Grateful Dead, including the Zodiacs and Mother MCree's Uptown Jug Champions (which is possibly one of my favorite band names of all time). After drummer Bill Kreutzmann was added, the band became the Warlocks – but not for long. Around 1965, Ron convinced the rest of the band to switch to electric instruments. Bassist Phil Lesh joined soon after and they became the Grateful Dead. Pigpen took over as the group's leader, singer, and front man.

Ron put together most of the Dead's early sets. They centered around blues and R&B covers, which grew tiring to his old friend, Jerry Garcia. By the end of 1966, Jerry had improved his skills and wanted to assert himself more as a leader, changing the band's direction and reducing Pigpen's lead role. In 1967, drummer Mickey Hart joined the band, followed by classically trained keyboardist Tom Constanten, considerably altering the band's style. Tom often replaced Pigpen on keyboards in the studio because he was having trouble adapting to the new material that Jerry and Phil Lesh composed for the band. Road manager Jon McIntire commented that "Pigpen was relegated to the congas at that point and it was really humiliating, and he was really hurt, but he couldn't show it, couldn't talk about it."

In October 1968, Pigpen and Bob Weir were nearly fired from the band after Jerry Garcia and Bob Lesh decided that their playing was holding the band back from lengthy and experimental jamming. Ron took

Ron "Pigpen" McKernan

it hard. Bob promised to improve, but Pigpen was resistant. He missed three Dead shows before vowing not to "be lazy" any more and rejoining the group.

Tom Constanten left the band in January 1970 over musical and lifestyle differences and Pigpen nominally resumed keyboard duties. He played on and off for the albums that followed, while Jerry continued to express frustration with Ron's missed rehearsals and his inability to keep up with new material. Bob Lesh was more forgiving, though, "It was okay for Pigpen to lay out... we kept wanting Pigpen to be there because he was 'one of us'."

By that time, the Grateful Dead was greatly changed from what it had started out as, much to the chagrin of Ron McKernan. The Dead had become famous for their long improvisational sets – under the influence of LSD – that became the epitome of psychedelic rock. Pigpen was never into drugs as much as the others. He was a boozer. He'd started drinking when he was 12 and by his mid-twenties had cirrhosis of the liver, ulcers, and other health problems.

After a lifetime with the bottle, Pigpen was admitted to the hospital with a perforated ulcer in 1971. Afterwards, her performed only occasionally with the band. Toward the end of his short life, he eased back on the drinking, but by then, it was too late. He was dying and he knew it.

In his last months, he wrote a song about "no tomorrow" and broke up with his girlfriend, explaining, "I don't want you around when I die." Pigpen was alone at his apartment in Corte Madera, overlooking San Francisco Bay, when he died on March 8, 1973. The end came from a massive intestinal hemorrhage, caused by cirrhosis. He had been dead for two days when his landlady found him.

Pete Ham of Badfinger

A little over two years later, another member joined the Club – this one by choice. Pete Ham, the singer, songwriter, and guitarist from the group Badfinger, hanged himself in his garage.

Pete was born and raised in Swansea, Wales. Around 1961, he formed his first band, a local rock group known as the Panthers. The group went through several name and line-up changes before it became the Iveys four years later. In 1966, they got a manager, Bill Collins, who encouraged them to move to London. He bought a tape recorder for Pete and convinced him to write original songs. It was Pete's music that grabbed the attention of Mal Evans – the Beatles' personal assistant – in 1968. This led to the Iveys getting signed to the Beatles' Apple Records label after approval from all four Beatles, who were reportedly impressed by Pete's songwriting abilities.

With the release of their single "Come and Get It" – written by Paul McCartney – the Iveys changed their name to Badfinger. Initially, Pete had balked at the idea of using a non-original song to promote the band, but he was quickly convinced that having a hit single could only bring positive attention to his own work. And he was right. His greatest songwriting success came with his co-written composition "Without You," a worldwide Number One when it was later covered by Harry Nilsson in 1972.

Despite their success, there was trouble in the band. Pete, along with his songwriting partner, Tom Evans, did not receive the royalties that they expected and became embroiled in disputes with management. Things got even worse after that. Warner Brothers Records sued Badfinger's business manager, Stan Polley, after an advance vanished and, after Polley disappeared, the band was left penniless.

Deeply depressed, Pete reached a point where only death seemed the solution to his problems. He met Tom at a pub on the evening of April 24, 1975 – three days before his 28th birthday – and told him, "Don't worry, I know a way out."

Fortified by drink, Pete went to his home in Woking, Surrey and hanged himself in his garage. He left a note telling his pregnant wife and her son that he loved them. It read, "I will not be allowed to love and trust everybody. This is better. Pete. PS Stan Polley is a soulless bastard. I will take him with me."

As a macabre end to the story, Tom Evans also hanged himself seven years later.

There were no new members inducted into the 27 Club until June 14, 1989, when Pete de Freitas, drummer for Echo and the Bunnymen died when his motorcycle collided with a car riding from Liverpool to London.

Pete had been born in Port of Spain, Trinidad and Tobago, but grew up in Somerset in the Southwest of England. He had joined up with the Bunnymen in 1979, replacing the drum machine they'd been recording with. He was with the band for their earliest successes, but temporarily left in 1985. He spent several months drinking in New Orleans while attempting to start a new band. Finally, in 1987, he returned to England and rejoined the Bunnymen as a part-time member. He also got married that year and his daughter, Lucie Marie, was born in 1988.

Pete de Freitas

On June 14, he was on his way to London on his 900cc Ducati motorcycle when he collided with a car. Pete was instantly killed, snuffing out a life that had just gotten back on track.

On July 7, 1993, Mia Zapata, singer for the punk band The Gits, was beaten, raped, strangled, and left for dead in Seattle. She would be the first of three 27 Club deaths to occur in the Seattle music community in the span of 11 months.

Mia was born in Louisville, Kentucky on August 25, 1965. By the time she turned nine, she'd already learned to play both guitar and piano. She loved all kinds of music, including punk, but had an affinity for jazz, blues, and for R&B singers like Bessie Smith, Sam Cooke, Billie Holliday, and Ray Charles.

In 1984, Mia enrolled at Antioch College, a liberal arts school in Yellow Springs, Ohio. In September 1986, she and three friends – guitarist Joe Spleen, drummer Steve Moriarty, and bassist Matt Dresdner -- formed a punk rock band they called The Gits. Within three years, they had relocated to the up-and-coming music scene of Seattle. They moved into an abandoned house and Mia got a job at a local bar to pay the bills.

Mia Zapata

In 1990 and 1991, The Gits hooked up with a local independent label and put out a series of well-received singles. They played a lot of area shows – usually with their friends' band, 7 Year Bitch – and put out their first album, *Frenching the Bully*, in 1992.

They were starting to make a name for themselves within the Seattle grunge scene and getting a lot of attention for their explosive shows and hard-edged lyrics. Soon they had a loyal following amidst the city's underground punk scene. Many grouped them together with bands like Nirvana and Pearl Jam, but Mia brought a feminine voice to the grunge scene that had not been seen yet.

Most wouldn't know that she was a rock star on her way up, though. Mia had come from an affluent family but preferred to live in poverty. As her father described it, "Mia lived in two different worlds. She lived on two different sides of the street—the straight side on one, with parochial schools, an affluent family, and tennis clubs. But when she crossed the street, material things didn't mean anything to her."

Mia's music was all about the rejection of financial comfort, and to hear it, most expected she would be anti-social and hard to deal with. The opposite was true. She was well-connected with her community and the hub of several social circles. She had a magnetic personality that drew all sorts of people together who never would have met.

That's what made what happened to her all the more tragic.

Around 2:00 AM on July 7, 1993, Mia left the Comet Tavern in the Capitol Hill area of Seattle. She was then staying in a studio space in the basement of an apartment building that was located a block away, and briefly visited with a friend who lived on the second floor.

This was the last time she was seen alive.

She may have walked a few blocks west, or north to a friend's apartment, or may have decided to take a walk south to her home. No one knows for sure.

What is known is that she was beaten, raped, and strangled, probably around 2:15 AM, or perhaps later. A woman found her body in the street around 3:30 AM, near the intersection of 24th Avenue South and South Washington Street in the Central District.

When her body was discovered, she couldn't be identified – Mia had no identification on her – but when she arrived at the morgue, she was recognized by the medical examiner, who was a fan of The Gits and had been to many of their shows. The autopsy report stated that, if she had not been strangled, she would have died from internal injuries that she suffered from the beating.

Mia's murder seemed an impossible crime to solve. There were no leads, no witnesses, and no clues. The Seattle music community, including its most famous bands – Nirvana, Pearl Jam, Soundgarden – helped raise $70,000 to hire a private investigator for three years. The funds dried up without any major breaks in the case, but the investigator, Leigh Hearon, continued to investigate on her own time without any luck. In 1998, after five years of investigation, Seattle police Detective Dale Tallman reported, "We're no closer to solving the case than we were right after the murder."

But time – and advances in DNA technology since the time of the murder – cracked the case in 2003. At the time of the original autopsy, medical examiners took swabs of saliva that was found on Mia's body. It had been kept in cold storage ever since. Technology in 1993 was too limited to extract a full sample from it, but that had changed with the dawn of the new century.

In 2002, a Florida fisherman named Jesus Mezquia was arrested for burglary and domestic abuse and his DNA was entered into a national database. When the DNA evidence from Mia's murder was put into the system, detectives got a match and Mezquia was soon under arrest in connection with the crime. It was soon discovered that he had a history of violence toward women and all his ex-girlfriends, and his wife, had filed charges against him over the years. There was also a charge of indecent exposure in his file that put him in Seattle within two weeks of Mia's murder.

One thing, though – there was never any link found between Mezquia and Mia Zapata.

At trial, Mezquia never took the stand in his own defense. He maintained that he was innocent – and still does – although his DNA was an exact match to that found on Mia's body. Prosecutors theorized that Mezquia saw Mia leave the bar on the night of the murder and followed her a short distance before he attacked her. She was wearing headphones and listening to music as she walked and was unaware of any danger until he grabbed her, forced her into his car, and assaulted her in the back seat.

Mezquia was found guilty at trial and sentenced to 37 years in prison.

Nine months after the promising career of Mia Zapata came to an end, on April 5, 1994, Nirvana lead singer Kurt Cobain committed suicide in his Seattle home. His body was not found until three days later. During the last years of his life, he had struggled with heroin addiction, depression, and difficulty coping with his fame and public image.

Until, finally, he just couldn't stand it anymore.

Kurt was born in Aberdeen, Washington, on February 20, 1967, the son of an auto mechanic, Donald, and a waitress, Wendy. He had a younger sister, Kimberly, who was born in 1970. When he was young, he was always described as a happy, excitable, yet sensitive child. He had a great talent as an artist, even from a very early age, and loved to draw his favorite characters from cartoon and films. This enthusiasm was encouraged by his grandmother, Iris, who was a professional artist.

He also developed a love for music. This is no surprise, considering that many of his family members were musicians. He had aunts and uncles who played in bands and a great-uncle, Delbert, who had a successful career as an Irish tenor. His aunt, Mari, who played guitar and sang in bands in the area, later recalled that Kurt began singing around the age of two. At four, he was playing the piano and wrote a song about a trip to the park.

But then at age nine, according to Kurt, his world came crashing down when his parents divorced. His family became part of the big wave of no-fault divorces that ended marriages in the 1970s. Up until that time there still had to be a party at fault to make a divorce legal. California led the way with no-fault divorces in 1969, and soon, other states also adopted the law, causing the American divorce rate to skyrocket. Like many other children of the era, the divorce had a profound effect on Kurt's life – and he probably took it harder than a lot of other children did. His mother noted that his personality changed drastically, and he became defiant, sullen, and withdrawn.

In a 1993 interview, he talked about the effect their divorce had on him: "I remember feeling ashamed, for some reason. I was ashamed of my parents. I couldn't face some of my friends at school anymore, because I desperately wanted to have the classic, you know, typical family. Mother, father. I wanted that security, so I resented my parents for quite a few years because of that."

Kurt's parents both found new partners after the divorce. Although his father had promised not to remarry, he wed Jenny Westeby, much to Kurt's dismay. Kurt, his father, Jenny, and her two children, Mindy and James, moved into a new home together. Kurt liked Jenny at first. She gave him a lot of attention – until she had a son of her own. In January 1979, Chad Cobain was born and this new family – which Kurt insisted was not his real one – was in stark contrast to the attention that he had been receiving from Jenny

Kurt Cobain

when he was the only boy. He quickly grew to resent his stepmother, along with the rest of his father's new family.

Kurt's mother, Wendy, began dating a man who was abusive. Kurt often witnessed the violence that he inflicted on her, including a broken arm that sent her to the hospital. Wendy refused to press charges and insisted on staying in the relationship.

Not surprisingly, Kurt began acting out. He started to behave badly toward adults and lashed out against other children, which led to him being disciplined for bullying other students in school. Things got so bad that Donald and Jenny took him to a therapist, whose only advice was that Kurt's mother and father should reconcile. Both sides of the family attempted to get his parents back together, but to no avail. Finally, on June 28, 1979, Kurt's mother granted full custody to his father, but there was only so much that Donald could take. He ended up placing his son in the care of the Reed family. Kurt's friend, Jesse, and the rest of his family were devout born-again Christians. While he lived with them, Kurt embraced Christianity and regularly attended church services. His devotion wouldn't last long, and he'd later become skeptical of any kind of organized religion. In fact, his song "Lithium" is about his experience living with the Reeds.

Kurt continued his love/hate relationship with his father, enrolling in sports because his father wanted him to and then failing on purpose so that he could disappoint him. He was bullied in school because one of his friends was gay, so it was assumed he was gay also. He wasn't, but in a later interview, he said that he liked being associated with a gay identity because he did not like people, and when they thought he was gay they left him alone. He continued to do all he could to be disruptive and troublesome, using his art to get attention and to upset his teachers with "unflattering" caricatures of celebrities and President Reagan. In time, he found escape within the thriving Pacific Northwest music scene, going to punk shows in Seattle.

During his second year in high school, Kurt moved in with his mother in Aberdeen. Two weeks before the end of his senior year, he dropped out of Aberdeen High School because he learned that he did not have enough credits to graduate. His mother gave him a choice – find a job or move out. After one week, Kurt found his clothes and other belonging packed into boxes. With no place else to go, he started crashing with friends, camping outdoors, sleeping under a bridge, and sneaking into his mother's basement when the weather got bad.

In 1986, Kurt moved into an apartment, paying the rent with part-time work. During his free time, he was traveling frequently to Olympia, Washington, to go to rock shows, which was how he met Tracy Marander. They had a close relationship, but one that was strained by financial difficulties. Tracy made most of the money, working at the cafeteria of the Seattle–Tacoma International Airport, often stealing food. Kurt, on the other hand, spent most of his time watching television, sleeping late, and working on art projects. The relationship didn't last long.

It was in 1986 that Kurt first experimented with heroin. Throughout most of his life, he had suffered from chronic bronchitis and intense pain caused an undiagnosed chronic stomach condition. He started smoking marijuana when he was 13 and graduated to oxycodone to control his pain. After his first taste of it, he used heroin sporadically for several years. He claimed that it was a way to self-medicate his stomach condition, but by 1990, it had become a full-blown habit.

Soon after his breakup with Tracy Marander, Kurt began dating Tobi Vail, an influential punk artist from the band Bikini Kill. After he met her, Kurt said that he vomited because he was so completely overwhelmed with anxiety caused by his infatuation with her. Kurt saw Tobi as his female counterpart, but their relationship didn't last for long. He wanted a traditional relationship, which she could never have – she regarded such a thing as sexist in the countercultural punk community. But while they were together, they did collaborate on some music and their relationship ended up inspiring many of the songs on *Nevermind*.

They spent a lot of their time together as a couple discussing political and philosophical issues. Once, while he was discussing anarchism and punk rock with friend Kathleen Hanna, another member of Bikini Kill, Hanna spray-painted "Kurt Smells Like Teen Spirit" on Cobain's apartment wall. Teen Spirit was the name of a deodorant Vail wore. Cobain, unaware of the deodorant's existence, interpreted the slogan as having some sort of revolutionary meaning – inspiring the title of what would become one of Nirvana's biggest hits.

On Kurt's 14th birthday, in 1981, his uncle had offered him either a bike or a used guitar – Kurt had chosen the guitar. Music had always been in his blood and, even though he saw himself as an artist, friends believed that he was destined to make a name for himself in the rock world. He'd formed several bands over the years but often had a hard time finding anyone to play with him. In high school, though, he'd met Krist Novoselic, a fellow devotee of punk rock. Krist's mother owned a hair salon and the pair occasionally practiced in a room above the salon. A few years later, Cobain tried to convince Novoselic to form a band with him, but Krist wasn't interested. After months of asking, though, Krist finally agreed to join him, forming the beginnings of Nirvana. Kurt was still flirting with the idea of religion at the time and the band's name, "Nirvana," was taken from the Buddhist concept, which Cobain described as "freedom from pain, suffering and the external world," a concept that he aligned with the punk rock ethos and ideology.

Even as the band was coming together, Kurt was already disenchanted with the idea of touring, their failure to draw substantial crowds, and the difficulty they were having making enough money to support themselves. In the first few years, Kurt and Krist went through a constantly rotating cast of drummers. Eventually, they settled on Chad Canning, with whom they recorded the album *Bleach* in 1989. But Kurt became unhappy with Canning's style, leading to a new drummer, Dave Grohl. It was with Dave that they recorded their 1991 major-label debut, *Nevermind*. The lead single from it was "Smells Like Teen Spirit," and with that, Nirvana entered the mainstream, helping to pioneer the subgenre of alternative rock called "grunge."

The album's success provided numerous Seattle bands – like Pearl Jam, Alice in Chains, and Soundgarden – access to a much wider audience. As a result, alternative rock became a dominant genre on radio and music television in the early 1990s. Nirvana was considered its "flagship band" and Kurt found himself reluctantly anointed by the media as the genre's "spokesman."

Kurt with his wife, musician Courtney Love

As far as he was concerned, they couldn't have picked a worse one. He struggled to reconcile the massive success of Nirvana with his underground roots. He felt persecuted by the media and began to harbor resentment toward people who claimed to be fans of the band, yet refused to acknowledge, or misinterpreted, the band's social and political views. He became a vocal opponent of sexism, racism, and homophobia and was proud that Nirvana played a gay rights benefit that opposed an Oregon ballot measure that would have allowed schools to teach against homosexuality. He was also a vocal supporter of the pro-choice movement, which led to him receiving death threats from anti-abortion activists.

With the band's success came more pressure on Kurt's personal life. He had his hands full between touring, playing shows, his growing heroin addiction, and his tumultuous relationship with Courtney Love, who he'd met in January 1990. Initially, Courtney had pursued Kurt, but he was unsure that he wanted to be in another relationship. He ignored her advances and canceled dates, but he was falling in love. He later said, "I was determined to be a bachelor for a few months. But I knew that I liked Courtney so much right away that it was a really hard struggle to stay away from her for so many months." By late 1991, they were together as often as possible and had bonded through their drug use.

On February 24, 1992, a few days after the conclusion of Nirvana's "Pacific Rim" tour, Kurt and Courtney were married on Waikiki Beach in Hawaii. Courtney wore a satin and lace dress that had once belonged to actress Frances Farmer and Kurt wore green pajamas because he was "too lazy to put on a tux." Eight people were in attendance at the ceremony, including Dave Grohl.

Courtney was pregnant when they got married and the couple's daughter, Frances Bean Cobain" was born on August 18, 1992. And even this event became controversial. In an article in *Vanity Fair* magazine, Courtney admitted to using heroin, not knowing she was pregnant at the time. After a public outcry, she claimed she'd been misquoted, but the damage was done. The couple was hounded by tabloid reporters, many wanting to know if Frances had been addicted to drugs when she was born. She wasn't, but the story refused to go away. Eventually, the Los Angeles County Department of Children's Services took the Cobains to court, stating that the couple's drug use made them unfit parents.

On August 24, 1992, six days after Frances's birth, the first court hearing was held. Though they hoped to retain custody of Frances as a couple, Kurt and Courtney were prepared for the possibility the court might put restrictions on one parent, and, therefore, had separate lawyers. It didn't matter. The judge ruled Kurt and Courtney would not be allowed to see their own child without the supervision of the court-appointed guardian. Kurt was ordered to undergo 30 days of drug treatment, and both parents were required to give random urine tests. Kurt had been clean for several days, yet he told Courtney he felt the ruling had broken his heart in two.

They had already planned on having a nanny, so they developed a complex plan to put Frances into the temporary care of nannies and relatives, as required by the judge. This presented another problem: What relative? Both Kurt and Courtney had so many issues with their own families, they weren't willing to trust Frances to their respective parents. Initially, Courtney's estranged half-sister cared for the infant, but this didn't last. Eventually, they found a new nannie through friends and she ended up with the primary care of Frances.

Two days after the court hearing, Kurt flew to England. Nirvana was headlining the 1992 Reading Festival, which included The Melvins, Screaming Trees, L7, Mudhoney, Eugenius, and Bjorn Again, an Abba-cover band Kurt adored. But most of the 60,000 fans were coming for Nirvana. New baby, drug rehab, *Vanity Fair* article, and court hearings aside, he was needed onstage.

The show turned out to be amazing. The band had not played together – or even rehearsed – for two months, and yet they performed a 25-song set that spanned their entire catalog. It even included a snippet of Boston's 1976 hit "More Than a Feeling" to introduce "Teen Spirit," appropriate since Kurt claimed in interviews that he'd stolen his riff from Boston.

But rehab was waiting for him back in the States. Heroin had turned things ugly, and not just for his personal life, marriage, and family. It had often affected the band. During the support tour for *Nevermind*, Nirvana had a photographic session booked on the same day as a *Saturday Night Live* appearance. Kurt was high when he showed up for the shoot and nodded off several times during it.

He checked into the Exodus facility when he returned. He spent his time there attending individual therapy, group therapy, and at 12-step meetings. Most nights he wrote in his journal, producing long treatises on everything from the ethics of punk rock to the personal price of heroin addiction. He was allowed to check out for brief day visits with Courtney and Frances, but his nights seemed endless. Their marriage had a dynamic that when Kurt was weak and needy, he romanced Courtney more. The letters he wrote her from rehab were a combination of poetry and stream-of-consciousness ranting. He covered them with candle wax, blood, and, occasionally, his semen.

But most of what Kurt wrote about was his struggle to free himself from heroin. Immediately prior to entering rehab, his journal entries reflected a growing state of denial, particularly in response to the media coverage of his drug problem. "I am not a heroin addict!" he penned one day, as if he were trying to convince himself. Yet as soon as Kurt kicked heroin long enough to break the physical addiction, he took on the opposite slant, displaying a hatred and disgust at himself for getting hooked in the first place. "Almost everyone who tries hard drugs, i.e. heroin and cocaine, will eventually become literally a slave to these substances," he declared in one journal entry.

He found even more success in his treatment when he began seeing Dr. Robert Fremont, a Los Angeles chemical dependency counselor, who was also treating Courtney. Fremont couldn't have been more controversial. In fact, he'd once lost his medical license after prescribing himself narcotics. After getting it back, he earned notoriety by treating some of Hollywood's biggest stars for their drug problems. But he was successful in a profession where relapse rates were extraordinarily high, largely by generously prescribing legal drugs to clients detoxing from heroin, which was what he did with Kurt.

In September 1992, Fremont began to use an experimental—and at the time illegal—treatment plan on Kurt that involved giving him daily doses of buprenorphine. This relatively benign narcotic stimulates the brain's opiate receptors, and thus can cut the craving for heroin, or so Fremont supposed.

It worked for Kurt – well, temporarily.

By early the next year, Kurt was once again punishing himself with heroin. Prior to a performance at the New Music Seminar in New York in July 1993, he overdosed in his hotel room. Rather than calling for an ambulance, Courtney injected him with naloxone, and he regained consciousness. Somehow, he managed to perform with Nirvana that night and the public was unaware of the near-death experience.

Kurt had slowly been killing himself with his heroin use for years, but now his efforts to end his life were becoming more serious. Following a tour stop in Munich, Germany, on March 1, 1994, Kurt was diagnosed with bronchitis and sever laryngitis. He flew to Rome the next day for medical treatment and was joined there by Courtney on March 3. The next morning, she woke to find that Kurt had overdosed on a combination of champagne and Rohypnol. He was immediately rushed to the hospital and was unconscious for the rest the day. He spent the next five days in the hospital before he was released to return to Seattle.

This was the beginning of the end for Kurt Cobain.

On March 18, Seattle police logged a call from Courtney, who informed them that Kurt was suicidal and had locked himself in a room with a gun. Officers arrived and confiscated several guns and a bottle of pills from Kurt, who insisted that he was not suicidal. He'd locked himself in the room to hide from Courtney, he said.

A week later, Courtney arranged an intervention for Kurt. Those involved included musician friends, record company executives, and one of his closest friends, Dylan Carlson. The intervention didn't go well at first. An angry Kurt insulted and yelled at everyone there and then locked himself in an upstairs bedroom. However, by the end of the day, he had agreed to a detox program. He returned to the Exodus Recovery Center in Los Angeles on March 30. The staff at the facility were aware of Kurt's drug program, but somehow, they were unaware of his history of depression and his suicide attempts.

His fans knew all about it but, amazingly, his doctors did not.

Friends who visited Kurt at the facility recalled that he seemed well. There was no indication that he was in any negative or suicidal state of mind. He spent the day talking to counselors about his drug abuse and personal problems and happily played with his daughter. These interactions at the facility were the last time that Frances saw her father alive.

On March 31, Kurt walked outside to have a cigarette and climbed over a six-foot-high fence to leave the facility. He took a taxi to the airport and got on the first flight back to Seattle. On the flight, he sat next to Duff McKagan of Guns N' Rose. Despite Kurt's hatred of the band – especially Axl Rose – he "seemed happy" to see Duff. They talked during the flight and Duff later stated that he knew from "all of my instructs that something was wrong."

At this point, none of his close friends or family members were aware that he was gone. The alert went out the next day. On April 2 and 3, Kurt was spotted in numerous locations around Seattle. He had become a ghost and sightings had to be questioned as to whether they were real or wishful thinking. On April 3, Courtney hired a private investigator to try and find him. Kurt was now nowhere to be found. Rumors swirled about Nirvana breaking up, especially on April 7, when the band pulled out of the 1994 Lollapalooza Festival.

But by that time, Kurt was already dead.

His body was found on April 8 in the living quarters above the garage of his Lake Washington Boulevard home. He was found by an electrician named Gary Smith, who had arrived to install a security system. At first, he thought Kurt was just sleeping – and then he saw the shotgun on his lap. A suicide note was found next to him. Toward the end he wrote, "I don't have the passion anymore, and so remember, it's better to burn out than to fade away."

There was a high concentration of heroin in his bloodstream, along with traces of diazepam. His body had been lying there for days – dead on April 5, 1994, at the age of 27.

There was a public vigil for Kurt on April 10, at a park at Seattle Center. More than 7,000 people showed up to mourn him, adding to the millions that were stunned by his death around the country.

No one was ready to let him go – not his wife, his daughter, his family, his friends, or his fans. Maybe that's the reason that so many controversies have raged about his death over the years.

Most believe that Kurt took his own life. He was clinically depressed, suffered from a persistent drug addiction, and left a handwritten suicide note behind that was addressed to his childhood imaginary friend. It's hard to believe that the note wasn't authentic. His friends believed it and so did most of his fans, even the ones who grieved over the loss.

But, as with so many other celebrity deaths, there were those who questioned the circumstances and suggested foul play and murder.

The first to publicly dispute the official report of suicide was Seattle public access host Richard Lee. A week after Kurt's death, he aired the first episode of a series he called "Kurt Cobain was Murdered," claiming there were discrepancies in the police reports, including problems with the nature of the shotgun blast. He claimed there was not enough blood at the scene for a point-blank shotgun blast to the head. But he had the story wrong. Kurt had put the shotgun in his mouth and pathology experts have explained that this usually results in less blood than a blast to the head.

But he wouldn't be the only one to question the story. The main proponent of the "foul play conspiracy" was Tom Grant, the private investigator that Courtney hired after Kurt disappeared from rehab. He was still working for her when the body was found, and he came to believe that Kurt was murdered.

His main contention was that, based on the amount of heroin in Kurt's bloodstream, he didn't think Kurt could have pulled the trigger. He believed the drug was used to incapacitate him so that the shotgun blast could be carried out by his killer. The issue was that this claim was based on estimates about heroin levels that were printed by the newspapers, not amounts that were in the official autopsy report. That information was not made available to the public.

While working for Courtney, Grant was given access to Kurt's suicide note and he used her fax machine to make a copy, which has since been widely distributed. He had his own take on what the letter meant. He claimed that it was a letter that Kurt wrote announcing his intention to leave Courtney, Seattle, and the music business and that the lines at the bottom – separate from the rest – were the only parts that implied he planned to commit suicide. The official report concluded that Kurt wrote the note, but Grant stated that the report did not distinguish these final lines from the rest of the note and assumed the entire thing was written by Kurt.

When the note was examined by handwriting experts, their findings didn't help clear up the confusion. Document examiner Janis Parker examined the original copy for two weeks and concluded that the note was written by Kurt. When *Dateline NBC* sent a copy of the note to four different handwriting experts, one concluded that the entire note was in Kurt's hand, while the other three said the sample was inconclusive – it was a photocopy, not the original note. That was the same problem that the series *Unsolved Mysteries* had when that show tried to clear up the issue, even though two of their experts found the writing, especially the last four lines, to be "suspicious."

Grant had other issues, too. He noted that the shotgun, a 20-gauge Remington Model 11, was not checked for fingerprints until May 6. The Seattle Police reports stated that the shotgun was inverted on Kurt's chest and his left hand was wrapped around the barrel. They managed to get four latent prints off the gun, but they weren't useable. Grant also claimed that Kurt's fingerprints were not found on the suicide note. Of course, none of this circumstantial evidence pointed to murder, but Grant believed that it supported his larger case.

Grant's main suspect? The woman who hired him – Courtney Love.

On March 3, 1994, Kurt was in a coma in Rome. At the time, his management agency, Gold Mountain Records, stated that Kurt had accidentally taken too many painkillers because he was suffering from influenza and fatigue. After his death, Courtney said this was a suicide attempt and told David Fricke from *Rolling Stone*, "He took 50 pills. He probably forgot how many he took. But there was a definite suicidal urge, to be gobbling and gobbling and gobbling."

But not everyone agreed. When contacted, Dr. Osvaldo Galletta, who treated Kurt after the incident, said that he didn't believe it was a suicide attempt. He said, "We can usually tell a suicide attempt. This didn't look like one to me." He also said that Kurt had not taken 50 pills, as Courtney claimed, although he did admit that Kurt's life had been saved by Courtney's intervention.

Grant, however, argued that. He believed that Courtney mixed a large quantity of pills into Kurt's champagne so that when he drank it, he unknowingly ingested the drugs – enough to kill him.

But if that's true, why did she call the police when she found him unconscious on the floor? If she wanted Kurt dead, why didn't she just leave him there until he died?

Grant couldn't be bothered with ideas that didn't fit his case. He insisted that the suicide attempt claims were not made until after Kurt was dead. He claimed that people close to Kurt, including his management agency, denied the characterization prior to his death. Grant believed that if the incident in Rome had truly been a suicide attempt, Kurt's friends and family would have been told so that they could have watched over him.

Others have asserted that the press spin that was put on the suicide attempt was simply to mask the efforts of what was happening with Kurt behind the scenes. Lee Ranaldo, guitarist for Sonic Youth, told *Rolling Stone*, "Rome was the latest installment of [those around Cobain] keeping a semblance of normalcy for the outside world."

In the end, Grant's claims – along with those of others who have tried to make the case that Kurt was murdered – have been dismissed, by the police and by the public at large.

Sergeant Donald Cameron, one of the homicide detectives involved in the case, specifically dismissed Grant's theory, stating, "[Grant] hasn't shown us a shred of proof that this was anything other than suicide."

It was easy to grasp at straws – to wish that things were different than they really were. Most of Kurt's friends and family understood that he had taken his own life. They hated it, but they understood it. Kurt had been on a downward spiral for years, maybe even dating back all the way to his parents' divorce. His suicide might even have been inevitable.

But that didn't make it hurt any less. Dave Grohl said that news of Kurt's death, "was probably the worst thing that has happened to me in my life. I remember the day after that I woke up and I was heartbroken that he was gone. I just felt like, 'Okay, so I get to wake up today and have another day and he doesn't.'"

Needless to say, I didn't know Kurt Cobain, but I remember when he died, and I remember how it felt to those of us who loved his music. I had been a fan of Nirvana, but it wasn't until their MTV *Unplugged* episode that I truly appreciated Kurt, I guess. The news was bad, but it wasn't surprising.

I mean, this had to be one of the least surprising rock deaths ever. Kurt had been threatening suicide for so long that it had become a guessing game as to when he would do it, and how. He'd posed for more photos with guns than the newspapers could print. The "celebrity" we knew as Kurt Cobain was gone -- as opposed to the musician who had written all his songs and sung them. The Kurt from the tabloids was dead, just like we expected, but the guy who played his music on *Unplugged* was a little harder to let go of.

I found it hard to connect the two sides of Kurt Cobain. His death wasn't a surprise, but it was hard to wrap my head around the idea that there would be no more new music. My favorite Nirvana song has always been "Heart-Shaped Box," about the fear of having someone in your life that you can't let go of. People like to claim that all his songs were all about the pressures of fame, but that one wasn't. That was a song we could all relate to – at least I could.

I still listen to him sing and I think I've grown to like him more the longer he's been dead. He was one of the few musicians that was my age, worrying about the same things that I was worrying about, in a fucked-up marriage and yet writing songs about it that seemed real. And he was about the same age I was when he died. Maybe that's why I can connect, I don't know.

But I do know that I've gotten older, while Kurt Cobain will always be 27.

The Seattle music scene had one more death to add to the 27 Club. On June 16, 1994, Kristen Pfaff, the bass player for the band Hole – which was fronted by Kurt Cobain's wife, Courtney Love – was found dead in her apartment, the victim of a heroin overdose. She died, like so many others in the Club, with her potential untapped.

Kristen Pfaff

Kristen Marie Pfaff was born May 26, 1967, in Buffalo, New York. Her mother remarried when Kristen was a toddler, taking the surname of her new husband Norman Pfaff. Together, the Pfaff's had a son, Jason. The Pfaff children seemed to have an aptitude for music. Kristen was a child prodigy of sorts, showing early skill as a cellist and a classical pianist. After graduating from Catholic school Buffalo Academy of the Sacred Heart in 1985, she spent a short time in Europe and briefly attended Boston College before ultimately finishing at the University of Minnesota, where she majored in Women's Studies with a minor in English. She was also DJ for the college radio station.

While at the University of Minnesota, Kristen volunteered to provide support for victims of sexual assault, rape, and domestic violence as a counselor. She was a part of Restore of the Sexual Violence Program, which offered a crisis line, counseling services, and training in self-defense programs. As an activist, she organized the 24-Hour No Rape Zone, which has, since 1990, been an annual event on campus.

While living in Minneapolis, Kristen circled back around to her love of music and, inspired by the spirit of punk rock, taught herself to play bass guitar. She later crossed paths with local musician Joachim Breuer and the two forged a songwriting partnership. With drummer Matthew Entsminger, they teamed up to start a band – Janitor Joe.

They soon became a staple of the Minneapolis sound, influenced by the Pacific Northwest's grunge sound and the sharper, faster post-hardcore scene. In 1992, they began touring the country and pressing singles to sell at their shows. By 1993, they had started to attract a lot of press attention and after a California show, Kristen was scouted by Eric Erlandson and Courtney Love of Hole, who were looking for a new bassist. Courtney invited Kristen to play with them, but Kristen passed and returned to Minneapolis.

But Eric and Courtney continued to pursue her. After thinking it over – and getting advice from her father, Norman – Kristen decided to move to Seattle and join the band. She became the bassist for Hole and contributed to the songwriting process. Those songs eventually turned into *Live Through This*, which became the band's most successful and acclaimed album.

While living in Seattle, Kristen formed close friendships with Eric Erlandson and Kurt Cobain. She and Eric dated for a time, staying together through most of 1993, and remaining close even after breaking up. But things weren't perfect. While living in Washington's "heroin capital," she developed a problem with drugs. As Courtney Love said about this period, "Everybody was doing it. Everyone, everyone. All our friends were junkies. It was ridiculous. Everybody in this town did dope."

By most accounts, Kristen's own drug use was relatively moderate. She had dabbled in drugs in Minneapolis and when she moved to Seattle, she felt disconnected from everything, so as she made friends, she also made drug connections, which led to her downfall.

Things got bad enough that Kristen decided to go back home. She entered a Minneapolis detox center for heroin addiction in February 1994. She took some time off from Hole that spring to tour with Janitor Joe – and then got the news that Kurt Cobain was dead.

She took it hard and in the wake of his suicide, decided to leave Hole and return to Minneapolis permanently. When the tour with Janitor Joe was finished, she returned to Seattle to retrieve her belongings and move home.

She never made it.

Around 9:30 AM on June 16, 1994, Kristen was found dead in her apartment by Paul Erickson, a friend with whom she planned to leave with for Minneapolis that day. On the floor, there was a bag containing syringes and drug paraphernalia. Kristen's death was attributed to "acute opiate intoxication."

Her death was a perfect example of so much wasted talent. Her father, Norman Pfaff, perhaps said it best: "She was a bright, personable, wonderful...very, very talented, smart, and she always seemed to be in control of her circumstances. Last night she wasn't."

Perhaps more of an unsolved mystery than an actual death, Richey Edwards, writer and guitar player for the alternative band the Manic Street Preachers, vanished on February 1, 1995, the day he was set to leave England and go to America for a promotional tour. No trace of him has ever been found – and he has been declared legally dead – so perhaps this is a case of the "curse" of the 27 Club after all.

Richey Edwards was born and raised in Blackwood, Wales. He had one younger sister, Rachel, who was born in 1969. After finishing at the Oakdale

Richey Edwards

Comprehensive School, he attended the University of Wales and graduated with a degree in political history.

There was one thing that Richey was not – a musician. He was initially a driver and roadie for the Manic Street Preachers, but he soon became accepted as the band's main spokesman and fourth member. He wasn't involved in the music so much as he was a huge part of the band's lyrics and design. He frequently pretended to play guitar during the band's early performances but was, along with bassist Nicky Wire, their principal lyricist. Musical input or not, there was no question that he contributed to the overall musical direction of the band.

He gained his first notoriety in 1991. On May 15, after an argument with a journalist who questioned the band's authenticity and values, trying to make sure that the punk ethic was not being abused, he asked about Richey's seriousness toward his art. In response, Richey carved the words "4 REAL" into his forearm with a razor blade. The wound ended up requiring 18 stitches, but I suppose he made his point.

Most will not be surprised to learn that Richey suffered severe bouts of depression and was open about it in his interviews. He also self-harmed, mainly putting out cigarettes on his body and cutting himself. As he told one interviewer: "When I cut myself, I feel so much better. All the little things that might have been annoying me suddenly seem so trivial because I'm concentrating on the pain. I'm not a person who can scream and shout, so this is my only outlet. It's all done very logically."

Things became so bad that after the release of the album *The Holy Bible*, Richey checked himself into The Priory psychiatric hospital. He missed out on some of the promotional events for the album and forced the band to perform without him at the Reading Festival.

After his release from the hospital, the Manic Street Preachers toured Europe for what was to be the last time. Richey's final appearance with the band was at the London Astoria on December 21, 1994. The show ended with the band infamously smashing their equipment and damaging the lighting system. At the end of the set closer, Richey violently destroyed his guitar before leaving the stage. No one can say that he didn't go out with a bang.

Then, on February 1, 1995, Richey disappeared.

He was scheduled to leave with James Dean Bradfield that day to fly to the United States on a promotional tour. But it's clear in hindsight that he had no intention of going. In the two weeks before the trip, Richey had withdrawn £200 each day from his bank account, which eventually totaled up to £2,800 by the day of the scheduled flight. On the night before he vanished, he also allegedly gave a friend a book called *Novel with Cocaine*, instructing her to read the introduction, which details the author staying in a mental asylum before vanishing.

On the night before the trip, Richey was staying at the Embassy Hotel in Bayswater Road, London. The next morning, he collected his wallet, car keys, some Prozac, and his passport. He checked out of the hotel at 7:00 AM, leaving his toiletries, packed suitcase, and some of his Prozac behind in his room. He then drove to his apartment in Cardiff and – officially, anyway – was never seen again.

However, in the two weeks that followed, Richey was apparently spotted in the Newport passport office and at the Newport bus station by a fan who did not know he was missing. On February 7, a taxi driver from Newport supposedly picked up Richey from the King's Hotel and drove him around, including to Richey's hometown of Blackwood. The driver reported that the passenger had spoken in a Cockney accent, which occasionally slipped into a Welsh one, and that he asked if he could lie down on the back seat. The driver was eventually directed to the Blackwood bus station but then the passenger reportedly said, "this is not the place." He then asked to be taken to the Pontypool railway station. He paid the £68 fare in cash.

On February 14, Richey's car, a Vauxhall Cavalier, received a parking ticket at the Severn View service station, and three days later, the vehicle was reported as abandoned. The police discovered the battery to be dead and noted that it looked as though the car had been lived in. Due to the station's proximity to the Severn Bridge – a known suicide spot – it was widely believed that Richey had taken his own life by jumping from the bridge.

His friends and family didn't believe it, though. They said that he was not the type to commit suicide, and in fact, Richey himself was quoted in 1994 as saying, "In terms of the 'S' word, that does not enter my mind. And it never has been done, in terms of an attempt. Because I am stronger than that. I might be a weak person, but I can take pain."

So, if Richey didn't kill himself, where did he go? Since his disappearance, he has been reportedly spotted in a market in Goa, India, and on the islands of Fuerteventura and Lanzarote. There have been many other alleged sightings of Richey, too, mostly in the years following his disappearance. However, none of them proved conclusive and none of them were confirmed by investigators.

Investigators who, by most accounts, didn't try very hard to find him. The police have been roundly criticized by fans, family members, and many journalists, who assert that detectives didn't prioritize his disappearance due to his ongoing mental issues. They even dismissed the idea of analyzing CCTV footage of the area where his car was found because, as one investigator allegedly said, "the idea that you could identify somebody from that is arrant nonsense."

Richey's family had the option of declaring him legally dead starting in 2002 but chose not to for many years. His status remained open as a missing person until 2008. At that point, he became officially "presumed dead," but they've never really given up hope.

Richey is still out there somewhere, many believe, but whether or not he'll ever choose to return to his old life remains another mystery.

In the early 2000s, Amy Winehouse became a commercial and critical hit with her eclectic mix of musical genres. But like so many other members of the Club, success only hastened her death. Long troubled by drugs and alcohol, she was found dead in her London home on July 23, 2011. After her death, her most popular album, 2006's *Back to Black* – which included her song "Rehab" – became the bestselling album in the UK in the twenty-first century.

This makes you wonder – what could she have achieved if she had lived?

Amy Jade Winehouse was born on September 14, 1983 in Chase Farm Hospital in North London. Her father, Mitchell, was a window panel installer, then taxi driver, and her mother, Janis, was a pharmacist. Amy's family was descended from Russian and Polish Jews who immigrated to London. When Amy was a girl, she attended Osidge Primary School and attended a Jewish Sunday school, but she never liked it. In fact, she begged her father not to send her. She was Jewish, but she wasn't religious and in interviews, said she only went to synagogue once a year, on Yom Kippur, "out of respect." When Amy was nine, her parents separated, and she lived with her mother and with her father and his girlfriend in Essex on weekends. Unlike Kurt Cobain, Amy wasn't shattered by her parents' split. Her life was probably better because of it.

Some would say that she had music in her blood. Several of her uncles were professional jazz musicians and her father often sang old Sinatra songs

Amy Winehouse

to her. Whenever she got into trouble at school, she would sing "Fly Me to the Moon" before going to the office of the headmistress.

In 1992, her grandmother, Cynthia, suggested that Amy attend the Susi Earnshaw Theatre School and it was there that she took vocal lessons and learned to tap dance. She stayed for four years before seeking full-time training at the Sylvia Young Theatre School but then left at 14. She was either expelled or changed schools, depending on which version of the story is being told.

That same year, Amy bought her first guitar and began writing music. Soon after, she started working for a living, spending time as an entertainment journalist and singing with a local group. In July 2000, she became the featured vocalist with the National Youth Orchestra. She was greatly influenced by jazz, soul and R&B music, which soon became apparent to friends like soul singer Tyler James, who started passing around a demo tape that Amy had made. In 2002, she was signed to Simon Fuller's 19 Management and was £250 a week against future earnings.

While Amy was being developed by the management company – singing jazz standards at the Cobden Club -- she was kept secret from the recording industry. Her future rep at Island Records, Darcus Beese, heard her by accident when the manager of the Lewinson Brothers was playing him some music that featured Amy as key vocalist. When he asked who the singer was, the manager told him that he was not allowed to say. Hoping to sign her, it took several months of asking around for Beese to eventually discover who she was. By then, however, Amy had already recorded several songs and was close to signing a publishing deal with EMI.

But Beese didn't give up. He introduced Amy to his boss, Nick Gatfield, who shared his enthusiasm for signing the young artist. Amy ended up with Island and work was started on her debut album, *Frank*, which was released in 2003. The album was influenced by jazz and, aside from two covers, every song was co-written by Amy. The album received positive reviews and entered the upper levels of the UK charts in 2004. It also received a number of awards and sent Amy out on her first national and international tours.

In the midst of her success, Amy's demons began to appear – and they would return many times over in the years to come. She battled with substance abuse, issues exacerbated by the media, who loved to draw attention to them. In 2005, she went through a period of drinking, heavy drug use and weight loss, however, friends who saw her during the end of that year and in early 2006 reported a rebound that coincided with the writing of her next album.

That album – *Back to Black* – stepped away from the jazz influence of her first album and shifted toward the girl groups of the 1950s and 1960s. Amy hired New York singer Sharon Jones's longtime band, the Dap-Kings, to back her up in the studio and on tour. The album, completed in five months was produced by Amy's producer for *Frank*, Salaam Remi and Mark Ronson. The album was released in October 2006 and went to number one on the UK charts. In the U.S., it entered at number seven on the Billboard 200. It became the best-selling album of 2007.

Back to Black produced a number of singles, not the least of which was "Rehab," a song about refusing to go to rehab to get help for what family and friends saw as a young woman dealing with dangerous addictions.

The song could not have been more on the nose.

Amy toured in conjunction with the album's release, performing headliners in September and November 2006, including a charity concert at the Union Chapel in Islington, North London. On New Year's Eve, she appeared on Jools Holland's Annual Hootenanny, live on the BBC, and covered Marvin Gaye's "I Heard it Through the Grapevine."

She began a run of another 14 shows, beginning in February 2007, and that's when things started going off the rails. At his request, actor Bruce Willis introduced Amy before her performance of "Rehab" at the 2007 MTV Movie Awards – a performance that no one was sure was going to happen. Amy had gone off on a Las Vegas jaunt in the hours before the show, making the awards organizers very nervous.

That summer, she performed at various festivals, including the Isle of Wight Festival and Glastonbury in England, Lollapalooza in Chicago, Belgium's Rock Werchter, and the Virgin Music Festival in Baltimore.

The rest of the tour, however, didn't go so well.

In August 2007, the opening night of a 17-date tour was marred by booing and walkouts at the National Indoor Arena in Birmingham. A newspaper critic said it was "one of the saddest nights of my life...I saw a supremely talented artist reduced to tears, stumbling around the stage and, unforgivably, swearing at the audience." Other concerts ended the same way with, for example, fans at her Hammersmith Apollo show in London saying that she "looked highly intoxicated throughout."

On November 27, it was announced that her performances and public appearances had been canceled for the remainder of the year. Her reps cited her doctor's advice that she needed a complete rest. In reality, she was in the hospital after an overdose of heroin, ecstasy, cocaine, ketamine, and alcohol. She had already spoken in interviews about having problems with depression and eating disorders but blamed drugs for her hospitalization. "I really thought it was over for me then," she said. Amy entered into a physician-supervised program to help with her addictions and then a rehabilitation facility for a two-week treatment program.

Some believed that Amy's problems grew worse when she started a relationship with Blake Fielder-Civil, a former video production assistant who had dropped out of school and went to live on his own at age 16. They had a tumultuous, often violent, relationship that involved both alcohol and drugs. In August 2007, they were photographed, bloodied and bruised, in the streets of London after an alleged fight, although she contended her injuries were self-inflicted. Despite the on and off relationship of fights and break-ups, they were married in Miami Beach, Florida in May 2007.

Amy Winehouse was now becoming known less for her music and more for her train-wreck private life, which was being played out very publicly in the tabloids.

Amy's parents – along with her new in-laws – publicly spoke out about their concerns over the marriage, later citing fears that the two might commit suicide together. Blake's father encouraged fans to boycott Amy's music, while Mitchell Whitehouse was arguing against that, saying it wouldn't help. Blake contributed to the chaos after being quoted by a British tabloid saying that he had introduced Amy to crack and heroine and said that he and Amy often cut themselves to ease the pain of withdrawal.

In July 2007, Blake was involved in a fight with a pub landlord which ended with the other man suffering a broken cheekbone. Blake ended up in jail – not for the fight but for the cover-up that ensued. According to the prosecution at his trial for perverting the course of justice and grievous bodily harm with intent, the prosecution stated that the landlord the accepted £200,000 as part of a deal to "effectively throw the [court] case and not turn up." Blake – again, not helping the situation – claimed that the money belonged to Amy, but she had pulled out of a meeting with the men involved in the plot so that she could attend an awards ceremony. Blake was imprisoned from July 21, 2008 to February 25, 2009.

In the months leading up to Blake serving his prison sentence, Amy spun further out of control. On April 26, 2008, Amy admitted to police that she had slapped a man in the face, a "common assault" offense, her first of two. She voluntarily turned herself in and was held overnight. The police said that, at her arrival, she was "in no fit state" to be interviewed. Ten days later, she was arrested on suspicion of possessing drugs after a view of her apparently smoking crack cocaine was given to the police. However, she was released a few hours later because it could not be confirmed just what she was smoking in the video. She was cleared by the Crown Prosecution Service, since they could not make their case, but did succeed in charging two London residents with conspiracy to supply Amy with cocaine and ecstasy.

Needless to say, her erratic behavior seemed to prove that Amy's drug rehabilitation efforts had been unsuccessful, leading her father and manager to seek assistance in having her detained under the Mental Health Act of 1983. Even though her physician would claim that she quit using illegal substances in 2008, her drinking continued to be a problem. She was treated for alcohol withdrawal and anxiety, but continued problematic behaviors made it clear that she frequently relapsed.

Although her father, manager, and various members of her touring team reportedly tried to dissuade her, Amy performed at the Rock in Rio Lisboa Festival in Portugal in May 2008. Although the set was plagued by a late arrival and problems with her voice, the crowd warmed to her. Amy also performed at Nelson Mandela's 90th Birthday Party concert at London's Hyde Park on June 27, and the next day at the Glastonbury Festival. In July, she performed twice in Ireland and on August 16, she played at the Staffordshire part of the V Festival, and the following day played another part of the festival in Chelmsford. Organizers said that Amy attracted the biggest crowds of the entire event – although audience reaction was mixed.

On September 6, she was the Saturday headliner for Bestival. Her performance was described as "polished" but was cut off by a curfew because the show was running late. Amy had started an hour behind schedule. She stormed off the stage when given the news that she had to cut her performance short.

The latter part of 2008 – while Blake was in jail and she was effectively cut off from him – was a good time for Amy. *Back to Black* was the world's seventh-biggest-selling album in 2008 and, for the most part, her performances were well-received.

When Amy was seen with actor Josh Bowman on holiday in Saint Lucia, in early January 2009, she said she was "in love again and I don't need drugs." She commented that her "whole marriage was based on doing drugs" and that "for the time being, I've just forgotten that I'm even married."

On January 12, Blake's attorney sued for divorce on claims of adultery, but two months later, Amy told a reporter, "I still love Blake and want him to move into my new house with me – that was my plan all along... I won't let him divorce me. He's the male version of me and we're perfect for each other."

Nonetheless, an uncontested divorce was granted on July 16, 2009, and became final on August 28. Blake received no money in the settlement.

Meanwhile, Amy's life was already crashing down around her.

On March 5 – around the time that Amy was under the delusion that she and Blake were going to patch things up – she was arrested and charged with common assault following a claim that she had punched a woman in the eye during an appearance at a charity ball in September 2008. Amy's rep announced the cancellation of her performance at the Coachella Festival in the U.S. in light of the new legal issue. Amy appeared in court on March 17 to enter a plea of not guilty. On July 23, her trial began with the prosecution charging that Amy acted with "deliberate and unjustifiable violence" while appearing to be under the influence of alcohol or some other substance. But Amy testified that she did not punch the victim, Sharene Flash, but tried to push her away because she was scared of her. She said Flash was much larger than she was and behaved very "rudely." On July 24, District Judge Timothy Workman ruled that Amy was not guilty, stating that all but two of the witnesses were intoxicated at the time of the incident and that medical evidence did not show "the sort of injury that often occurs when there is a forceful punch to the eye."

Amy managed to avoid prosecution that time, but she wouldn't be so lucky in December when she was arrested again. This time around, she was charged with common assault, plus another charge of public order offense after assaulting the front-of-hour manager of the Milton Keynes Theatre after he asked her to move from her seat. Amy pled guilty and was given a conditional discharge.

Amy continued to perform but things didn't always go well. At one point, at a jazz festival where she was unsteady on her feet and had trouble remembering lyrics, she apologized to the audience for being "bored" and ended the set in the middle of a song. Later in 2010, she performed the song "Valerie" with Mark Ronson at a movie premiere but forgot some of the song's lyrics. In January 2011, she played five dates in Brazil, with opening acts of Janelle Monae and Mayer Hawthorne, but in February, she cut short a performance in Dubai after she was booed by the crowd. Amy was reported to be tired, distracted, and "tipsy" during the performance.

In June 2011, Amy started her 12-nights European tour in Belgrade. Local media described her performance as a "scandal" and "disaster." She was booed off the stage because she was too drunk to perform. It was reported that she was unable to remember what city she was in, the lyrics of her songs, and – when she tried to introduce them – the members of her band. Reporters also claimed that Amy was forced to perform by her bodyguards, who didn't let her leave the stage when she tried to do so. In the wake of the show, she pulled out of performances in Istanbul and Athens, which had been scheduled for the following week. On June 21, it was announced that she had canceled all the shows on the tour and would be given "as long as it takes" to get things sorted out.

But, tragically, Amy would never get things sorted out.

Amy's bodyguard, Andrew Morris, said that Amy drank vodka on the last day of her life. He wouldn't say that she was "drunk." He'd seen Amy drunk too many times to use the word lightly. She was drinking moderately – for Amy.

He was at the house all day, aside from leaving for a few minutes to pick up some milk from the store. When he returned, Amy was in the kitchen having a snack of celery and a dip. Then she went up to her room, where she listened to music, watched TV, and surfed the internet.

Amy hated to be alone but had trouble finding company that day. She talked with a friend who was busy with a show and didn't have time to talk. She spoke with a member of her band. Her attempts to get in touch with other friends failed. It was a busy music festival weekend and many of them were in Cambridgeshire.

There were a lot of missed calls and to comfort herself, Amy drank. She drank vodka more or less constantly during the last three days of her life. It's sad that this had become ordinary for Amy's life. Her entourage considered it normal behavior. "She was drinking normally. She didn't appear drunk," Andrew Morris later said.

It was also a mark of how low Amy had fallen -- and how strange her life had become – that her doctor came regularly to her home. Around 7:00 PM, Amy received a final home visit from Dr. Cristina Romete, who said, "She was tipsy, I would say, but she didn't slur her words, and she was able to hold a full conversation." She told the doctor that she was drinking because she was bored. The doctor was satisfied that she wasn't suicidal. "She specifically said that she didn't want to die," she later told the police, adding that Amy said she had things that she still wanted to do.

Amy spent much of the rest of the evening watching You Tube with Andrew Morris. About 2:30 AM, Andrew went to his own room to watch a movie. He could still hear Amy moving around upstairs.

Amy was alone at the end. Andrew was in the house, but she was alone in her room. As a result, there's no way to know what she did at the last, or what she consumed, but it's likely that she drank more vodka, judging by the postmortem results and the empty bottles found in her room.

She drank herself into a stupor in the early morning hours and then she laid down to sleep as the sky was starting to brighten with the dawn. She went to sleep, and she never woke up again.

Andrew Morris checked on Amy around 10:00 AM on Saturday, July 23. She was lying on the bed and he assumed she was asleep, so he left her alone. Amy usually slept late, so this was not out of the ordinary.

He went about his day and after realizing that Amy was still not out of bed, he returned to her room, shortly after 3:00 PM. She was in the same position as before and he attempted to wake her up. Amy didn't stir. And then he realized that she wasn't breathing and called emergency services.

Two ambulances arrived at Amy's house at 3:54 PM. She was pronounced dead at the scene. Once the Metropolitan Police announced her death, media and camera crews descended on the scene. Crowds gathered on the streets outside to weep, mourn, gawk, and to pay their respects. When her autopsy report was made public, it was discovered that Amy's blood alcohol content was more than five times the legal limit. As the coroner understated it, "The unintended consequences of such potentially fatal levels was her sudden death."

Amy made a big impact on popular music in a short career without doing very much or going very far. She lived her whole life in London, her homes within a few miles of each other, a short distance away from the cemetery where she was buried.

Amy had told her doctor that she still had things that she wanted to do. Sadly, she would never do them. Her life was cut short by her own excess, just like almost all the others who will be forever linked to her by the "curse" of the club that none of them wanted to join.

For those of you who are playing along at home, I'm sure you're thinking that I forgot one of the most famous members of the 27 Club -- Doors lead singer, Jim Morrison.

Jim Morrison

Well, I didn't forget. I left him out on purpose. And you're probably wondering why.

The official story says that on July 3, 1971, the body of Jim Morrison was discovered in a bathtub in his Paris apartment. He had died from a heroin overdose – a drug he supposedly never used – and his death certificate was quickly signed by a French doctor who apparently never existed. The official word says he was quickly buried in a Paris cemetery and the story of Jim Morrison was over. But was it really?

There are many who insist that Jim didn't die that day in Paris. They claim that he vanished into history – exactly as he always planned to do. Tired of the life of a rock star, he simply walked away from it one day and let the world believe he was dead. Did Jim fake his death in order to escape a life that he had grown to despise?

Consider the evidence – or, in some cases, lack of it – and decide for yourself.

Jim Morrison was known for living life on the edge. He was rock singer, poet, and some say, a shaman who was haunted by a vision that he had when he was only four-years-old. Later in life, he told the story of being with his family as they drove across the desert. At dawn, they came upon a terrible accident that involved a group of Native American workers. Jim described the scene in the song "Dawn's Highway," claiming that he was able to see the spirits of the Indians that died on the road that day, and that one or two of them leapt into his soul. He carried them with him for the rest of his life, he said, and they became his spirit guides, often guiding his movements during concerts. On stage, Jim controlled an audience like no other singer, before or since. His lyrics became almost hypnotic and when he called for action, the crowd responded. Promoters often feared that Doors' concerts could easily turn into riots since Morrison seemed to have an eerie ability to get the audience to do anything he wanted.

Jim had a difficult childhood. His father was an admiral in the U.S. Navy, but Jim, even at an early age, was a nonconformist. He never got along with his parents, and later, after achieving stardom, lied to interviewers and told them his family was dead. He was a voracious reader with a high IQ and was inspired by the works of Nietzsche, Kerouac, Ginsberg, Plutarch, Dylan Thomas, James Joyce, and Moliere, but his greatest inspiration came from Arthur Rimbaud.

Rimbaud was a nineteenth-century French poet who believed that all poets should live their lives in derangement of the senses. The poet must know all kinds of love and suffer through the most incredible pain. By living a life of excess, the poet would then receive his greatest visions. Rimbaud completed his poetry by the time that he was 19 and then disappeared to follow his teachings. He traveled the world, gladly living in squalor, sleeping on the streets and seeking out the tragedy that he believed he was destined to face. Rimbaud only returned to his former life when he became ill with cancer. He died at age 37.

Jim tried to remain faithful to Rimbaud's example. After The Doors had achieved success, he lived in filthy conditions in the cheap hotels and sought his own destiny in excessive drinking and in copious amounts of sex. Jim's favorite quote was from William Blake – "The road to excess leads to the palace of wisdom."

While searching for his own voice, Jim wound up at UCLA studying filmmaking. It was there that he met Ray Manzarek and The Doors were formed. Manzarek became the keyboardist who composed the musical scores for Jim's poetry. The name of the band came from Aldous Huxley's book, *The Doors of Perception*, which described his drug experiences with mescaline and LSD.

As the band achieved fame, Jim began pushing everything to the edge. Others saw his brazen stunts and wild drinking binges as a death wish. They told tales of high-speed drunken car rides and walks on building ledges high above city streets. Jim was willing to try anything once, including the occult. In June 1970, he was allegedly married to Patricia Keneally, a practicing witch,

The Doors: Jim Morrison, Ray Manzarek, Robbie Krieger, and John Densmore

in a blood-letting ceremony that ended with them drinking their combined blood in a chalice.

Even though Jim was involved with countless women, Pamela Courson provided a haven for him to replenish his creative powers. She believed him to be a great poet and he took care of her for reasons known only to himself. It was not a perfect relationship and, at times, each seemed to be determined to bring as much pain upon the other as possible, but both seemed to embrace the idea that love and hate are our two strongest emotions. Pamela and Jim were part of a symbiotic relationship that lasted throughout their tragic – and possibly short – lives.

The Doors shot to fame almost in spite of themselves – or at least in spite of Jim, who claimed that he never wanted to be a rock star. Regardless, his reputation as the "Lizard King" and his masterful control of audiences begged otherwise. But Jim had never stopped trying to challenge his own success and on March 1, 1969, at the Dinner Key Auditorium in Miami's Coconut Grove neighborhood, Jim gave the most controversial performance of his career – one that almost derailed the band for good. The auditorium was a converted seaplane hangar that had no air conditioning on that hot night, and the seats had been removed by the promoter in order to boost ticket sales. Jim had been drinking all day and had missed connecting flights to Miami, and by the time he eventually arrived, the concert was over an hour late in starting. Jim was drunk, the audience was restless, and the situation was boiling out of control.

Pamela Courson

The crowd of 12,000, packed into a facility designed to hold 7,000, was subjected to Jim's lack of interest in singing soon after starting "Break on Through (To the Other Side.)" He taunted the crowd, calling them idiots, and then begging them to love him. At one point, Jim removed the hat of an onstage police officer, who was there for security, and threw it into the crowd. The officer, in turn, removed Jim's hat and tossed it into the crowd. Things were still good-natured at this point, but it was turning ugly fast. Doors' manager Bill Siddons would later remember the night as "bizarre" and "circus-like."

An audience member jumped onto the stage and poured champagne on Jim, so he took off his wet shirt and encouraged the audience to "get naked." Moments later, some of them began taking their clothes off. Having removed his shirt, Jim held it in front of his groin area and started to make hand movements behind it. Even though he never exposed himself, some onlookers believed that he had. It would be an incident that would have stunning repercussions for the band.

On March 5, the Dade County Sheriff's Office issued a warrant for Jim's arrest claiming he had deliberately exposed his penis while on stage, shouted obscenities to the crowd, simulated oral sex on guitarist Robby Krieger, and was drunk at the time of his performance. Jim turned down a plea bargain that required The Doors to perform a free Miami concert. He was later convicted, sentenced to six months in jail, with hard labor, and ordered to pay a $500 fine. Jim remained free pending an appeal of his conviction, and due to his reported death, the legal matter was never resolved. Band members John Densmore, Robby Krieger, Ray Manzarek, and even some of the police officers present that night denied the allegation that Jim exposed himself on stage.

During the recording of their next album, in November 1969, Jim once again found himself in trouble with the law after harassing airline staff during a flight to Phoenix, Arizona to see The Rolling Stones in concert. The charges against Jim were dropped in April 1970, after an airline flight attendant reversed her testimony to say she had mistakenly identified Jim's friend, Tom Baker, as Jim.

In 1970, The Doors released their fifth album, *Morrison Hotel*, and their first live album, *Absolutely Live*. The critics called *Morrison Hotel* a "return to form," but by this time, Jim was burning out. The Doors performed in arenas throughout the summer, and even though Jim faced trial in Miami in August, the group made it to the Isle of Wight Festival on August 29. They performed alongside artists such as Jimi Hendrix, The Who, Joni Mitchell, Leonard Cohen, Miles Davis, Emerson, Lake & Palmer, and Sly and the Family Stone.

On December 8, 1970, his 27th birthday, Jim recorded another poetry session, but fans were anxious for the release of the new Doors album, *L.A. Woman*. The tour to promote the new album-- by Jim's demands -- would be only two dates. The first was held in Dallas on December 11. During the band's last public performance with Jim, at The Warehouse in New Orleans on December 12, 1970, Jim apparently had a breakdown on stage. Midway through the set he slammed the microphone numerous times into the floor until the platform beneath it was destroyed, then sat down, and refused to perform for the remainder of the show. After the New Orleans show, the band decided to end their live act, mutually agreeing that Jim was ready to retire from performing.

L.A. Woman turned out to be one of the band's greatest albums. It contained two Top 20 hits and went on to be their second best-selling studio album, surpassed in sales only by their debut. The singles "L.A. Woman," "Love Her Madly," and "Riders on the Storm" remain mainstays of rock radio programming, with the last of these being inducted into the Grammy Hall of Fame for its special significance to recorded music. In the song "L.A. Woman," Jim scrambled the letters of his own name to chant "Mr. Mojo Risin' " – a phrase that would soon have special significance to some of the band's insiders.

On March 13, 1971, Jim took a leave of absence from The Doors and moved to Paris with Pamela Courson. He had visited the city the previous summer and was interested in moving there to become a writer in exile. They took up residence in a third-floor apartment at 17 Rue Beautreillis. Jim went for long walks through the city. He had left the United States to concentrate on writing poetry. After all, he had always considered himself a poet first and never seriously regarded himself as a rock star. In Paris, Jim seemed to be

Jim and Pamela – it was said that she'd have done anything for him.
Would she have helped him fake his death?

making peace with himself. He shaved his beard and lost some of the weight he had gained in the previous months.

It is here where the ultimate legend surrounding Jim Morrison begins.

On the night of July 2, 1971, Jim attended a movie, *Pursued*, starring Robert Mitchum – or so some believe. Where he went after the movie is a matter of speculation. The reports of his activity that evening are filled with contradictions. Some say he went to the Rock 'n' Roll Circus, a hangout for heroin addicts, where he bought some heroin and overdosed in the club's bathroom. This story claims he was carried out the back door and dumped at his apartment. Others say that he left home, telling Pamela that he was going to a movie and instead went to the airport, where he was seen boarding a plane. Or maybe he just walked all night. Or he went to the movie and returned to the apartment, where he complained that he wasn't feeling well and was going to take a bath. It was this last story that gained the most exposure, but whatever happened on that Friday night, by Monday morning, July 5, Jim was rumored to be dead.

Newspapers in England began calling the London offices of Elektra Records, The Doors' record label. No one there could verify that Jim was alive. The papers had heard that he had died in his Paris apartment.

The big questions were – how did the rumor start? And was it really true this time?

Jim had been reported to be dead many times before. Clive Selwood, who ran Elektra's London office, called the company's office in France for verification. No one in the Paris office even knew that Jim was in the city. Clive then called the American Embassy and the Paris police. Both denied any knowledge of the death of an American named Jim Morrison. Clive then decided to call Doors' manager Bill Siddons, who laughed when he heard Clive's concern, knowing that Jim was supposed to have died dozens of times before – and still hadn't.

Siddons promised to call Jim and set things straight. Pamela answered the phone and said that he'd better come right over, as if Paris was just down the street. Concerned that something might really be wrong, Siddons booked a seat on the next flight. Before leaving, he called Ray Manzarek and told him that Jim might be dead. Manzarek was skeptical but he told Siddons to call as soon as he knew anything for certain.

Siddons arrived in Paris on Tuesday, July 6. He was met at the apartment by Pamela, a sealed coffin, and a signed death certificate. Funeral arrangements had been quickly – and secretly – made. On July 7, Pamela filed the death certificate with the American Embassy, identifying Jim as James Douglas Morrison, a poet. She said that he had no living relatives. The official cause of death was a heart attack.

The burial took place the following day at Pere Lachaise, the Paris cemetery where many famous people are buried. Jim had recently visited there, seeking the graves of Edith Piaf, Oscar Wilde, Balzac, and Chopin. Only five mourners were present at the service: Pamela, Siddons, and three Paris friends. When it was over, Siddons helped Pamela pack up her and Jim's belongings. On Thursday, they returned to Los Angeles, where Siddons announced what little he knew. Pamela, reportedly, was in shock and resting.

Jim Morrison, by all accounts, was dead.

But was he really?

Even now, decades later, people still wonder if Jim is dead and if so, how did he die?

Even before he died – assuming that he really did die, and the jury is still out on that one – Jim was the sort of figure about whom death rumors often circulated. When he was at the peak of his fame, he "died" nearly every weekend, usually in a car accident, often falling from a hotel balcony where he was showing off for friends, or from an overdose of something alcoholic or sexual.

So, how did he die in Paris? Over the years there have been countless theories of overdoses in clubs and even accusations of murder. Many claimed that it was totally out of character for Jim to have died of a heart attack in the bathtub, or to have overdosed on heroin, a drug he didn't use because he was afraid of needles. Perhaps he snorted it, some have suggested. And perhaps he did, but the lingering questions about his death put everything into doubt.

The official story stated that Pamela and Jim were alone in the apartment and that sometime after midnight on July 3, Jim threw up a small amount of blood. He had done this before, Pamela said, and although she was concerned, she was not particularly upset. Jim claimed that he was okay and said that he was going to take a bath. Pamela fell asleep soon after. At 5:00 a.m., she woke up and found Jim had not come to bed. She went to check on him and found him in the tub, his arms resting on the porcelain sides, his head thrown back, and his long, wet hair falling over the rim. He had a smile on his face. At first, Pamela thought he was playing a joke. When he failed to respond to her calling his name, she called the fire department's resuscitation unit. A doctor and the police followed, she said, but they were too late.

One thing that caused much of the initial disbelief in Jim's death was the timing. Siddons told his story to the media six days after Jim allegedly died, two days after the funeral. He read to reporters from a prepared statement: "I have just returned from Paris, where I attended the funeral of Jim Morrison. Jim was buried in a simple ceremony, with only a few close friends present. The initial news of his death and funeral was kept quiet because those of us who knew him intimately and loved him as a person wanted to avoid all the notoriety and circus-like atmosphere that surrounded the death of other rock personalities as Janis Joplin and Jimi Hendrix. I can say that Jim died peacefully of natural causes – he had been in Paris since March with his wife, Pam. He had seen a doctor in Paris about a respiratory problem and had complained of his problem on Saturday – the day of his death."

In the days that followed, Siddons offered no more information about Jim's death because he had none. He had never seen the body. When he arrived at the apartment, he found a sealed coffin and a death certificate with one doctor's signature – a doctor that it was later discovered did not exist. No autopsy was conducted. All he had was Pamela's word that Jim was dead and there was little doubt that Pamela would do anything to protect Jim. Would she lie and say that he was dead, even if he wasn't? Probably.

Jim Morrison's story should have ended with his death, but it has not. For every person that claims Jim died in his Paris apartment in 1971, there are three others who point at the strange evidence that seems to show that he didn't die after all. If there was ever a man who was ready, willing, and able to walk away from his life and start over, it was Jim Morrison. It would have been perfectly in keeping with his unpredictable personality for him to stage his death as a way to escape from public life. He was tired of an image that he had outgrown and yet could not live down. Perhaps he didn't die on that July weekend – perhaps he just dropped out to start a new and anonymous life.

The seeds of this sort of hoax had been planted as early as 1967. At the Fillmore Auditorium in San Francisco in early 1967, before The Doors even had a hit record, Jim suggested pulling a death stunt to bring the band to national attention. Jim also told close friends that he someday wanted to radically change his life. He even came up with a name that he planned to use – "Mojo Risin,'" the same name that appeared in "L.A. Woman." He told his record company officials that if they received a message from a Mr. Mojo Risin' in Africa, the message would be from him.

The idea of such a plan was given to Jim early in his life. While studying the life and poetry of Arthur Rimbaud, he was gripped by the fact that Rimbaud had written his poetry when he was young and then had disappeared to North Africa to become a gun runner and slave trader.

Doors keyboardist Ray Manzarek once claimed that if anyone could get away with faking his own death, it would be Jim. A few days after the announcement of his death, a few fans claimed that they saw Jim on a flight leaving Paris. Newspapers and magazines ran stories of individuals who looked like Jim cashing checks and buying property. In 1994, Jim's brother-in-law, Alan Graham, stated that he was not sure that it was Jim who was buried at Pere Lachaise Cemetery. He said that the body in the bathtub had been blue and bloated, and when the police arrived, Pamela did not say that it was Jim. Eventually, though, she produced his passport to identify the body. Graham suggested that the body might have belonged to a mysterious German acquaintance of Jim's, who apparently looked so much like the singer that they could have passed as brothers. At Jim's urging, Pamela passed off the body as Jim, and he took the opportunity to disappear.

All of Jim's close friends agreed that not only was such a stunt something that Jim would have done, but, with Pamela's help, could actually pull off.

Before Bill Siddons had left Los Angeles for Jim's funeral, he had spoken to Ray Manzarek on the phone. What Manzarek said to him must have haunted him in the days to come. "I don't mean to sound morbid," Ray had said, "but please make sure."

"Make sure of what, Ray?" Siddons had asked.

"I don't know, man, just make sure."

But Bill Siddons had not made sure of anything when he arrived in Paris. He never asked that the coffin be opened, and he never checked to make sure the story that Pamela told was true. Why? Perhaps he really didn't want to know for sure.

On April 25, 1974, Pamela Courson died of a heroin overdose. She took the secret of Jim's death – real or a hoax – with her to the grave.

I know, I know... this probably all sounds crazy. But is it possible? Yes, it certainly is. I can't say for sure that Jim Morrison faked his death and disappeared to start a new life, but I'd like to think that he did.

Perhaps it's for this reason that every July 3, I raise a glass in honor of Jim Morrison on the day that he either ended his life – or he started a new one.

PART THREE:
THE "DEVIL'S MUSIC" REDUX

The rockabilly of the 1950s and the "beat combos" of the early 1960s eventually gave way to the psychedelic movement, whose foremost exponents experimented with mind-altering substances and promoted the exotic philosophies of the East. As the '60s wore on, the music got harder and heavier, staying in tune with the upheaval of the nation at that time.

The search for something new and something different by the young people of America exploded in wildly different ways. Some sought out drugs and sex, while others began to dabble in the occult and the metaphysical.

Eastern philosophies like Transcendental Meditation and Zen Buddhism became all the rage, along with Native American Shamanism, and even good, old-fashioned witchcraft saw a resurgence in interest. The new fascination for witchcraft was largely brought about by writer Gerald Gardner, who reinvented it in England after the Witchcraft Act was repealed in 1951. The lifting of the law left Gardner and his followers free from any legal reprisals and witchcraft was introduced to a new generation of followers.

Gardner, who had spent most of his life as an adventurous customs agent in Borneo, British Malaysia, Singapore, and other far-off trading posts of the British Empire, retired on the southern English coast in the 1930s. He used his retirement to study folklore and tribal rites that he had encountered in the Far East. He also delved into the research of anthropologist Margaret A. Murray, who suggested that an ancient "witch cult" had survived through the centuries in England and Western Europe. An American folklorist named Charles G. Leland had promoted a similar idea in the early 1900s, linking folk magic and nature cults as the "old religion." Gardner later claimed that he was initiated into one of these covens during World War II and they secretly met in the forest to cast binding spells against Hitler and the Nazis.

In 1954, Gardner published a book that would become a bestseller in both England and America, a slender volume called *Witchcraft Today*. It laid out the surviving beliefs and seasonal rituals of the nature-based cults that he claimed still existed. Gardner called their members "Wica," an Old English term for "wise" or "clever folk." In America, this new faith became known as Wicca. Gardner's new and old theology was borrowed, invented, half dreamed up and half grounded in a wide mixture of folklore and traditional practices. It was, above all, a new religion that met the needs of the times. Wicca was based in nature, sexually free, and female-affirming. By the late 1960s, its message of a do-it-yourself spirituality was embraced by hundreds of thousands of young people. Wicca – or paganism – became one of America's fastest-growing religious movements, even gaining recognition as an official religion in the United States military.

But not everything to do with witchcraft in the 1960s was immersed in nature and the old religion. It was during this period that a darker element began to seep into the popular culture. In England, the so-called "King of the Witches," Alex Sanders told an array of wild stories to the press about his initiation into witchcraft as a child in the 1930s and about meeting infamous magician Aleister Crowley. He also invited reporters to attend black masses, where the participants – mostly young women – were always naked. Sanders was an unrepentant narcissist, with a larger-than-life ego, and an insatiable need for attention. When the press pestered him for salacious accounts of nude rituals and magical spells, he willingly obliged. And the more media attention he got, the more followers he attracted. By 1965, he claimed 1,623 initiates in 100 covens. A romanticized biography and a film about his largely fictional exploits led to greater publicity, guest appearances on talk-shows, and public speaking engagements. All of this was to the chagrin of other witches, who saw Sanders as exploiting their faith and dragging it through the gutter of the sensational press.

While Sanders was quite the attraction in England, America had its own black magic ringmaster in the 1960s. His name was Anton Szandor LaVey and he founded the Church of Satan in 1966 and grabbed national headlines. His image as a charming Mephistopheles lured in fans and followers, including many who moved in Hollywood circles. He was a showman, con artist, and the face of a new American movement.

LaVey -- whose real name was Howard Stanton Levey – was born in Chicago in April 1930. His family relocated to San Francisco and he spent most of his early life in California. He learned about witchcraft, spirits, and the occult from his grandmother and developed a deep interest in dark literature and in the pulp horror fiction of the era. He also developed musical skills and was especially adept at the organ and the calliope. LaVey dropped out of high school and began working in circuses and carnivals, first as a roustabout and later as a musician. He played the calliope for the "grind shows" on Saturday nights, and played the organ on Sunday mornings for the tent revivals. He later noted seeing many of the same men attending both the strip shows on Saturday night and the church services on Sunday mornings, which reinforced his cynical view of religion. When the carnival season ended, LaVey began earning a living playing the organ in Los Angeles bars, nightclubs, and burlesque theaters.

Moving back to San Francisco, LaVey worked as a police photographer for a time. A short time later, he met and married Carole Lansing, who bore him his first daughter, Karla Maritza, in 1952. They divorced in 1960 after LaVey began seeing Diane Hegarty. They never married, but she was his companion for many years, and bore his second daughter, Zeena Galatea

LaVey in 1964. LaVey's final companion was Blanche Barton, who gave him his only son, Satan Xerxes Carnacki LaVey, in 1993.

During the 1950s, LaVey dabbled as a psychical investigator, looking into what his friends on the police force cheerfully referred to as "nut calls." LaVey soon became known as a San Francisco celebrity. Thanks to his paranormal research and his live performances as an organist, he attracted many California notables to his parties. Guests included Michael Harner, Chester A. Arthur III, Forrest J. Ackerman, Fritz Leiber, Dr. Cecil E. Nixon, and filmmaker and nutcase Kenneth Anger. He began presenting lectures on the occult

Church of Satan founder Anton LaVey

to what he called his "Magic Circle," which was made up of friends who shared his interests. It was a member of the circle who suggested, perhaps jokingly, that he could start his own religion based on the ideas that he was coming up with.

LaVey took this suggestion seriously, and on April 30, 1966 -- Walpurgis Night -- he launched his new religion. He shaved his head, declared the founding of the Church of Satan, and proclaimed 1966 as "the Year One," Anno Satanas - the first year of the Age of Satan. He exhibited a flair for self-promotion that would have impressed P.T. Barnum. In the years that followed, Satan rewarded him well. He acquired numerous properties, a fleet of classic cars, and even a yacht. In the interviews, articles, and books that followed, it became obvious that LaVey had put together a mish-mash of ideologies, ritual practices, and beliefs. His church did not literally worship Satan, but a personification of man's carnal nature. The motto was stolen from Aleister Crowley – "Do What Thou Wilt" – and as long as no one got hurt, all was well. Essentially, the Church of Satan was more about the publicity that it generated than about any kind of black magic or devil worship – but boy, the rituals and trappings of it all sure looked scary in the photographs that began showing up in national magazines and on television.

Media attention followed the founding of the Church of Satan, leading to coverage in newspapers all over the country and the cover of *Look* magazine. The *Los Angeles Times* and the *San Francisco Chronicle* were among those that dubbed him the "Black Pope." LaVey performed Satanic weddings, Satanic baptisms (including one for his daughter Zeena), and Satanic funerals. He released a record album entitled *The Satanic Mass*. He appeared on talk shows with Joe Pyne, Phil Donahue, and Johnny Carson, and in feature-length documentaries. Since its founding, LaVey's Church of Satan has attracted scores of followers who shared a jaded view of organized religion, including celebrities like Sammy Davis, Jr., Marilyn Manson, director Robert Fuest, ufologist Jacques Vallee, author Aime Michel and many others.

But not all the publicity was good.

One of the converts to LaVey's Church of Satan was Jayne Mansfield, one of America's top pinup girls. On June 29, 1967, she died a horrible and violent death along a lonely roadway near Biloxi, Mississippi. Her death had a sobering effect on the Hollywood film community and strange repercussions in the occult community of the time, as well. Jayne's death was said to have been caused by a curse gone awry. Jayne was involved in a violent relationship with an abusive boyfriend named Sam Brody and she asked LaVey for help. Allegedly, LaVey cursed the man and told Jayne to stay away from him if she didn't want to become collateral damage from the curse. She didn't follow his advice and was killed, along with Brody, in the terrible crash.

The publicity that followed Jayne Mansfield's death attracted what LaVey felt were the "wrong sort of people" to the church. These were the people that even LaVey feared – the sick, the mentally ill, and the ones mad enough to believe that they could commit crimes and have the protection of the Devil himself. LaVey saw himself as a shameless schemer and manipulator, which he believed the Devil would also be. His "black masses" were more for entertainment than devil worship. It was pure theater for the curious, who were treated to the sight of a naked girl tied down on an altar while people in black robes chanted and sang.

Devout Christians and moralists were outraged by LaVey's shameless self-promotion and the inflammatory nature of his widely-publicized beliefs, but the truth of the matter was that they needed a "devil" like him to complain about. They needed LaVey to be a real "evil" or their crusade against him would lose its meaning. LaVey might have been Satan's best promoter, but he made a valid point when he wrote, "Satan has been the best friend the Church has ever had. He's kept them in business all these years."

The Christians lost their adversary on October 29, 1997, when LaVey died at St. Mary's Hospital in San Francisco of pulmonary edema. For reasons open to speculation, the time and date of his passing were listed incorrectly on his death certificate, stating that he died on Halloween. LaVey's funeral was a secret, by-invitation-only, Satanic service held in Colma, California. His body was cremated, with his ashes eventually divided among his heirs.

LaVey had played a very important part in ushering in an era of the paranormal in American pop culture. The 1960s and 1970s saw a rise in books, magazines, and films that dealt with the occult, witchcraft, and, of course, the Devil himself, like *The Exorcist*, *Rosemary's Baby*, and many others. The Devil seemed to be alive and well in America.

And who would the Devil be without his music to dance to?

THe PIPeR aT THe GaTes OF DaWn

In 1967, an audience that went to see Pink Floyd was ready for anything.

The band revolutionized the live experience as they played long mind-altering jams as movie projectors flashed images and smoke swirled around the swaying crowds of people who were flying high on acid. Usually, the crowd moved to their individual rhythms as much as they did with the collective shimmer of the entire audience and rode whatever wave the band was on. Every show was like staring into a kaleidoscopic fun house of mirrors – a reflection of the occult's influence on rock-n-roll.

Pink Floyd --- founded by students Syd Barrett on guitar and lead vocals, Nick Mason on drums, Roger Waters on bass and vocals, and Richard Wright on keyboards and vocals – was part of a new energy that swept across England in the mid-1960s. American rock-n-roll was in a tough spot at the time. It's sexual and spiritual rebellion had been neutered. Even though there were kids across the United States going into garages, plugging in their cheap, electric guitars, and banging on drums, trying to re-ignite the flame, it was in England that new, loud, crass bands were cooking up a new sound. Bands like the Beatles, the Who, and others of what was soon to be called the "British Invasion" were finding rock-n-rolls roots in the blues and reminding people why they'd loved music in the first place.

From there, it was the LSD experience – endorsed by Eastern mysticism, mythology, and the occult – that transformed rock's sound with clothing, stage design, and an ability to convince fans that it was a transmitter for some new spiritual truth. Pink Floyd's Sid Barrett believed that he was a messenger for this new form of enlightenment.

Syd Barrett (right) with Pink Floyd

Through Pink Floyd, Syd conjured up a mystical dream for his audience to inhabit, created from his own drugged imagination, which was fueled by his interest in mysticism, as well as popular fascinations of the era like J.R.R. Tolkien's *Lord of the Rings* and the *I Ching*, an ancient Chinese form of divination.

Even more essential, said Rob Young in his book *Electric Eden*, was Syd being "strangely pulled between nostalgia for the secret garden of a child's imagination and the space-age futurism of interstellar overdrive."

Whoa. I have to say this probably makes more sense if you're really, really high.

Anyway, Syd's idea was to try and pierce the veil between these two worlds, and while this nostalgia and futurism seem opposed, according to Young, they are actually two ideas at the heart of magic. The practice of real magic requires a link to both the past and future. Syd added this directly to the lyrics of his songs and into his live performances., experimenting with light and sound to try and put his audiences into a trance. It was a new way of doing what was an ancient system. It was old magic being worked by a musician – or magician, if you prefer.

Before taking the stage with the first of his grand experiments in 1967, Syd poured the contents of a bottle of hair gel, mixed with crushed Quaaludes onto his head. Under the hot lights of the stage, the gel and pill mixture slowly dripped down his face. To the sick astonishment of his audience and bandmates, his face appeared to be melting. But that was the idea – except on this night it went wrong. Syd stood at the edge of the stage in a trance of his own, playing the same monotone chord over and over again.

The rest of the band was worried, but they weren't really surprised. Syd's behavior had become more and more erratic. He had been maniacally consuming so much LSD that it was inducing -- or at least aggravating – some kind of mental illness.

By this time, they were finally afraid for Syd. He had become so unpredictable that they had no idea what might happen next. Later that year, Syd walked out on stage and just stood there, silently, not moving at all. Suddenly, he put his hands on his guitar and everyone thought he was finally ready to perform – but he just stood there, "tripping out of his mind," as Pink Floyd friend June Bolan put it.

LSD and the pressures of fame are often blamed for Syd Barrett's downfall, but his drug use was all part of his delving into the occult.

He was born as Roger Keith Barrett in Cambridge, England to an ordinary middle-class family. His father, Arthur, was a pathologist. As a boy, he played piano occasionally, but usually preferred drawing and writing during his early years. Then, it all changed. He got a ukulele at 10, a banjo at 11, and an acoustic guitar at 14. A year later, he bought an electric guitar and built his own amplifier. Somewhere, he picked up the nickname "Syd." Some claim that it was named after an old local jazz bassist, Sid "The Beat" Barrett, and changed the spelling to differentiate himself from his namesake. No matter where it came from, he used it interchangeably with his real name through his school years. His sister said that he was never "Syd" when he was at home.

On December 11, 1961, his father died of cancer. It was less than a month before Syd's 16th birthday. He left that page of his diary blank. Syd was the last of the Barrett children still at home and eager to help her son recover from his grief, she encouraged his band – Geoff Mott and the Mottoes – to practice in their front room. One of the frequent visitors at these rehearsals was Syd's childhood friend, Roger Waters. Helping out his friend, he organized a gig for them at a benefit in 1962, but shortly afterwards, Geoff Mott joined another band and the Mottoes broke up.

Syd enrolled in the Cambridge Technical College's art department in September 1962, when he met David Gilmour. It was soon after this that he discovered the music of the Beatles and he began playing covers of their songs at parties and picnics. When the Rolling Stones came along, Syd became a fan and began writing his own songs. He and David Gilmour had started playing some acoustic shows together and he also did some paid musician work for the Those Without and the Hollerin' Blues. But music was nothing to build a future on, he believed, so he decided to apply for the Camberwell College of Arts in London. He enrolled in the summer of 1964 to study painting.

But music always pulled him back in. Starting in 1964, the band that would become Pink Floyd evolved through various lineups and name changes, including The Adbabs, The Screaming Adbabs, Sigma 6, and The Meggadeaths. When Syd joined up in 1965, it was known as The Tea Set. Unbelievably, one night they found themselves playing a show with a band that had the same name, so Syd came up with The Pink Floyd Sound. It later became the Pink Floyd Blues Band, and finally, Pink Floyd. Not long after that, they went into the studio for the first time when a friend of Richard Wright gave the band some free time to record.

During this same summer, Syd took his first LSD trip – and came back for more. During one trip, he and a friend, Paul Charrier, ended up naked in a bathtub, chanting "No rules, no rules!"

Syd wanted to expand his consciousness – as so many others did who experimented with acid – and he became involved with a group that practiced Sant Mat, an occult mixture of Sikhism, Hinduism, and Sufism. The Sant Mat philosophy required initiation into its teachings and Syd was not considered spiritually fit. The order required abstinence from sex, alcohol, and drugs, plus a commitment to mediation, none of which appealed to a young up-and-coming rock star.

Syd was saddened by the esoteric group's rejection of him, but he had plenty of other distractions, like LSD and Pink Floyd. He also pursued occult knowledge on his own, as well as working on some do-it-yourself mind expansion. He delved into *Grimm's Fairy Tales*, the works of Tolkien, the *I Ching*, and Carlos Castaneda's *The Teachings of Don Juan*, which purported to document the author's apprenticeship with a Yaqui Indian sorcerer from Sonora, Mexico in the early 1960s.

Syd didn't really use the drugs and literature to pursue spiritual life, though. He tested the limits of sound and lyrics, crafting songs about the cosmic consciousness from his own psychic landscape. It mirrored the spiritual yearning of the counterculture of the time and changed the nature of Pink Floyd. Before this, they had been playing cover versions of American blues songs but now they were carving out their own style of improvised rock that was nothing like anyone had heard before.

Syd wrote most of the songs for Pink Floyd's first album, *The Piper at the Gates of Dawn*, which was a direct reference to a chapter in Kenneth Grahame's 1908 book, *The Wind in the Willows*, where the animal characters unexpectedly find themselves in the presence of the nature deity, Pan. Rat and Mole are traveling in a boat along the river and Rat hears the piping first. Mole is skeptical, until he comes across Pan himself. In a moment that is not in any way related to the main story of the book, Mole and Rat have a religious epiphany as they are seemingly initiated into the cult of Pan.

Yeah, it's just as weird as it sounds.

And the connection to Pink Floyd? Well, the music of the 1960s was sort of a revival in interest for Pan. It wasn't the first one either. The Romantic poets and writers of the nineteenth century had done it, too. They used pagan and natural imagery to tell their stories, as Percy Bysshe Shelley did in "Hymn of Pan," in which the god suggested that the use of drugs could offer a window into Pan's ancient realm – the same way that Samuel Taylor Coleridge did with his opium-infused poem "Kubla Khan."

The counterculture of the 1960s revived the Romantic belief that the use of reason and the age of industry were counter to the existence of the natural world and the spirit of myth and poetry. This was the experience that the seekers of the 1960s were looking for – a direct connection with nature and the universe. Art and music were vessels for both the Romantics and the hippies. The piper at the gates of dawn was playing his panpipe for those who needed to hear – and those who would listen. The youth of the 1960s were happy to be pulled toward this new siren song. Music was urging them toward transcendence and toward creating their own inner landscapes.

All they needed was good music – and good drugs.

The Piper at the Gates of Dawn is a trip – and I don't mean the LSD kind, or well, maybe I do. Even if you're not really a fan of Pink Floyd, it's worth a listen, even as a time capsule of an era when the psychedelic movement was just getting started. It's filled with what sounds like Gregorian chants, pagan folk images, and Eastern mysticism, making it a product of its time.

Syd Barrett didn't invent this kind of music, but he certainly took it to the next level. And there is no denying that he wouldn't have gotten there without LSD and the occult. His embrace of LSD as a path to enlightenment was common for the era. By 1967, mystical consciousness and psychedelic drugs had become synonymous. LSD and other hallucinogenic drug experiences seamlessly aligned with the occult and with Eastern religious imagery and ideas. A sense of "becoming one with the universe" – a common phenomenon for those who took acid trips – was much like pantheism, where God is believed to be in all things, and all things are in God.

Of course, none of this is to suggest that an LSD trip somehow communicates special spiritual knowledge, but many people thought so. Acid experiences could be overwhelming and Eastern religion and occultism seemed to help people make sense of an otherwise inexplicable occurrence.

The connection between LSD and the East was made in the 1966 book and – well-suited to the time – companion record *The Psychedelic Experience: A Manual Based on the Tibetan Book of the Dead* by Timothy Leary, Ralph Metzner, and Richard Alpert. In the book, the authors make two simultaneous – and opposing – claims: first, that the psychedelic experience is remarkably similar to classic mystical experiences described in Eastern traditions, and second, that LSD could take the place of religious discipline when achieving a mystical state of consciousness.

This idea was first introduced by Aldous Huxley in his book, *The Doors of Perception*, a wildly popular book in the 1960s that also served as the inspiration for the band that was put together by Jim Morrison and Ray Manzarek. Huxley, who had once been a follower of the Hindu philosophical system known as Vedanta and wrote strongly against attempts to go around rigorous spiritual discipline to attain a union with the divine, took a little less than half a gram of mescaline – the psychoactive ingredient found in the peyote cactus – and changed his mind. He came to believe that psychedelic drugs bypassed any need for religion. It was a radical idea, but for a generation desperately seeking some divine connection without being pinned down to any kind of tradition, it was just the thing that the hippies wanted.

But Leary and company recognized that their audience of novice acid trippers would be well-served by having a religious framework for what could be an unpredictable and sometimes terrifying journey, so they threw in *The Tibetan Book of the Dead*, as a guidebook. It was exotic, unfamiliar, and was nothing like the religious teachings of your parents. But he qualified the use of the religious text so he wouldn't scare off the skeptical. Leary wrote in the liner notes of the album: "Today psychedelic drugs such as LSD make it possible for anyone to propel himself out of his mind into unknown, uncharted neurological regions. The yogas and spiritual exercises of the past are no longer needed to escape the inertia of the symbolic mind. Exit is guaranteed."

Leary had spoken and had said that the mystical experience could be untethered from religion. That was good enough for some people, but not for most. Despite this freedom given to the new consciousness explorers, occult and Eastern mystical imagery continued to dominate the scene. The occult offered ways of making sense of a world that was spinning out of control. It was not enough to just change the political and social situation – one had to change one's very being and relationship to the universe. Only a direct experience with the divine could do that.

The spiritual rebellion needed a soundtrack, so two editors of the influential London underground magazine *International Times*, Joe Boyd and John "Hoppy" Hopkins, opened the UFO Club (pronounced YOU-FOE, by the way) on Tottenham Court Road in December 1966. During only one year in business, the UFO Club helped shape the look and feel of the new mysticism and revolutionized rock concerts by turning them into spectacles with the use of film, lights, and shape-morphing slides that were projected on the walls.

It was the show posters, however, that gave the counterculture an occult-filled aesthetic that can still be found in rock posters today. The posters became an alchemy of various nineteenth-century art movements, including Romanticism, Art Nouveau, and Symbolism.

The nineteenth century had been, in many ways, the last truly enchanted time for artists and musicians until the 1960s. It's natural that the artwork of the time was so embraced in this era. In the late 1800s, there had been what was called the Occult Revival, when a number of artists, free-thinkers, society people, and intellectuals joined magical fraternities, and writers like Arthur Conan Doyle and William James became interested in psychic research and Spiritualism.

Artists painted the nineteenth century in mystical symbolism, often hidden from plain view unless you knew where to look. For the Symbolists, art was a method to transmit secret meaning in an effort to undermine the realism that was starting to dominate modern art. Many of the artists and musicians who associated with Symbolism were members of various Rosicrucian orders and used their artwork to outwardly embrace the occult – if you knew how to interpret what they had created.

The Decadent movement, closely linked to Symbolism, often incorporated more explicit sexual and taboo elements into their works. The illustrator Aubrey Beardsley was well-known for his drawings of Oscar Wilde's play *Salome* and for dramatic and graphic renderings of the works of Edgar Allan Poe. Other drawings referred to pagan and mythological themes, many of which were at the heart of occult ideas of the time. Beardsley's drawing *The Mysterious Rose Garden*, found in a literary journal that Beardsley edited called *The Yellow Book*, shows a nude young woman in a garden, listening to secrets from the wing-footed god Hermes, who became a core figure in Hermetic doctrine, which shaped nineteenth century occult thought.

The more obvious influence on the UFO Club's posters – and really, most rock posters of the late 1960s – was the Czech artist Alphonse Mucha, who came to define the Art Nouveau style. A Freemason with a penchant for Spiritualism, he was true to the spirit of the time. Mucha believed that the purpose of art was to communicate hidden spiritual realities. Although Mucha earned a living painting elaborate advertising pieces, much of his work was very complex. One piece, *La Pater*, a series of drawings of the Lord's Prayer spoken by Jesus in the New Testament Gospels, is filled with visionary figures, devils, and heavenly visitations. Mucha used the prayer to reflect on the divine evolution of humanity and believed – like the hippies of the 1960s – that a new spiritual age was dawning. Even his advertising poster art illuminated the idea of spiritual perfection, often using women, surrounded by florally decorated halos, dressed in long, ethereal fabrics, and with expressions of spiritual peace on their faces.

These elements found their way into almost every poster of the UFO Club, reviving the nineteenth-century idea that art could change the spiritual condition of the world.

The bands that played the UFO Club – The Soft Machine, The Crazy World of Arthur Brown, Pink Floyd – played against a projected backdrop created by the art collective known as the Boyle Family – Mark Boyle and Joan Hills. In early performances, they projected bodily fluids like blood, semen, and vomit onto screens. During UFO shows, acid was poured onto zinc slides and the destruction was projected. Colored liquids were also used, and sometimes entire evenings would use one color as a theme and colored fabric, paint, and confetti would be thrown during the shows.

It was all meant to be part of the massive cultural change that was in the air. Change was in the very look and sound of the time. Rock posters like the ones that began at the UFO Club spread to every facet of music, to magazine and television ads, and into the general consciousness. It was as though the mystical transformation of the era was too powerful for the counterculture to contain. A 7UP commercial by artist Peter Max – reminiscent of the Beatle's film *Yellow Submarine* – featured a character in bell-bottoms, walking on clouds, imagining prizes, each presented in a brightly colored, mystical settling. A Brim commercial for its decaffeinated coffee suggested that the drink contained a special ingredient. Each person who drank from a cup was shown going wide-eyed as colorful animated thoughts swirled from the top of their heads, revealing Mucha-like swirls and flowers. A 1969 Pepsi ad

Just two of the thousands of rock posters that were created in the late 1960s that were influenced by the psychedelic posters at the UFO Club

featured a bottle of the soft drink surrounded by floral mandalas and lighted by a rainbow-colored sun.

People were ready for change and Pink Floyd wanted to give that to them. But as the band continued its upward momentum in 1967, Syd Barrett was spiraling downward. The other members of Pink Floyd could never rely on him to perform. He would detune his guitar and stare blankly into space. His appearances on TV were just as unpredictable. While he still had some ability to perform in the studio, by 1968, the band had voted to replace him with David Gilmour. Syd was soon out of the music business completely, but not before recording a few solo records with Gilmour's production help.

His albums were uneven, at best, with his last one, *Barrett*, in 1970. It has been described as "an overly produced mess with only a smattering of brilliance." Soon after, he performed for the last time in front of an audience – backed by Gilmour – at the Olympia Exhibition Hall. Unfortunately, 15 minutes into his set, Syd carefully put down his guitar and walked offstage.

He became a recluse, rarely appearing in public. When he did, it was often a strange experience for everyone, including Syd. In 1975, a hollow-eyed, overweight version of the young man they once knew showed up unexpectedly at the recording studio where the now world-famous Pink

Floyd was recording a follow-up to *The Dark Side of the Moon* called *Wish You Were Here.* The band was then working on "Shine on You Crazy Diamond," a suite of songs about Syd, with lyrics that predicted the man who came to visit them, as well as capturing the brilliant musician they'd once all known: "Now there's a look in your eyes, like black holes up in the sky. Shine on your crazy diamond."

And one more, more eerie than the rest: "You reached for the secret too soon, you cried for the moon."

Sometimes madness and mystical experience are impossible to tell apart. What some believed to be religious experiences were later understood to be chemical imbalances. For many occultists, the distinction is meaningless. But during the psychedelic '60s, it wasn't enough to simply be seized by visions over and over again. There would always be a danger of creating a religion of nothing more than a series of religious experiences.

Syd Barrett had a consciousness that was always seeking occult connections, but all he found was a wealth of meaning with no single truth. For a time, his music offered the perpetual state of being turned on to a creative outlet, and audiences quickly identified their own hallucinogenic experiences in the occult storybook that Syd created with his music. But, eventually, it all came crashing down for him.

The mystical transformation of the world would happen without him.

I am THe WaLRUS

The Beatles were, without question, one of the most iconic bands in rock-n-roll history. And while they never journeyed down the same kind of rabbit holes that members of bands like Pink Floyd and Led Zeppelin did, their connections to the occult, murder, mayhem, prophecy, and (unsolved) mysteries are many.

To start with, they became one of the first bands to truly give Transcendental Meditation (TM) a wide audience, largely thanks to George Harrison, who had been studying it with his wife, Pattie. He had heard that the long-haired, giggling guru, Maharishi Mahesh Yogi, who had founded the movement was going to be in London and he wanted The Beatles to go and hear him speak. It wasn't hard to convince them. Paul McCartney recalled that the band was already in psychic disarray, heightened by personal struggles, and already experiencing the tensions that would ultimately split them apart. So, one night, George, Paul, and John Lennon, along with Pattie and Paul's then-girlfriend Jane Asher, went to listen to the Maharishi talk about the benefits of TM. This event turned out to be one that would begin a shift in the spiritual aspirations of a generation.

Transcendental Meditation offered an easy way to achieve enlightenment. After being interviewed by the Maharishi or one of his disciples, a student was given a personal mantra – usually a Sanskrit word – that was "attuned to your own vibrations." The mantra was not cheap, but the promise of a life free from stress seemed worth it. It was said that after a certain amount of time, some practitioners were even able to levitate. And if that's not worth the time and energy then, hey, what is?

The need for Westerners to find a guru from the East dated back to the dates of the Occult Revival in the nineteenth century. Helena Petrovna Blavatsky was a theatrical woman with a powerful personality and a flair for the dramatic, but she popularized the idea that true knowledge had to come from the exotic East in the middle and late 1800s.

She had been born in Russia in 1831 to German parents with excellent social credentials. She married young but later abandoned her husband to explore both the physical and spiritual worlds. She visited an odd assortment of places such as Canada, Mexico, Texas, and India and made a first attempt to enter the forbidden country of Tibet. A short time later, she vanished. For a decade between 1848 and 1858, Madame Blavatsky was not heard from and she would often refer to that period as her "veiled years." Her cloudy allusions to this time period were always vague and always intriguing. She may – or may not – have spent seven years at a mountain retreat in Tibet, but she truly did learn much of Indian mysticism and acquired more than a dabbler's knowledge of the Jewish Kabbalah. From this learning, she would later piece together the novel religion of Theosophy, a curious mixture of many faiths and philosophies.

Madame Blavatsky returned to the world scene in 1858. At home in Russia, she began offering Spiritualist séances, mixed with overtones of the East. She came to America and soon established herself as one of the best-known practicing mediums and occult teachers in the country. In 1861, she published her acclaimed book *Isis Unveiled*, a classic text of Theosophy that attracted more than 100,000 followers around the world. Always drawn to India, she went to Madras in 1879, where she established the world headquarters of the Theosophical Society. The anniversary of her death in 1891 is still remembered today and referred to as "White Lotus Day."

Later, the Vendata movement brought great Hindu teachers like Swami Vivekanada to the United States after the turn of the century, and this became the religion of choice for many intellectuals and writers in the 1940s and 1950s, like Aldous Huxley and Christopher Isherwood. In the 1950s, Beats like Jack Kerouac began exploring Zen Buddhism and Alan Watts turned Eastern mysticism into pop psychology with a psychedelic vibe. By the 1960s, there was a fascination in the West with the occult and it seemed natural to be dependent on the ideas of teachers from the East.

Mixing magic with LSD in the 1960s was shaking a lot of people to the core – and they needed someone to explain how and why it all worked. After the lecture in London, the Maharishi met with The Beatles and invited them to a retreat in Bangor, North Wales.

This time, all four of them went along, with friends and girlfriends in tow. Media and fans mobbed the group as they tried to board the train, and while they eventually made it to their destination, John's wife, Cynthia, was left behind. Mistaken for a fan by the police, she was kept back, and the train left without her. Less interested in the spiritual pretensions of the popular band, the newspapers snapped photos of the upset young woman and printed stories about her being stranded at the station.

Author Peter Bebergal notes that Cynthia being stranded at the station was symbolic of The Beatles' spiritual journey – forever trying to cast off the chains of celebrity as they explored altered states of religious and chemical consciousness, but having access to anything they wanted to explore, chant, and swallow because they were famous. That privilege was part of why rock-n-roll and the occult were so easily connected. Rock stars had money and cultural connections that gave them access to ideas and people that others did not. A private meeting with the Maharishi and being invited to a retreat is only one such example, but it's definitely a glimpse into how society's elite are able to easily break free of mainstream religion.

Fans who didn't have access to such things but still wanted something different could use The Beatles as a guide. The infamous newspaper article where John Lennon was quoted as saying, "We're more popular than Jesus" shared an observation that was more far-sighted than anyone could have imagined at the time. For many, The Beatles were precisely, in theological terms, mediators between heaven and earth, a bridge between the drudgery of middle-class life to something greater, like cosmic awareness and inner peace. It was a lot like the popularity of Hollywood films about the rich and successful during the Great Depression of the 1930s. People who had nothing flocked to theaters to see Fred Astaire in a tuxedo dancing on the deck of a luxury ocean liner. It was a glimpse into what was possible.

In the 1960s, though, cultural anxiety was not about money – it was about sex, war, race, and religion. And even though the public often looked to bands like The Beatles to show them something beyond the confusion, the chaos created by their celebrity status was a small version of the chaos that was all around them. People wanted to know every detail of their lives, not

The Beatles in 1967

only because of how much fun it all looked, but because The Beatles were also a cultural mirror. And in 1967, when Cynthia was left at the train station, people saw the chaos that existed between their need for spiritual wisdom and the demands placed on them by the world.

In Bangor, though, The Beatles were taken with the quiet meditative rhythm of what was happening. Never shy of the press, they were quick to speak about the benefits of TM. By the end of the first day, they were ready to sing the praises of the Maharishi. At the press conference, Paul told reporters, "I had given up drugs before becoming interested in the yogi's teachings. The only reason people take drugs is because they heard so much about experiences that can expand the mind. By meditating, this expansion can be done without drugs and without their ill effects. Meditation is a way of expanding the mind naturally."

Great, right? Except just a few months before, Paul had been lauding the benefits of LSD: "After I took it, it opened my eyes. We only use one-tenth of our brain. Just think what we could accomplish if we could only tap that hidden part. It would mean a whole new world."

An anti-LSD position was pretty radical for a band in 1967, even if they were The Beatles. But even as they denounced drugs, George Harrison wasn't straying far from the hippie position of not wanting to be preached at. It wouldn't work to start proselytizing for any kind of religion., even one from the East. "We don't know how this will come out in the music," he said.

"Don't expect to hear Transcendental Meditation all the time." He explained that he didn't want to sound "like Billy Graham."

The Beatles claimed to have found a new sense of peace, but it was tested right away when their trip was cut short by devastating news – beloved friend and manager Brian Epstein had died from an overdose of barbiturates mixed with alcohol. Brian was supposed to meet the band at the retreat and become initiated into TM practice. He killed himself instead.

The Beatles, in a state of shock, headed back to London. They couldn't help but feel that the trip to learn from the Maharishi and to make a commitment to a spiritual discipline in the midst of their incredibly chaotic lives, had to mean something, especially now. Brian Epstein's death pushed The Beatles further toward the charismatic teachings of the Maharishi. The ever-smiling guru was a safe place for them – away from their fans, from the press, and from the tragic loss of their friend. But always ready to meet with the media, The Beatles could not withhold even their most private moments. Despite George's promise that they were not going to become the Maharishi's missionaries, TM had become too important, and too life-changing, to keep to themselves. A month after Brian's overdose, Lennon told the press: "This is the biggest thing in our lives at the moment, and it's come at a time when we need it... We want to learn the meditation thing properly so we can propagate it and sell the whole idea to everyone."

In the 1960s, the culture of rock-n-roll and the lives of the musicians and the music they made was inseparable. It was imperative that The Beatles be able to reflect the interests and obsessions of their audience. George Harrison became the spiritual face of the band. His interest in Hindu spirituality had been evolving ever since, George said, he'd first heard Indian music. Once be began his friendship with sitar player Ravi Shankar, he realized that the music of The Beatles and spiritual intentions didn't have to exist separately. When the two men met, Shankar later admitted that he was confused. "It was strange to see pop musicians with sitars," he said. He never thought their collaboration would cause such an explosion in interest in Indian music on the rock scene.

For three days in June 1967, the Monterey Pop Festival became a fusion of Eastern and Western Spirituality. It had been designed to present music as a method for transcendence. The official logo even used a satyr playing panpipes in a bed of flowers. The lineup for the weekend was a who's who of music for the time – Jimi Hendrix, Janis Joplin, Otis Redding, Simon and Garfunkel, The Mamas and the Papas, The Who, The Byrds, and many others. Beyond including some of the most iconic performances in rock history – The Who destroying their instruments, Hendrix setting his guitar on fire – the atmosphere of the festival was both thick from pot smoke and a collective consciousness that was tuned in to a spiritual vision. Eric Bordon of the Animals even spelled it out: "To me, Monterey wasn't a pop music festival. It wasn't a music festival at all, really. It was a religious festival. It was a love festival."

Ravi Shankar at the Monterey Pop Festival

Photographs and film footage from the weekend showed stoned and tripping faces beaming as if they're illuminated from within. Reviews in the rock and popular press described something that was like bearing witness to an ancient rite. And it was the performance by Ravi Shankar – his first public appearance in America – that gave the festival a sense that something really special was taking place. He played raga for three hours on his sitar – literally an improvised plinking melody – to a crowd of thousands. And they actually listened. If that's not proof of some sort of religious experience – or really great drugs – I'm not sure what is.

Shankar appreciated the reception that he got at Monterey. He also respected George Harrison and the passion that The Beatles had for his music, but he was skeptical about the hippie movement in general. He drew a line between the religious roots of his music and the drug culture, but it was too late – most people were accepting it as music with which to get high and to reach for the gods.

But Shankar need not have worried that his pure music would be corrupted. He had his fans, but alone he would not have the impact that was achieved by mixing sitar playing with popular music. Not only were these songs presented to the youth culture by The Beatles, in the context of rock, especially psychedelic rock, but the sound itself resonated with them. The sitar gave the LSD experience something authentic, both culturally and musically. By this point, it was impossible to separate the mystical from the psychedelic and the magical from the drugs. It became part of the consciousness revolution. And the sound of the sitar in the hands of a genius like George Harrison elevated the music beyond anything else that it had been before. It spread, like all of rock's important milestones, into commercial and marketing efforts of the most cynical kind, but more important, it changed rock's sound and reception in the 1960s. The Beatles' explicit expression of mysticism created an even deeper connection between the band and their audience.

But like so many good things, it eventually turned ugly.

Eastern mysticism soon became all the rage in the counterculture of the 1960s. If a Beatle believed in it, well, it must be true. This made many in the religious establishment uneasy. While other spiritual ideas might offer some hope, they are ultimately in opposition to Christian teachings.

You guessed it – it was the "Devil's Music" all over again.

Church leaders took their pulpits and let it be known that it's often "spiritually undeveloped people" who are drawn to mysticism and the occult. The Beatles were a perfect example of how so many tragically turn away from the teachings of Christ.

Although unconnected to the criticism leveled against them, The Beatles soon experienced their own disillusionment for the movement that had so recently endorsed. In February 1968, the band, along with musician Donovan, and Mike Love from the Beach Boys went to see the Maharishi at his ashram in New Delhi. Boredom, and rumors that the giggling yogi was making sexual advances toward the female guests, sent The Beatles back home to London, confused and angry.

The Beatles' short-lived embrace of the Maharishi and other Hindu practices helped to keep just about every kind of alternative religion in the public consciousness in the late 1960s. The Western view at the time was that mysticism and the occult were mostly synonymous. Their fame – along with their explicit statements about spirituality and religion – worked to inspire the idea that they must be hiding something. Many believed there must be some unseen force working to shape their life and music, or they were willing participants in various – often thought to be dark – conspiracies that both benefited and cursed them in equal measure.

Like Robert Johnson, they were just too good to have achieved fame on their own. They must have made a deal with the Devil, some thought, and from this, The Beatles became the subject of every kind of occult speculation imaginable.

The cover of their *Abbey Road* album – the now famous image of The Beatles crossing the street – was a departure from their previous two outlandish covers: *Sgt. Pepper's Lonely Hearts Club Band*, with its collage of saints and sinners, and *The Beatles* – better known as *The White Album* – which was just that, a white, blank slate. Perhaps just for that reason, *Abbey Road* became the subject of intense conjecture.

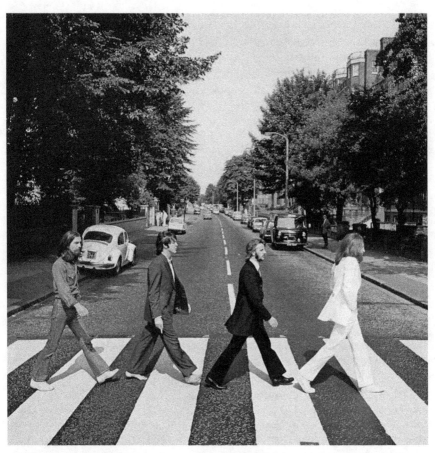

The Beatles' *Abbey Road* album cover, which was filled with clues that some fans used to create the "Paul is Dead" conspiracy

There was a secret hidden there, many people claimed, and it was perhaps the most shocking secret that any Beatles fan could imagine – Paul McCartney was dead. It's true! All you had to do was play the record backward and you'd see – Paul is dead.

The story was that in 1966, Paul was in a fatal car crash. But the band had to go on, so the remaining members of The Beatles covered up his death by hiring a replacement, who also looked just like Paul. Still, known for their witticism – and being the angst-ridden artists they were – the rest of the band hid secret messages and clues in their music that alluded to what really happened.

The conspiracy – as wild as it seems – did have its roots in the truth. There was no reported car crash in 1966, but there was an accident involving Paul's Mini Cooper in 1967. The driver – who was not Paul, who wasn't even in the car – however, was not killed. Even so, rumors that Paul was dead began to pop up, but that were quickly refuted in the *Beatles Book Monthly* magazine and that seemed to be the end of it.

A few years later, though, the story came back. College and underground publications began printing stories, again claiming that Paul was dead. The articles, which spread rapidly, alleged there were various clues in several recent Beatles albums that confirmed the story. One of the more popular claims was that by playing the track "Revolution 9" off the *White Album* backward the telling message would be revealed: "Turn me on, dead man."

This all culminated in a call on October 12, 1969, from Tom Zarski, a student at Michigan University, to Detroit disc jockey Russ Gibb. Zarski wanted to discuss the stories about Paul being dead. Gibb was initially dismissive of the rumors, but then Zarski convinced him to play "Revolution 9" backward on air. Everyone who tuned into WKNR that night heard it, over and over again, "Turn me on, dead man... Turn me on, dead man." The radio station's lines rang off the hook and the previously underground story began reaching a national audience.

In the weeks that followed, more "clues" emerged and new "secret messages" were unearthed. "Strawberry Fields Forever" played backward contained the message, "I buried Paul." And the *Abbey Road* album cover was a symbolic funeral procession with Paul's bare feet indicating his role as the corpse.

In November 1969, immediately after the rumors began to spread, albums from The Beatles saw a substantial increase in sales. Two albums – *Sgt Pepper's Lonely Hearts Club Band* and *Magical Mystery Tour*, re-entered the Billboard chart after being off it for nine months.

Hoping to clear the air, Paul did an interview with *Life* magazine. In it, Paul said, "Perhaps the rumor started because I haven't done much in the press lately." The conspiracy lost some traction after the interview, but not everyone was buying it – then or now. It has continued to crop up in many ways throughout the years.

As recently as 2009, the Italian version of *Wired* magazine featured an article about a study that was done by two forensic scientists who used computer technology to compare the measurements of Paul's skull before and after the car accident. They took on the project so that they could prove, using scientific evidence, that the "Paul is dead" story was a lie.

Uh oh.

What they shockingly discovered was that the point where the nose detached from the face was actually different in the two skulls. The position of the ears was different in a way that couldn't be explained by surgery, and the shape of the palate was dissimilar.

Was Paul really dead? Nope, but old death rumors apparently die hard. To this day, there are still people out there who are devoted to the legend.

After all this time, Paul McCartney has stopped taking the "Paul is dead" story seriously. He even had a laugh over it when he named his 1993 album *Paul is Live.*

You know, if that musician is actually Paul McCartney...

While the "Paul is dead" rumors didn't involve any occult elements, the obsessive looking for clues in Beatles album covers inspired what would become a regular part of the activity of listening to rock-n-roll – searching for hidden meanings in the album covers. The band always denied ever deliberately helping to perpetuate the myth, but the covers of many of their albums certainly kept people guessing, whether it be about whether Paul was still breathing or other things. There is no telling what all those people and items on the cover of *Sgt. Pepper* meant to the band, if anything at all, but there's no denying that the faces, objects, and symbols there appealed to those who were searching for meanings other than musical ones. There were many people in 1967 who stared at that cover for hours, unlocking special, secret clues, and then debating them with their friends.

It was a lot of fun for most enthusiasts, but there was also a negative side to how rock inspired this kind of obsessive behavior. Those with enough time and inclination could read Beatles album covers as if they were guidebooks to occult terror, step-by-step handbooks to helping Satan and his demons take over the world.

And I'm not kidding with this.

Even today, the search continues. At least one blogger has gone to the trouble of compiling every esoteric reference that can be found on a Beatles cover – or at least what they believe is such a reference. For instance, there's the cover of *A Hard Day's Night* – Eight eyes, and the number 8 means "sun worship." From *Help!*, you have the letter "H", which is the eighth letter, which is again the sun worshipper's number. "HE" equals 13, which is occult. "ELP" equals 33, which stands for the number of Masonic degrees. So, the record is an "occult sun-worshipper's record." From *Yellow Submarine,* John is making the "devil's horns" with his hands and, of course, *Sgt. Pepper's* is an encyclopedia of hidden occult symbols, like a hookah (drugs), a purple velvet snake (Satan), Snow White (Walt Disney was a Freemason), a Mexican Tree of Life (usually depicting Satan offering forbidden knowledge in the Garden of Eden), a Saturn trophy (stand-in for Satan), and the list goes on.

It was almost too easy for anyone with a particular religious agenda to find all the evidence they needed to "prove" The Beatles were part of some vast occult conspiracy, sending out subliminal messages through mass media. The Beatles' fame made them either willing participants or unwitting dupes under the control of a Satanic master plan. The band pushed every fundamentalist button with a history that included a guru and admission of drug use, and even the tragedy of John Lennon's death – and we'll get to that – was seen as proof of their infernal dealings. But this is more often than not the voice of someone preaching to other believers. It's a delusion that feeds itself.

Unfortunately, this kind of confused occult interpretation can take a darker turn. When it did so, in Los Angeles in 1969, it shook The Beatles, Hollywood, and the music industry to the core.

The connections first began to be made when the police arrived at the home of Leno and Rosemary LaBianca at 3301 Waverly Drive and were shocked not only by the brutal way the couple had been killed, but with the words that had been written on the walls with their blood. One phrase was familiar: "Helter Skelter." It was the title of a Beatles song from the *White Album* and what turned out to be the rallying cry for charismatic cult leader Charles Manson.

Manson has earned his place as one of the most sinister criminals in American history. As the leader of the "Family," a quasi-commune and cult, he was found guilty of a series of murders that were carried out by his followers on his orders. He called the killings "Helter Skelter" because he believed The Beatles were speaking to him directly – offering direction to start an apocalyptic race war that murders he committed would set in motion. This connection with rock music, and the fame of one of his victims, linked him to the counterculture of the 1960s, for which he became a dark symbol of murder, insanity, and the macabre.

Born Charles Maddox to unmarried, 16-year-old Kathleen Maddox in Cincinnati in 1934, Manson never knew his real father. For a time, after her son's birth, Kathleen Maddox was married to a laborer named William Manson and the boy was given his last name. Manson's mother, allegedly a heavy drinker, once sold him for a pitcher of beer to a childless waitress, from whom his uncle retrieved him a few days later. When his mother was sentenced to five years in prison for robbing a Charleston, West Virginia, service station in 1939, Manson was placed in the home of an aunt and uncle. His mother was paroled in 1942 and he was returned to her, faced with a life of run-down hotel rooms and flophouses. Kathleen could only handle the boy for about five years, and in 1947, she tried to have him placed in a foster home. With no spaces available, the court sent him to the Gibault School for Boys in Terre Haute, Indiana. After 10 months there, he fled and returned to his mother, who wanted nothing to do with him.

Charles Manson

Soon after, Manson had his first brush with crime and he spent the next few years in and out of reformatories and boys' homes, often escaping or being released to simply break the law and wind up incarcerated again. He was tested by psychiatrists and social workers who found Manson to be intelligent but labeled him "aggressively antisocial." After being transferred from one institution after another, each more secure than the last, because of continued disciplinary problems, he finally became a model prisoner and was paroled from his last reformatory, in Ohio, in 1954.

After temporarily honoring a parole condition that he live with his aunt and uncle in West Virginia, Manson sought out his mother again. He moved in with her for a time and then in January 1955, he married Rosalie Jean Willis, a 17-year-old waitress with whom, by his own account, he found genuine, but short-lived happiness. He supported them by working at a series of low-paying jobs that included parking lot attendant and bus boy – and by stealing cars. In October of that same year, Manson stole a car and moved his pregnant wife to Los Angeles. The unlucky Manson was caught again and, this time, was charged with interstate theft. After a psychiatric evaluation, he received five-years probation. His subsequent failure to appear at a Los Angeles hearing on an identical charge filed in Florida resulted in his March 1956 arrest. His probation was revoked, and he was sentenced to three years imprisonment at Terminal Island in San Pedro, California.

During his first year at Terminal Island, Manson received visits from his wife and mother, who were now living together in Los Angeles. In March 1957, though, the visits ceased, and Manson's mother informed him that Rosalie was now living with another man. Manson was caught trying to escape less than two weeks before a scheduled parole hearing and his parole was denied.

During this time, however, Manson began attending prison classes that were focused around the popular Dale Carnegie book, *How to Win Friends and Influence People*. What was essentially a self-help book for potential salesmen became a how-to guide for Manson on the best ways to manipulate people and twist them around to his way of thinking. He befriended the pimps and the hustlers that he was locked up with, pumping them for information and methods to convince people – especially women – to do what he wanted.

In September 1958, Manson was freed, and he immediately began putting what he learned in prison into practice – pimping a 16-year-old girl and getting additional money from her wealthy parents. It didn't take long before the chronic lawbreaker was in trouble again. In September 1959, he entered a guilty plea to attempting to cash a forged U.S. Treasury check but received a 10-year suspended sentence after a young woman with a history of prostitution arrests tearfully told the court that she and Manson were in love and would get married if he were freed. The young woman, whose name was Leona, actually did marry Manson before the year was out and Manson took her and another woman from California to New Mexico to work as prostitutes.

There, Manson was held and questioned for violation of the Mann Act, which prohibited taking women across state lines for the purposes of prostitution. Though he was released, Manson was convinced he was still being investigated and he disappeared. Now in violation of his probation, a bench warrant was issued, and he was arrested in Laredo, Texas, when one of his girls was picked up for prostitution. Manson was returned to Los Angeles, and for violating his probation for the check-cashing charge, he was ordered to serve his 10-year sentence.

Manson spent a year trying to appeal the revocation of his probation and ended up being transferred from the Los Angeles County Jail to the federal penitentiary at McNeil Island. In 1963, Leona divorced him.

In June 1966, Manson was sent to Terminal Island in preparation for an early release. By the time he got out, on March 21, 1967, he had spent more than half of his 32 years incarcerated in one institution or another.

After his release, Manson moved to San Francisco, where, with the help of a prison friend, he obtained an apartment in Berkeley. It was here, during the famed "Summer of Love" that Manson began to develop the influence that he had over women, which had started to emerge a few years before. He would also begin the early formation of the Family.

Manson was mostly panhandling in San Francisco, until he met Mary Brunner, an assistant librarian at UC Berkeley. They moved in together and in a short time, Manson overcame her resistance to bringing other women into bed with them. Before long, they were sharing Brunner's apartment with a dozen or more other young women. Manson quickly established himself as a guru of sorts in San Francisco's Haight-Asbury. Using his age -- he was normally several years older than his followers -- and some of the techniques that he learned in prison, he soon had his first group of cult followers, most of them young and female.

Dennis Wilson of the Beach Boys

Before the summer was over, Manson and a group of his followers piled into an old school bus that had been renovated in hippie style. The seats had been removed and colored rugs and pillows were placed on the floor. Hitting the road, they roamed through California, Mexico, and the Southwest. When they returned to L.A., they continued to move from place to place, living in Topanga Canyon, Malibu, and Venice.

The events that would culminate in the murders were set in motion in the spring of 1968. According to accounts, Dennis Wilson of The Beach Boys picked up two hitchhiking Manson girls one night and brought them to his Pacific Palisades home. Returning home in the early hours of the morning following a late-night recording session, Dennis was approached in his driveway by Manson, who had walked out of the house. Nervous, Dennis asked the bearded, shaggy-haired Manson if he intended to hurt him. Assuring the musician that this was not his intention, Manson dropped down and started kissing Wilson's feet. Inside the house, Dennis discovered 12 strangers, mostly girls.

At first, Dennis was flattered by the attention and was happy to have a group of pretty young women -- whose belief in "free love" was enthusiastic – as houseguests, but those feelings undoubtedly changed when, over the next few months, their number doubled. Family members who crashed at Wilson's Sunset Boulevard home cost him at least $100,000. This included a large medical bill for the treatment of gonorrhea and $21,000 for the accidental destruction of a borrowed car.

Dennis and Charlie became friends and Dennis paid for studio time to record songs written and performed by Manson. He even took one of

Charlie's songs, changed it up, and used it on one of the Beach Boys albums – neglecting to credit Manson for the lyrics. Dennis also introduced him to friends in the entertainment business, like songwriter Gregg Jakobson, record producer Rudy Altobelli, and producer Terry Melcher, who was the son of actress Doris Day.

By August 1968, Dennis's patience with the dirty band of hippies had reached its limit. He got his manager to clear Manson and his Family out of his house, and soon after, Manson established a home for the group at Spahn's Ranch, not far from Topanga Canyon. The ranch had once been a location for shooting Western films, but by 1968, the old sets were deteriorating and largely abandoned. It was primarily doing business offering horseback rides and Manson convinced the elderly, nearly blind owner, George Spahn, to allow the Family to live at the ranch in return for doing work around the place. It was not hard to convince him. Manson had Lynette Fromme, one of his girls, act as Spahn's eyes and she, along with other girls, serviced the old man sexually. Because of the tiny squeal that Lynette would emit when Spahn pinched her thigh, she acquired the nickname "Squeaky."

The Family was joined at Spahn's Ranch by Charles Watson, a Texan who had met Manson while he was still living at Dennis Wilson's house. Watson had quit college and moved to California where he met Wilson when he gave the hitchhiking Beach Boy a lift after his car had broken down. Watson's southern drawl earned him the nickname "Tex."

In early November 1968, Manson established the Family at alternative headquarters in Death Valley, where they occupied two old ranches, Myers and Barker. The former was owned by the grandmother of a new girl in the family and the latter was owned by an elderly local woman who believed that Manson was a musician in need of a place to work. She agreed to let them stay, provided that they fixed things up.

In December, Manson was introduced to the *White Album.*

He and Watson were visiting a friend who lived in Topanga Canyon and he played the album for them. Manson became obsessed with The Beatles and believed that some of the songs played right into some of the crazed rhetoric that he had been spouting for some time: that America was going to become embroiled in a race war between blacks and whites. He told the Family that the social turmoil he had been predicting was also foreseen by The Beatles. The *White Album* songs, he said, spoke to him in code. In fact, he said, the album had been intended for the Family, a carefully selected group that was being instructed to preserve the world from the coming disastrous events.

In early 1969, the Family positioned itself to monitor the tension that was allegedly coming to L.A. by moving into a bright yellow house in Canoga

Park, not far from the Spahn Ranch. Manson believed that the house would allow the group to remain "submerged beneath the awareness of the outside world" and he called it the "Yellow Submarine," another Beatles reference. At this house, the Family prepared for the apocalypse, which Manson had termed "Helter Skelter" after the Beatles' song.

Within a couple of months, Manson's vision was complete. The Family would create an album with songs that would trigger the predicted chaos. Ghastly murders of white people by black attackers would be met with retaliation and a split between the racist and non-racist whites would bring about the white race's annihilation. The blacks would then turn to the Family to lead them after the storm had cleared. They were, Manson believed, unable to govern themselves. The Family would survive by riding out the conflict in a mysterious cave called the Devil's Hole in Wingate Pass, hidden away in Death Valley. Legend had it that an underground city was below the earth there, and the family planned to stay there until the war had ended – no matter how long it took.

At the yellow house, family members worked on vehicles and studied maps, preparing for their desert escape. They also worked on songs for their "world-changing album." When they were told Terry Melcher was coming to the house to hear the material, the girls cleaned up and prepared a huge meal, but Melcher never arrived.

On March 23, 1969, Manson went –uninvited – to 10050 Cielo Drive, which he knew was the home of Terry Melcher. The house was actually owned by Rudy Altobelli, and Melcher had once been a tenant but no longer lived there. The new tenants were film director Roman Polanski and his wife, actress Sharon Tate.

Manson was confronted by Shahrokh Hatami, a photographer and Tate friend, who was there to photograph Sharon before she left for Rome the next day. He saw Manson through a window as he approached the main house and went out onto the porch to ask him what he wanted. When Manson told Hatami he was looking for someone whose name Hatami did not recognize, Hatami informed him the place was the Polanski residence. Hatami advised him to try the guesthouse, beyond the main house. Manson made no effort to move and a moment later, Sharon Tate appeared in the doorway to ask who was calling. Hatami said that it was a man looking for someone and they watched as Manson, without a word, went back to the guesthouse, returned a minute or two later, then left.

That evening, Manson returned to the property and again went back to the guesthouse. He walked into the enclosed porch and spoke with Rudi Altobelli, who was just getting out of the shower. Although Manson didn't ask for Melcher, Altobelli got the impression that the man was looking for him. Through the screen door, he told Manson that Melcher had moved to Malibu, but he lied and said that he did not know his new address. In response to a question from Manson, Altobelli said he himself was in the entertainment business, although, having met Manson the previous year, at Dennis Wilson's home, he was sure Manson already knew that. At the time, he had lukewarmly complimented Manson on some of his musical recordings.

Manson decided to try and get Altobelli to listen to the Family's new recordings but Altobelli told him that he was going out of the country the next day. When Manson said he'd like to speak with him upon his return; Altobelli lied and said he would be gone for more than a year. Altobelli also told him not to come back to the property because he didn't want his tenants disturbed.

Manson left. As Altobelli flew with Tate to Rome the next day, Sharon asked him whether "that creepy-looking guy" had gone back to the guesthouse the day before. He admitted that he had, but assured Sharon that she'd never see him again.

A short time later, Manson did manage to track down Terry Melcher, who reluctantly agreed to visit the Spahn Ranch and hear a performance by Manson and the girls. He brought along a friend who owned a mobile recording unit and the Family performed. Melcher wasn't interested in producing anything for them, but he did give Manson a little money because he thought that the Family members "looked hungry."

Manson was no closer to recording his "world-changing album." Perhaps the Family's music was not going to change things after all. He might need to find another way.

By June, Manson was telling the Family that they might have to show the blacks how to start "Helter Skelter" – they wouldn't be able to figure it out without their music to show them the way. When Manson gave Tex Watson the job of getting money together to help the Family with the conflict to come, Watson ripped off a black drug dealer named Bernard "Lotsapoppa" Crowe. The dealer responded with a threat to wipe out everyone at the Spahn Ranch, but Manson got to Crowe first. He shot him in his Hollywood apartment on July 1. Manson assumed that Crowe was dead, and this mistake was seemingly confirmed by a news report that announced the discovery of the body of a "Black Panther member" in Los Angeles. Although Crowe was not a member of the Panthers, Manson concluded that he had been and expected retaliation from the radical group. He turned Spahn Ranch into an armed camp, putting out night guards, and passing weapons around.

The Family was convinced that "Helter Skelter" was coming.

Still looking for money, Manson sent occasional Family member Bobby Beausoleil -- along with Mary Brunner and Susan Atkins -- to the home of

Manson followers Bobby Beausoleil and Susan Atkins

acquaintance and music teacher Gary Hinman on July 25, 1969. Manson had heard rumors that Hinman had recently inherited some money and Manson wanted it. The three Family members held an uncooperative Hinman hostage for two days, during which Manson showed up to threaten him and used a sword to slash his ear. After that, Beausoleil stabbed Hinman to death, acting on Manson's instructions. Before leaving the Topanga Canyon residence, Beausoleil -- or one of the girls -- used Hinman's blood to write "Political piggy" on the wall and to draw a panther paw, a Black Panther symbol. He wanted to convince the police that black radicals had committed the crime. If he could inflame white resentment against African-Americans, Manson believed his race war would begin.

But detectives weren't buying it. Beausoleil was arrested on August 6, 1969, driving Hinman's car. The murder weapon was found in the tire well. Two days later, Manson told the Family members at Spahn Ranch, "Now is the time for Helter Skelter." He wanted things to escalate. By planning a murder that was similar to Hinman's – including the racial graffiti – he could not only put the blame on black killers, he could also make it look as though the police got the wrong man when they arrested Beausoleil. He couldn't commit an identical murder if he was locked up in jail.

On the night of August 8, Manson directed Watson to take Susan Atkins, Linda Kasabian, and Patricia Krenwinkel to "that house where Melcher used to live" and "destroy everyone... as gruesome as you can." The girls were instructed to do whatever Watson told them to do. When the four

Tex Watson

of them arrived at the entrance to the Cielo Drive property, Watson climbed a telephone pole and cut the telephone lines.

It was now just after midnight on August 9, 1969.

They parked at the bottom of the hill and walked up to the gate. Assuming that it might be alarmed or electrified, they climbed up an embankment and dropped over the fence onto the grounds. Just then, headlights came their way from within the property and Watson ordered the girls to hide in the bushes. He stopped the approaching car and shot the driver, 18-year-old Steven Parent, to death. After cutting the screen of an open window of the main house, Watson told Kasabian to keep watch down by the gate. He removed the screen, entered through the window, and let Atkins and Krenwinkel in through the front door.

The first person to encounter the intruders was a friend of Polanski, Wojciech Frykowski, who was sleeping on the living room couch. When he awoke, Watson kicked him in the head. The man asked who he was and what he was doing there, and Watson replied, "I'm the devil, and I'm here to do the devil's business."

Susan Atkins found the house's three other occupants and, with Krenwinkel's help, brought them into the living room. The three were Sharon Tate, who was eight and a half months pregnant; her friend, Jay Sebring, a noted hairstylist; and Frykowksi's girlfriend, Abigail Folger, heiress to the Folgers Coffee fortune. Roman Polanski was in London at the time, working on a film project.

Watson tied Tate and Sebring together by their necks with a rope that he'd brought with him, and he threw it up over a ceiling beam. When Sebring protested about his rough treatment of the pregnant Tate, Watson shot him. After Folger was taken back into the bedroom to get her purse, which held about $70, Watson stabbed the wounded Sebring seven times with a large knife.

Frykowski, whose hands had been tied together with a towel, managed to get free and he began struggling with Atkins, who stabbed him in the legs with a knife she was carrying. Frykowski got loose and began running for the front door, but Watson caught up with him on the porch and struck him several times with the gun, breaking the gun's right grip in the process, stabbed him repeatedly, and then shot him twice. Around this time, Linda Kasabian came up from the driveway after hearing "horrifying sounds." In a vain effort to halt the massacre, she lied to Atkins, telling her that someone was coming.

Inside the house, Abigail Folger escaped from Krenwinkel and ran out a bedroom door to the pool area. Krenwinkel pursued her and tackled her in the yard. Folger was stabbed several times by Krenwinkel and then Watson joined in with his own knife. Abigail Folger died after being stabbed 28 times. Frykowski had been stabbed 51 times. Atkins, Watson, or both, killed Sharon Tate, who was stabbed 16 times. She pleaded with her killers to let her live long enough to have her baby and she cried, "mother... mother..." until she finally died.

Sharon Tate, preparing for a baby that she would never have.

Earlier that night, as the four Family members had left Spahn Ranch, Manson told the girls to "leave a sign... something witchy," at the house. After the murders, Atkins wrote "pig" on the front door of the house in Sharon Tate's blood. Then they fled, changed out of their gore-soaked clothing, and dumped the clothes and the weapons in the hills.

The next night, six Family members, including the four from the previous night's murders plus Leslie Van Houten, and Steve "Clem" Grogan, were sent out to commit more murders. This time, Manson went along with them. He gave Kasabian directions to 3301 Waverly Drive, home of supermarket executive Pasqualino "Leno" LaBianca and his wife, Rosemary, who was co-owner of an upscale women's clothing store. Located in the Los Feliz section of L.A., the LaBianca home was next door to a house at which Manson and Family members had attended a party the year before.

Manson and Watson went into the house first and, according to Watson's later version of the events, Manson ordered him to bind Leno LaBianca's hands with a leather cord. Rosemary LaBianca was brought into the living room and Watson followed Manson's instructions to put pillowcases over the couple's heads. Manson then left, sending Krenwinkel and Leslie Van Houten into the house with instructions that the couple be killed.

Rosemary was sent back into the bedroom with the girls and Watson began stabbing Leno LaBianca with a bayonet, which had been given to him by Manson when Watson complained about the inadequate weapons that had been provided for the previous night's murders. Watson's first thrust went into LaBianca's throat. Suddenly, he heard noises in the bedroom, and he went in to find Rosemary LaBianca was keeping the girls away from her by swinging a lamp that they had tied to her neck. Watson charged forward and stabbed the woman several times with the bayonet, knocking her to the floor. He then went back into the living room and renewed his attack on Leno, stabbing him a total of 12 times. He then carved the word "war" on the man's abdomen.

Manson had been irritated that the messages left behind at the Polanski house had been too vague. He wanted it to be clear that the murders were the start of an "uprising."

Returning to the bedroom, where Krenwinkel was stabbing Rosemary LaBianca with a kitchen knife, Watson, who had been told by Manson that each of the girls needed to play a part in the murders, ordered Van Houten to stab her, too. She did so, jamming the knife into the woman's back and buttocks. Rosemary LaBianca died after being stabbed 41 times.

While Watson cleaned off the bayonet and showered in the LaBianca's bathroom, Krenwinkel used the victims' blood to scrawl "Rise" and "Death to Pigs" on the walls and "Healter Skelter" on the refrigerator door – she'd heard the phrase repeatedly but didn't know how to spell it.

She also stabbed Leno LaBianca 14 times with an ivory-handled, two-tined carving fork, which she left jutting out of his abdomen. She jammed a steak knife into his throat and left it there when she and her companions left the house.

Planning to carry out two murders on the same night, Manson sent Kasabian to the Venice home of an actor acquaintance of hers. Manson dropped off the second set of Family members at the man's apartment building and then drove back to the Spahn Ranch, leaving all of them to hitchhike home. Kasabian deliberately thwarted this murder by knocking on the wrong apartment door and waking a stranger. As the group abandoned the murder plan and left, Susan Atkins defecated in the stairwell.

The bloody writing on the wall of the LaBianca house

On August 10, as the bodies from the Tate murders were being autopsied and the LaBiancas' bodies were yet to be found, detectives from the L.A. County Sheriff's Department, which had jurisdiction in the Hinman case, informed LAPD detectives assigned to the Tate case of the bloody writing that had been found at the Hinman house. They even mentioned that their suspect, Beausoleil, hung out with a group of hippies led by "a guy named Charlie."

Tate detectives ignored the information. They believed their murders were connected to a drug deal gone bad.

Steven Parent, the young man who had been killed in the Tate driveway, had no connection to the other victims. He was an acquaintance of William Garretson, who had been hired by Rudi Altobelli to watch over the property while Altobelli was out of town. When the killers arrived, Parent had been leaving Cielo Drive, after visiting Garretson. Held for a short time as a possible murder suspect, Garretson told the police that he was living in the guesthouse but had neither seen nor heard anything on the night of the murders. He was released on August 11, after a polygraph exam showed that he was not involved in the crimes.

On August 12, the LAPD announced to the news media that it had ruled out any connection between the Tate and LaBianca murders.

On August 16, sheriff's deputies raided the Spahn Ranch and arrested Manson and 25 others – but not for murder. They were picked up as suspects in an auto theft ring that had been stealing Volkswagens and converting them into dune buggies. Weapons were seized, but because the warrant had been misdated, the Family was released a few days later.

By the end of August, virtually all leads in both cases had gone nowhere. As it turned out, a report by LaBianca detectives -- younger than those assigned to the Tate murders -- noted a possible connection between the bloody writings at the LaBianca house and the latest album by "the singing group of the Beatles" but nothing further was done to follow up on this.

In mid-October, the LaBianca team, still working separately from the Tate team, checked with the sheriff's office about any possible similar crimes and learned of the Hinman murder, which had been ignored by the detectives on the Tate case. They also learned that Hinman detectives had spoken with Bobby Beausoliel's girlfriend, Kitty Lutesinger, who had been arrested a few days earlier with members of the Manson Family.

Those arrests had occurred at the desert ranches, to which the Family had moved while they searched for the Devil's Hole in Death Valley and access to the secret underground city. A joint force of National Park rangers and officers from the California Highway Patrol and the Inyo County Sheriff's Office had raided both the Myers and Barker ranches after following clues left behind when Family members burned an earthmover owned by Death Valley National Monument. The officers had found stolen dune buggies and other vehicles and had arrested two dozen persons, including Manson. A Highway Patrol officer found Manson hiding in a cabinet under a bathroom sink at the Barker Ranch.

LaBianca detectives spoke with Lutesinger and also made contact with members of a motorcycle gang that she'd told them Manson tried to hire as guards for the Spahn Ranch. While gang members were providing information that suggested a link between Manson and the murders, a cellmate of Susan Atkins informed the LAPD of the Family's involvement in the crimes. Atkins had been arrested at Barker Ranch and while at the Sybil Brand Institute, an L.A. detention center, she spoke to bunkmates Ronnie Howard and Virginia Graham about the crimes she had taken part in.

On December 1, 1969, acting on the information from these sources, the LAPD announced warrants for the arrest of Watson, Krenwinkel, and Kasabian in the Tate case. The suspects' involvement in the LaBianca murders was also noted. Manson and Atkins, already in custody, were not mentioned. At this point, it was not known that Leslie Van Houten, also arrested near

Death Valley, had been involved in the LaBianca case. Watson and Krenwinkel had also been arrested. Both had fled from L.A. but authorities in McKinney, Texas, and Mobile, Alabama, had picked them up after being notified by the LAPD. Informed that there was a warrant out for her arrest, Linda Kasabian voluntarily surrendered to authorities in Concord, New Hampshire, on December 2.

Soon, physical evidence -- like Krenwinkel's and Watson's fingerprints, which had been found at Cielo Drive -- was enhanced by evidence recovered by the public. On September 1, 1969, the distinctive .22-caliber Hi Standard Buntline Special revolver Watson used to shoot Parent, Sebring, and Frykowski had been found and given to the police by a 10-year-old who lived near the Tate home. In December, when the *Los Angeles Times* published an account of the crimes based on information from Susan Atkins, the boy's father made several telephone calls to the police and they finally connected the gun to the murders – almost three months later. Acting on the same article, a local ABC television crew located the bloody clothing that had been discarded by the killers.

At the trial, which began on June 15, 1970, the prosecution's main witness was Linda Kasabian, who, along with Manson, Atkins, and Krenwinkel, was charged with seven counts of murder and one count of conspiracy. Since she did not take part in the actual killings -- and even tried to stop some of them -- she was granted immunity in exchange for testimony that detailed the events that occurred on the nights of the crimes.

Because of his conduct, including violations of a gag order and submission of "outlandish" and "nonsensical" pretrial motions, Manson's permission to act as his own attorney, which had been reluctantly granted in the first place, was withdrawn by the court before the trial ever started.

His strange behavior continued once the trial began. On Friday, July 24, the first day of testimony, Manson appeared in court with an "X" carved into his forehead and issued a statement that said that since he was considered to be inadequate to represent himself, he had placed an "X" on his head to cross himself out of the "establishment's" world. That weekend, all the female defendants duplicated the marks on their own foreheads and within a day or two, most of the other Family members did, too.

Prosecutor Vincent Bugliosi cited Manson's interpretation of "Helter Skelter" as the main motive in the murders. The crime scene's bloody *White Album* references were correlated with testimony about Manson's predictions that murders that blacks committed at the outset of the race war would involve the writing of the word "pigs" in their victims' blood. Testimony that Manson said, "Now is the time for Helter Skelter" was backed up by

Kasabian's testimony that, on the night of the LaBianca murders, Manson considered leaving Rosemary LaBianca's wallet lying on the street in a black neighborhood. His plan was for someone to pick up the wallet and use the credit cards inside, making it seem that "some sort of organized group killed these people." Manson directed Kasabian to leave the wallet in the ladies' room of a gas station near a black neighborhood. "I want to show blackie how to do it," Manson told Family members after the LaBianca murders.

During the trial, Family members lurked in the entrances and corridors of the courthouse. To keep them out of the courtroom itself, the prosecution subpoenaed them as prospective witnesses. That way, they were unable to enter the courtroom while others were testifying. The Family established a vigil on the sidewalk outside and each of them carried a large, sheathed hunting knife. Since it was carried in plain sight, it was legal. The knives, along with the "X" carved into his or her forehead, made Family members easily identifiable.

On August 4, despite precautions taken by the court, Manson flashed the jury a *Los Angeles Times* front page with a headline that read "Manson Guilty, Nixon Declares," a reference to a statement made the previous day when U.S. President Richard Nixon complained about what he saw as the media's glamorization of Manson. When questioned by the judge, the jury members stated that the headline did not influence them. The next day, the female defendants stood up and said in unison that, in light of Nixon's opinion, there was no point in going on with the trial.

And this was not the end of the disruptions. On October 5, after the court refused to allow the defense to question a prosecution witness that they had earlier declined to cross-examine, Manson jumped over the defense table and tried to attack the judge. He was wrestled to the floor by court bailiffs and was removed from the courtroom with the female defendants, who had risen to their feet after Manson's outburst and began chanting in Latin.

On November 19, the prosecution rested its case – and so did the defense, without ever calling a witness. Lawyers for the women were unwilling to let their clients testify and assume all the guilt, believing that Manson had instructed them to do this. The next day, Manson was permitted to testify, but because his statements would possibly violate a California statute by implicating his co-defendants, the jury was removed from the courtroom. Manson spoke for more than an hour, blaming everything on music, which was instructing young people to rise up against the establishment. He also stated that he didn't ever recall telling the girls to "get a knife and a change of clothes and go do what Tex says."

As the trial was concluding, attorney Ronald Hughes, who had been representing Leslie Van Houten, disappeared during a weekend trip. Hughes tried to separate the interests of his client from those of Manson, a move that angered Manson and may have cost Hughes his life. He hoped to show that Van Houten was not acting independently but was completely controlled in her actions by Manson.

Despite Hughes' disappearance, Judge Charles Older ordered the trial to proceed and appointed a new attorney, Maxwell Keith, for Van Houten. Keith was appointed to represent Van Houten during Hughes' absence, but this caused a two-week delay as Keith familiarized himself with the case. The girls angrily demanded the firing of all their lawyers and asked to reopen the defense. The judge denied the request and the trial resumed just before Christmas. However, disruptions caused by the defendants during the closing arguments forced the judge to ban them from the courtroom.

Not long after this, Ronald Hughes' decomposed body was found wedged between two boulders in Ventura County. Due to the severe decomposition, he had to be identified by dental records and the cause and nature of his death was ruled as "undetermined." His murder was never solved.

On January 25, 1971, guilty verdicts were returned against Manson, Krenwinkel, and Atkins on all counts. Van Houten was convicted on two counts of murder and one of conspiracy. During the trial's penalty phase, Manson shaved his head and told the press that he was the Devil. Once the jury retired to weigh the state's request for the death penalty, the female defendants shaved their heads, as well. On March 29, 1971, the jury returned verdicts of death against all four defendants. The judge agreed with their findings and on April 19, sentenced them to death.

The lengthy proceedings to extradite Charles Watson from Texas, where he had returned a month before he was arrested, resulted in his being tried separately for the murders. The trial began in August 1971, and by October, he had been found guilty on seven counts of murder and one of conspiracy. He was sentenced to death.

The death penalties were never carried out. In February 1972, the sentences of all five parties were automatically reduced to life in prison by California v. Anderson, a case in which the California Supreme Court abolished the death penalty in the state.

In a 1971 trial that was held after his convictions in the Tate and LaBianca murders, Manson was found guilty in the murders of Gary Hinman and Donald "Shorty" Shea and was given a life sentence for those crimes. Shea, a Spahn Ranch stuntman and horse wrangler, had been killed about 10 days after the August 16, 1969, sheriff's raid on the ranch. Manson, who suspected that Shea had helped set up the raid, believed that the stuntman was trying to get the Family removed from the ranch. In separate trials, Family members Bruce Davis and Steve "Clem" Grogan were also found guilty of Shea's murder.

With the murders solved and the defendants safely locked behind bars, it seemed the Family would fade away for good. But neither Manson, nor many members of the Family, could remain out of the spotlight. On September 5, 1975, the Family found national attention again when Lynette "Squeaky" Fromme attempted to assassinate U.S. President Gerald Ford. The attempt took place in Sacramento, where she and fellow Manson follower Sandra Good had moved to be near Manson while he was incarcerated at Folsom State Prison. A subsequent search of the apartment shared by Fromme, Good, and a Family recruit turned up evidence that, coupled with later actions on the part of Good, resulted in Good's conviction for conspiring to send death threats through the U.S. mail. The threats were against corporate executives and government officials for what she saw as their neglect of the environment.

Manson himself seemed to enjoy his role as the "crazed cult leader" and made a number of notable television appearances in the 1980s. He appeared on all three major networks from the California Medical Facility and San Quentin and was interviewed by Tom Snyder, Charlie Rose, and Geraldo Rivera, who spoke with Manson as part of a prime-time special on Satanism.

On September 25, 1984, while imprisoned at the California Medical Facility, Manson was seriously burned by a fellow inmate who poured paint thinner on him and then set him on fire. The prisoner later stated that Manson had threatened him. Despite suffering second and third-degree burns on about 20 percent of his body, Manson recovered from his injuries.

Thanks to the court case that nullified all California death sentences in 1972, Manson was eligible to apply for parole after just seven years in prison. His first hearing was in 1978, and he was continually denied release until his death on November 19, 2017.

Manson continued to relish his notoriety until the day he died.

The Beatles? Well, they were not fans.

At the trial, Manson himself stated, "Helter Skelter is confusion. Confusion is coming down fast. If you don't see confusion coming down fast, you can call it what you wish. It's not my conspiracy. It's not my music. I hear what it related. It says 'Rise!' It says 'Kill!' Why blame it on me? I didn't write the music. I am not the person who projected it into your social consciousness."

The band was devastated that their music was interpreted in this way, and thanks to Manson, became increasingly sensitive about how they were being perceived by the public.

The Beatles had become a mirror of the 1960s, a decade that had seen a deep and almost desperate need for spiritual meaning and for a religious experience that was not governed by Christianity. When the Manson killings painted their music in a way they never could have imagined, they wanted no more of it. By the end of the decade, the band members had each gone their separate ways, musically and spiritually.

The Beatles were over, but their story lived on.

And for one of them, so did his connection to the strange and the occult.

John Lennon met his soulmate, Yoko Ono, on November 9, 1966 – strangely, the same date as the car crash that started the "Paul is dead" rumors. Friends and biographers have stated that John and Yoko were fascinated with the occult. At times, John would buy out entire sections of occult literature in bookstores. He was intrigued by portents and prophecies and sought out the advice of tarot readers and psychics. During the evening, he would follow the example of author James Joyce and read seven pages from seven different books before falling asleep. He read everything from books about ancient history, to religion, nautical history, and especially loved books on psychic phenomena, the occult, and death.

When the Lennons moved to New York, they acquired an apartment at the famed Dakota, which had long had a reputation for being haunted. Author Stephen Birmingham wrote a fascinating book about the Dakota, detailing its history – and its ghosts.

One legendary ghost was said to be that of a little girl who appeared in nineteenth-century dress. One worker in the building reported seeing the girl a few years before John and Yoko moved in. She was bouncing a ball and excitedly told the man, "Today's my birthday!" and then walked away. When the man told his co-workers about the mysterious girl, they tried to figure out who she was, believing she was a child of one of the occupants. But there was no child at the Dakota who matched her description.

A few days later, the workman who saw her fell to his death down an open stairwell.

John Lennon didn't know anything about this story, but when he and Yoko moved into apartment 72, he became so worried about the stairwell outside their apartment that he laced it shut with heavy clothesline to keep their son, Sean, from falling through the opening.

Another phantom that haunted the Dakota was the one that residents called the "man with a wig" who would appear at times and threaten the

The Dakota Apartment Building in New York

work staff. Some said that the ghost resembled Edward Clark, the man who had built the Dakota in 1884. He died before it was completed – explaining why he might have stuck around – and records show that the eccentric millionaire wore a wig and had a strong resemblance to the spirit that was seen in the hallways.

Some of the living occupants of the Dakota could be as frightening as the ghosts.

One of them was a resident known simply as Miss Leo. When her favorite carriage horse died, she had it stuffed and put on display in her parlor. At the age of 100, she walked the halls completely naked, with her long, dyed-red hair hanging down her back. At some point, neighbors became very curious about an odd odor that came from inside her apartment. Miss Leo had lived with her bachelor brother for many years and when the puzzling odor became a noxious stench, they entered her apartment to find the corpse of her brother still sitting in his favorite chair. He had been dead for days, but Miss Leo just couldn't let him go.

The Dakota was home to many celebrities. Judy Garland had lived there, as had Edward R. Murrow, Lauren Bacall, Rex Redd, Leonard Bernstein, Roberta Flack, among others. Many had died there, like Judy Holiday, Boris Karloff, actor Robert Ryan, and his wife, Jessie.

Apartment 72, where the Lennons lived, had once belonged to the Ryans. When John and Yoko moved in, they decided to hire a medium to see if there might be any spirits lingering behind. The medium almost immediately made contact with Jessie Ryan, who announced that she was happy to share her home with John and Yoko and promised to cause them no trouble. Yoke decided that it would be a good idea to let the Ryans' daughter, Lisa, know of her mother's presence in the apartment.

Lisa Ryan was not exactly thrilled with the news.

There was also one bit of other sinister history connected to the Dakota – it was used as a filming location for Roman Polanski's *Rosemary's Baby*. In fact, a series of apartments on the seventh floor were used for the film – including apartments that were purchased by John and Yoko a decade later.

John Lennon in 1980

Of course, shortly after the release of the movie, Polanski's wife, Sharon Tate, was brutally murdered by the Manson family, who claimed to be inspired by the Beatles song, "Helter Skelter."

Friends say that John was convinced that he would suffer an early death. He had his personal assistant, Fred Seaman, search his genealogy for the cause of his ancestors' deaths. In a number of his recordings, there are disturbing coincidences that hint at his tragic death at an early age – if you want to interpret them that way. In "I Am the Walrus" the song ends with a burial scene from Shakespeare's *King Lear*. One voice in the fadeout says, "Bury my body." Another voice exclaims, "Oh, untimely death?" while the last voice says, "What? Is he dead?" John's death was untimely at the age of only 40, but that's a hard sell to convince me that the song predicted it.

This one is weirder, but still could be a coincidence... maybe.

In the LP booklet for *Magical Mystery Tour*, John is standing next to a sign that says, "The Best Way to Go is by M & D Co." Fans say that the mysterious M & D Co. was a funeral home in London. It was meant as a joke until someone pointed out that MDC are also the initials of the man who murdered John, Mark David Chapman.

Fred Seaman said that John often talked about weird, recurring dreams in which he suffered a violent death. Sounding grim and apprehensive, he said that he assumed that because he had led a life filled with violence, both in thought and deed, he was destined to die a violent death.

John's life ended when he was gunned down in the Dakota's gothic gateway on December 8, 1980. Perhaps all the really weird stuff about the death of John Lennon deals with his assassin, Mark David Chapman.

Chapman initially claimed that he killed John because of Lennon's 1966 statement that The Beatles were more popular than Jesus. He later admitted that he felt like the character Holden Caulfield from J.D. Salinger's book, *A Catcher in the Rye*. Like Caulfield, Chapman claimed to be protecting the innocence of childhood. He stalked Lennon and even adopted his name for a short while. He would lead church youth group sing-a-longs, including his own version of "Imagine," where he would sing "Imagine there's no John Lennon."

Hilarious, right?

But it gets weirder. While in Hawaii just weeks before killing Lennon, Chapman attended a film lecture given by film maker Kenneth Anger – we'll get back to him later – and he stayed after the lecture to ask Anger many questions about John and Yoko Ono. Allegedly, after he left the lecture, Chapman went down to the beach, took off all his clothes, and began playing a recording of "Lucy in the Sky with Diamonds." Then, he began to pray to Satan – or so he claimed – asking for the powers of darkness to help him kill John Lennon.

A short time later, the world lost a musical legend when John was gunned down outside of the Dakota by Chapman.

Earlier that morning, Chapman left his room at the Sheraton Hotel, leaving personal items behind which the police would later find, and bought a copy of *The Catcher in the Rye* in which he wrote "This is my statement," signing it "Holden Caulfield." He then spent most of the day near the entrance to the Dakota, talking to fans and the doorman. Early in the morning, a distracted Chapman missed seeing Lennon step out of a cab and enter the Dakota. Later in the morning, Chapman met Lennon's housekeeper who was returning from a walk with their five-year-old son, Sean. Chapman reached in front of the housekeeper to shake Sean's hand and said that he was a beautiful boy, quoting Lennon's song "Beautiful Boy (Darling Boy)."

Around 5:00 PM, John and Ono left the Dakota for a recording session at Record Plant Studios. As they walked toward their limousine, Chapman shook hands with John and asked for him to sign a copy of his album, *Double*

John Lennon signing an autograph for his killer – Mark David Chapman

Fantasy. Photographer Paul Goresh took a photo of Lennon signing Chapman's album.

Around 10:49 PM, the Lennons' limousine returned to the Dakota. John and Ono got out, passed Chapman, and walked toward the archway entrance of the building. From the street behind them, Chapman fired five shots from a .38 special revolver, four of which hit John in the back and left shoulder.

Chapman remained at the scene, reading from *The Catcher in the Rye*, until the police arrived. The NYPD officers who first responded, recognizing that Lennon's wounds were severe, decided to transport him to Roosevelt Hospital. Chapman was arrested without incident. In his statement to police three hours later, Chapman stated, "I'm sure the big part of me is Holden Caulfield, who is the main person in the book. The small part of me must be the Devil."

John Lennon was pronounced dead at 11:07 PM at St. Luke's-Roosevelt Hospital Center and the world became a little less of a good place without him in it.

SYMPATHY FOR THE DEVIL

When the British Invasion began, The Beatles were like the boys next door. They were well-groomed, even if their hair was a little long, and polite, and their songs talked about just holding young girls' hands. The Rolling Stones, though, well, that was something else altogether. They wanted a lot more than your daughter's hand – they wanted to spend the night together. Most audiences were in shock when it seemed as though a band that was the opposite of The Beatles was climbing the charts and appearing on America's television sets.

The Stones were the rebellious side of rock-n-roll. They were playing the "Devil's Music" and they didn't seem to care.

The Rolling Stones rank as one of rock's greatest bands and most prolific bands, with music that now spans an incredible six decades. Perhaps their longevity is due in part to their ability to adapt to changing styles of music and their willingness to experiment with varying themes in their songs. While they have consistently portrayed an image as "bad boy rock-n-rollers," there is a period of their music in the 1960s that flirted with the occult in a way that is downright chilling in retrospect.

The Rolling Stones were the creation of Brian Jones, the shag-haired blond guitarist and member of the sinister "27 Club." Brian had always loved music and his parents always believed that he would pursue a career in classical music. But at a young age, he became a disciple of American blues, devoting his energies to mastering the tunes of Muddy Waters, Howlin' Wolf, and Robert Johnson. He became one of the first British guitarists to take up the slide guitar.

Eventually, he met up with Mick Jagger and Keith Richards, and the resulting chemistry, after some personnel changes, gave birth to the Stones. They managed an early appearance at the Crawdaddy Club and altogether split a grand total of £24. There were only 66 people in the audience that night, but they witnessed the start of a musical legend.

It wasn't easy for the Stones to duplicate the American success of The Beatles. Decca Records had released the Stones' version of Chuck Berry's "Come On" and Willie Dixon's "I Want to be Loved," but both tracks sold poorly. Their American tour became even more frustrating when their single "Little Red Rooster" was banned by certain U.S. stations because they considered it obscene. Even the group's first performance on *The Ed Sullivan Show* in 1964 was so bad that Sullivan himself remarked, "I promise they'll never be back on our show."

The Rolling Stones in 1967

The band managed to record at Chicago's Chess Studios during their first American tour. The loved the great American blues artists, and to the Stones, the label was rock-n-roll heaven. When they arrived at Chess Studios, they met Muddy Waters for the first time. The blues guitarist was dressed in white overalls, standing on a ladder, painting the wall. It wasn't a hobby – he was doing it for the paycheck. That was when the Stones realized how tough the music business could be. As Keith Richards later put it, "Here's one of your gods painting the ceiling, and you're making a record of some of his songs."

But things changed drastically for the Stones after the release of their first big singles, "The Last Time," and "(I Can't Get No) Satisfaction." It was now 1965 and the British Invasion was in full swing. Hit singles helped put The Rolling Stones on the same level as The Beatles. The public was soon split into two opposing camps, each arguing constantly about which band was better. The competition seemed to bring out the best in both bands. New instruments like the sitar and the dulcimer found their way into both Beatles and Stones recordings. Brian Jones could pick up just about any instrument and master it within minutes. The Stones were matching the Beatles' creative output until 1967, the year The Beatles released *Sgt. Pepper's Lonely Hearts Club Band*.

It was now the "Summer of Love" and psychedelic music was hitting the airwaves. It was a new era for music and The Beatles had once again led the way with an innovative collection of songs that was unlike anything else on the radio at the time. The Stones would have to venture into the unknown waters of psychedelic music, and away from their blues roots, if they were going to keep up with the changing times.

Newfound fame had brought new relationships to the band and these new associates provided unusual avenues of escape for the often-bored musicians, who had, by now, tasted just about every pleasure of life that the world had to offer. So, why not venture out beyond this world and toward the next one?

Film maker and Satanist Kenneth Anger

This is when The Rolling Stones began their foray into the dark side – embracing a fascination with witchcraft and magic. They did so in the company of an American filmmaker named Kenneth Anger.

Anger was born in Hollywood, California, in 1930. He made his first film appearance in *A Midsummer Night's Dream* when he was four-years-old. Later in his career, he danced with Shirley Temple, and in 1947, he completed his first film at age 17, using his parent's home movie camera. It was in his teenage years that Anger developed an interest in occultist Aleister Crowley – we'll get back to him later, too – and stated that he intended his films "to cast a spell, to be a magical invocation of his fusion of dreams, desire, myth, and vision." Using film, he wanted to astound audiences with his mystical beliefs.

In 1960, Anger published what became a best-selling book called *Hollywood Babylon*, which was banned in the United States until 1975. The book was a hodge-podge of legends and lore about the scandalous behavior of the beautiful people who achieved success in the film capital of the world. Anger's grandmother had once worked as a studio wardrobe mistress and passed on all the sordid gossip and the details of scandals that occurred among Hollywood royalty. Anger turned it into a book. It's an entertaining

Anger in a scene from his occult experimental film, *Scorpio Rising*

read – as long as you don't mistake the stories for gospel truth. He also wrote a sequel a couple of years after the original book was allowed in U.S. bookstores.

During the late 1960s, Anger – now considered a renegade avant-garde filmmaker – took up residence in England and began hob-knobbing with rock stars. Anger first met Mick Jagger at the home of art gallery owner Robert Fraser. He had become enamored with the almost supernatural power that the Stones held over their audiences and was soon impressed by Mick's personal charisma. Anger was the one who got Mick interested in the occult.

Mick was obsessed with matching the success of The Beatles' *Sgt. Pepper* album and this served as a major power play to get Brian Jones out of the band. Brian was a blues purist and was convinced that an uncharted journey into psychedelic sounds was a terrible mistake. He was sure that the Stones would alienate their fans and told his friend, Tony Sanchez, "If he insists on recording this kind of crap, the Stones are dead."

But Mick was sure this was the direction in which they needed to go. "It's psychedelic, man," he said. "Pretty soon everything is going to be psychedelic, and if we aren't in there on our next album, we will be left behind. No one is going to want to listen to rhythm and blues anymore."

Mick Jagger in the late 1960s

Just keep in mind that this is the same guy who also steered the band toward disco when that was in style. Ouch.

Mick easily convinced Keith Richards to make the leap and work began on their next album, *Their Satanic Majesties Request*. During the recording, Brian did little to contribute to the swirling psychedelic sound. At times, cruel jokes were played on him, such as having him attempt to overdub guitar lines while the recorders were off. Brian was in pretty bad shape by this point in his life, but the bitterness made things worse. One thing he was sure of – Brian had lost control of his own creation.

The album's cover art was designed by Michael Cooper – who had also photographed the *Sgt. Pepper* cover – and portrayed the Stones dressed as wizards and magicians, complete with a pointed wizard's hat. Mick had purchased books to keep with the theme, occult texts like *The Secret of the Golden Flower, Morning of the Magicians,* and *The Golden Bough*. A special camera was flown in from Japan to shoot a 3-D image for the cover. If you look closely, you can see the image of the four Beatles in the shrubbery. This was done to repay the plug that The Beatles had given them on the cover of *Sgt. Pepper*, where you can find a stuffed doll wearing a "Welcome The Rolling Stones" sweatshirt.

Their Satanic Majesties Request became a critical failure for the band. Brian had been right. Critics claimed it had been made just to cash in on the success of *Sgt. Pepper*. The Stones would return to their musical roots, but for Brian, his time in the band was almost over, and tragically, his death was near.

The Stones moved on and when production began on *Beggars Banquet*, they were much deeper into their studies of black magic, heavily influenced by Kenneth Anger. It was Anger who was said to have suggested creating a rock anthem to Satan – "Sympathy for the Devil."

And, of course, things got weirder.

In 1970, Mick starred in a cult film called *Performance*. In it, he played the role of Turner, a rock star who wore makeup and dressed in feminine clothing. The character also studied the occult and was obsessed with black magic. You're right if you believe this role shaped Mick's persona in the years that followed – a case of life imitating art. The occult props from the movie set constantly disappeared, swiped by Anita Pallenberg, the beautiful blond who had been Brian's lover and then started living with Keith. Anita had also gotten caught up in the band's fascination with the supernatural.

The concept for "Sympathy for the Devil" was based on Mikhail Bulgakov's book about Satanic fantasy called *The Master and Margarita*. During this time, Anger was developing a concept for his salute to Satan. His plan was to create a film called *Lucifer Rising* and he wanted to film it with the Stones. He wanted Mick to play Lucifer and Keith to play Beelzebub, a sort of crown prince and henchmen to the Devil. Mick agreed to compose a musical score for the film, but he didn't want to play the role of Lucifer. Anger used his brother, Chris Jagger, instead and cast Marianne Faithfull as Lilith. But Anger dropped Chris after just one day of filming and kept looking for the perfect actor to play the part.

Mick helped with the production of the film, which was shot in exotic places, using Egypt as the main focal point. Marianne Faithfull later stated that she didn't believe that Kenneth Anger possessed any psychic or magical powers, but she did believe in his work as a filmmaker. One of her scenes took place in Giza, with the Sphinx as the backdrop. It was here that she sensed that Anger's creative powers were overrated. She said, "Even as inept as Kenneth was, I knew he was dangerous in a way. I knew that simply by being in the film I was involving myself in a magic act far more potent than Kenneth's hocus-pocus Satanism." After smearing herself with stage blood, Marianne filmed a sequence where she crawled around an Arab cemetery shortly before dawn, as the sun rose over the pyramids. Years later, she claimed, "If I'd been my normal self, I would have just laughed, but by then I was a hopeless junkie. I used to feel a lot of bad luck in my life came from that film."

Later, during a scene filmed at an ancient Neolithic site in Germany, Marianne climbed to the top of a mountain and passed out. She believed it was because she ran out of heroin and blacked out – it was nothing to do with the film sequence – but she took a long fall and should have been badly injured. She was rushed to the hospital but didn't even end up with a concussion. She always claimed that Anger likely wished that she had died in the fall – it would have been better for the film.

Marianne Faithfull with Mick Jagger around the time of his dabbling in the occult

Marianne always claimed that Mick hadn't taken the role in *Lucifer Rising* because his interest in Satan was all an act – she called it "Satanic pantomime." But even if Anger misread Mick's interest, he knew that other kindred spirits lurked within the group. According to Anger, "The occult unit within the Stones was Keith, Anita, and Brian. I believe that Anita is, for want of a better word, a witch. You see, Brian was a witch, too. I'm convinced. He showed me his witch's tit. He had a supernumerary tit in a very sexy place on his inner thigh. He stated, 'In another time they would have burned me.' He was very happy about that. Mick backed away from being identified with Lucifer. He thought it was too heavy."

Witch's tit? Yes, it was really a thing – sort of. In the seventeenth century, this was also referred to as a "Devil's Mark." The mark was made when the alleged witch pricked her or his finger with a silver pin in order to sign a contract with the Devil in blood. Early witch finders believed that this "witch's tit" could take the shape of a mole, freckle, or third nipple. The legends said that the mark would emit no sensation so witch-finders would stab them with a needle to determine the guilt or innocence of an accused witch.

I can make this a little weirder.

The ultimate test for witches was to throw the accused into a body of water to see if they would float. Water was a purity symbol of baptism and

Anita Pallenberg with Keith Richards in 1969

would cause a servant of Satan to rise up out of the water. If the accused sank – and drowned – then they were obviously innocent. If they didn't, then they could be hanged or burned as a witch.

Rather strange that Brian Jones drowned in his pool in 1969, isn't it? By this logic, I guess he wasn't a witch after all.

But what about Anita? When it became obvious that Keith was falling in love with Anita, tension mounted between Keith and Brian. Marianne Faithfull was living with Mick at the time and remembered, "Anita was certainly into black magic. And although I really can't say whether she was a witch or not, there's no denying the fact that Anita was some sort of black queen, a dark person, despite her blond looks. It's very hard to define wickedness, but when Anita looked at you sometimes with that incredible smile on her face, it was not a smile you had ever seen before, it was a smile that seemed to be camouflage for some dark secret that she was hoarding. The best way that I can describe Anita is that she was like a snake to a bird and that she could transfix you and hold you in place until she wanted to make her move."

Yikes. But Anita took it in stride. When told of Marianne's description of her powers, she said, "Oh, she's probably referring to the spell that I put on Brian. She knew about that."

Brian and Anita had a terrible fight and Anita was forcibly thrown out of the house. She fled to a friend's house and the longer she sat there, "scraped and bloody," the angrier she got. And since revenge is a great motivator, she explained, "I was sitting there, in tears, angry, getting my wounds treated, feeling terrible, and I decided to make a wax figure of Brian and poke him with a needle. I molded some candle wax into an effigy and said whatever words I said and closed my eyes and jabbed the needle into the wax figure. It pierced the stomach."

Well, "whatever words" Anita said, they had the desired effect. When Anita returned to Brian's house the next morning, she found him very sick – suffering from severe stomach pains. He had been up all night, in severe agony, swallowing every kind of medicine he could find. Nothing helped and it took several days for him to get better.

Anita admitted, "I did have an interest in witchcraft. The world of the occult fascinated me, but after what happened to Brian, I never cast another spell."

According to Stones insider Tony Sanchez, though, this wasn't exactly true. Tony remembered an incident in which there was an old man dying on a road outside of Marrakesh. His cart had been struck by a truck and turned over. As a crowd gathered around, Anita pushed her way through and dipped a handkerchief in the old man's blood. Tony swore, "Later Anita attempted to use that same handkerchief to put a curse on a young man that angered her. Subsequently, he died."

That young man had been Joe Monk, a former friend of Keith Richards. After a drug bust in the summer of 1973, Anita became convinced that Monk had been an informant for the police. She swore revenge – she'd put a curse on him, she said. A short time later, Monk was driving along a lonely cliff-top road in Majorca when his car crashed, and he was killed. No one saw it and there were no other vehicles involved. The police were unable to explain how the accident had occurred.

Coincidence? Maybe, but I'm going to say that it didn't pay to have Anita Pallenberg mad at you.

The influence of Kenneth Anger continued to grow and, as it did, the Stones began to fear the powers of their guru. Anger claimed to be a magus – a magician of the highest order – and while most people have always believed he was little more than a con artist of the highest order, the Stones were said to have witnessed enough strangeness around him to make them more than a little uneasy.

Mick's musical compositions for *Lucifer Rising* were used as a soundtrack for another Anger work, *Invocation of My Demon Brother*. This short film included scenes of magic, the Stones in concert, and American soldiers fighting in Vietnam. The starring role went to a California musician who had become Anger's new choice for the starring role in *Lucifer Rising*. He was cast as Lucifer, but after a few months of filming, he became involved in a terrible argument with Nager. It has been suggested that he stole some of the film negatives and used them to try and extort money from Anger. As a result, Anger was said to have responded with a "ritualistic curse."

That musician's name? Bobby Beausoleil.

A short time after being fired by Anger, he drifted into the Manson family and murdered Gary Hinman. After the murder, he scrawled the words "Political Piggy" on the wall with Hinman's blood. He was soon arrested while driving his victim's car, with the murder weapon in it.

No doubt this was one of the reasons that the Stones began to break away from Kenneth Anger. Tony Sanchez recalled, "We were all a little afraid of him. Again, and again, inexplicable things involving him would happen."

Once, the Stones and Beatles friend Robert Fraser hosted an opening party for some sculptures created by John and Yoko Lennon. Since the statues were white, guests were asked to dress in white for the party. Sanchez noticed that Kenneth Anger was at the party, but said that when he walked toward the filmmaker, Anger seemed to vanish into thin air. Strangely, Anita Pallenberg, Marianne Faithfull, and Keith Richards all had the same experience. Each saw Anger moving through the crowd but as each of them approached him to have a conversation, he just seemed to disappear. Anita added that seeing him there was strange because Anger had told her that he couldn't come to the party because he was going to be in Germany on business.

Anger was gone for two weeks, but by the time he returned, numerous people who had been at the party – including John, Yoko, Robert Fraser, and artist Jim Dine – all remarked that they had seen him across the crowded room but had been unable to speak to him. Tony Sanchez later had the chance to ask Anger if he had been there that night. "He only laughed," Sanchez said.

When Keith and Anita suggested that they'd like to get married but didn't want the legal paperwork hassle of a marriage between an English citizen and a German-Italian, Kenneth Anger suggested a pagan service. He said that the door to their house needed to be painted gold with a special paint that was enriched with magical herbs. The newly painted door would represent the sun and would bless the marriage. Keith laughed at the idea and had no intention of paying to have the work done. But early the next morning, Anita awakened him with her screams – the heavy, three-inch mahogany door had been painted gold during the night. To have accomplished such a flawless job, the door would have had to have been removed from its hinges, but this would have been impossible because of the heavy lock on it.

Somehow, they believed, Anger had entered their home by his mere will alone.

Several Stones insiders came to believe that Kenneth Anger's presence cast a sort of pall over the band, perhaps leading to Brian's death and other dark events in the band's history that brought a close to the 1960s.

Brian's last performance took place during the production of *The Rolling Stones Rock and Roll Circus*, to which the Stones invited a who's who of rock royalty to star in what Mick hoped would be the rock film to end all rock films. The greats in attendance included John and Yoko Lennon, Eric Clapton, The Who, and Jethro Tull. Many of the performers dressed in costume. Bill Wyman and Charlie Watts were dressed as clowns, Yoko was a witch, Mick and Keith were ringmasters, and Brian wore a silver top hat with horns. He represented the Devil. The Stones closed the show with "Route 66," Jumpin' Jack Flash," and finally, "Sympathy for the Devil." As the song reached its peak, Mick tore off his red shirt to reveal a temporary tattoo of Satan.

On July 3, 1969, a few weeks after Mick and Keith replaced him with Mick Taylor, Brian was discovered dead in his swimming pool.

Two days later, the Stones performed a large free concert at Hyde Park. Of course, Mick claimed that this was a tribute to their fallen friend and bandmate, but most fans had no idea of the animosity that had grown between Brian, Mick, and Keith. Jagger and Richards would both grow to regret the things that happened with Brian, but never felt any guilt about his death. As Mick said in one interview, "I do feel that I behaved in a very childish way, but we were very young, and in some ways we picked on him. But, unfortunately, he made himself a target for it; he was very, very jealous, very difficult, very manipulative, and if you do that in this kind of a group of people you get back as good as you give, to be honest. I wasn't understanding enough about his drug addiction."

The concert at Hyde Park went on as scheduled and the English charter of the Hell's Angels served as the band's security. Hundreds of thousands of fans listened with tears in their eyes as Mick read the poem "Adonais" by Shelley in tribute to Brian. After the reading, thousands of white butterflies were released from cages on the stage. It was meant to represent the soul of Brian Jones, being released from earth to soar toward the heavens – but instead it had a somber effect on the crowd. The heat had been too much for the delicate creatures and instead of flying away, most of them flittered upward and then died, falling on the audience like snowflakes.

The Rolling Stones prepared for their 1969 American tour with a desire to upstage the Woodstock festival. It was the Age of Aquarius and the dawning of a new era of peace and love – but it turned out to be anything but that when they made it to Altamont. The Stones had decided that the tour would be filmed as a testament to rock-n-roll. If they were to offer a free

The Rolling Stones at Altamont

concert in San Francisco, it would smash the attendance records at Woodstock, and the Stones would live up to their reputation as the world's greatest rock-n-roll band.

But the entire venture turned out to be a disaster.

Everything was in short supply – doctors, food vendors, bathrooms – but the greatest concern was the show's security. The Grateful Dead had suggested that the Stones use some California charters of the Hell's Angels. It's been claimed that the Stones paid the motorcycle club with a truckload of beer to provide security at the concert. It was all done in a hurry so that the concert and documentary could take place on schedule.

Mick had been uneasy throughout the tour. He'd heard about an underground college play in which a famous rock performer was stabbed to death at a concert at the conclusion. There was no doubt who the character was supposed to be since one of the other players shouted, "He's killed Mick!" during the climax. He'd received a number of letters threatening death – including one from a self-professed student of the occult who claimed that his murder has been astrologically predicted. On the day after the letter arrived, Mick never left his hotel room and stayed surrounded by a security detail, just in case.

Mick knew of the existence of a lunatic fringe in California but felt safe in a city of peace and love – you know, where "gentle people lived with flowers in their hair," as the song went. There was no way of knowing that all hell was going to break loose that night.

The Rolling Stones arrived at the Altamont Speedway by helicopter. The concert was already in full swing and featured Santana, Jefferson Airplane, The Flying Burrito Brothers, and Crosby, Stills, Nash & Young. The Stones were supposed to take the stage last as the final act. The Grateful Dead were also scheduled to perform but declined to play shortly before their scheduled appearance due to the increasing violence as the crowd slowly went out of control. "That's the way things went at Altamont—so badly that the Grateful Dead, prime organizers and movers of the festival, didn't even get to play," staff at *Rolling Stone* magazine wrote in a detailed narrative on the event, calling it "rock and roll's all-time worst day, December 6th, a day when everything went perfectly wrong."

When the Stones finally took the stage, Mick – who had been punched in the head by a concertgoer within seconds of getting off the helicopter – was visibly intimidated by the unruly crowd. Tony Sanchez later recalled naked audience members trying to crawl onto the stage, only to be pummeled by Hell's Angels with pool cues. Mick urged everyone to "Just be cool down in the front there, don't push around."

During the third song, "Sympathy for the Devil," a fight erupted in the front of the crowd at the foot of the stage, prompting the Stones to pause their set while the Angels restored order. After a lengthy delay and another appeal for calm, the band restarted the song and continued their set with less incident until the start of "Under My Thumb."

That's when things went from bad to horrific.

Some of the Hells Angels got into a scuffle with an 18-year-old African-American man named Meredith Hunter, who was trying to get onstage with other fans. One of the Hell's Angels grabbed Hunter's head, punched him, and chased him back into the crowd. After a minute's pause, Hunter returned to the stage where, according to the producer of the documentary film about the show, *Gimme Shelter*, Porter Bibb, Hunter's girlfriend Patty Bredehoft found him and tearfully begged him to calm down and move further back in the crowd with her; but he was reportedly enraged, irrational, and "so high he could barely walk."

After his initial scuffle with the Angels, Hunter – as seen in the concert footage wearing a bright, lime-green suit -- returned to the front of the crowd and drew a long-barreled .22 caliber revolver from inside his jacket. Hell's Angel Alan Passaro, seeing Hunter drawing the revolver, drew a knife from his belt and charged Hunter, knocked aside the pistol, and stabbing him to death.

The documentary crew was unaware of having caught the killing on film. This was discovered more than a week later when raw footage was screened in the New York. In the film sequence, lasting about two seconds, an opening appears in the crowd, leaving Patty Bredehoft in the center. Hunter enters the opening from the left. His hand rises toward the stage, and the silhouette of a revolver is clearly seen against Patty's light-colored dress. Passaro is seen entering from the right and delivering two stabs with his knife as he parries Hunter's revolver and pushes him off-screen. Passaro was reported to have stabbed Hunter five times in the upper back, although only two stabs are visible in the footage. Witnesses also reported Hunter was stomped on by several Hells Angels while he was on the ground. The gun was recovered and turned over to police. Hunter's autopsy confirmed he was high on methamphetamine when he died. Passaro was arrested and tried for murder in the summer of 1971, but was acquitted after a jury viewed concert footage, showing Hunter brandishing the revolver and concluded that Passaro had acted in self-defense.

The Stones were aware of the skirmish, but not the stabbing. Mick later said, "You couldn't see anything, it was just another scuffle." But it soon became apparent they could see something of what had happened because the band stopped playing mid-song and Mick was heard calling into his microphone, "We've really got someone hurt here... is there a doctor?"

After a few minutes the band began playing again. Mick said they all agreed that if they abandoned the show at that point, the crowd would have become even more unruly, perhaps turning into a full-scale riot.

Even without the riot, there was a death toll. Four were dead after Altamont – one by stabbing, two were run over after Hell's Angels rode their bikes into a crowd, and one LSD drowning in a dirty drainage ditch. Hundreds of other people were injured, some of them seriously.

One audience member wrote to *Rolling Stone*: "To those that know, it's obvious that the Stones, or at least some of them, have been involved in the practice of magick ever since the *Satanic Majesties Request* album. But there at least the colour was more white than black. Since then the hue had gone steadily darker and darker. At Altamont He appeared in his full majesty with his consort of demons, the Hell's Angels. It was just a few days before the Winter Solstice when the forces or darkness are at their most powerful. The moon was in Scorpio, which is the time of the month when the Universal vibration is at its most unstable. It was held in a place dedicated to destruction through motion. Then Mick comes on only after it is dark enough for the red lights to work their magick. I don't know if they are sadder and wiser from the experience. But an agonizing price was paid for the lesson. And we are all guilty because we have eaten of the cake the Stones baked."

After their return to England, a black cloud seemed to follow them. Keith and Anita's young son died tragically and Keith's addiction to heroin worsened to the point that the two of them eventually split up. Mick burned all his books on magic and stopped taking calls from Kenneth Anger, who later made snide mention of the fact that when Mick married Bianca Pérez-Mora Macías "he wore a rather prominent cross about his neck."

Perhaps the Stones really were "sadder and wiser" after Altamont. If nothing else, they'd certainly learned a lesson.

THE WICKED DISCIPLE

As has already been documented, the 1960s produced a lot of stellar rock groups. However, none of them came close to unleashing the kind of furious sound that Led Zeppelin did. Their signature sound was conjured up from the blues guitars of the American South and combined with the force of John Bonham's thunderous drums. Steppenwolf may have been the first band to use the term "heavy metal" but Led Zeppelin defined it.

As the band grew in legend, fantastic rumors surfaced, like whispers of blood pacts, mortal curses, black magic, and a quest for forbidden knowledge. It probably seems to most readers that such stories were likely just clever marketing, appealing to a legion of fans who spent a lot of their time reading J.R.R. Tolkien, but in this case, that's not necessarily true.

It wasn't just the music being performed by Led Zeppelin that was crossing the line to the dark side.

But it all started innocently enough. In 1957, on a British television variety show, two young boys performed "Mama Don't Wanna Play No Skiffle No More." One of the guitarists was a 12-year-old named James Patrick Page. He had just been given his first guitar – a musical instrument that had to be confiscated from him at school each day. Like so many other young guitarists of the day, he had been inspired by Elvis Presley, although Jimmy never had dreams of being a professional musician. He lived in the suburbs and had grown up on his uncle's farm. He wanted to be a lab technician, but his love of music eventually led him to stardom.

Jimmy first went on the road with Neil Christian and the Crusaders in the early 1960s. He was still in school but convinced his parents to let him follow his music and see where it led. However, after getting sick from playing night after night in clubs, he decided to return to school. He majored in art and put away his guitar for a time, but his resolve to stay away from music didn't last. Between 1963 and 1965, Jimmy performed as a session

Led Zeppelin in 1969

musician, playing on many of the biggest hits of the era, from "Baby, Please Don't Go" to "Sunshine Superman."

His first real break came when he joined the Yardbirds. They were known for their incredible guitar work, and other alumni from the group included Eric Clapton and Jeff Beck. At first, Jimmy was a replacement for bassist Paul Samwell-Smith, but for a short time, he shared guitar duties with Jeff Beck. When the Yardbirds became victims of their own excesses, Jimmy was left with the name but none of the original members. So, he started recruiting new members – Robert Plant on vocals, John Bonham on drums, and musician and arranger John Paul Jones on bass and keyboards. It was during the fulfillment of the Yardbirds' final concert contract that The Who's drummer, Peter Moon, informed Jimmy that his new band was going to go over like a "fucking lead balloon."

And the band's new name was born.

The first Led Zeppelin album was released on January 12, 1968, three days before Jimmy's 25th birthday. The Beatles' *White Album* was at the number one spot at the time, but *Led Zeppelin* entered the charts at 99 and had soared to number 10 by May of that year. It stayed on the charts for an incredible 73 straight weeks. Their first American tour turned out to be remarkable. At times, they were billed only as the "supporting act" but they blew more established bands off the stage. The pounding sounds of British blues were a hit with audiences and Zeppelin quickly became one of the most revered bands in rock history.

Led Zeppelin II was released in October 1969 and was certified gold on the day of its release. Even more incredibly, their first album was still on the charts at number 18. Both albums were now certified million sellers, and with Led Zeppelin II, the band had managed to replace the Beatles' Abbey Road as Billboard's number-one bestselling album. The biggest single off the album was "Whole Lotta Love," but it was a song that the band tried to keep from being released as a single. A middle section of it had been removed for more conservative radio airplay and Zeppelin felt compelled to stand up against radio and market exploitation.

Many other musicians had no idea how to explain the Led Zeppelin sound. Eric Clapton once said, "I don't know about them. I've heard their records and I saw them play in Milwaukee – we were on the same bill. They were very loud – I thought unnecessarily loud. I liked some of it; I really did like some of it. But a lot of it was just too much. They overemphasized whatever point they were trying to make, I thought."

What Clapton called "overemphasis" led the band to experimenting with different textured sounds. On their third album, they departed from their established sound for a lighter acoustic feel. Many rock critics hammered them for this, but Led Zeppelin, they explained, was a constantly changing entity, filled with creative power. And this was coming from a band whose meteoric rise to fame defined all popular convention. Jimmy Page and John Paul Jones were respected musicians, but only known for their session work. Robert Plant and John Bonham were relative unknowns.

This never slowed them down, though, and the band embraced their new "rock gods" status. When they went on tour, their offstage escapades became legendary. Groups flocked to the band. Television sets were thrown out hotel windows, there were drinking binges, fights, and more naked women than any one band could handle – okay, maybe not that last part.

Seasoned professional musicians combined with raw, youthful energy was what gave birth to the Led Zeppelin sound but, course, there were many who compared the seemingly magic way that they rose to success with the legend of Robert Johnson. Jimmy and Robert were devoted to Johnson's music and some of the bluesman's lyrics borrowed and placed into Zeppelin songs. Robert Plant eerily tried to imitate Johnson's voice on "Bring it on Home" and in one interview, Robert claimed to have a bottle of dirt that had been filled at the crossroads where Johnson was said to have made his deal with the Devil.

Rumors spread that Led Zeppelin had struck their own bargain with Satan. This mythical contract was allegedly drawn up in 1968, and in it, band members pledged to follow the Left Hand Path of black magic in exchange for musical success. Three of the band members quickly signed, but the third – John Paul Jones – refused. For that reason, he seemed to be untouched by the so-called "Zeppelin Curse" that plagued the band in the 1970s.

Needless to say, there's no evidence any kind of pact like this ever existed, but it's no surprise that the rumors got started. Most of those people, though, weren't attributing the group's success to a devilish deal, they were linking it to the peculiar fascinations and hobbies of Jimmy Page.

Jimmy Page was a serious collector of the occult. He once even owned an occult bookstore and bought thousands of books, artifacts, and objects with sinister connections. His fascination centered around one of the

Jimmy Page

leading figures in the occult world, who had seen such a resurgence in interest about him in the 1960s that even The Beatles placed him on the cover of their *Sgt. Pepper* album.

His name was Aleister Crowley and he was the man who helped shape the mythology of sex, drugs, and rock-n-roll.

'MR. CROWLEY"

The man with the clean-shaved head that peered out ominously from a crowd of onlookers on the cover of *Sgt. Pepper's Lonely Hearts Club Band* was Aleister Crowley, a man the British press called "the wickedest man alive." He became the most infamous practitioner of what he called "sex magick" in

Aleister Crowley

history, and with his carefully cultivated reputation as the Anti-Christ – he even adopted the moniker "Great Beast 666" – he both revolved and fascinated people. Crowley regularly practiced his magical rites with both male and female acolytes, was known for drinking menstrual blood, and was in the habit of eating his own semen, which he regarded as a potent magical elixir.

Cynics claimed that Crowley's claims to be a seeker of occult wisdom were entirely fabricated to enable his debauchery, while others regard him as a true visionary of the early twentieth century. Either way, he remains a remarkable and compelling figure whose views changed both the world and the mythology of music in the 1960s.

He was born Edward Alexander Crowley in England on October 12, 1875 – that much we do know. Beyond that, much of Crowley's life remains shrouded in mystery. This is not because documentation of his life does not exist, but because most of that documentation was provided by Crowley himself. As a shameless self-promoter, Crowley undoubtedly invented whole sections of his life, magnifying the occult aspects of his existence to appeal to his followers and devotees. We'll never know for sure just how much of his biography is fact -- and how much is fancy -- but the following has been pieced together from the most reliable sources that I could find.

His father, Edward Crowley, had made his fortune from Crowley's Ales, and had retired to become a minister, preaching the conservative evangelical doctrine of the Plymouth Brethren. The family lived in Leamington, a small peaceful town, and Crowley made it clear that his "diabolism" later in life was a revolt against the religious repression of his childhood. However, his youth was not a bitter one and his parents were very affectionate and indulgent, spoiling their son. Crowley admired his father and imitated his leadership abilities, a skill that would serve him well as an adult. His father died when Crowley was 11 and the boy began getting into trouble. He was sent to a private, religious school and it was here that his seeds of rebellion began to be sown in earnest.

As Crowley became a teenager, his interest in sex began to grow. His mother was a puritanical woman and so straitlaced that she once argued violently with Crowley's cousin, Agnes, because the younger woman had a book by Emile Zola in her house. As an outright revolt against such attitudes, Crowley lost his virginity to a servant girl on his mother's bed when he was 14-years-old.

Just a year later, Crowley's life almost came to an early end on Guy Fawkes Night in 1891. Guy Fawkes Night (or Fireworks Night) is an annual celebration on the evening of November 5 to celebrate the foiling of the Gunpowder Plot in which a number of Catholic conspirators, including Guy Fawkes, attempted to blow up the Houses of Parliament in London. As Crowley tried to light a 10-pound, homemade firework, it exploded, knocking him unconscious for 96 hours. His followers believe that the accident may have awakened some sort of latent psychic abilities in him, which is how they explain the dark career of his adulthood and the powerful influence that he obtained over the occult community of the day.

After recovering from the fireworks accident, Crowley began attending public school at Malvern, and then went on to Oxford, where he lived lavishly on his inheritance and published his own poems. Crowley was not a poet, but he certainly believed that he was. At one point, he referred to the small town where he grew up and its proximity to Stratford-on-Avon and noted that it was "a strange coincidence that one small county should have given England her two greatest poets – for one must not forget Shakespeare." He discovered rock climbing while in college and for many years, this satisfied his adventurous nature.

But the lure of the occult continued to call to him.

As a student, he discovered *Kabbalah Unveiled*, which fascinated him because it was all so incomprehensible. It was perhaps at this time that the first inklings of what lay ahead of him in life began to surface, especially after his discovery of A.E. Waite's compilation on ceremonial magic, *The Book of Black Magic and of Pacts*. Crowley continued to pen his own poetry -- including an uplifting cycle of poems about a sexual psychopath who becomes a murderer -- but his writings began to take on a more supernatural feel. But sex was never far from his mind and he also wrote a short sadomasochistic novel called *Snowdrops from a Curate's Garden*.

Through a fellow student, Crowley was introduced to an "alchemist" named George Cecil Jones, and through Jones to the Order of the Golden Dawn, a magical cult that practiced arcane rituals for spiritual development. The Order had been founded by retired physician Dr. William Robert Woodman; Dr. William Wynn Westcott, a London coroner, and Samuel

Liddell MacGregor Mathers. They were Freemasons and Rosicrucians, both prominent secret societies of the era. Westcott, also a member of the Theosophical Society, was the initial driving force behind the establishment of the Golden Dawn.

The Golden Dawn was formed along the lines of a Masonic Lodge; however, women were admitted on an equal basis with men. The Golden Dawn is technically only the first or "outer" of three orders, although all three are often collectively described as the "Golden Dawn." The First Order taught esoteric philosophy based on the Kabbalah, as well as the basics of astrology and tarot reading. The Second taught magic proper, including scrying, astral travel, and alchemy. The Third Order was that of the "Secret Chiefs," who were said to be powerful adepts no longer in human form, but who directed the activities of the lower two orders through spirit communication with the people in charge.

Sorry, it's all a bit muddled, but bear with me.

By the middle 1890s, the Golden Dawn was well established in England, with membership rising to over 100 from every class of Victorian Society. This was considered the heyday of the order and many celebrities of the time boasted membership within its ranks, including actress Florence Farr, Annie Horniman (who sponsored the Abbey Theatre in Dublin), occult novelist Arthur Machen, William Butler Yeats, Evelyn Underhill, and many others.

Crowley was introduced to the Golden Dawn during this period and right away, announced himself disappointed by the mediocrity of the members and about how boring and commonplace the ceremonies were. He was admitted to their ranks anyway but found himself at the lowest of the order's levels. He quickly began working hard to rise in status.

Around 1897, Dr. Westcott broke off all ties to the Golden Dawn leaving Samuel Mathers in complete control. He appointed Florence Farr to be Chief Adept in Anglia. This left Mathers as the only active founding member and in charge of the order. Thanks to personality clashes with other members, and his frequent absences from the center of order activity in England, challenges to Mathers' authority as leader began to develop among the members. Many of them were unhappy with Mathers' leadership and were anxious to make contact with the Secret Chiefs on their own, instead of receiving "wisdom" through Mathers.

It was Crowley who antagonized the situation. In his struggle to rise in the order's ranks, he had applied to a higher level in the London temple, but was rejected. Mathers overrode their decision and initiated him at a temple in Paris instead. For the London leaders, this was the last straw. Crowley's initiation led to a general meeting that called for Mathers' removal as chief and his expulsion from the order. It took many months, but it was eventually decided that the revolt against Mathers was unjustified, and by 1908, he was working closely with J.W. Brodie-Innes, who had been part of the council that ran the order in his absence.

During this time, Mathers began extending the order's connections in America. The first Golden Dawn temple had been established in Chicago around 1900. It was located in a small building on Halsted Street, which is now home to a bar. Renovations in the building in recent years revealed ritual paintings in the basement and a dagger that had been buried under the floor to purify the location.

The Order of the Golden Dawn eventually faded out of existence. Most of the temples closed down by the 1930s, with the exception of the Hermes Temple in Bristol, which operated sporadically until 1970. The group has been revived several times over the years and a modern version still survives today.

But Crowley had abandoned the Golden Dawn when Mathers was kicked out. He also got into a very public disagreement with W.B. Yeats -- who Crowley maintained hated him because Crowley was a much better poet. The problem emerged over money, of which Crowley had plenty, thanks to his inheritance. However, Crowley shared with Mathers a curious habit of pretending to be an aristocrat. Mathers was given to dressing in kilts and calling himself the Chevalier MacGregor or the Comte de Glenstrae, both of which were titles he created himself. Crowley rented a flat in London shortly after joining the Golden Dawn, started using Russian accent, and called himself Count Vladimir Svareff. He explained later that he did this in the interests of psychological observation. He had observed how tradesmen deferred to his because of his wealth and he wanted to see how they behaved with a Russian nobleman. This may or may not have been the case since Crowley continued such charades long after the "experiment" in London.

When he moved to a house that overlooked Loch Ness in Scotland, he dubbed himself "Lord Boleskine"

Crowley's Boleskine House at Loch Ness

and imitated Mathers by adopting a kilt. While living in the house, he concentrated on the magic of Abra-Melin the Mage, whose ultimate aim was to establish contact with one's guardian angel. Crowley claimed that in London, he and George Cecil Jones, his alchemist friend, succeeded in materializing the helmeted head and left leg of a spirit called "Buel," and that on another occasion, a group of semi-formed demons spent the night marching around his room.

Have I mentioned that Crowley was a frequent opium user?

At Loch Ness, the lodge and terrace of his house allegedly became haunted by shadowy shapes and the lodge keeper went mad during Crowley's tenancy and attempted to kill his wife and children. Crowley claimed that the ritual room of the house became so dark while he was trying to copy magical symbols that he would have to light lamps, even when the sunshine was blazing outside.

After his quarrel with Yeats, Crowley went to Mexico, where he claimed that his concentrated effort almost made his reflection vanish from a mirror. In the dry, hot climate of Mexico, Crowley continued to work to create his own mystical religion, greater than any that he had encountered before, but he was at a loss as to how to continue. He said that he put out a great call for help from the cosmos and a week later, he received a letter from George Cecil Jones, suggesting a new course of study. Oddly enough, it was an old mountain climbing companion of Crowley's who suggested his next move. He advised him to give up magic and simply develop a power of intense concentration. Crowley followed his friend's suggestion and spent months involved in what constituted yoga training.

More mountain climbing followed, as well as travels to San Francisco, and Ceylon (now Sri Lanka), and a love affair with a married woman that resulted in his book *Alice, An Adultery*. In Ceylon, he found his close friend Allan Bennett, a colleague from his Golden Dawn days and a student of Buddhism. Bennett later became the founder of the British Buddhist movement, and he was one of the few people of whom Crowley remained consistently fond. He spent months teaching Crowley all that he knew of Eastern mysticism, and after his recent period of intense thought control, Bennett's teachings came as a revelation to him. Crowley now believed that he could harness all his psychic energies and do amazing things with such a force.

Meanwhile, Bennett, who had been working as a private tutor to the solicitor-general in Ceylon, decided that he was going to renounce the world and become a Buddhist monk. With his friend out of commission, Crowley went on a big game hunt, penetrated a secret shrine at Madura, explored the

Irrawaddy River in a canoe, and finally, visited Bennett at his monastery, where he claimed to see Bennett levitating in the air during a period of intense meditation.

Crowley, now in his mid-twenties, was still basically a rich playboy and sportsman, not much different from the Golden Dawn members that he had such disdain for when he joined the order. In 1902, he was one of a party that attempted to reach the summit of the Chogori (now known as K2), the world's second-highest mountain, in India's Karakoram range. Bad weather and illness prematurely ended the expedition.

Crowley returned to Paris and called on Mathers, hoping that his mental accomplishments would earn his respect. Mathers was not in the least bit interested in yoga and dismissed his one-time ally, which greatly cooled Crowley's respect for him. Crowley set about becoming an eccentric character in the artistic circles of Paris and W. Somerset Maugham wrote about him in his 1908 novel, *The Magician*. In this tale, the magician, Oliver Haddo -- a caricature of Aleister Crowley -- attempts to create life. Crowley wrote a critique of this book under the pen name Oliver Haddo, where he accused Maugham of plagiarism.

After a time in Paris, he returned to Boleskine House at Loch Ness and became friendly with a young painter named Gerald Kelly. Crowley soon met Kelly's unstable sister, Rose, an attractive young woman with a score of emotional issues. Already a widow, she had involved herself with a number of men who wanted to marry her, and she encouraged them all. Crowley's odd sense of humor offered her a solution to her dilemma: marry him and she could leave the marriage unconsummated if she wished. She could have his name and be free of her admirers. They were married by a lawyer the next morning.

Crowley had pretended to be uninterested in sex with Rose, but he could not pass up the opportunity to work his "sexual magick" on her. In addition, there was something about Rose's mental weakness that appealed to the sadist in him and he couldn't help but take advantage of her. Their decision to keep the marriage platonic lasted for only a few hours. The two became fervent lovers and Crowley claimed that he "ravished her over and over again, much to his new bride's delight."

He soon learned that Gerald Kelly and the rest of Rose's family were not happy about the marriage, which delighted Crowley, who loved drama of any sort. He took Rose to Paris and then they traveled on to Cairo, where they spent a night inside the Great Pyramid.

Soon after occurred the event that Crowley would call the most important in his life: Rose became pregnant. Her behavior, already bizarre, became even stranger. Crowley didn't blame hormones on her personality

In 1903, Crowley married Rose Kelly, the unstable sister of a friend.

change. He claimed that the spirits of the air that he had invoked for her benefit put her into a peculiar mood. She told him that she had offended the Egyptian god Horus, of whom, Crowley said, she knew nothing. In a museum, she showed him a statue of Ra-Hoor-Khuit, one of the forms of Horus, and he was impressed to find that the number of the exhibit was 666, the number of the Beast in the Biblical Book of Revelation. Rose, whom he began calling Ouarda, now began to instruct him on how to invoke Horus. The ritual did not seem to make sense, but he tried it anyway, and later claimed that it was a complete success. Horus allegedly told him that a new epoch was beginning, a statement that many other occultists also believed. Crowley was ordered to write and a "musical voice" from out of the corner of the room dictated *The Book of the Law* to him, assuring him that the volume would solve all religious problems and would be translated into many languages.

The *Book of the Law*, with its fundamental theme of "Do What Thou Wilt," became what Crowley considered one of his central pieces of writing. He attached enormous importance to it. For the rest of his life, he began all of his letters with the assertion "Do what thou wilt shall be the whole of the Law." He believed that the old era of gods and demons was over and that a new epoch was beginning that would force man to stand on his own and come into his own power. Crowley saw himself as a potential new god, gradually coming to understand his own powers. The book became Crowley's major achievement, and when he had finished it, he likely felt that he had at last produced his masterpiece, a work that towered above everything that he had previously written, and one that was worth devoting his life to making known.

The next portion of Crowley's life was filled with anger and perhaps even madness.

After he completed The Book of the Law, he wrote Mathers from Paris and told him that the Secret Chiefs had appointed him the head of the Order of the Golden Dawn. The letter was obviously meant to antagonize Mathers -- Crowley said that he "declared war on him" -- and it succeeded. According to Crowley, malevolent magical currents swept from Mathers in Paris to Loch Ness, where he had taken Rose to give birth to their child. He believed Mathers was out to get him and was responsible for killing off his dogs and causing a workman to go insane and try to attack Rose. In response, Crowley invoked 49 demons -- which Rose allegedly saw -- and sent them off to torment Mathers. When Rose gave birth to their daughter, Crowley named her Nuit Ma Ahathoor Hecate Sappho Jezebel Lilith.

After his daughter was born, Crowley returned to traveling. He took on another mountaineering expedition, this time to Kanchenjunga in Nepal. In 1905, he led a group that attempted to scale the peak. His personality soon set the others on edge. After the party had reached a height of about 24,000 feet on the main peak, a conference was called to formally depose Crowley as the leader of the team, thanks to his sadistically cruel treatment of the porters. One of the expedition members, noticing the porters were climbing the icy mountain barefoot, accused Crowley of failing to provide them with shoes, as he had agreed. Crowley insisted that he had given the "economical natives" footwear but they preferred to pack them away for future use rather than wear them "unless there is some serious reason for putting them on."

Crowley refused to accept the demotion and the expedition was called off. Everyone but Crowley and a Swiss climber named Reymond started down the mountain toward the lower camps. There was a slip that set off an avalanche and all of them were swept down the mountain and buried under the snow. A few of the men managed to dig themselves out and called to Crowley to come and help as they searched for the porters and the other climbers, who later turned up dead. Reymond ran to help, but Crowley refused to leave his tent, where he was drinking tea. That evening, he wrote a letter, which was later printed in English newspapers, commenting that he "was not over-anxious in the circumstances to render help. A mountain accident of this kind is one of the things for which I have no sympathy whatever." The next morning, he ascended the mountain, avoiding his former companions, and proceeded to Darjeeling by himself.

He went on to Calcutta, where he described an incident in which he was attacked in the street by a gang of thieves. Crowley claimed that he fired his revolver at them and then "made himself invisible." He explained that this was not literally true; it was simply that he possessed an odd power that caused a blank spot in the minds of those who were looking at him.

Crowley and his magical symbols

The next day, Rose and the baby arrived in India. Crowley had fallen out of love with her, he said, and had little interest in the child. Regardless, he took his family with him to China. After four months, he sent Rose back to England by way of Calcutta, so that she could pick up some luggage they had left there. Crowley, meanwhile, returned through New York. When he arrived back in Liverpool, he learned that his daughter had died of typhoid in Rangoon.

Rose gave birth to another child not long after, Lola Zaza, who almost died of bronchitis soon after she was born. The birth and illness caused a permanent falling out with Rose's family and shortly after, his marriage to Rose came to an end. Rose became an alcoholic and later went insane.

Strangely, this was a pattern that seemed to occur over and over again with people who became too intimate with Crowley.

Left to his own devices, Crowley began seeking disciples. His first was a man named Lord Tankerville and together, they traveled in Morocco and Spain. Tankerville footed the bill for these trips because Crowley's fortune was finally beginning to run out. They parted ways, but Crowley soon found another follower, a poet named Victor Neuberg. Crowley published more of his own poetry, wrote a book praising himself called *The Star in the West*, and started a bi-annual journal about magic called *The Equinox*. Crowley also decided to start his own magical society, which he called the Silver Star and made use of some of the rituals from the Golden Dawn. He knighted himself, claiming that he had received the title in Spain, and shaved his domed head. Rose was, by now, completely insane, and he divorced her.

In 1910, he discovered the use of mescalin and -- probably with assistance from the drug -- devised a series of seven rituals, which he called the Rites of Eleusis. He hired a hall for their performance on seven successive Wednesdays. Admission was five guineas and the aim of the rituals, he said, was to induce religious ecstasy. Crowley's mistress, Austrian violinist Leila

Waddell, provided musical accompaniment for the shows. Newspapers and magazines were harshly critical of the performances and one magazine even devoted three issues to attack Crowley personally. This was the beginning of what Crowley referred to as the "persecution" that plagued him until his death in 1947.

At the same time, he was again having trouble with his former friend, Samuel Mathers. Crowley was being sued to try and stop the publication of the third issue of his magic journal, *The Equinox*, because it contained a full description of the secret rites of the Golden Dawn, which Crowley had taken an oath never to reveal. The judge found in favor of Mathers, but Crowley later claimed that he performed a series of magic rituals and appealed the case. This time, he won. The issue was published, and Mather's secrets were revealed, affording Crowley a small bit of revenge.

Crowley was now beginning to fear that the high point in his life was over. His existence was becoming a series of repetitive events – magical ceremonies, mistresses, frantic efforts to raise money, and newspaper attacks on him, followed by attempts to justify himself in the press. But everything changed in 1912, when Crowley met German occultist and Ordo Templi Orientis leader Theodor Reuss. At first, Reuss was angry with Crowley because he had revealed in his *The Book of Lies* that sex could be used magically. When he realized that Crowley's revealing of the secret had been inadvertent, he authorized him to set up his own branch of the O.T.O., an idea that Crowley heartily embraced. He launched his branch of the order by sodomizing disciple Victor Neuberg as part of a magical ceremony in 1913.

Crowley's need for debauchery now had an outlet and he began practicing sex magick with a new diligence. One of his companions in this was a friend of Isadora Duncan, Mary D'Este Sturges. They rented a villa in Italy for a lengthy bout of rituals. He also took a troupe of chorus girls, the Ragged Ragtime Girls, to Moscow.

He continued to irritate the British press and opened a Satanic Temple in a studio on London's Fulham Road. The newspapers had a field day, especially after an American journalist was allowed to visit the Temple and wrote an article about the number of rich British women who frequented it.

Crowley had filed his two canine teeth to a sharp point and when he met women, he was inclined to give them the "serpent's kiss," biting them on the wrist, and occasionally the throat, with his fangs. He also developed a new kink: defecating on carpets. He explained to one man, who was offended that Crowley had done this in his home, that his waste was sacred, like that of the Dalai Lama.

When World War I broke out, Crowley, now 39, was caught in Switzerland. He claimed that he tried to get the British government to employ him as a spy, but they refused.

He decided to go to America and after a year of unsuccessful magical activities – apparently Americans were not yet ready for Crowley's version of weird -- he developed a new role: the anti-British Irishman. He was, of course, not Irish, and had never been to Ireland, but this didn't matter to him. He made a speech at the foot of the Statue of Liberty and tore up what he claimed was his British passport. After this, he began to write anti-British propaganda for a German-leaning newspaper; a bit of treason that he later explained was actually to help the British cause during the war. He said that he tried to make his propaganda so absurd that it would provoke the opposite effect.

The British were not impressed and dismissed Crowley as a man looking for attention who would do anything to keep his name before the public. But it was likely more accurate that Crowley was becoming increasingly disgusted with England, a country from which he felt that he had been exiled and rejected. He had never been given any recognition at home and he struck out in the only way that he could.

Crowley described his period in America as a time of poverty and humiliation. Humiliated or not, he managed to live quite well in the states. A report in a New York newspaper, *The Evening World*, described a fairly luxurious studio in Washington Square, most likely provided for him by his followers. Crowley was an expert at cadging money from his disciples. American writer on witchcraft and voodoo, William Seabrook, who was introduced to Crowley, said that Crowley always had a retinue of followers and disciples around him. He witnessed several of the group's rituals and admitted that some of the invocations were "quite beautiful." Seabrook also remarked that Crowley seemed to be a "man of power" and a person of great inner strength. He recalled that Crowley would eat and drink until he became bloated and then starve himself down to a healthy weight again.

Seabrook recounted an amusing story of how Crowley one day announced that he was going off to spend 40 days and nights in the wilderness. Seabrook and some other friends decided to fund his trip, since Crowley was broke. They gave him some money and found him a canoe and a tent. When they went to see him off, they discovered that he had spent all the money they had given him on huge cans of red paint and rope. He told them that, like the prophet Elijah, he would be fed by the ravens. Crowley spent the 40 days and nights painting in huge red letters on the cliffs south of Kingston the inscriptions EVERY MAN AND WOMAN IS A STAR and, of course, DO WHAT THOU WILT SHALL BE THE WHOLE OF THE LAW.

He was fed by local farmers, who periodically brought him eggs, milk, and sweet corn. He returned to New York after his time in the "wilderness" looking healthy and well.

Seabrook told another story about Crowley, an incident that marked one of the strangest examples of his alleged powers. After his return to New York, Crowley told Seabrook that he had gained strength during his time away and Seabrook asked for a demonstration of this. Crowley took him along Fifth Avenue, on a sparsely populated stretch of the sidewalk, and fell into step with a man, walking behind him, and imitating his walk. Suddenly, Crowley buckled at the knees, squatted on his haunches for a moment, and then stood upright again. At the same time, the man in front of him collapsed onto the pavement as his own knees gave out. Seabrook and Crowley helped him to his feet and the man nervously went on his way, unable to explain why he had fallen.

Was this a real example of Crowley possessing a supernatural power? Was it merely the power of suggestion? Or did Crowley imply stage the event for the benefit of Seabrook, who he knew would write about it and generate publicity for the charismatic cult leader?

Towards the end of his time in America, Crowley discovered yet another "Scarlet Woman," as he referred to the numerous women who became involved with him. An acquaintance named Renata Faesi called on him one day in the company of her younger sister, Leah, a thin, not very attractive girl with a wide mouth, strangely sharp teeth, and a bony, angular body. She seemed ordinary and plain but something almost magnetic occurred when she and Crowley saw one another. Crowley immediately seized Leah and began to kiss her violently, much to Renata's astonishment. Within hours, Leah was agreeing to be painted in the nude and Crowley created a ghoulish picture that he called "Dead Souls." In due course, Leah, whom Crowley called Alostrael and The Ape of Thoth, in reference to the companion of the god Tahuti, who enabled his ideas to become reality, became pregnant.

In December 1919, Crowley finally returned to England, but was not happy there. He now suffered from asthma and bronchitis every winter and his periodic indulgence in all kinds of drugs, from mescalin to hashish, cocaine, and opium, had lowered his physical resistance to the British cold and dampness.

He had lost many of his English friends and contacts during the war. His former disciple, Victor Neuberg, had married and settled down, but he remained obsessed with Crowley for the rest of his life. Crowley had cursed him when they separated before the war and Neuberg was very nervous for years after, blaming his many health problems on Crowley's incantations.

Leah, one of Crowley's abused and manipulated "Scarlet Women"

There was no one else in London from whom Crowley could get money, but as luck would have it, he received a fairly large sum of money around this time and decided to leave England for a warmer climate. Crowley and Leah found a farmhouse in Sicily and were accompanied there by a Ninette Shumway, who doubled as a nursemaid and Crowley's mistress. She brought her young son, Hermes, and cared for the two children that Crowley had with Leah: a boy named Dionysus and a newborn girl named Anne Leah. Crowley, now in his middle 40s, seemed to have developed a few normal human feelings. He wrote of his family: "I love Alostrael; she is all my comfort, my support, my soul's desire, my life's reward..." He also expressed deep affection toward Anne Leah, whose health had been feeble since the time she was born.

At first, life in Sicily was idyllic, with swimming in the ocean, long hours of meditation, and magical sex rituals. Crowley covered the walls of the farmhouse with paintings of people having sex in every position, and painted his studio, which he called the "Chamber of Nightmares," with pictures of demons. He became convinced that one could only free one's self from the need for drugs by taking them as much as a person wanted, so piles of cocaine were left around the house for anyone to take and Crowley arranged for opium to be supplied to him by a trader from the mainland.

The only thing that seemed to spoil the scene was the jealousy of his two "Scarlet Women." One peace-shattering incident occurred on the day that the sun entered the sign of Taurus (April 20, 1920). Crowley celebrated the event with a sex ritual in which both women participated. In the middle of the proceedings a violent argument broke out between Leah and Ninette and the latter, bursting into tears, snatched up a cloak to cover her nakedness, and ran out into the dark, rainy night. Crowley wandered all over looking for her, afraid that she had fallen off one of the nearby cliffs. After calling her name for almost an hour, he found her, and dragged her back to the house. Meanwhile, Leah had opened a bottle of brandy and was now raging drunk. She cursed at Ninette when Crowley brought her back and the fight started all over again. Crowley managed to get Ninette to go to bed, and then Leah, as if to have the last word, vomited and passed out.

Crowley tried hard to convince the two women that possessiveness was an evil, and that they should rise above such a trivial thing, but they were unconvinced. However, they continued to take part in his magic sex rites, including one ceremony when Leah allowed herself to be penetrated by a goat. The animal's throat was then cut as a sacrifice.

Visitors -- both disciples and curiosity-seekers -- began to arrive at the Sicily farmhouse, which Crowley had dubbed the Abbey of Theleme. American film star Elizabeth Fox was among the first visitors. Crowley looked forward to introducing her to sex magick, but she turned out to be a disappointment, he said.

The mathematician J.N.W. Sullivan arrived with his wife, Sylvia. He found he liked Crowley and staying up talking with him all night. Sylvia liked him, too, and stayed on for another day to practice sex rituals after her husband left.

But life at the Abbey was becoming too complicated with personal issues, arguments, and tragedies – something that visitors were becoming aware of. Crowley's daughter, Anne Leah, died after a long illness and Crowley was shattered. Soon after, a young American, an ex-naval officer named Godwin, arrived and Crowley re-named him Brother Fiat Lux. The strain of life around Crowley and his mistresses became too much for him after another disciple, Australian businessman Frank Bennett, arrived at the Abbey. Crowley asked Godwin to let Bennett have his room. This resulted in a violent argument. Godwin returned to America with the sanity that he had left, and in 1931, he founded the Chortonzon Club, which was named for a demon. Godwin rejected Crowley's magic rituals and invented his own type of sex magic, which involved sexual intercourse that would be continued indefinitely without orgasm. The aim of it was to produce long and drawn-out ecstasy and intoxication. Godwin operated in California for many years.

Another rebellious Crowley disciple was Jack Parsons, a brilliant rocket scientist who was obsessed with the sexual side of ritual magic. He was an early follower of Crowley but went on to become fascinated with the idea of incarnating the Whore of Babylon, described in the Book of Revelation. He believed this creature would be the bride of the Antichrist and the Mother of

All Abominations. His chosen method of doing this was known as "Babylon Working," which essentially involved him impregnating his mistress, the actress Marjorie Cameron, under occult conditions. Parsons hoped that the resulting "moonchild" would be the Whore's incarnation on earth. Parsons collaborated with L. Ron Hubbard, the founder of Scientology, in the magical exercises that followed, which included Parsons having sex with Marjorie while Hubbard "magically" described what was happening on the astral plane. Parsons claimed that his "Left-Hand Path" magic had been successful in creating the child, but there is no evidence to substantiate this claim. Increasingly identified with the Beast 666, in his later years Parsons legally changed his name to Belarion Armiluss Al Dajjal Antichrist. He was killed in a mysterious lab explosion in 1952.

Whew, I know what you're thinking but I promise we'll get back to the music soon. Crowley had such an impact on music in the late 1960s that we have to wade into this stuff.

But Crowley did succeed with some of his disciples, especially Frank Bennett. Like Crowley, Bennett had lived through a repressive childhood. When Crowley explained to him that the sexual organs were the image of God, and the best way to free the hidden powers of the subconscious mind was through sexual magic, Bennett found the revelation so startling that he ran out into the ocean and began to swim frantically up and down the beach. After further discussion that same night, he walked barefoot into the mountains. Then, after a day of bewilderment, he lapsed into a trance-like state of pure delight as he began to grasp the idea of allowing the subconscious to free itself. After all of this, Bennett departed and went back to Australia, filled with the gospel of the "Beast."

Crowley's health and financial status began to suffer. The doses of heroin that he had begun to take would have killed a normal man. Periodically, he would force himself to go without all drugs for days, resulting in sickness and pain. After a period of intense depression and misery, he would begin to paint and write again with his old excitement. He always returned to the drugs, though, claiming that he could take them or leave them whenever he wanted. The result was long periods of listlessness and increasing insomnia, which troubled him for years.

In addition to his drug problem, he was out of money again. In Sicily, there were no rich disciples to sponge off; on the contrary, his steady streams of visitors sapped his finances. J.N.W. Sullivan suggested that he write his memoirs, but Crowley wanted to write a novel first and managed to get a small advance for a book called *Diary of a Drug Fiend*. The novel was about an aristocratic couple that became slaves to heroin, met Crowley, retired to his Abbey, and were miraculously cured. The book appeared in 1922, and was violently attacked by newspapers that revealed that the Abbey was a real place and denounced Crowley as a seducer of young people. Crowley was not entirely displeased by the publicity, but the publisher allowed the book to go out of print and balked at the idea of publishing Crowley's autobiography, even though he had been given a good-sized advance.

While in London for the release of his book, Crowley met an enthusiastic, but slightly unbalanced, young man named Raoul Loveday, who was married to a pretty model. Loveday had read Crowley's works, and within hours, he was an enthusiastic disciple. When Crowley returned to Sicily, Loveday and his wife, Betty May, followed. Loveday's wife had strong misgivings about Crowley. She hated the Abbey, hated the food, the lack of bathrooms, the obscene paintings, and most of all, her husband's total infatuation with Crowley.

Loveday's stay at the Abbey lasted three months – and ended with his death. Both he and Crowley came down with the same ailment, similar to hepatitis, caused by bad water. In February 1923, Crowley decided that a cat should be sacrificed to save their health. He hated cats and chose one to kill that had scratched him badly when he threw it out of a room. Allegedly, he found the animal in a pantry, made the sign of a pentagram over it with his staff, and ordered it to stay there until the hour of sacrifice. Crowley claimed that the animal never moved. Even when Betty May took it somewhere else in the house, it came back to the same spot, petrified, and refusing food.

Loveday was selected to perform the sacrifice. The cat was placed on an altar, incense was lit, and incantations were performed for two hours. Finally, Loveday slashed the animal's throat with a knife, but the cut was too shallow, and the cat ran from the room. It was captured and slain and then Loveday was made to drink a cup of its blood. He subsequently collapsed and was taken to his bed. Crowley consulted his horoscope and predicted that Loveday was going to die, on February 16.

Several terrible arguments with Betty May followed. One day, she stormed out of the Abbey after calling Ninette a whore but returned the next day at her husband's request. On February 16th – the day that Crowley had predicted – Loveday died. Betty May was stunned and recalled that on their wedding day, he had dropped the ring as he was about to put it onto her finger, a bad omen. She also remembered a photograph of the two of them that had been taken at St. John's College, Oxford, in which the ghostly outline of a young man appeared, his arms stretched out over his head. This was the same position that Loveday had been in when he died.

Betty May departed Sicily and returned to England, where she gave newspaper interviews about her disastrous visit to the Abbey. The British public was both shocked and delighted with more gossip about the infamous Crowley. More newspaper attacks followed and by the time they appeared, Crowley was also taken ill with the same sickness that had killed Loveday. He was semi-conscious for three weeks before slowly recovering. But the adverse publicity over Loveday's death had its effect on the new ruler of Italy. A short time later, Mussolini ordered Crowley to vacate the Abbey and leave the country.

Once again, a strange turn of events saved Crowley from poverty and homelessness. Norman Mudd, a young man who had known Crowley since 1907 at Cambridge, came back into his life. Mudd had been introduced to the Beast through Neuberg, but when Crowley's unsavory reputation and pornographic books got him kicked out of the college where he was a student, their friendship cooled. Mudd had become a professor of mathematics in South Africa but was unable to forget about Crowley. As Crowley was being attacked by the British press, and being kicked out of Sicily, Mudd appeared at the Abbey, presented Crowley with his life savings, and begged to be accepted as his disciple.

Crowley moved to Tunis, hoping that the Italian government would change its mind. Leah went with him, as well as his five-year-old son, who reportedly smoked cigarettes all day long and declared that he would become the Beast when his father died. Ninette had borne Crowley another daughter, and Crowley's horoscope for the child ended with the prediction, "She is likely to develop into a fairly ordinary little whore." Norman Mudd accompanied the party and he and Leah became lovers, a development that Crowley did not mind. He was too preoccupied with recovering his health, and with his drug addiction, which he realized he was unable to shake.

When Crowley became bored, he abandoned the group and went to Paris, leaving Leah and Mudd to starve in Tunis. Crowley fared no better in the City of Lights. He was drug-addled and wandered the city in a daze. Eventually, he was kicked out of the hotel where he was living on credit. Leah and Mudd followed him to Paris and then Mudd moved on to London, where he took refuge at the Metropolitan Asylum for the Homeless Poor. Crowley and Leah stayed together for a few months, but Crowley had grown tired of her and her inability to survive under any conditions, as he was able to do. When a rich American woman named Dorothy Olsen fell under his spell, Crowley named her his new "Scarlet Woman," and deserted Leah. Leah's sister, Renata, had already taken away her son and took him to America. Leah was furious and hysterical. Mudd returned to her and they lived on the streets of Paris together while Crowley and his new mistress traveled in North America.

Both Leah and Mudd became bitter about Crowley, although there was nothing to stop them from finding work and continuing a life together. But Crowley's abandonment of them seemed to break something inside of the pair. Leah worked as a prostitute for a while, then as a waitress. Mudd remained in a state of despair, but even after all that had happened, his main concern seemed to be whether Crowley would remain faithful to *The Book of the Law*. Crowley's new lover soon ran out of money after a few months of supporting him in the luxurious style to which he was accustomed and had to write to friends in America to borrow money.

But Crowley, once again, had another stroke of incredible luck. Theodor Reuss, his old friend from the Ordo Templi Orientis, died and his successor turned to Crowley as one of the elite members of the Order. The O.T.O. paid off all of Crowley's debts in Paris, and even gave money to Mudd and Leah, who eventually grew to hate Crowley. Leah was so angry that she wrote him a letter renouncing her vow of obedience to him. What eventually happened to her is unknown. In 1934, Mudd committed suicide by drowning himself in the Channel Islands. He closed the bottom of his pants with bicycle clips and then filled them with rocks as he walked into the sea.

Crowley still enjoyed his reputation as the "wickedest man in the world", but this was a double-edged sword for him. He loved the infamy, but it meant that no major publisher would touch the autobiography that he had been working on. Eventually, a small press put out the book, but they were unable to get bookstores to place orders for it.

In 1929, Crowley was ordered to leave France. He tried to go back to England but his two chief disciples, an American secretary that he called "The Serpent" and his latest mistress, Maria Teresa de Miramar, were not allowed to enter Britain. Finally, Crowley got Maria into England by marrying her in August 1929. He was supposed to lecture at Oxford in early 1930, but was banned from the college. He tried to present an exhibition of his paintings at a rented house in Langham Place, but bad newspaper publicity caused the owner to cancel his lease. His marriage to Maria became a series of vicious arguments and soon fell apart, but there were plenty of others who wanted to be his "Scarlet Woman."

Crowley took a new mistress, a 19-year-old German girl named Hanni, who he called "The Monster." They went to Lisbon together, but Hanni soon became disenchanted with Crowley and his sex magic rituals. She deserted him and returned to Berlin. To be abandoned was a new, and shattering experience for Crowley. He pursued the girl to Berlin and a reconciliation took place. Before leaving, he left a suicide note at the top of Hell's Mouth, a high cliff, and the result was a flattering uproar in the world's press, which delighted in the fact that the "world's wickedest man" had taken his own life. But after lying low in Berlin for a few days, Crowley attended the opening of an exhibition of his paintings, ending the speculation about his "death." Hanni became Crowley's magical assistant and Crowley maintained that she became a skilled "scryer" and once saw the Devil's face looking up at her from inside of a crystal. Their sex magic was so successful that she became pregnant, but she left him soon after.

Remember Crowley's wife, Maria? She went insane and was hospitalized for the rest of her life. At least one Crowley biographer claims that Hanni also went insane. While some might assert there was a supernatural cause behind the reports of insanity and suicide connected to those who were close to Crowley, there is a simpler explanation. Crowley's powerful, dominant personality attracted people to him who were much weaker than he was, and in many cases, already mentally unstable. Crowley's rejection and abandonment, or perhaps simply their exposure to his magical rituals, often sent them over the edge and drove them to suicide and into asylums.

As far as magic is concerned, the remainder of Crowley's life was anticlimactic.

In the 1930s, Crowley became involved in a court case against his old friend Nina Hammett. He got a taste for litigation when he saw a copy of his novel *Moonchild* displayed in a bookstore window with a sign next to it stating that an earlier novel (*Diary of a Drug Fiend*) had been withdrawn from publication after a newspaper attack. This was not true, it had simply gone out of print. Crowley sued the bookseller and received a small settlement.

This legal victory gave him the idea to raise money by suing Nina Hammett, the Soho personality who had referred to Crowley as a "black magician" in her autobiography. She had raised the idea, only to dismiss it, and hinted that a baby (possibly used as a sacrifice) had disappeared from the Abbey. Crowley knew that Hammett had no money, but her publisher, Constable & Co., certainly did, and they would have to pay. Whether he expected to win the case, or merely thought that it would garner him more publicity remains a matter for speculation, but he hired the lawyers to pursue it. Unfortunately, none of his friends would appear for the defense and his attorneys warned him that if the courts got a look at any of his pornographic writings, the case would be thrown out of court. As it turned out, things never got that far. When several witnesses appeared on the stand and described

Crowley's magical activities, the judge halted the case and declared that he had "never heard of such dreadful, horrible, blasphemous, and abominable stuff as that which has been produced by a man who describes himself as the greatest living poet in the world." The jury found against Crowley and he was bankrupted, although he really had no assets anyway. The publicity for the case, though, was tremendous – and that might have been just what Crowley wanted in the first place.

Crowley spent his last days living in a boarding house called Netherwood at the Ridge, Hastings. Photographs of him from the years after World War II show a thin old gentleman, dressed in tweeds, smoking a pipe, and looking more like a retired British military man than one of the infamous men in history. He was a bored, lonely old man who was more interested in heroin than food. He lived until 1947 on the generosity of old friends and fading disciples, who couldn't bear to see the Great Beast starve during his final days on earth. He continued, as he had throughout his life, to impose on the kindness of friends, taking whatever he desired from them. The irate wife of one of his disciples pointed out to him in a letter that he had spent £15,000 of her money on expensive cigars, cognac, cocktails, taxis, dinners, and mistresses and concluded "God Almighty himself would not be as arrogant as you have been, and that is one of the causes of all of your troubles."

And she was right.

Until the very end of his life, Crowley possessed a withering arrogance, a lofty view of his own value that paled in comparison to the admiration that even his most devoted followers felt toward him. This explained why he could so easily turn on faithful disciples like Norman Mudd and his mistress, Leah, totally convinced in his own mind that some action of theirs had forfeited their rights to his divine presence.

But no matter what you might think of Crowley – lunatic or visionary – it cannot be denied that, in spite of his over-the-top self-promotion, his haughty arrogance, and his exaggeration and outright lies about his magical abilities, he not only changed the course of occult history with his ideas, but he set the stage for every rock god that followed in his path. Doesn't most of the things that we can say about Crowley also apply to some of the great rock musicians of all time?

And like some of them, he also crashed and burned. It's almost tragic to saY that Crowley died of something as common as pneumonia on December 5, 1947. He died unrepentant about his life of sin and scandal. The novelist Louis Wilkinson read aloud Crowley's lurid "Hymn to Pan" at the funeral service, as gleefully and shamelessly as Crowley might have expected it to be read for such an occasion. The city council of Brighton, the town in which he was buried, angrily stated that it would take steps to see that such an incident was never, ever repeated again.

It was a fitting, scandalous end for the "wickedest man in the world."

STAIRWAY TO HEAVEN

There had been other rock musicians who had been interested in the life and exploits of Aleister Crowley, but none with the fervor of Jimmy Page. He named his occult bookstore, The Equinox, after Crowley's short-lived magazine. He had financed a reprinting of some of Crowley's books and spent thousands at rare book shops and auction houses buying Crowley manuscripts, hats, clothing, and art that had belonged to him.

And look who's back – Kenneth Anger.

Jimmy met him in the late 1960s, when Anger was hanging around with rock stars that he could work his "black magician schtick with. Jimmy was taken with him, just as Mick Jagger and the Stones had been. He kept Jimmy spellbound with tales about Crowley's magical prowess. Anger first met the guitarist when he outbid him for an original Crowley manuscript at Sotheby's. Jimmy was delighted to show him his Crowley memorabilia collection of books, canes, and especially his ceremonial robes.

Jimmy became such a collector that he decided to add the one missing piece to his vast collection – Crowley's house, Boleskine, on the shores of Loch Ness. The frightening legends that surrounded the place scared off most buyers, but Jimmy considered it perfect for his needs. Anger was a frequent visitor and loved to tell other guests about how restless the spirits of the house were.

Jimmy never spoke much about his private life, but he did talk about Boleskine in an interview with *Rolling Stone*: "It was owned by Aleister Crowley. But there were two or three other owners before Crowley moved into it. It was also a church that was burned to the ground with the congregation in it. And that's the site of the house. Strange things have happened in that house that had nothing to do with Crowley. The bad vibes were already there. A man was beheaded there and sometimes you can hear his head rolling down. I haven't actually heard it, but a friend of mine who is extremely straight and doesn't know anything about anything like that at all, heard it... So that sort of thing was there before Crowley got there. Of course, after Crowley there have been suicides and people carted off to mental hospitals."

When the interviewer asked Jimmy whether he had any contacts with the spirits, he replied, "I didn't say that. I just said I didn't hear the head roll."

After purchasing Boleskine, Jimmy hired Satanist Charles Pierce to decorate the house with mystical symbols befitting the new Lord Boleskine. The house did have many secrets. It was claimed that Crowley had misplaced his original copy of *The Book of the Law* and that it had been hidden in the house for years. He was also supposed to have summoned demons there, which resulted in the caretaker going insane and trying to murder his family – like the Scottish version of *The Shining*.

Even though Jimmy told an interviewer that he'd bought the house because he loved the unknown, but took the necessary precautions so that he wouldn't walk into things blind and unaware, one of the caretakers said that Jimmy would never spend the night alone in the house.

That same caretaker was also convinced the place was haunted. One night when the caretaker was sleeping in one of the rooms, he heard a sound at the door. It was heavy breathing like a large dog was on the other side of the door, trying to get into the room. The breathing was followed by a sound like claws scraping against the wood and then a heavy impact that shook the door. The caretaker stayed in bed, waiting for the sun to come up.

There were no actual dogs in the house on that dark night.

It was when *Led Zeppelin III* was released that the fans first became aware of Jimmy's unusual pastime. It was released by Atlantic Records on October 5, 1970, while the last album was still on the charts after 52 weeks. This was the album that was so widely panned by critics because of its acoustic tracks, but its also the first in which the presence of Aleister Crowley can be found. If you look closely in the runout grooves of the early pressings, you can see a very distinct "Do What Thou Wilt" in the vinyl. Some editions had the phrase on both sides, while later pressings only had the slogan on side two. Some of the early pressings also had the phrase "So Be It Mote," which was described as a binding spell from a magician's book of incantations.

But if the spell was supposed to make the album successful, it failed.

Led Zeppelin III still had great music, but the critics slammed it and it left the charts after only 31 weeks. This was the shortest amount of time on the charts for any of the first five Zeppelin albums.

For the recording environment that was wanted for the production of the band's fourth album, a mobile unit was transported to Headly Grange, a 200-year-old mansion. It had once served as a workhouse during the Victorian era. When the band members first arrived, they complained of a chilly presence throughout the house – and not just because it was an unheated pile of old stone. One night, Jimmy reported seeing a gray, ghostly figure at the top of the stairs. He was convinced the place was haunted, thanks to its terrible past, filled with stories of the neglected poor. He also noticed that the sheets in his bedroom always seemed to be damp. As far as Plant and Bonham were concerned, they agreed there was an uneasy darkness in the halls. After the recordings were made, though, Jimmy stated that the house had a much lighter feel, as though the music had helped purge the darkness from inside its walls.

When the album was released, there was little concern about the opinions of critics. The band wanted the music to speak for itself. For that reason, the fourth album was released with no title on November 8, 1971. Led Zeppelin didn't want their name – or the album name -- on the cover. Atlantic Records went along with the demand. Jimmy had suggested that each member of the band create a specific symbol for the album art. Some critics claimed these occult symbols were Icelandic runes that contained cryptic metaphysical meanings, but they were trying way too hard.

The band made them up, based on Native American and ancient symbols that they just happened to like. John Bonham's three circles were said to be representative of the Trilogy – man, woman, and child – but someone else pointed out that it was also the emblem for Ballantine beer. A friend suggested that Bonham's symbol also might be the wet circular rings left on a bar by placing beer bottles down in a pattern. After all, Jimmy had once claimed that John was the champion beer drinker in all of England.

Jimmy's symbol was the only one that was really mysterious. Robert once claimed that Jimmy told him the meaning, but he forgot it. The symbol was so dominant that many fans refer to the fourth album as *Zoso*. At one time or another, fans suggested that the symbol was in the shape of 666, the "Mark of the Beast," which is unlikely. Others have suggested that the symbol is taken from Cerebos, the guardian at the gates of Hell, or that the Zoso symbol bears a resemblance to the alchemical symbol for mercury.

And then there's my favorite explanation – that the name is from *Curious George*, the monkey, also known as Zoso, in the popular children's book series.

It's also possible – as Jimmy hinted – that the symbol crosses into the mystical world between the living and the dead. The term *Zoso* sounds a lot like the name of the first pharaoh of Egypt, Zoser, who established the first dynasty and built the first step pyramid. Early civilizations believed the steps on these structures were like ladders from which man could climb to visit the gods.

In this case, the original "stairway to heaven." Get it?

The much-debated symbols from the fourth Zeppelin album

Jimmy said that the symbol was not a pronounceable word, so no one is ever going to know what it means until he decides to announce it. But that sure didn't end the speculation.

Page and Plant designed the cover art for the fourth album. The old man carrying sticks on his back was said to represent harmony with the natural world. When the album jacket was opened, the old man's picture was found hanging on the wall to suggest the cycle of past, present, and future. The old man completed a cycle of unity with nature. He took from the land, but through death, decayed slowly back into nature, becoming one with the world.

This album also contained a hidden, cryptic message in the vinyl run-offs – two of them, in fact. On side one was the word "porky" and on side two, the term "pecko duck" could be seen. These were not phrases from the works of Aleister Crowley. Instead, they were humorous notes left behind by record engineer George "Porky" Peckham, who often left these little inscriptions etched into the run-out grooves of albums he worked on.

But Crowley did make a return to this album – in its number one song "Stairway to Heaven." It's a song that we all know and have probably heard 1,000 times or more, usually later at night, in the days of early FM radio, when deejays used its eight-minute run time to have a drink, a smoke, a bathroom break, or a quick shag. It has been voted the all-time favorite rock favorite of FM radio. When it came out, one station in Florida became so enamored with it that they played it 50 times in a row.

The song was groundbreaking – there had never been anything quite like it. It had a light melodic beginning that built to a thundering climax of guitar and drums. There had never been anything else that had the texture and raw energy of "Stairway to Heaven."

In the U.S. in the late 1970s and early 1980s, there was a movement that formed to investigate the hidden messages in rock recordings. The number one target was, of course, "Stairway to Heaven." Everyone was convinced that it was the "Devil's Music."

Knowing Jimmy's fascination with the occult and Aleister Crowley, some fans believed that "Black Dog" was an invitation to the dark side. John Paul Jones said that the song got its name because of a black dog who had wandered into the recording space during a session. They named a song in his honor.

But that was too simple of an answer for fans who wanted a juicy conspiracy. Books on the occult suggested that religious prayers were often recited backwards as a tribute to Satan and what was "dog" but a reversal of the word "God"? With this logic – or lack of it – they claimed the song served as a salute to the "Black God," who was the Devil.

Sure.

If you listen to the lyrics, they seem to talk more about Robert Plant's feelings about large "big-legged" women than about this devotion to the Devil.

But there may be a hidden message in "Stairway to Heaven." The lyrics mention there are "two paths to go by" and that "there's still time to change the road you're on." To followers of the occult, this seemed to speak of the "right-hand and left-hand paths" of Satan and God, evil and good. There is also mention of a piper that "leads us to reason." The piper, to some listeners, was Pan, the pagan god with horns and cloven hoofs. Was this another reference to Crowley and the "Hymn to Pan" that was read at his funeral?

One of Crowley's statements was that if a magician truly wanted to practice magic that he had to "train himself to think backward by external means – let him learn to write backward, let him learn to walk backward, let him constantly watch, if convenient, films and listen to records reversed."

This might have been the true purpose of the infamous hidden message in "Stairway to Heaven," along with the Zeppelin lyric that reminds us that "sometimes words have two meanings." In this case, the meaning can be determined by listening to the vocal forward and then backward, in the way that perhaps Crowley would have done with a Zeppelin album.

The hidden message occurs in the verse that states," If there's a bustle in the hedgerow, don't be alarmed now. It's just a spring clean for the May Queen." Many listeners pondered what a "bustle in the hedgerow" meant. The answer may be in two explanations. First, the track is not a true backward mask. In a backward mask a recording is simply played backward. This is the case in a lot of recordings said to contain hidden messages – and we'll come back to that later. The "Stairway to Heaven" track was created with a phonetic reversal. The "hidden" message could be recorded and then turned over. As the tape was heard backwards, new lyrics could be composed with the same basic sounds, creating what seemed to be weird wordplay. Starting with the verse that starts with "If there's a bustle in your hedgerow..." and carrying on until "and it makes me wonder," people swore that a hidden Satanic prayer was heard.

I know, you're skeptical. Me too.

Personally, I have been able to pick up some key phrases, although I suspect that this is because my mind has been programmed to do it after reading and writing about this for so long. I believe I can hear, "Here's to my sweet Satan. The one will be the one who makes me sad whose power is in Satan." The last vocal phrase is, "And she's buying a stairway to Heaven," but if reversed, some listeners claim that the backward phrase states, "Play music backward, hear words sung."

A lot of this is garbled, but some of it's pretty clear. I admit that it's unnerving when you're listening to this late at night. But even so, I keep wondering how many hours were spent listening to this over and over by people, trying to figure it out. There seems to be a much better use for just about anyone's time.

I should mention that there is another, more mundane explanation for "bustle in your hedgerow" – it's a sexual innuendo about female genitalia. The "spring clean for the May Queen?" a reference to a young girl's coming of age with the start of her first menstrual cycle.

You can decide which explanation is the weirdest.

The use of Led Zeppelin's occult references continued with the release of *Houses of the Holy* in March 1973. The album art depicted two fair-skinned, blond, naked children, climbing up a mysterious mountain. The cover photograph was taken by Aubrey Powell and was said to be based on the science-fiction novel *Childhood's End.* When the album jacket was opened, it showed a man holding one of the children above his head in what some described as looking like a sacrificial rite. The two children looked eerily like Robert Plant's children, Karac and Carmen. There would soon be claims that the image was a prophetic one – Karac died mysteriously within a few years of the album's release.

The album's lyrics – printed on the inner sleeve, as they used to do in the good old days -- contained many allusions to the occult. "Walking side by side with death, the devil mocks every step" from "No Quarter," were a chilling premonition of the tragedies that would soon befall the band.

The next turning point in Jimmy Page's study of the occult was in 1974, when he decided that he could produce the soundtrack for Kenneth Anger's *Lucifer Rising.*

Yes, that thing was still kicking around out there.

Jimmy felt that it was an honor to work with someone who had such a great understanding of Crowley's ideas. Though Jimmy had agreed to write the soundtrack – I'm assuming this was a new one since he was far from the first musician tasked with the job – he was upfront with Anger about his time restrictions. Jimmy allowed Anger to use the cellar of Boleskine for filming and his Tower House residence as an editing facility for this cinematic tribute to Satan. Jimmy even paid for an expensive film editing table and tried to help him find financing for the project. After Mick Jagger bailed out of the project, Anger was happy to have Jimmy on board and praised his use of a violin bow and reverse echo in capturing the proper mood for the film.

You can guess how this is going to turn out, right?

Time passed and Anger became upset because Jimmy didn't set aside everything to finish the soundtrack. In all, he'd written and recorded a 28-minute score of strange sounds and chants, but Anger wanted more. When Jimmy was unable to meet Anger's schedule, the filmmaker tried to shred Jimmy's reputation in the press: "The selfishness and inconsideration were appalling... It was like rapping on inch-thick glass. Jimmy had more or less turned into an undisciplined, rich dilletante, as least as far as magic and any serious belief in Aleister Crowley's work was concerned. Page had only completed twenty-eight minutes of music in three years' work on the project. The way he has been behaving is totally contradictory to the teaching of Crowley and the ethos of film."

Anger went on to say that Crowley had been a habitual user of heroin and cocaine and his strong physical condition allowed the drugs to increase his power. Jimmy Page, however, "couldn't handle it."

Anger also claimed that he had put a curse on Jimmy and the other members of Led Zeppelin. Of course, that's what all these guys say after something bad happens to something and they recall, "oh yes, I placed a curse on them." That was easy for him to do since bad things were coming around the bend for the band.

In the meantime, Jimmy had to defend himself in the press: "I must start by saying I've lost a hell of a lot of respect for Anger. He's implying that he received nothing from me, which is totally untrue. I gave him everything in plenty of time... Then one day this whole thing just blew up and that's all I know about it... All I can say is: Anger's time was all that was needed to finish that film. Nothing else! I had a lot of respect for him. As an occultist, he was definitely in the vanguard. I just don't know what he's playing at. I'm totally bemused and really disgusted. It's truly pathetic. He is powerless – totally. The only damage he can do is with his tongue."

Eventually, Anger went on to complete *Lucifer Rising* in 1980. He spent more than 10 years making it and the finished film was 28 minutes in length. The film turned out to be the same running time as the score that Jimmy had contributed, but Anger didn't use it – he used music performed by Bobby Beausoleil instead. The recordings were done at Tracy Prison, where Beausoleil was serving a life sentence for his part in the Manson murders. The role of Lucifer was played by Leslie Huggins. Marianne Faithfull still appeared in her part as Lilith and Anger himself played the Magus. In a promotional release for the film, Anger claimed that he was "showing actual ceremonies in the film, not reenactments, and the purpose was to make Lucifer rise."

I promise that I won't bring back Kenneth Anger again in this book.

Jimmy moved on. His traumatic break with Anger did little to change his interest in the occult. Anger's "curse" didn't seem to do any damage to the success of the next Led Zeppelin album, *Physical Graffiti*. This new release was a double album with a new collection of musical sounds, from standard rockers to songs like "Kashmir," which was influenced by the mysterious East. The cover was of a building at 97 St. Mark's Place in New York, complete with open window cutouts. Through the windows, fans could find the individual band members, Marilyn Monroe getting undressed, King Kong, Charles Atlas, Queen Elizabeth, Jerry Lee Lewis, Elizabeth Taylor, Neil Armstrong and, of course, a zeppelin airship in flight. When *Physical Graffiti* came out, Led Zeppelin did something that no other band had done before – they had six albums on the charts at the same time.

Some listeners searched out the occult references in the lyrics on the album. In "Houses of the Holy" Robert Plant sings, "Let the music be your master, won't you heed the master's call? Oh, Satan and man!" For fans who wanted to dive into the album's symbolism – as the "Paul is dead" crowd did with *Abbey Road*, there is a strange coincidence on the cover that should be noted. The male figure sitting on the steps looked like John Bonham. He was sitting in front of two doors that fans with wild imaginations claimed stood for the "two paths you can go by" from "Stairway to Heaven." The back of the album had the two doors presented again. One door was closed but radiated a bright light. The other was opened to a dark hallway. It looked like Bonham had to make a choice, you know, if it was really him. It wasn't, as much as some fans wanted it to be after this death in 1980.

The release of *Physical Graffiti* also launched the Led Zeppelin label, Swan Song. The concept of having their own label came up when their contracts with Atlantic Records expired. Early suggestions of the label's name included Slut, Slag, Superhype, and Eclipse, but finally, Swan Song was agreed upon.

Some thought it sounded awfully grim, but Jimmy thought that if Zeppelin were to die, they should go out still producing incredible music.

The artwork for the Swan Song label was based on a painting by William Rimmer that depicts the Greek sun god Apollo, but rumors persisted that this angelic-looking being was actually Lucifer, being cast out of heaven.

Led Zeppelin signed acts like Bad Company and Pretty Things to the label and threw lavish parties to celebrate each release. After the release of the Pretty Things album *Silk Torpedo*, Zeppelin hosted a Halloween party at some caves along the coast. Band manager Richard Cole recalled, "There was enough food and booze (mostly wine) to meet the needs of the entire British army... Much more eye-catching were the topless and, in some cases, fully naked women who mingled among the guests and rolled around in vats of cherry Jell-O. Other nude women played the parts of virgins sacrificed on makeshift altars. Strippers arrived dressed as nuns and peeled off their habits in an act that, if the Vatican were making the decisions, would have doomed us to an eternity in hell."

After the Montreux Jazz Festival in July 1975, the band went their separate ways on vacation – and it was at this time that Led Zeppelin's incredible luck started to run out.

On August 4, Robert Plant, his wife Maureen, their two children, and Jimmy Page's daughter, Scarlet, were in Rhodes on holiday when Maureen lost control of their rental car and had a terrible accident. At first, Robert was convinced his wife was dead. Luckily, that turned out not to be the case, but she was badly hurt. Robert broke his ankle and elbow. His children were also seriously injured, but Scarlet came through unscathed. Manager Richard Cole immediately chartered a private plane, flew to Rhodes, picked up the family, and got them to Rome. Cole had managed to bring fresh blood for Maureen and made sure she was given a transfusion on the way to the airport. Robert was convinced this saved her life.

Of course, some Zeppelin devotees were convinced that Scarlet Page was spared any injury in the accident because of her father's close relationship with the Devil. This was as ridiculous as the rumors that Jimmy had named her in tribute to Aleister Crowley's many "Scarlet Women." But it didn't help to dispute this after fans found out why Jimmy had not been with his daughter on the day of the accident – he had gone to Sicily to check out some property that had once belonged to Crowley.

After the accident, Robert Plant was confined to a wheelchair. This was during the time of the writing and recording of the album, *Presence*, which was released on March 31, 1976. Plant performed from his wheelchair and with his

Robert Plant in 1975

broken ankle, it seemed especially fitting that the opening song on the album was "Achilles' Last Stand."

After the completion of the album and time was taken for Robert to heal from his injuries, Led Zeppelin decided to turn their attention to producing their own concert documentary, *The Song Remains the Same.* It was meant to be more like the Beatles' *A Hard Day's Night* than a rock documentary like *Woodstock*, but concert sequences that were used had been filmed at New York's Madison Square Garden in July 1973.

I have to tell you, if you haven't seen it, this film is weird, even for fans of Led Zeppelin.

It opens with the band's managers dressed in gangster clothing from the Roaring 20's. There had been a real resurgence of interest in that era at the time. They use machine guns to tear up a house and there's one scene in which a faceless man is machine-gunned over a table covered with money.

In the next section of the film, Led Zeppelin band members appear. Plant with his wife, Maureen, and his children, Carmen and Karac show up next to a running stream. John Paul Jones is first seen reading "Jack and the Beanstalk" to his children. Their eyes are wide in wonder as he imitates the gruff voice of the Giant. John Bonham appears driving a farm tractor. Jimmy makes the last appearance, sitting in the garden at Boleskine House on a sunny afternoon. His acoustic guitar is lying next to him and he is playing a hurdy-gurdy, a stringed instrument that produces sound by a hand crank-turned, rosined wheel rubbing against strings. His back is to the camera. When he turns, his eyes flash with an eerie, burning red light. The scary eyes with the creepy sound of the hurdy-gurdy is very unsettling.

The Song Remains the Same also includes dream sequences for each band member – and this is where it gets even weirder. In Jones' segment, a group of masked men ride through what appears to be an eighteenth-century English countryside. It's filmed at night and one major scene is set in a graveyard. When one of the masked men, Jones, returns home, he takes off his mask and his family greets him as though he were returning from a day at the office. I'm not sure what this is supposed to represent, but director Joe Massot said that it was John's idea. He wanted to do a horror tale about the leader a group of masked riders who terrified villagers, raped women, and acted horribly, but when he gets home to his family, and removes the mask, he has a peaceful life.

Plant's dream sequence occurred during the band's performance of "The Song Remains the Same." In it, he becomes a medieval hero on some sort of quest. He was filmed on a sailing ship with ancient banners, trying to reach the shore. At the end of his journey, he is met by his lady, played by Maureen, who presents him with a sword. After he prepares himself for battle, he attacks a castle ruin and frees a damsel in distress, only to have her disappear. With his deed completed, he returns to the lady, who rewards him with gold.

The strangest film sequence belongs to, naturally, Jimmy Page. It's meant to be a recreation of the cover art from the band's fourth album. In it, Jimmy is a young seeker of wisdom who climbs a mountain to find out the secrets held by the hermit of tarot cards. When he reaches the top, he finds the hermit is actually himself and he watches his regression from old man into a fetus in his mother's womb – and then he turns back again into the old hermit. The filming had been done at Loch Ness, near Boleskine. Of course, he had to wait until the full moon to complete the imagery, which becomes all about light and shadow, in a way that only films made in the 1970s can achieve.

"Jimmy's film was strange," said director Mosser in a bit of an understatement. "He felt he wanted to say something about time and the passage thereof. There's a mountain out in back of his place, Boleskine, on the shores of Loch Ness in Scotland. So, Jimmy decided that he would climb it and act out a symbolic tale of a young man fighting his way to the top to meet with the old man of the mountain at the summit, Father Time in symbolism. Jimmy plays both parts in the film. He insisted that his segment be shot on the night of the full moon. It was quite difficult lighting that mountain at night – we had to build special scaffolds on the side of it and put cameras on and mount arc lamps. It was a weekend and overtime for the crew, but Jimmy wanted it to be right."

There are no occult references in John Bonham's segment. He drag races in a hot rod around town. That was him, being himself. There is also a scene where he practices his drums next to his young son, Jason, who has a matching, scaled-down drum set of his own.

The interacting of the three film sequences creates an atmosphere of illusion as it drifts back and forth to the sounds of Led Zeppelin in concert. It's supposed to make it difficult to tell the difference between what's fantasy and what's reality. I can't say that I think it succeeds with that, but regardless, fans loved it when The Song Remains the Same was released on September 28, 1976.

Less than a year later, Robert Plant was again struck by tragedy.

During the band's American tour in 1977, Robert received an emergency telephone call at his hotel in New Orleans. The staggering call with Maureen lasted for two hours and when he hung up the phone and returned to his friends, he had terrible news – his son, Karac, was dead. He had only been five-years-old. The little boy had contacted a respiratory infection on July 26, and it became so bad that he had to be taken by ambulance to the hospital. Karac died on the way. The doctors said that the infection was "strange" and "extremely rare." Robert was devasted and later said to a reporter, "All this success and fame, what's it worth? It doesn't mean very much when you compare it to love of a family."

Robert flew home and the remainder of the tour was canceled. The funeral was held one week later, but Richard Cole and John Bonham were the only Zeppelin team members who attended. When Robert asked where Jimmy and John were, Cole told him that they were uneasy about death and funerals. Robert's reaction was understandable: "Maybe they don't have as much respect for me as I have for them. Maybe they're not the friends I thought they were."

"What the hell is going on?"

That was the question that some people were asking. The press and the tabloids made the bad things happening to Led Zeppelin front-page news. Some fans recalled the rumors of the pact with Satan, finally catching up with them. Others pointed to the "curse" placed on them by someone whose name I promise not to mention again. Or maybe it was bad karma? Jimmy Page gave the only answer he had: "It's [karma] just the wrong term to use, and how somebody could write that down, knowing the full facts about what has happened, I don't know. It shocks me. The whole concept of the band is about entertainment. I don't see any link between that and karma, and yet I've seen it written a few times about us, like 'yet another incident in Zeppelin's karma – John Paul Jones has a broken hand.' It's nonsense – that was years back. It's all crap. The thing about karma really bothers me. Where's the clue? Why are they using that term? It's a horrible, tasteless thing to say."

A disk jockey from Detroit claimed that "if Jimmy Page would just lay off all that mystical, hocus-pocus occult stuff, and stop unleashing all those evil forces, Led Zeppelin could just concentrate on making music."

Rumors claimed that Robert Plant blamed his son's death on Jimmy's fascination with the occult, but this was only a rumor and Plant never acknowledged that publicly. It was certainly the last thing that he wanted to think about right after his son passed away.

Jimmy angrily responded, though: "The people who say things like that don't know what in the hell they are talking about. And Robert sure doesn't need to hear that kind of crap. A lot of negative things have occurred recently, but tragedies happen. Why do they have to make it worse by talking that way? Why don't they let Robert mourn in peace?"

But as it turned out, Karac's death was only the start of a series of bizarre events.

The following month, in August 1976, Elvis Presley died. Led Zeppelin had always considered Elvis one of their greatest inspirations and had met their idol one time. Elvis wanted to know if all the stories that he'd heard about Zeppelin on tour were really true.

The next month, in September, John Bonham suffered two broken ribs in a car accident.

Things were quiet for the next year while Robert remained in seclusion with his family, but in September 1978, Zeppelin friend Keith Moon of The Who died from an overdose of medication that had been prescribed to help him stop drinking. In one year, the man who had inspired the band and the man who named it had both died.

It was two years before Zeppelin began recording *In Through the Out Door*. It was released on August 15, 1979. The album's artwork was designed in a series of six shots. Each album was placed in a shrink-wrapped paper bag so that the buyer wouldn't know which artwork it contained. The albums were numbered on their spines with the letters A to F. And yes, there was a hidden message – some of the early pressings had the word "strawberry" inscribed into the runoff grooves. As a final touch, if the album jacket came into contact with warm weather – although, why would you want it to? – it supposedly changed color.

The recording again contained some brilliant work, including "All of My Love," written by Jones and Plant. Side one, however, ends with "In the Evening," which has musical passages inspired by themes leftover from Jimmy's soundtrack for *Lucifer Rising*.

The release of a new album brought renewed attention to the band during the promotional tour. It had now been over two years since Zeppelin had toured in America. A few concert dates in England seemed to rekindle their creative spark and they were ready for something new. A rehearsal schedule was put together – and then another tragedy struck.

On September 24, 1980, John Bonham was driven down to Jimmy's new Windsor mansion, the Mill House, for rehearsals. On the way, John had stopped at a pub and drank what was believed to have been four quadruple vodkas. When he arrived at Jimmy's house, he continued to drink. After that, he went to a reunion party and drank some more. He passed out on the couch at midnight and Zeppelin associate Rick Hobbs helped the very intoxicated drummer to a bedroom. He placed John on his side and left him to sleep it off. But when John had not made an appearance by midafternoon of the next day, Robert's assistant, Benji LeFevre, went to wake him up. After shaking him, he

John Bonham

realized that John's body was blue and cold. An ambulance was called and while the crew worked hard to resuscitate him, John was dead. He was only 31-years-old.

The news of John's death set off another round of Satanic rumors about the band. One fan claimed to see thick black smoke coming from Jimmy's house on the night John died – a story that shouldn't have made the tabloids, but did. Other fans swore they'd heard Jimmy speaking in strange, unknown languages. Another rumor popped up about the existence of a Zeppelin "black album" – a mysterious recording that was said to contain death chants translated by a German writer from ancient languages. The *London Evening News* ran a headline about the "Zeppelin 'Black Magic' Mystery." An unnamed source, who was allegedly close to the group, said, "It sounds crazy, but Robert Plant and everyone around the band is convinced that Jimmy's dabbling in black magic is responsible in some way for Bonzo's death and for all those other tragedies... I think the three remaining members of Zeppelin are now a little afraid of what is going to happen next."

John Bonham's death was not declared as the result of "black magic" by the coroner – it was an accident. John had consumed 40 measures of vodka in a 12-hour period. The body was cremated a few days later and a memorial service was held for him on October 10.

In the end, John's death killed the band.

A few weeks after his service, it was determined by unanimous decision that Led Zeppelin was no more. In 1982, a few outtakes and some unreleased recordings were made available on an album called *Coda*. In musical compositions, a coda is the closing section of a song or movement. It was a fitting end to a turbulent era of music.

Jimmy, Robert, and John went their separate ways and recorded their own solo projects and performed with other bands. John retired to the studio and became a successful writer and producer. In time, Jimmy and Robert patched up whatever differences were between them and put out some new Zeppelin music. The band has since been inducted into the Rock and Roll Hall of Fame and the two have taken their place as a couple of the grand old men of rock.

Jimmy Page has – at least as much as the rumors are to be believed because he doesn't speak about it publicly – given up his interest in the occult.

But who knows?

The glory days of Zeppelin are past, even though you can easily relive them on FM radio, any music streaming service, or on a vinyl LP, the way their music was always meant to be heard.

If you do decide to dust off their fourth record some night, turn down the lights and see if you can play "Stairway to Heaven" backward. You just never know what you might hear.

"MR. CROWLEY" AND
"ZIGGY STARDUST"

We're not quite finished with Aleister Crowley.

David Bowie had one of the most successful careers in music, and he remains today one of the most important figures in the world of art and pop, but how much of that had to do with his connection to the occult – and more specifically, to Aleister Crowley? Throughout his career, he used bits of chaos magic, Gnosticism, and paganism to craft a densely layered artistic persona that remains as mysterious now as it was back in the 1970s.

Bowie's interest in the arcane began long before he started writing songs. In the 1960s, he flirted with the idea of Buddhism, even going as far as to try and join a monastery. He was dissuaded by a monk who insisted that he would make a better musician. In the late 1960s, he became interested in Aleister Crowley – a passion that stayed with him literally until the end of his life. At some point between his albums *Space Oddity* (1969) and *The Man Who Sold the World* (1970), he began developing his darker interests. *The Man Who Sold the World* is filled with songs that reference forbidden knowledge, and he began to intertwin his occult beliefs into his songwriting process and life. Even on his final album, *Blackstar*, his occult beliefs were on full display. Each of his albums reference the occult in one way or another, with the overarching theme of much of his early work being his belief in Gnosticism, or transcendence reached by looking into yourself to find a personal religious experience.

In an interview, Bowie explained, "My overriding interest was in Kabbalah and Crowleyism. That whole dark and rather fearsome never-world of the wrong side of the brain."

Bowie even imitated Crowley, dressing up like the magician in a series of photo shoots, specifically taking on the look that Crowley used for photographs in Egyptian garb for the Order of the Golden Dawn.

But it wasn't just Crowley that influenced Bowie's views on the occult. Dion Fortune was an English practitioner who disseminated a philosophy rooted in psychic warfare that she claimed was taught to her by a group known as the "Ascended Masters." Throughout the 1970s, Bowie kept a copy of Fortune's book, *Psychic Self Defense*, with him at all times and her work even inspired him to wear a silver cross while living in L.A. He began wearing the cross while filming *The Man Who Fell to Earth* and continued to do so through the sessions for *Station to Station*.

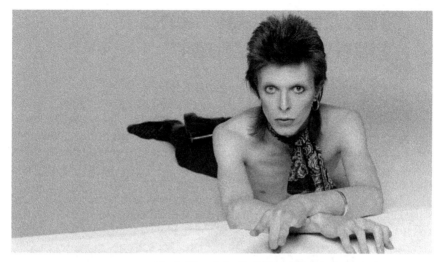

David Bowie in the 1970s

Bowie's 1971 breakthrough album, *Hunky Dory*, is steeped in occult lore, but the singer put his mystical foundations on display in the song "Quicksand," which openly references Crowley and the Golden Dawn.

By the early 1970s, Bowie was following Crowley's example in ways that had nothing to do with magic. In 1917, Crowley had written, "Give cocaine to a man already wise and if he be really master of himself, it will do him no harm. Alas! The power of the drug diminishes with a fearful pace. The doses wax; the pleasures wane. Side-issues, invisible at first, arise; they are like devils with flaming pitchforks in their hands."

Bowie admits that his love affair with cocaine led to a downward spiral of psychosis. By the time he recorded *Station to Station* in 1975, he was using so much cocaine that he later claimed not to remember any of the production. If this is true, it makes the lyrical content of the album even more intriguing because it heavily invokes a Kabballah influence. The Kabbalah system is known as the "septhiroth," or a station, each of them separating the realm of spiritual transcendence from the physical realm.

Bowie used a certain technique to pen many of his lyrics, which made their inherent magical nature even more fascinating. There's nothing otherworldly about the cut-up technique, which was made popular by author William S. Burroughs, but what results from it can be eerie, especially in light of all of Bowie's occult references. The technique is similar to automatic writing – a method used by Spiritualist mediums to obtain information from the next world – but instead of random writing on a black sheet of paper, a cut-up writer takes a section of text and then puts the pieces back together at random. It can be a page from a book, something the writer wrote previously, or anything similar to that. The outcome can often be meaningless gibberish, but in some cases, it's brilliant. The question remains whether this is random – or guided by otherworldly hands.

One of the things that Bowie became most-known for during his career was his use of playing different characters. He did this for a specific reason, he said. Regardless of what he was embodying at the time – or what was embodying him – Bowie considered these personas to be something that existed outside of him – a kind of projection of his mental space at the time. In the occult, these are referred to as "tulpas." For instance, when he felt the world needed a "plastic rock and roller," he gave it Ziggy Stardust.

Bowie also saw these characters as a way to expunge negative energy. He explained this in a 1993 interview: "There was a theory that one creates a doppelgänger and then imbues that with all your faults and guilts and fears and then eventually you destroy him, hopefully destroying all your guilt, fear and paranoia. And I often feel that I was doing that unwittingly, creating an alternative ego that would take on everything that I was insecure about."

During his time living in Los Angeles in the middle 1970s, Bowie was deep in his phase of ingesting only cocaine and red peppers. It was during this time that he became acquainted with one of the few other major rock stars who was as open about his love of the occult as Bowie was – Jimmy Page. The two bonded over their fascination with Aleister Crowley – at first. But then, somehow, Bowie became terrified of Page. He came to believe that the guitarist was casting spells on him. Bowie's paranoia began after an incident when Page drew "Kabbalistic symbols" on Bowie's studio floor, sending the cocaine addled singer into a tailspin.

Bowie later told his wife, Angie, that he was going to retaliate against Page with "the dark side of Buddhism" – whatever that is – but apparently nothing ever developed into a battle of wizardry between them.

But then there was that pesky demon.

Around this same time, Bowie came to believe there was a demon in his swimming pool. Keep in mind, he was still on the "cocaine diet" at the time. Hoping to alleviate his fears, Angie put him in contact with Walli Elmlark, a "white witch" from New York who gave Bowie instructions for an exorcism over the phone. Angie said that a Greek Orthodox church offered to perform the ceremony, but Bowie had a "no strangers" rule in place in his home, so he bought the necessary supplies and got to it.

In her autobiography, Angie later wrote: "So, there we stood, with just Walli's instructions and a few hundred dollars worth of books, talismans, and assorted items from Hollywood's comprehensive selection of fine occult emporia. I had no idea what was being said or what language it was being said in, I couldn't stop a weird cold feeling rising up in me as David droned on and on. There's no easy or elegant way to say this, so I'll just say it straight. At a certain point in the ritual, the pool began to bubble. It bubbled vigorously (perhaps "thrashed" is a better term) in a manner inconsistent with any explanation involving air filters or the like."

Pretty weird, right? Well, Bowie later said that after performing this ritual, he knew it was time to pull himself together.

Even though his artistic output slowed – and then sped up again – late in his life, Bowie's interest in the occult never waned. His final album, *Blackstar*, represented a "meticulously planned" ending for the story of his life. The imagery behind the album delved into the concept of a person leaving earth and ascending to another realm, where he becomes a god. Bowie doubled down on this imagery in the video for "Blackstar." In the piece, a woman discovers a skull hidden in an astronaut's helmet, a direct reference to Bowie's early hit, "Space Oddity." Following this discovery, a magical ritual breaks out around the skull of Major Tom.

The video's director, Johan Renck, told *Vice*: "I'm a huge Crowley fan, I've always been. I tried to make a movie on his life a few years ago but we didn't manage to put it together. I love Crowley for being an audacious man at a certain point in time. I think he's greatly misunderstood. He was a good guy, but he was portrayed as an evil man and he wasn't."

Even though he didn't plan it this time, Crowley had crept into the life – and death – of David Bowie one last time.

MR. CROWLEY'S LAST NOD

As we have seen, rock-n-roll has enjoyed a strangely symbiotic relationship with the occult since the Beatles included a photograph of Aleister Crowley on their *Sgt. Pepper* album, and the Rolling Stones credited Anton LaVey and Voodoo priests for their inspiration in creating "Sympathy for the Devil." It was perhaps inevitable that the hippie era of the late 1960s, with its emphasis on "acid rock" and Eastern mysticism would initiate a change in classic rock, evolving over time into the current "heavy metal" scene.

Heavy metal, which gets its name from its reliance on electric guitars cranked to ear-splitting decibels, has become inextricably linked to Satanism in the public eye, thanks in equal parts to lyrics, deliberate marketing strategy, and the exaggerated claims of some Christian fundamentalist groups. Beyond the stage lights and amplifiers, in the daily lives of the rabid fans who become obsessed with heavy metal, the police and religious groups claim that the music has a disastrous effect. They claim that fans commit crimes ranging from petty vandalism to murder – all directly inspired by the message of occult-oriented bands. But, of course, such claims are nothing new – the "Devil's Music" strikes again -- and not all of them can be attributed to the blasting chords of heavy metal.

In the late 1960s, the press had labeled Mick Jagger as the "Lucifer of Rock," but as we discovered, the Stones were more interested in sex, drugs, music, and their public image than they were in worshipping the Devil. Their satanic image was nothing more than a clever marketing ploy during a time period when the public was titillated by the occult. But the Stones found out that even playfully evoking a Satanic image could prove fatal at Altamont. They learned their lesson.

Other less mainstream bands, however, found the satanic imagery too tempting to resist and by the end of the decade, bands like Black Widow and Coven summoned the faithful to the Black Mass.

The Chicago band Coven can lay claim to being the first overtly satanic band to release an album. The closing track of *Witchcraft Destroys Minds and Reaps Souls* is a thirteen-minute Black Mass that uses a Latin chant that the sleeve notes claim is authentic. The cover of their 1969 debut album also featured what might have been the first appearance of the "Devil's sign," a hand gesture that was later popularized by Ronnie James Dio. He claimed that he learned it from his Italian grandmother, who told him it was a traditional protection against the "evil eye." The gesture was subsequently used en masse by metal fans as a way of showing tribute to the performers. Incidentally, Dio also fronted Ritchie Blackmore's band Rainbow, another group with a passing interest in the occult.

Coven was made up of vocalist Esther "Jinx" Dawson, bassist Greg "Oz" Osborne, guitarist Chris Neilsen, keyboardist Rick Durrett, and drummer Steve Ross. Dawson and Osborne, after playing together in the group Him, Her and Them, formed Coven with Ross in Chicago in the late 1960s. In 1967 and 1968 they toured, playing concerts with artists including Jimmy Page's Yardbirds, the Alice Cooper band, and Vanilla Fudge. They signed with Mercury Records in 1969 and released their first album, *Witchcraft Destroys Minds & Reaps Souls*.

The music on the album – it's pretty bad, sorry – was considered "underground rock" with heavy emphasis on diabolical subject matter. It included songs like "The White Witch of Rose Hall," "For Unlawful Carnal

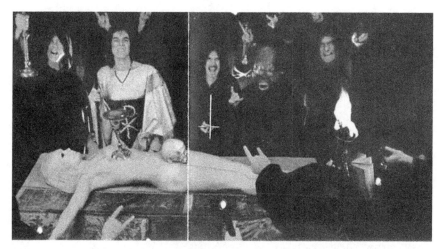

Coven's "awesome" Black Mass poster, included with the album

Knowledge," "Black Sabbath," "Dignitaries of Hell," and, of course, the 13-minutes track of chanting and Satanic prayers that was sure to liven up any party. The album also came with a bonus Black Mass poster, showing members of the group displaying the sign of the horns as they prepared for a Satanic ritual over a nude Dawson lying on an altar.

See what you kids missed out on if you didn't grow up in the days of vinyl LPs?

But all the occult stuff didn't last long. The band got a lot of unwanted publicity when an issue of *Esquire* magazine came out in March 1970 with a cover story called "Evil Lurks in California," which linked the counterculture's interest in the occult to Charles Manson and the Tate-La Bianca murders. It also specifically mentioned Coven's album and its Black Mass material. As a result, Mercury pulled the album from circulation.

A year later, Jinx Dawson recorded the vocals for "One Tin Soldier," the title theme for the 1971 film *Billy Jack*, which was credited as "sung by Coven." The song was a hit and in 1972, the band put out a new, self-titled album that included "One Tin Soldier."

By this point, the occult posturing was toned down to just one spooky black cat and a band member surreptitiously flashing the sign of the horns on the album cover.

Black Widow came around at the same time as Coven. Their debut album, *Sacrifice*, also featured several songs with satanic themes, including "Conjuration," "Come to the Sabbat," and the title track. Their stage act included a faux ritual, complete with a naked female dancer, which they claimed was choreographed by Alex Sanders, the so-called "King of the Witches." As it turned out, though, you needed more than just a good stage act to make it in rock-n-roll. Their music proved to be too unremarkable to make much of a lasting impression.

In contrast, British metal band Black Sabbath embraced the "schlock horror" aspect of witchcraft and devil worship wholeheartedly. They named themselves after a stylish Italian horror film starring Boris Karloff, and they served up the musical version of Hammer horrors in tracks like "The Wizard," "Children of the Grave," "War Pigs" and "Paranoid."

In his solo career, lead singer of the band, Ozzy Osbourne, even released a song called "Mr. Crowley," which was dedicated to Crowley himself. The lyrics include a section that goes: "You fooled all the people with magic, you waited on Satan's call."

Black Sabbath was certainly intent on fooling people with their "black magic" antics and devilish imagery – they never thought anyone would take it seriously. However, the band soon realized they had inadvertently started something that couldn't be stopped. Fans began reading invocations to Satan into every lyric. "N.I.B.," for example was interpreted to mean "Nativity in Black," but it had actually been a reference to the drummer's nickname, Nibby. The negative attention that they attracted from seriously disturbed fans led the group to write songs that warned against dabbling in the occult.

They later admitted that they had been uncomfortable with the subject from the start, as evidence by a story told by bassist Geezer Butler.

In 1966, he began reading black magic magazines and black magic novels by British author Dennis Wheatley. Raised as a Catholic, he believed in the existence of the Devil and so when he started having precognitive dreams, he wondered if they had been sent to him by dark forces. He started putting upside-down crosses on his walls, painted his apartment black, and decorated the place with pictures of Satan. But his avid interest would soon come to an end.

One of Geezer's supernatural experiences inspired the title track of the band's debut album. He had been lying in bed one night after reading a book on the occult when he sensed what he called a "malign presence." When he opened his eyes, he was terrified to see a large black shape that looked like a hooded monk standing at the end of his bed. After a moment or two, it disappeared, but it left behind an unsettling atmosphere. The next morning, Geezer discovered that the occult book he had been reading was gone. He knew that the thing, whatever it was, had been drawn by the book and he vowed never to read anything on the subject again.

Black Sabbath in the 1970s

And he didn't. But he did become part of a band that played up their "connection" to the Devil for years. The point was, though, they didn't take it seriously.

Ozzy Osbourne, who also made the most of Black Sabbath's satanic image ended up becoming America's favorite eccentric uncle as he shuffled around his Hollywood mansion in his slippers, mumbling his way through a reality show. As a working-class lad from Birmingham, Ozzy always had his tongue firmly wedged in his cheek when it came to being the "Prince of Darkness." He seemed a frightening figure until TV viewers saw him struggling with television remotes and taking abuse from his kids. After that, he hardly seemed like a threat to the nation's youth.

As for the rest of the band, he now admits that the members of Black Sabbath were so shaken after watching *The Exorcist* that they had to sleep in the same bed. "That's how satanic we were!" he now laughs.

Black Sabbath might have been a "hell of a band" in their prime but never reached the levels of Led Zeppelin, who, as we know, was plagued with rumors of pacts with the Devil and curses caused by Jimmy Page's fascination with the occult.

Outwardly, though, the band's albums only contained fleeting, obscure references to the occult and even those are ambiguous and open to interpretation. Jimmy Page might have been under Crowley's spell, but he was astute enough to realize that overt references to magic and the Devil would only appeal to a minority of listeners.

Other bands of the era knew this, as well. Alice Cooper is regarded today as the godfather of Gothic rock and was at one time the purveyor of the most perversely pleasurable stage show in the business. Cooper, born Vincent Furnier, allegedly borrowed his stage name from a seventeenth-century witch, after consulting a Ouija board. He used a satanic image in his shows and advertising, but in reality, he is a family man who loves golf. Today, he is far from the image of every parent's worst nightmare than he was in the 1970s.

By the middle 1970s, showmanship was clearly the key for heavy metal bands, epitomized by the fire-spitting, tongue-wagging performances of KISS. Guitarist Gene Simmons described the band's style to an interviewer: "We wanted to look like we crawled out from under a rock somewhere in Hell. We wanted parents to look at us and instantly want to throw up."

Within a few short years, satanic emblems, lyrics, and tattoos became the standard trappings of successful heavy metal bands. Taking their cue from Black Sabbath, would-be successes began calling themselves Iron Maiden, Venom, Slayer, Sodom, Anti Christ, Hellhammer, Nocticula, Megadeth, and Possessed. A small-time band from Denver, Satan's Host, boasted performers with stage names like Satan Patrick Evil, Belial, D. Lucifer Steele, and Leviathan Thisiren. Publicists worked overtime to exploit the "witchy" angle of their bands, creating Black Metal, Death Metal, and Thrash Metal – each louder, faster, and perhaps more profitable than anything that had come before. The vocals were an unintelligible growl – often sounding like the Cookie Monster from *Sesame Street* with a microphone inserted in his gullet - - the guitars were a screaming level of distortion, and the drummers needed the stamina and speed of an Olympic athlete to keep up the insanely fast tempo. This was the unholy sound of bands like Acheron, Angel Witch, Anaal Nathrakh, Bathory, Cloven Hoof, Cradle of Filth, December Moon, Hecate, Hell Satan, King Diamond (Mercyful Fate), Lord Belial, Megiddo Bal Sagoth, Onslaught, Pagan Altar, Reign of Erebus, Sabbat, Venom, Warhammer, Witchfynde, and many other so-called legions of the damned. It was not like music anymore, it was more like war.

Some began to feel like the apocalypse had finally arrived.

Critics of this new wave of demonic music noted its preoccupation with Satanic themes and kinky sex, brute force, and bloodshed. On the Christian talk show circuit, word began to circulate that certain heavy metal bands -- as opposed to the ones that were blatantly demonic with their names and images -- were hiding secret messages in their names and lyrics. Thus, it was suggested that KISS really stood for "Knights in Satan's Service." AC/DC's logo was said to be shorthand for "Anti-Christ / Devil's Child." By the same logic, WASP became "We Are Satan's People." Heavy metal performers denied the claims, but by the time these "secrets" were spilled, it was too late.

It is difficult, if not impossible, to gauge the true measure of occult / satanic belief among heavy metal performers. For some bands, like Motley Crue, pentagrams and inverted crosses were simply part of the act, along with lipstick, eye shadow, and women's underwear. At the other end of the spectrum was King Diamond from the band Mercyful Fate, who openly proclaimed his devotion to Satan. This was a rare thing in the fading days of the 1980s, but by the 1990s, the horrific side of metal was slapping people right in the face.

Band members of Venom stated, "We are not here to entertain you but to preach the ways of Satan." Their manifesto was declared in the song "Possessed," which stated, "I am possessed by all that is evil. The death of your God I demand I... I sit at Lord Satan's right hand."

I know I've said it before, but – yikes.

But what the critics failed to take into account was that artists perform "in character." Their lyrics don't necessarily represent their personal beliefs. Did Mick Jagger really believe that he was Lucifer incarnate when he asked for sympathy for the devil? No, he was acting the part for the sake of the song. And when Vincent Furnier beheaded dolls and sang "No More Mr. Nice Guy," he did it as his alter ego and stage persona, Alice Cooper. Only someone who believes that rock is the "Devil's Music" would assume that the spirit that moves and inspires artists in mysterious ways is anything other than their figurative muse.

That said, some of the Black Metal bands took themselves very seriously indeed.

Acheron recruited Peter Gilmore from the Church of Satan to act as master of ceremonies for their album *The Rites of the Black Mass*, but then again, how evil is the Church of Satan? LaVey's creation was sort of the religious equivalent of most heavy metal bands.

But then Morbid Angel boasted that they were "Satan's sword" on a mission to "rid the world of the Nazarene" and frontman Trey Azagthoth claimed to be a genuine vampire. He proved it by biting himself on stage and drinking his own blood.

Showmanship or insanity? Who can say?

But in reality, if the bands had been serious practitioners of the black arts, they might have released some pretty incredible forces with the energy conjured up by the number of leather and black t-shirt clad fans who came to "worship" them every week. Whipped into a frenzy, horrific things would have occurred in the course of what should have been Satanic rituals – but, of course, nothing did.

However, this didn't stop the religious fanatics from "crucifying" the bands for everything they did. Little did they know, but their criticism simply brought the artists more attention, more press, and a legion of new fans.

"SaTanIC PanIC"

It was in the 1980s when all the trouble started.

I guess you could say it started long before that, perhaps as far back as when the Church first decided that music that it didn't like was the "Devil's Music." It was music and then it was behavior and, finally, your beliefs that could get you into trouble.

In Salem, Massachusetts, in 1692, being accused of witchcraft had fatal results. But, of course, most Americans believed that nothing like that could ever happen again. But it did. In fact, in the 1980s, witches and Satanists were everywhere. A hysteria – much like the one that gripped the people of Salem – seized the country. The hysteria was spread by fundamentalist Christians, radical religious groups, television talk show hosts, and many otherwise well-intentioned people and organizations who lived in fear that a vast Satanic underground network was infiltrating the country.

They claimed that Satanic groups were spreading their evil message through rock-n-roll music, kidnapping and abusing children, and might even be responsible for murdering thousands of people who went missing every year. Those missing persons, they believed, had fallen victim to Satanic cults who used them for blood sacrifices to the Devil. The evidence for such an underground was obvious, they claimed, and pointed to a handful of murders carried out by pseudo-Satanists in black t-shirts, child abuse cases that would turn out to be more than a little questionable and, of course, "recovered memories" of what came to be known as Satanic Ritual Abuse.

The end result of the "witch hunts" of the 1980s and early 1990s were scores of people being accused of crimes they did not commit, the destruction of families caused by "repressed" memories of things that never happened, and a nationwide panic that cultists were waiting on every corner to kidnap children.

See what you missed, kids? Not only did you miss out on the original era of vinyl records by not being around in the 1980s, you also missed on being accused of worshipping Satan because you liked rock-n-roll.

If there was a single thing that can truly be credited with starting what became known as "Satanic Panic" in the 1980s, it was the publication of a book called *Michelle Remembers*, co-written by a Canadian psychiatrist named Dr. Lawrence Pazder and his patient, Michelle Smith. I discovered this book when I was starting my first year of high school and confess to being terrified by the contents. Not only did I believe that what I was reading was possible, I was convinced that it had all taken place. Like so many others at the time, I was fooled by the startling, horrific contents of the book, but my gullibility would not last for long.

Within a few years, I began to realize, as many others also did, that the Satanic hysteria of the 1980s had very little basis in truth. Unfortunately, though, the movement was only just beginning. It was just too colorful and too sensational for the talk show hosts and television evangelists to let go of, and they found that by ignoring the facts and spreading half-truths, they could keep their audiences glued to their seats – and utterly terrified that devil-worshipping boogiemen were around every corner waiting to get them.

In a nutshell, *Michelle Remembers* tells the story of a little girl whose mother turns her over to a Satanic cult in Vancouver in the 1950s. The book is put together as a narrative, flashing back and forth between the past and present, and offers the version of events that Smith retrieves from her "recovered memories" during her therapy. It documents her mother's involvement with the cult, the many Satanic rituals that the young Michelle was forced to attend and participate in, and the many horrifying events that occurred during a time when she was literally held prisoner by the cult. During the rites, Smith was allegedly tortured, locked in cages, sexually assaulted, witnessed several murders, and was covered in the blood of slain infants and adults. She was eventually rescued thanks to the intervention of Jesus and the Virgin Mary. The archangel Michael then shows up and erases all her memories of the events "until the time is right."

I know what you're thinking – but I swear it seemed real to 13-year-old me.

Anyway, when people started looking closer at the story, it began to fall apart. It took years, but eventually the book was completely debunked. By then, though, the damage was done.

Michelle Remembers was the first book of its kind, but its success would inspire dozens of copy-cat titles and it would become an important part of the controversies regarding Satanic Ritual Abuse and repressed memories. Satanic Ritual Abuse first made headlines after the publication of the book and referred to physical and sexual abuse that reportedly occurred during occult or satanic ceremonies. The phenomenon began in the early 1980s, mostly in the United States, but spread to other parts of the world, impacting how the legal, therapeutic, and social work professions dealt with allegations of abuse.

Other books about repressed memories followed, and in the hysteria that accompanied their publication, no one thought to ask why earlier cases of ritual abuse had not come to light. Too many people just accepted that the stories were true. They provided the model for all the allegations of ritual abuse that followed, like the McMartin Preschool case in California.

The case began in 1983 when the mother of one of the Manhattan Beach preschool students alleged to the police that her son had been sodomized by Ray Buckey, a teacher at the school. Buckey was the grandson of school founder Virginia McMartin and son of the school's administrator Peggy McMartin Buckey. According to the mother, her son made other startling accusations about the school, like teachers at the daycare center had sex with animals and that Ray Buckey "flew in the air." Bucky was questioned but was released due to lack of any evidence of the claims. Unbelievably, though, the police sent an open letter to about 200 parents of children at the McMartin school, stating that abuse might have taken place at the school and asking parents to question their children. In the letter, parents were supposed to check and see if their children had been involved in oral sex, fondling of the genitals, sodomy, and child pornography. Ray Buckey was named in the letter as a suspect.

The letter created an uproar – even though it later turned out the mother who accused Ray Buckey had been diagnosed with acute paranoid schizophrenia. Children from the school were interviewed by the Children's Institute International, a Los Angeles-based abuse therapy clinic. The interviewing techniques used during the investigations were highly suggestive and misleading, and by the spring of 1984, claims were being made that as many as 360 children had been abused. The children were asked repetitive, leading questions that almost always yielded positive results, making it impossible to know what the alleged victims experienced.

Not surprisingly, the often "bizarre" accusations included elements of Satanic Ritual Abuse. It was alleged that, in addition to having been sexually abused, the children saw witches fly, traveled in a hot air balloon, and were taken through underground tunnels. When shown a series of photographs by the McMartins' attorney, one child identified actor Chuck Norris as one of the abusers. Some of the abuse was said to have occurred in secret tunnels under the school, which evidence proved didn't exist. There were also claims of orgies taking place at car washes and at airports, and of children being flushed down toilets to secret rooms where they would be abused, cleaned up, and then given back to their unsuspecting parents.

On March 22, 1984, Virginia McMartin, Peggy McMartin Buckey, Ray Buckey, Ray's sister Peggy Ann Buckey and teachers Mary Ann Jackson, Bette Raidor, and Babette Spitler were charged with 115 incidents of child abuse, later expanded to 321 incidents of child abuse involving forty-eight children.

The trial went on for years and eventually everyone involved was acquitted on all accounts. Ray Buckey spent five years in jail without ever being convicted of anything.

It was the media and social workers who helped to fan the flames of the witch hunt in the McMartin case, and they continued to spread the word about so-called Satanic Ritual Abuse in the months and years to come. Psychologists began speaking at conferences about Satanic Ritual Abuse as a nationwide conspiracy. Best of all, those who denied the existence of an underground Satanic movement were probably part of the conspiracy. In 1986, a social worker named Carol Darling argued in a grand jury hearing that the conspiracy reached into the highest levels of the government. Her husband, Brad Darling, gave conferences about the satanic conspiracy, which he alleged dated back for centuries.

By the late 1980s, the recognition that mental health workers had given to Satanic Ritual Abuse led to the formation of Christian psychotherapy groups, exorcist organizations, multiple personality claims, and the development of groups for "survivors" of abuse. Thanks to all the attention, federal funding was provided for conferences supporting the idea of Satanic Ritual Abuse, offering an opportunity for prosecutors to exchange ideas on the best ways to secure convictions on cases that might be many years old. Many cases were prosecuted based on an adult's "recovered memories" of alleged childhood assaults.

Perhaps predictably, given its "wacky" reputation and its history of weird cults, California generated the majority of the ritual abuse reports. In Concord, a mechanic was named by his stepdaughter as part of a cult that forced her to eat feces and murder a baby. His trial ended with a hung jury. Nearby, in Antelope Valley, three children horrified their foster mother with stories of their father having taken part in ritual murder and cannibalism. No bodies were ever found, but the accused was convicted of felony child abuse. Several children at a fundamentalist Christian preschool in Mendocino claimed they had been raped, tied to crosses, and forced to chant, "Baby Jesus is dead!" In Pico Rivera, a 10-year-old named David Tackett accused six neighbors of being involved in orgies, urine-drinking, and the sacrifice of infants. Nine other children supported the story, but no charges were ever filed. Similar investigations in Torrance, Whittier, and Covina failed to produce any hard evidence. In Fremont, a five-year-old boy complained of being removed from his preschool by strangers who took him to a church where he was injected with drugs, sexually abused, and forced to watch the candlelit mutilation of humans and animals. At Fort Bragg, five children from a church daycare center claimed bizarre activities took place at the center involving drugs, pornography, black candles, pentagrams, and sacrificed pets. In Redwood City, two victims described adults wearing black robes and cremating a sacrificed infant, whose burned body "really stunk." In Atherton, a 17-year-old girl outlined abuse rituals performed by her stepfather and 10 strangers.

Meanwhile, allegations of abuse were spreading beyond California. In Memphis, Tennessee, a routine pediatric check-up exposed charges of ritual abuse when a three-year-old girl told her doctor that a preschool teacher had fondled her genitals. The girl named three other victims for the police, and those children in turn named others, all from the church-run Georgian Hills Early Childhood Center. Prosecutors ultimately charged a 54-year-old female staff member, her son, and Reverend Paul Shell with sexually abusing 26 children, torturing some, and baptizing others in "the Devil's name." Reports from the children included the now-familiar descriptions of black robes and masks, burning candles, plus mutilations of gerbils, hamsters, and a human infant. What might have been a legitimate report of abuse spun out of control during the frenzy of the times and likely led to people who had nothing to do with any sort of abuse becoming targets of the investigation. The congregation of the church stood behind the accused minister, but the prosecution refused to abandon the case. Bewildered jurors deadlocked on the case in 1987, causing a mistrial.

The media continued to add fuel to the fire. In 1987, Geraldo Rivera produced a national television special on Satanic cults, claiming that "there are over one million Satanists [in the United States] linked in a highly organized, secretive network." This show, along with others that began appearing at the time, were subsequently used by religious groups, psychotherapists, social workers, and law enforcement agencies to promote the idea that Satanic cults were engaged in a conspiracy to commit serious crimes across the country.

Perhaps the groups that benefited the most from the claims of satanic conspiracies were conservative Christian organizations, which were enthusiastic in promoting rumors of Satanic Ritual Abuse. Just as the Church had been quick to condemn the accused during the witchcraft scares hundreds of years before, religious fundamentalists in the late 1980s were using Satanic Panic to frighten believers and to bring new members into their churches. Christian psychotherapists began working with patients to "recover" lost and repressed memories and soon after, lurid stories of black robes and murdered babies began to appear. Religious groups were instrumental in starting, spreading, and maintaining rumors about Satanic Ritual Abuse through sermons about its dangers, by way of lectures by purported experts, and by prayer sessions and special showings of programs like Geraldo Rivera's 1987 "exposé."

Eventually, though, even the sensationalistic media couldn't ignore the fact that there was little in the way of hard evidence that would confirm the thousands of alleged accounts of Satanic abuse, or that a vast underground conspiracy existed that was covering everything up. Media coverage began to turn negative toward the end of the 1980s and the Panic finally came to an end between 1992 and 1995. By the end of the 1990s, allegations of ritual abuse were finally being met with skepticism and belief in Satanic Ritual Abuse finally stopped being given much credence in mainstream professional psychological circles.

But, as I said earlier, the damage was already done.

Rock-n-roll sustained a lot of collateral damage during the Satanic Panic era.

By the 1980s, occult symbols and satanic song titles were everywhere. Every metal band seemed to be laboring under the impression that having a pentagram on the cover of their album, or the number 666 in a lyric, was a more effective marketing gimmick than posing with a naked model in leather and chains. As the bands became more outrageous in their celebration of Satanic imagery, society's moral watchdogs became increasingly indignant about what they saw as their insidious influence on impressionable fans.

Finally, the righteous could repress their rage no longer and launched an aggressive campaign against a score of iconic rock acts accusing them of deliberately planting subliminal satanic messages in their music. Of course, the messages were said to be audible only when the albums were played backward.

We talked about backward masking in the section about Led Zeppelin. It's a process when bands deliberately record words or music backwards on an album. It'd been around for years and fans knew about it – especially the "Paul is dead" folks – but no one ever thought much about it. Musicians who acknowledged its use defended it as an enhancement of their music range or, in some cases, as a gimmick to sell more records.

But in the 1980s, it became the hot topic of the day with evangelists, politicians, and right-wing parents' groups alleging deliberate attempts to "brainwash" young people with hidden advertisements for sex, drugs and, of course, Satan. In fact, fundamentalist Jacob Aranza cited "expert sources" in his 1984 book *Backward Masking Unmasked* who claimed that backward masking used subliminal persuasion to convert fans of rock and roll to the occult without their conscious knowledge.

This was happening when I was in high school, so yeah, thanks for that.

The hysteria about backward masking in the 1980s started with a *CBS Evening News* report in April 1982. Dan Rather ran a report commenting on the discovery of supposedly hidden Satanic messages in pop songs.

By "pop" I assume they meant bands that did not have pentagrams on their album covers.

Rather played the infamous Zeppelin "Stairway to Heaven" backward track, as well as sections of songs by Electric Light Orchestra and Styx. Many viewers were shocked by what they heard and fundamentalist groups blamed the record companies, who must have been involved in the Satanic conspiracy.

Hilariously, Electric Light Orchestra had a number of recordings with hidden messages – although none of them were Satanic. On their album *Face the Music*, the song "Fire on High" had a secret message – that wasn't very secret since it's obviously garbled when played normally -- that when played backwards said, "The music is reversible, but time is not. Turn back! Turn back! Turn back!"

The B-52's – perhaps one of my least favorite bands – used the same approach at subliminal humor by placing a backward track in "Detour Through Your Mind." When the track is reversed, the listener can hear Fred Schneider's voice say, "I buried my parakeet in the backyard. No, no, you're playing the record backward. Watch out, you might ruin your needle."

But ELO was still in the hotseat with "Satanic messages." It was claimed that their song "Eldorado" had a sequence that went, "He is the nasty one. Christ you're infernal. It is said we're dead men. All who have the mark will live." Jeff Lynne laughed at the suggestion that this was real. "It doesn't say anything of the sort," he said in an interview. "That was totally manufactured by the person who said it. Because, anybody who can write a song forward and have it say something else backward is some kind of genius, and I ain't. And at first, I was upset by the accusation. But now I think it's funny. I was just going to say again, categorically, that we are totally innocent of all those claims of devil stuff, it's a load of rubbish."

ELO decided to make a sport of it after that. On the back cover of their third album, they reversed all the band member's names in the album credits. There is a series of dots and dashes on the album that spells out ELO in Morse code. The opening song of the album was appropriately called "Secret Messages" and at the start of it, a keyboard methodically tapped out ELO again in Morse code. After that keyboard section, a backward track can be heard with the phrase "come again. There's even a voice that intones secret message to help the first-time listener discover the location of the secret track. When it was reversed, it said, "Welcome to the big show." There's another backward track at the end of the album – a very cordial "Thank you for listening."

Not everyone saw the humor in ELO's *Secret Messages* album. Those who had always blamed the excesses of rock-n-roll for all of society's ills came up with a bunch of garbled word salads of phonetic sounds as evidence of the Devil's work.

The Eagles were accused of hiding a Satanic message in "Hotel California" – a song, which I have to confess, scared the hell out of me as a child when I first heard it playing late at night on my AM radio. Anyway, in the lyric "This could be heaven, or this could be hell," some listeners claimed that, when reversed, it said, "Yeah Satan. How he organized his own religion. Yeah, well he knows he should. How nice."

What the...?

Of course, to the detractors who believed the bizarre rumor that "Hotel California" was merely a code word for "Church of Satan," this was more proof of the band's diabolical agenda.

The fundamentalists also came after Cheap Trick. Some listeners were convinced that a backward mask in "Gonna Raise Hell" actually said, "Satan holds the keys." But Cheap Trick had the last laugh. On their *Heaven Tonight* album, the track "How Are You?" contained a high-speed subliminal message that rushed by during some of the lyrics. When that garbled message was slowed down, it becomes "The Lord's Prayer."

Other groups targeted included the Cars, whose "Shoo Be Doo" reversed was supposed to state "Satan" 11 times, and Jefferson Starship, whose song "A Child is Coming" supposedly contained the hidden message of "son of Satan." It was claimed that the song "Snowblind" by Styx allegedly contained the command, "Satan, move in our voices." Black Oak Arkansas was targeted for their song "When Electricity Came to Arkansas," which reportedly hid the message, "Satan, Satan, Satan. He is God, God, God." What's really great about this one is that the album was recorded live, which means the grunting syllables would have had to be well thought out in advance and then pronounced very clearly and phonematically – in front of a live audience – to give the hidden message.

It would take a genius to do that and hey, we are talking about Black Oak Arkansas here.

No song was safe. In April 1986, evangelist Jim Brown convinced Ohio teenagers to burn their records of television's Mister Ed theme song -- how many copies could there have been? -- because he somehow persuaded them that a reversal of "A Horse is a Horse" contained the words "Someone sung this song for Satan."

It was the 1980s. What can I say?

We've already established that some "hidden" messages were less garbled than others, and some were even comically deliberate, but was there ever any proof that a conspiracy existed to brainwash fans of rock music? No – but that doesn't mean that a lot of people believed it and were serious enough about it to file a case in court.

In October 1984, John McCollum, 19, shot himself in the head with a .22-caliber handgun after listening to a number of Ozzy Osbourne albums, including *Blizzard of Oz*, which features the song "Suicide Solution." When the police arrived on the scene, they found the young man still wearing headphones, gun still in his hand, which suggested that his death was spontaneous and had a direct link with the music that he was listening to at the time. It was said that he had been suffering from depression and had an alcohol problem. Grief-stricken and angry at what they believed to be the rock star's irresponsible and reckless indifference to the effects of his music, McCollum's parents initiated legal proceedings against Osbourne and his label, CBS records. It was one of three similar lawsuits that Ozzy was forced to defend himself against at the time.

Two other teenagers had killed themselves in similar circumstances, also allegedly under the influence of Osbourne's satanic spell. When the McCollum case came to trial in January 1986, the media – as well as the radical religious right – saw it as a critical test case.

Dressed conservatively in a tailored suit, Osbourne took the stand to protest that the song was in fact inspired by his own self-destructive drinking habit and was intended as a warning against over-indulgence. The word "solution" in the title, he said, referred to alcohol, not the ending of one's life as a solution to life's problems. In other words, alcoholism was a form of suicide. Osbourne also argued that his image as a devil-worshipping occultist was just a part of his act. He had no wish to convert the youth of America to Satanism. Rock was entertainment, nothing more.

Unimpressed, the prosecution alleged that Osbourne had hidden subliminal messages in an instrumental section of the song, which encouraged listeners to "Get the gun – shoot," a suggestion that the singer strenuously denied. Under pressure from relentless questioning, Ozzy barked at the prosecutor, "I swear on my kid's life I never said 'get the fucking gun!'"

Neither the judge nor the jury could make out what was being said in the passage in question, which was totally obscured by guitar feedback, bass, and drums, so they turned to the experts from the Institute for Bio-Acoustics Research to dig into it a little deeper. The IBAR techs subjected "Suicide Solution" to intense scrutiny in their laboratory, filtering it through state-of-the-art sound equipment to isolate Ozzy's mumblings, which they claimed had been recorded at one and a half times the normal rate of speech, presumably to avoid detection by the casual listener. Their report concluded that the "meaning and true intent" of the subliminal lyrics "becomes clear after being listened to over and over again." The offending lines were said to be "Why try, why try? Get the gun and try it! Shoot, shoot, shoot," followed by a demonic laugh. Anticipating the argument that the defense might offer, that these words were ad-libs, the scientific experts revealed that they had identified something far more sinister in the track – the presence of high frequency signals had been detected. These signals are a patented process that was developed to aid the assimilation of information by the human brain. They could not have been incorporated into the recording accidentally.

This was disputed by the defense, who argued that Ozzy had been messing around at the mixing desk, so the so-called "lyrics" were merely a sound effect. Besides, he was free under the First Amendment of the U.S. Constitution to write and record anything that he wished, unencumbered by the worry that someone might misinterpret what he had said.

The judge agreed and the court of appeal concurred that the Devil might have all the best tunes, but his lyrics are unintelligible, so there's no risk to any of his fans.

The acquittal in Osbourne's trial didn't stop a civil action from being brought against Judas Priest in 1990. According to the prosecution, James Vance, 20, and Raymond Belknap, 18, attempted to end their lives with a shotgun after listening to Judas Priest's music. Belknap was successful, but Vance only managed to blow away part of his face.

When the case came to court in Nevada, part of the prosecution's case was that one of the band's songs contained the command "do it" when played backwards. The bands defense team responded by demonstrating that the same song – again played backwards – also contained what sounded like, "I asked for a peppermint, I asked her to get me one."

At the end of the trial, the judge dismissed the case. He told the court that when the speech is played backwards those who wished to hear intelligible phrases will interpret the garbled sounds into whatever they want to hear. However, it was unintentional on the part of the artist. The point was simple – no artist can be held responsible for what their listeners might hear—or do – when in a disturbed state of mind.

That finally closed the book on the "Satanic Panic" era and the Satanic conspiracy of backward masking.

But the Devil is still alive and well and dancing to the tunes that rock-n-roll conjures up.

By the middle 1990s, the first generation of heavy metal bands were history, having gotten old, split up, or having been sidelined by the next big thing. Their demise was no doubt hastened by the Satanic Panic that tainted bands by association, even those who protested that their devil worship was all just an act. However, after the dust had settled, Satanic rock became louder than ever before in the form of Marilyn Manson, Slip Knot, Rob Zombie, Slayer, and even a resurrected Ozzy Osbourne, whose reality show had made him even bigger than ever before.

As in the past, making the "Devil's Music" was more about marketing than reality. However, some artists professed to believe in what they sang about. One of them was Marilyn Manson, who was reputedly ordained as a priest in the Church of Satan and had close ties with the late Anton LaVey.

For most bands, though, being all about the Devil was all part of the branding and marketing of their music, which is something that religious groups and moral watchdogs have always failed to understand. No true Satanists or black magicians would ever publicize their methods or indulge in self-promotion. The simple reason would be that the attention of outsiders would be an unwelcome distraction.

Success in the art of magic has always depended on the ability to focus the will on what the magician wishes to bring into being. The same could be said for the artist. Music and the Devil may go hand in hand, but don't be fooled into thinking that just because something looks and sounds Satanic that is necessarily is Satanic.

The "Devil's Music" will always endure. It always has, and well, it always will.

BIBLIOGRAPHY

Aftel, Mandy – *Death of a Rolling Stone: The Brian Jones Story*; 1982

Altschuler, Glenn – *All Shook Up: How Rock 'n Roll Changed America*; 2003

Amburn, Ellis – *Buddy Holly: A Biography*; 1996

Azerrad, Michael - *Come as You Are: The Story of Nirvana*; 1994

Bebergal, Peter – *Season of the Witch*; 2014

Birmingham, Stephen – *Life at the Dakota*; 1979

Brant, Marley – *Freebirds: The Lynyrd Skynyrd Story*, 2002

Buckley, Peter - *The Rough Guide to Rock*, 2003

Bukszpan, Daniel - *The Encyclopedia of Heavy Metal*, 2003

Burlingame, Jeff - *Kurt Cobain: Oh Well, Whatever, Nevermind*; 2006

Burt, Olive Woolley – *American Murder Ballads*; 1958

Clapton, Eric -- *Clapton, The Autobiography*; 2007

Cole, Richard – *Stairway to Heaven: Led Zeppelin Uncensored*; 1992

Cope, Andrew L. - *Black Sabbath and the Rise of Heavy Metal Music*; 2010

Cross, Charles - *Heavier Than Heaven: A Biography of Kurt Cobain*; 2001

Davis, Stephen - *Hammer of the Gods: The Led Zeppelin Saga*; 1985

---------------- - *Old Gods Almost Dead*; 2001

Echols, Alice – *Scars of Sweet Paradise*; 1999

Faithfull, Marianne – *Faithfull: An Autobiography*; 1994

Fast, Susan - *In the Houses of the Holy: Led Zeppelin and the Power of Rock Music*; 2001

Freeman, Scott – *Midnight Riders: The Story of the Allman Brothers Band*; 1995

Friedman, Myra – *Buried Alive: The Biography of Janis Joplin*; 1992

Gaar, Gillian G. - *The Rough Guide to Nirvana*; 2009

Garofalo, Reebee - *Rockin' Out: Popular Music in the USA*; 2008

Green, John – *Dakota Days*; 1983

Guinn, Jeff – *Manson: The Life and Times of Charles Manson*; 2013

Gulla, Bob - *Guitar Gods: The 25 Players Who Made Rock History*; 2001

Guralnick, Peter – *Searching for Robert Johnson*; 1989

Henderson, David – *'Scuse Me While I Kiss the Sky: The Life of Jimi Hendrix*; 1978

Herman, Gary – *Rock 'n' Roll Babylon*; 1982

Hopkins, Jerry and Daniel Sugerman – *No One Here Gets Out Alive*; 1980

Hoskyns, Barney – *Hotel California*; 2006

Hotchner, A.E. – *Blown Away: The Rolling Stones and the Death of the Sixtie;* 1990

Jackson, Laura - *Golden Stone: The untold life and tragic death of Brian Jones;* 1992

Jones, Jack – *Let Me Take You Down;* 1992

Katz, Gary J. – *Death by Rock and Roll;* 1995

Karnbach, James and Carol Benson - *It's Only Rock 'n' Roll: The Ultimate Guide to the Rolling Stones;* 1997

Krist, Gary – *Empire of Sin;* 2014

Lachman, Gary – *Aleister Crowley: Magick, Rock and Roll, and the Wickedest Man in the World;*2014

------------------ – *Turn Off Your Mind;* 2003

Lewis, Dave - *The Complete Guide to the Music of Led Zeppelin;* 1994

Longstreet, Stephen – *Sportin' House: New Orleans and the Jazz Story;* 1965

Milward, John – *Crossroads: How the Blues Shaped Rock 'n' Roll;* 2013

Mitchell, Corey – *Hollywood Death Scenes: True Crime and Tragedy in Paradise;* 2001

Newton, Michael – *Raising Hell: An Encyclopedia of Devil Worship and Satanic Crimes;* 1993

Nolan, A.M. – *Rock 'n' Roll Roadtrip;* 1992

Norman, Phillip – *Sympathy for the Devil: The Rolling Stones Story;* 1984

Oakley, Giles – *The Devil's Music: A History of the Blues;* 1977

Patterson, R. Gary – *Hellhounds on Their Trail;* 1998

------------------ – *Take a Walk on the Dark Side;* 2004

------------------ - *The Walrus was Paul;* 1996

Richards, Keith – *Life;* 2009

Rawlings, Terry - *Who Killed Christopher Robin?: The Life and Death of Brian Jones;* 1994

Sanchez, Tony – *Up and Down with the Rolling Stones;* 2011

Schaffner, Nicolas – *Saucerful of Secrets: The Pink Floyd Odyssey;* 1991

Seaman, Frederick – *The Last Days of John Lennon;* 1991

Shadwick, Keith - *Led Zeppelin: The Story of a Band and Their Music 1968–1980;* 2005

Slade, Paul – *Unprepared to Die;* 2015

Sounes, Howard – *27;* 2013

Stephens, Randall - *The Devil's Music: How Christians Inspired, Condemned, and Embraced Rock 'n' Roll;* 2018

Taylor, Troy – *The Devil and All His Works;* 2013

Thompson, Dave – *Better to Burn Out: The Cult of Death in Rock 'n' Roll;* 1999

Tosches, Nick – *Hellfire: The Jerry Lee Lewis Story;* 1982

Walker, Michael – *Laurel Canyon;* 2006

Wall, Mick - *When Giants Walked the Earth: A Biography of Led Zeppelin*; 2008
Welch, Chris - *Led Zeppelin*; 1994
Winehouse, Mitch - *Amy, My Daughter*; 2012
Winer, Richard and Nancy Osborn – *Haunted Houses*; 1979
Witmer, Scott - *History of Rock Bands*; 2010
Wyman, Bill, with Ray Coleman -- *Stone Alone: The Story of a Rock 'n' Roll Band*; 1997

Special Thanks to:

April Slaughter: Cover Design and Artwork
Lois Taylor: Editing and Proofreading
Lisa Taylor Horton and Lux
Orrin Taylor
Rene Kruse
Rachael Horath
Elyse and Thomas Reihner
Bethany Horath
John Winterbauer
Kaylan Schardan
Maggie Walsh
Cody Beck and Leah Hentrich
Tom and Michelle Bonadurer
Becky Ray

And to the hundreds of musicians who have created the great music that inspired me so much throughout the years and to the countless people who introduced me to those artists – this book certainly could not have been written without you.

CPSIA information can be obtained
at www.ICGtesting.com
Printed in the USA
LVHW021603150419
614228LV00010B/310/P

9 781732 407954